TRANSATLANTIC TELEVISION DRAMA

TRANSATLANTIC TELEVISION DRAMA

Industries, Programs, & Fans

Edited by

Matt Hills, Michele Hilmes, and Roberta Pearson

OXFORD
UNIVERSITY PRESS

OXFORD

UNIVERSITY PRESS

Oxford University Press is a department of the University of Oxford. It furthers
the University's objective of excellence in research, scholarship, and education
by publishing worldwide. Oxford is a registered trade mark of Oxford University
Press in the UK and certain other countries.

Published in the United States of America by Oxford University Press
198 Madison Avenue, New York, NY 10016, United States of America.

Library of Congress Cataloging-in-Publication Data
Names: Hills, Matt, editor. | Hilmes, Michele, editor. | Pearson,
Roberta E., editor.
Title: Transatlantic television drama : industries, programs and fans /
edited by Matt Hills, Michele Hilmes, and Roberta Pearson.
Description: New York, NY : Oxford University Press, [2019] | Includes
bibliographical references and index.
Identifiers: LCCN 2018014434 | ISBN 9780190663124 (hardcover) |
ISBN 9780190663131 (paperback) | ISBN 9780190663162 (companion website) |
ISBN 9780190663148 (Updf) | ISBN 9780190663155 (Epub)
Subjects: LCSH: Television series—United States—History and criticism. |
Television series—Great Britain—History and criticism. | Television
broadcasting—United States—History—21st century. | Television
broadcasting—Great Britain—History—21st century.
Classification: LCC PN1992.3.U5 T723 2019 | DDC 791.450973—dc23
LC record available at https://lccn.loc.gov/2018014434

9 8 7 6 5 4 3 2 1

Paperback printed by Webcom Inc., Canada
Hardback printed by Bridgeport National Bindery, Inc., United States of America

CONTENTS

CONTRIBUTORS

Christine Becker is Associate Professor in the Department of Film, Television, and Theatre at the University of Notre Dame specializing in film and television history and critical analysis. Her book *It's the Pictures That Got Small: Hollywood Film Stars on 1950s Television* (2009) won the 2011 IAMHIST Michael Nelson Prize for a Work in Media and History. She is currently working on a research project comparing contemporary American and British television production and programming. She is also the Associate Online Editor for *Cinema Journal* and runs the *News for TV Majors* blog.

Jonathan Bignell is Professor of Television and Film at the University of Reading. He specializes in the history of television drama, especially in Britain, and also works on children's media and toys. His articles about television include contributions to *Critical Studies in Television, Historical Journal of Film, Radio and Television, Media History*, and *Screen*. His books include *Beckett on Screen, Big Brother: Reality TV in the Twenty-First Century, Postmodern Media Culture, A European Television History* (edited with Andreas Fickers, 2005), two editions of *British Television Drama: Past, Present and Future* (edited with Stephen Lacey), and three editions of *An Introduction to Television Studies*. His recent research has been on science fiction TV of the 1960s and the history and legacy of Harold Pinter's television dramas and film screenplays.

Paul Booth is Associate Professor at DePaul University, Chicago. He is the author of *Crossing Fandoms* (2016), *Digital Fandom 2.0* (2016), *Playing Fans* (2015), *Game Play* (2015), *Time on TV* (2012), and *Digital Fandom* (2010). He has edited *Seeing Fans* (2016, with Lucy Bennett), *Controversies in Digital Ethics* (2016, with Amber Davisson), and *Fan Phenomena: Doctor Who* (2013). His most recent editorial work involved compiling and introducing thirty-four chapters for *A Companion to Media Fandom and Fan Studies* (2018).

Gary Cassidy is Senior Lecturer in Acting at Bath Spa University. He has recently completed his AHRC-funded doctoral research at the University of Reading. His thesis explored the rehearsal process of playwright Anthony Neilson, using filmed footage of rehearsals and interviews. He trained as an actor at the Royal Scottish Academy of Music and Drama (now Royal Conservatoire of Scotland) and has thirteen years of acting experience—Equity name Cas Harkins—covering film, theater, television, and radio. He has published in the *International Journal of Scottish Theatre and Screen*, and coauthors the blog strand "What Actors Do" for *CSTOnline*. Plans for future research focus on using his research methodology to explore the working processes of other contemporary theater practitioners.

Lincoln Geraghty is Reader in Popular Media Cultures in the School of Film, Media and Communication at the University of Portsmouth, United Kingdom. He is the author of multiple books, including *Living with "Star Trek"* (2007), *American Science Fiction Film and Television* (2009), and *Cult Collectors* (2014). He has also edited numerous titles, including *The Influence of "Star Trek" on Television, Film and Culture* (2008) and, with Mark Jancovich, *The Shifting Definitions of Genre* (2008). His most recent collection, *Popular Media Cultures: Fans, Audiences and Paratexts*, was published by Palgrave Macmillan in 2015, and he has recently contributed chapters to the *Companion to Media Fandom and Fan Studies* (2018) and the *Routledge Companion to Media Fandom* (2018).

Matt Hills is Professor of Media and Film at the University of Huddersfield, where he is also Codirector of the Centre for Participatory Culture. Matt is additionally coeditor (with Dan Hassler-Forest) of the Transmedia book series for Amsterdam University Press. This published its first title, *Fanfiction and the Author* by Judith Fathallah, in 2017, and four further volumes in the series are now available. Matt has written six sole-authored monographs himself, starting with *Fan Cultures* in 2002 and coming up to date with *"Doctor Who": The Unfolding Event* in 2015, as well as editing *New Dimensions of "Doctor Who"* (2013) for the program's fiftieth anniversary year. He has also published more than a hundred book chapters and journal articles on media fandom and cult film and TV. Among other projects, Matt is currently working on a follow-up to his first book for Routledge, entitled *Fan Studies*.

Michele Hilmes is Professor Emerita of Media and Cultural Studies at the University of Wisconsin–Madison. Her research and publication focus on media history, with an emphasis on radio and sound studies and on transnational media flows. Her books include *Radio Voices: American Broadcasting, 1922–1952* (1997), *Network Nations: A Transnational History of British and American Broadcasting* (2011), and *Only Connect: A*

Cultural History of Broadcasting in the United States (4th edition, 2013). In 2017 she received the Distinguished Career Achievement Award from the Society for Cinema and Media Studies.

Simone Knox is Associate Professor in Film and Television at the University of Reading. Her research interests include the transnationalization of film and television (including audiovisual translation), aesthetics and medium specificity (including convergence culture, and acting and performance), and representations of minority and marginalized identities, as well as the lived experience of screen culture. She sits on the board of editors for *Critical Studies in Television*, and her publications include essays in *Film Criticism*, *Journal of Popular Film and Television*, *New Review of Film and Television Studies*, and the *Historical Journal of Film, Radio and Television*, as well as the coauthored blog strand "What Actors Do" for *CSTOnline*.

Lori Morimoto is an independent researcher of transcultural fan cultures and transnational media marketing. She has published influential essays on transcultural fandom and Japanese female fandom for overseas stars, in *Transformative Works and Cultures* and *Participations*, as well as contributing work on transnational Japanese cinema to *Scope* and *Asian Cinema*. Lori's recently published book chapters have included coauthored and sole-authored contributions to the likes of *Fandom* (2nd edition, 2017), the *Routledge Companion to Media Fandom* (2018) and the *Companion to Media Fandom and Fan Studies* (2018).

Robin Nelson remains a Professorial Fellow at the University of London, Royal Central School, where until semi-retirement (January 2015) he was Director of Research and Professor of Theatre and Intermedial Performance. He is also Professor Emeritus at Manchester Metropolitan University, where he held a number of posts over twenty years. He has published widely on the performing arts and media and on "practice as research" as a research methodology. His books include *Practice as Research in the Arts* (2013), *Stephen Poliakoff: On Stage and Screen* (2011), *Mapping Intermediality in Performance* (coedited with S. Bay-Cheng et al., 2010), and *State of Play: Contemporary "High-End" TV Drama* (2007). Professor Nelson is also a cofounding editor of *Critical Studies in Television*, for which he guest coedited a special issue on archiving (5:2, November 2010).

Roberta Pearson is Professor of Film and Television Studies at the University of Nottingham. Among her most recent publications are the coauthored *"Star Trek" and American Television* (2014), and the coedited *Many More Lives of the Batman* (BFI, 2015) and *Storytelling in the Media Convergence Age: Exploring Screen Narratives* (2015).

She is in total the author, coauthor, editor, or coeditor of fourteen books and author or coauthor of over eighty journal articles and book chapters.

Karen Petruska is Assistant Professor of Communication Studies at Gonzaga University. Her research interests include digital distribution, television history, and regulatory policy. A graduate of Georgia State University, Dr. Petruska has published in *Creative Industries, Spectator, Popular Communication,* and *The Velvet Light Trap.* She has also coedited a special issue of *Convergence,* contributed to four anthologies, and published online through *In Media Res, Flow, Antenna,* and *MIP Research.*

Eva N. Redvall is Associate Professor in film and media studies at the University of Copenhagen, where she founded and headed the research priority area Creative Media Industries from 2012 to 2016. Her research focuses on European film and television production, for example, screenwriting practices, coproduction strategies, and specific production frameworks. She has published widely in international books and journals. Among her latest books are the monograph *Writing and Producing Television Drama in Denmark: From "The Kingdom" to "The Killing"* (2012), the edited collection *European Cinema and Television: Cultural Policy and Everyday Life* (with Ib Bondebjerg and Andrew Higson, 2015), and *Transnational European Television Drama: Production, Genres and Audiences* (coauthored with Ib Bondebjerg et al., 2017). She has been a film critic for the daily Danish newspaper *Information* since 1999 and has been a member of the Adjudication Committee for the Nordic Council Film Prize since 2011.

Paul Rixon is Reader in Radio and Television at the University of Roehampton. He specializes in the field of broadcasting with a particular interest in American TV programs and popular and professional TV criticism, and has published two sole-authored monographs on these subjects: *American Television on British Screens: A Story of Cultural Interaction* (2006) and *TV Critics and Popular Culture: A History of British Television Criticism* (2011). Paul has also published a number of articles and chapters on newspaper television critics, American TV programs, and the Iraq war.

Sam Ward is Project Director at the branding and cultural insight consultancy Canopy Insight. He completed a PhD in the Institute for Screen Industries Research at the University of Nottingham, before becoming a lecturer at the University of Roehampton. He moved to Canopy in 2016, where he has led research projects for international clients across the media, communications, and publishing industries.

Faye Woods is Lecturer in Film and Television at the University of Reading. Her monograph, *British Youth Television*, was published by Palgrave (2016). Her work has appeared in the journals *Television & New Media, Cinema Journal, Critical Studies in Television,* and *Journal of British Cinema and Television,* as well as the edited collections *From Networks to Netflix, Television Aesthetics and Style, Shane Meadows: Critical Essays,* and *Multiplicities: Cycles, Sequels, Remakes and Reboots in Film and Television.*

TRANSATLANTIC TELEVISION DRAMA

INTRODUCTION

Flying the Flag for Contemporary Transatlantic Television Drama

MICHELE HILMES, ROBERTA PEARSON, AND MATT HILLS

A tide of high-quality transnational television drama is currently sweeping the world, according to critics and scholars as well as the popular press.[1] Speaking what has become the global language of serial television, often coproduced, and available on a range of both terrestrial and digital platforms, the new transnational television drama has developed not only global appeal but innovative new modes of production, distribution, and reception. Nowhere is the transnational exchange of television drama more vital than between Britain and the United States, where it builds on a more than sixty-year history of transatlantic import, adaptation, and coproduction.

This book explores the British-American connection in the context of contemporary transnational television drama, focusing on key programs and practices that reflect the current situation in the transatlantic television industry, its programs, and its audiences. Subsequent chapters will analyze some of the most widely discussed and highly rated programs on the transatlantic circuit, from recent series like *Game of Thrones, Black Mirror, Orphan Black, Episodes, Elementary*, and *Sherlock*, to those like *Masterpiece* and *Doctor Who* that have long and active histories of transnational circulation, to others whose transnational success speaks to more specific underlying currents in the process of exchange, adaptation, and cooperation, such as *Supernatural, Downton Abbey, Rome*, and *Parade's End*.

THE TROUBLE WITH TELEVISION

The transatlantic relationship that produces such programs and sends them out world-wide is just one part of the larger transnational exchange that also circulates films, music, literature, theater, art, and virtually every form of modern culture. But television drama is, in many ways, a uniquely contentious kind of transnational space. Because of the historical development of television as an institution and expressive form deeply tied to the nation—to national culture, national mandates, national politics, national regulation, national viewership, and, in many cases, national ownership—it has long walked a difficult and highly debated line between the national and the not-national, between creating and broadcasting programs produced in the home nation that reflect and support home culture, and importing programs and practices from elsewhere, most ubiquitously and contentiously from the United States. Until recently, most public service systems limited nonnational programs to a certain percentage of the broadcast schedule—in Britain until the 1990s it was 14 percent, most but not all from the United States—and transnational coproduction was a controversial practice.[2] However, UK audiences have always had more access to US programs than their US counterparts did to UK programs. In the 1950s both the BBC and ITV turned to the United States for content to expand their schedules, and US programs remained prominent through the 1970s. The channel fragmentation of the 1980s resulted in the main terrestrial broadcasters, the BBC and ITV, branding around domestically produced drama, but smaller channels (C4, Channel Five, and the Sky channels) frequently used US content in their branding. Today, with relatively rare exceptions, most peak-time content on the BBC and ITV is British, but US content is readily found elsewhere.[3]

In the United States, television's national bias was more a matter of economics than public policy. Hollywood rarely saw much profit in importing programs from elsewhere and instead favored Americanized adaptations of shows originated in other countries. Such adaptations were potentially far more remunerative to their producers than simply buying and airing an imported show "off the shelf," since the "new" wholly owned version could be sold internationally as well as domestically with profits going to its American producer. A good recent example of this practice is *Ugly Betty*, the US version of the originally Colombian show *Yo Soy Betty la Fea*, which became a global hit in its own right.[4] Some US adaptations, much altered from the original, succeeded—like *All in the Family*, adapted from the British original *Till Death Us Do Part*, or more recently the US version of *The Office*—and went on to earn their American producers vast sums, as intended. Most sank without a trace, proving that the textual integrity of creative drama and comedy can't always be stretched to fit. But with a very few exceptions—*Masterpiece Theatre* on PBS after 1971, the Arts and Entertainment (A&E) cable network after 1984—until recent decades US viewers had little access to drama and comedy from Britain, or from anywhere else, for that matter, at least not on mainstream channels.[5]

The rise of new distribution platforms, beginning with cable, satellite channels, and videocassettes in the late 1980s and going on to DVDs, expanded cable, and, most transformatively, the digital streaming services so widely available today, have facilitated the distribution of international content in both countries. Platforms like Sky, Netflix, Amazon, iTunes, HBO, and many others, as these chapters discuss, not only distribute programs originated in national contexts to broader audiences around the world, but in many cases have become active producers of original television drama, often through coproduction deals that can range from upfront distribution guarantees, to joint ventures that contribute funding to national broadcasters for transnationally oriented shows, to series commissioned and coproduced by the (largely) US-based services themselves, often working with international partners. In this kind of complex network of relationships, the meanings of both "national" and "transnational" have become contentious. As Karen Petruska and Faye Woods explore in their chapter, a program's "original" identity can no longer be understood as solely the property of a text (a show about Americans set in New York), or of the location or ownership of its production company (a show produced by British creators working in London), or even of its primary audience (a show originally broadcast in Canada but with a large international audience) but as a product of a complex system of transnational negotiations that occur at many levels, from national policy to financing to producing to writing and acting to postproduction and marketing, as well as in reception conditions determined both by national broadcasters and by global internet platforms. Such practices began to demand a new term, less restrictive than "international," less vaguely comprehensive than "global," designating a new way of not only performing but thinking about cultural flows and relationships.

PUTTING THE "TRANS" IN TRANSNATIONAL

The term "transnational" has been used to designate a wide variety of phenomena, from transnational corporations to transnational flows of people, money, ideas, and media. Most uses position it in contradistinction both to the "international" and the "global" and note that it implies "going beyond" the nation and the national in some way, while still drawing on national identity for at least part of its coherence. Pierre-Yves Saunier, in his essay on the term in the *Palgrave Dictionary of Transnational History*, points out that its first use in English occurred as early as 1862 in the *Princeton Review*, reviewing work done by a German scholar of philology on the "transnational" constitution of languages;

he also notes that it was frequently employed as a synonym for "transcontinental" when talking about highways in the 1910s and 1920s—actually an incorrect usage, since "trans" as a prefix means going beyond, not across.[6] But, he argues, it was Randolph Bourne's use of the term in his article "Trans-national America" in the *Atlantic Monthly* in July 1916 that set it into sociological and political use, a bit ahead of its time. "America is coming to be, not a nationality but a transnationality, a weaving back and forth, with the other lands, of many threads of all sizes and colors," claimed Bourne.[7] Saunier mentions that Bourne's editor was not very happy with the failure of this definition to adhere to the white Anglo-Saxon Protestant identity project then dominant in the United States. But it is significant that the term first arises and then spreads in relationship to the United States and its culture, making it particularly apt in talking about an area of media research often associated with a rampant kind of American cultural imperialism.

Saunier finds that "transnational" remained primarily an American usage through the 1950s and 1960s, until it was taken up by the larger academic community in the early 1970s, in Europe in particular as the beginning of the assertion of a pan-European identity sparked by the emergent European Economic Community. In 1971 the conference "Transnational Relations" brought social and political scientists from around the world to Harvard, but in the United States the field called "international relations" quickly replaced this term, reasserting the primacy of the nation as the essential, foundational unit of politics. In Europe the transnational persisted, however, and began to be used alongside "globalization," often without making any key distinctions. In the 1980s the influential work of Arjun Appadurai attached the prefix "trans" to a variety of phenomena,[8] including the Center for Transcultural Studies, established in 1986 under Appadurai's direction in cooperation between the Universities of Chicago and Pennsylvania, out of which arose the Project for Transnational Cultural Studies and the journal *Public Culture*. In the field of anthropology it also gained ground in the context of discussing migratory populations and diasporas. By the 1990s, according to Saunier, it even attained a political opposition: conservatives used the term "transnational progressives" to indicate a group that, in his words, "includes academics, NGOs, activists, philanthropic foundation officers, European Union and United Nations civil servants . . . a global elite on the march to wash away national citizenship and democracy in favour of world government."[9]

In media studies, "transnational" has most often been used in the sociocultural sense to denote flows of influence, dispersion of media through technology, and trade in textual formats and forms. It is not hard to recognize a transnational corporation, a transnational business deal, a transnational satellite network. Many references are made to the transnational circulation of texts and to the transnational circuits of production that may center on Hollywood or on other media capitals, to use Michael Curtin's term.[10] Creative personnel in film and television frequently have transnational careers, and it is recognized that transnational capital underwrites everything. However, when it comes to critical cultural analysis, the acknowledgment of transnational intertextuality—the way that the national and "beyond national" interact in specific texts and practices of production and reception—has largely been reserved for literary studies and the realm of the "serious" arts, where it is not perceived as threatening that texts might have not only national and local but also transnational authorship, narratives, references, and meanings. In fact, such elements are valued. Not so for the television text, where the dominance of the national framework has rendered elements of transnationality deeply suspicious, evidence of cultural imperialism and even of a dangerous "denationalizing" of culture.

TRACING THE TRANSATLANTIC

Yet such programs belong to an ongoing system of production that has always been transnational, with long-standing flows of influence between nations and regions, foremost among them the transatlantic relationship between the United Kingdom and the United States. Beginning in the 1960s but accelerating since the rise of digital distribution, the United Kingdom and the United States forged a system of transnational negotiation of dramatic and documentary forms that shaped television programming in both nations and led to types of cooperation and coproduction that contributed to a broader transnationality worldwide.

All of the chapters in this volume deal in some way with the struggles of industries, producers, programs, and audiences to negotiate the tensions between the national and transnational that arise in the new digital environment. When the BBC coproduces with *Masterpiece*, is it using British license fees to make programs for Americans? When Netflix declares that a production originated by the United Kingdom's Channel 4 and broadcast in Britain has become a "Netflix Original," has "original" lost all sense of its traditional meaning rooted in national origins? What does it mean when the leading show on a channel branded as British and aimed at Americans—BBC America—is produced by Canadians, as with *Orphan Black*? When American fans of British shows display ignorance about British culture and idioms, should British fans object, or just give in to American monoculture? These are some of the questions addressed in the following chapters.

Film theorist Mette Hjort's work provides terms that are useful for understanding these blurred lines. In her essay "On the Plurality of Cinematic Transnationalism," Hjort argues that transnationalism must be understood, first, as a matter of degree.[11] There are both "strong" and "weak" types of transnationalism, relating not only to circumstances of production, distribution, and reception but also to the textual project of the film itself. The question here is how central the various national negotiations are to the film's conception and authorship: how much the film deliberately brings issues of national and transnational cultural positions into both its production processes and the narrative and diegesis. Clearly, a program like *Episodes*, explored in this volume by Jonathan Bignell, falls into the "strong" category, since not only is it made by British producers working for HBO in Los Angeles, but exploration of British and American perceived cultural differences (in television, no less, for true reflexivity!) forms the fundamental premise of the text. A program like *Elementary*, on the other hand, though it draws fairly obviously on the classic Sherlock Holmes original, rarely references its British roots, is entirely produced and set in the United States, and in fact significantly reimagines key elements of the original text, as Roberta Pearson describes: fairly weak transnationalism.

A further distinction made by Hjort pertains to the amount of transnational involvement the text itself admits to, or *marks*: are its transnational qualities overtly visible within the text or can they only be discovered by an investigation of its production circumstances? In other words, is transnationality *strongly marked, weakly marked*, or *unmarked* in the text itself: is it clearly perceptible to the viewer, is it perceptible but relatively unimportant to the project of the text, or is it hidden? A text might be strongly marked as transnational—clearly a product of different national production spaces and personnel, dealing with issues relating to the interaction of transnational identities, again like *Episodes* or like *Black Mirror*, as argued by Matt Hills in his chapter—or it might be completely unmarked, its transnational elements invisible or irrelevant to the viewer, as in *Game of Thrones*. Analyzing television production, texts, and reception along these lines reveals much about the ways that national identity functions in today's televisual context.

We might also need to add another category: the falsely marked. As far back as the 1950s, British television offered *The Adventures of Robin Hood* as an "original" British television program; even the most attentive viewer could not have known that it was largely written and produced by blacklisted American writers relocated to England, writing under pseudonyms. Until very recently, PBS played down its growing influence on *Masterpiece*'s primarily UK-produced period dramas, a tactic useful on both sides of the Atlantic since Americans valued precisely the show's Britishness, and UK viewers found the idea of American influence on such shows objectionable. By strongly, yet somewhat misleadingly, marking such productions as "British" and minimizing the growing amount of American influence, *Masterpiece* helped to ensure the survival of a certain kind of quality drama in both countries, as Michele Hilmes argues in her chapter. With *Rome*, this transnational erasure was reversed, as the BBC highlighted HBO's involvement, while HBO minimized the show's British production, with the Italian broadcaster RAI's participation completely erased, as Robin Nelson points out. Netflix's marking of certain shows as "original" seems to be a clear case of this, as mentioned above. Such marking occurs not only in the shows themselves, as chapters in the second part discuss, but in the discourse surrounding them. This includes both industry discourse, the focus of chapters in the first part, and audience/reception discourse, as found in the third part.

BEHIND THE SCREENS: THE IMPORTANCE OF THE TRANSATLANTIC MARKET

However acknowledged or obscured, there is no doubt that few other channels of trans-national exchange have been, and continue to be, as lucrative and globally influential as the UK-US connection. Collectively, the United States and the United Kingdom strongly dominate the international television trade. In 2007, the United States "accounted for an estimated 76 percent of all finished programs exported worldwide, compared to 7 per-cent from the United Kingdom, which followed in second place."[12] Ten years later, the two countries remain "the dominant creative markets, with the US the largest exporter of scripted content and the United Kingdom the world leader for exported formats."[13] In 2014, the five distributors accounting for the top fifteen best-performing fictional se-ries per territory were CBS Studios International, Warner Bros. International Television Distribution, Twenty-First Century Fox Television Distribution, BBC Worldwide, and Disney Media distribution, more evidence of Anglo-American dominance.[14]

The six major US television production studios (Warner, Disney, Fox, Universal, Columbia, and Paramount) rely on television licensing for their profit margins. In 2004, licensing revenues amounted to around $16 billion, "the studios' single richest source of profits."[15] By 2012, international sales brought in "as much as half of the revenue that [the studios] get for new dramas."[16] Despite benefiting from one of the larger and more profit-able domestic markets, the studios increasingly look overseas for the television licensing fees now so central to their business models. As Shawn Shimpach states,

> Facing the saturation of domestic markets . . . the global audience is now an increas-ingly integral part of programming and fiscal strategy for the US television industry. International distribution deals have become a necessity for deficit-financed televi-sion productions, particularly expensive hour drama series.[17]

American television networks place similar emphasis on international sales and distri-bution. CBS Corporation (formerly Viacom), in its 2016 annual report to the Securities and Exchange Commission, stated that its "principal strategy is to create and acquire premium content that is widely accepted by audiences, and to generate both advertising and non-advertising revenues from the distribution of this content on multiple media platforms and to various geographic locations," and that its primary opportunities for revenue growth include "expanding the distribution of its content internationally."[18]

The CBS report offers some insights into its international television licensing revenues and strategies. Since the typical network licensing fee charged to first-run buyers is lower than actual production costs, the company recoups costs and earns a profit through secondary distribution, which includes domestic syndication, digital streaming, and international licensing.[19] International sales are usually made within one year of the US network run,[20] although in some cases such as *Elementary*, programs are sold to international buyers before their domestic debuts. In 2015, international sales of *NCIS*, *Elementary*, and *CSI* significantly boosted the CBS bottom line, while in 2014 a 3 percent decrease in domestic licensing revenues was "partially offset by higher international television licensing revenues."[21] CBS reports that the UK market yields a higher percentage of revenues than any other single national territory—17 percent in 2015 and 15 percent in 2016. The second and third most profitable territories are Canada (13 percent in 2015 and in 2016) and the combined category of "other Europe" (35 percent in 2015 and 39 percent in 2016)—the combination indicating that besides the United Kingdom and Canada, no other single country represents a sufficiently large market to be broken out.[22]

Just as the United Kingdom is the single most important market for the largest American producers, the United States is the single most important market for the UK industry. Like the US studios, the UK television production sector receives a significant share of its profits from the international market. In 2016, sales totaled 1.3 billion pounds, up 10 percent from the year before. Exports of "finished television programming" (as opposed to formats), represented £668 million pounds of that total.[23] The United States was, as always, the United Kingdom's largest export market, with £497 million in sales, up 16 percent from the year before.[24] BBC Worldwide, the commercial distribution arm of the nonprofit public service BBC and one of the biggest players in the international television trade, made £305.7 in the North American market in 2016.[25] The company's annual report does not provide the percentage of the profits deriving solely from the US market, but it's probable that Worldwide's activities contributed significantly to the £497 million UK distributors earned in the United States in that year, since Worldwide is the most significant UK player in the international market.

It is increasingly the case that the production patterns of US and UK television industries cannot be understood without reference to international distribution. As Roberta Pearson argues in her chapter in this book, US television series are now being renewed despite poor domestic ratings if their international sales remain healthy. Hence global distribution has a direct influence upon domestic television production, which may conceivably lead to programs designed to succeed in the international as well as the domestic markets. Such programs might, for example, feature international casts or locations, as was the case with *Lost* and *Heroes*, or conform to well-established and successful genres, such as the procedural. UK domestic production is similarly impacted by decisions concerning potentially profitable international content. For example, over the five years from 2011 to 2016, BBC Worldwide deposited almost £1.3 billion in revenues into the BBC's coffers, "money that has supplemented the licence fee to keep audiences in the UK informed, educated and entertained."[26]

However, these audiences may now be consuming programs designed not for their own information, education, and entertainment but for the rest of the world, as producers come under pressure to produce less locally specific content in favor of content that travels well—a concern that has affected the transatlantic TV trade since its earliest decades. This may mean more programs resembling *Downton Abbey* and *Sherlock* and fewer resembling *Broken*, the recent BBC series about the travails of a priest and his parishioners in Merseyside in the age of austerity, which some may argue better serves the needs of domestic viewers than the international hits. In addition to affecting domestic production patterns, the transatlantic television trade also has an impact on domestic distribution, with imported content used to attract niche audiences and brand domestic channels, a topic addressed by several of this volume's authors. Clearly it is no longer possible to talk about television from a primarily national perspective; television studies' traditional focus on national industries and national content has recently given way to a "third wave" of scholarship with a more transnational approach.

ROOTS OF TRANSATLANTIC SCHOLARSHIP

Three distinctive "waves" of scholarship mark our understanding of television's global circulation. During the first wave of international television scholarship, from the 1960s into the 1980s, the main emphasis of research centered on the impact of imported American television on national cultures, linked to fears of "Americanization" more generally. Broadcasters around the globe struggled to develop a national television culture and a domestic industry despite the lure of cheap US imports (and those from other, regionally dominant nations), even as an international trade in programs began to prosper.[27] The enormous global success of the prime-time serial drama *Dallas* in 1980–1981 brought such fears to a head, giving rise to iconic terms of anxiety like "wall-to-wall Dallas" and "Dallasification."

The second wave of international television research, from the mid-1980s to the late 1990s, responded to political and technological developments of the period, including

Thatcher/Reagan-era deregulation and the rise of cable and satellite television, with their promise of more channels and increased commercial competition. Anxieties over the erosion of the public sphere and the shift of emphasis from citizen to consumer circulated globally as well, as public service broadcasters were mandated to downsize their operations and outsource production, and the tide of American programs continued to increase.[28] However, as cultural studies began to make an impact on the academy, more scholars turned their attention to how viewers actually used and responded to global television.[29] We also begin to see some of the first uses of the term "transnational" over the more common "global," as in the Skovmand and Schroder volume *Media Cultures: Reappraising Transnational Media* (1992).

By the late 1990s, a third wave of scholarship began to develop out of the growing collision of digital media with traditional broadcasting, as well as the impact of increasing population migrations and the expanding influence of the European Union and its transnational project. As new media capitals rose (Bombay, Hong Kong, Lagos, Seoul), new ways of theorizing cultural flows began to appear,[30] and with them considerations of media culture willing to reconsider the old oppositions and to analyze ever more complex circuits of exchange. Scholars began to explore aspects of the international television trade from a more transnational perspective, providing a background to this volume's focus on the US/UK relationship, including the function of key transaction nodes of the transnational television industry, such as MIPCOM (Marché International des Programmes de Communication), held each year in Cannes, where buyers and sellers from around the world come together to bargain for global TV properties and exchange ideas.[31] Timothy Havens examines distribution, acquisition, and scheduling, with a primary focus on "gatekeepers," the "executives who make decisions about global trade"[32] and serve as mediators between transnational media conglomerates and national audiences. Others began to examine how practices formed in the era of strong nationalism had shifted to accommodate new transnational imperatives, such as coproduction,[33] and the ways that broadcasters integrated transnational texts into their domestic environments.[34]

Another strand of third-wave research gathered around the late 1990s' "format revolution," as Jean Chalaby terms it.[35] During this period, "Concepts adapted from territory to territory began to cross borders in great numbers," establishing the format trade as a "thriving global industry"[36] and turning scholarly attention to the transnational television trade through a focus on the development, circulation, and reception of globally successful "reality programs" such as *Big Brother, Survivor,* and the various *Idols*. Since the format trade is based on licensing not a finished program but a structuring concept or set of "rules" (often organized around some kind of competition), it is designed to be effectively transnational, adaptable to a wide range of international languages, cultures, and topics, breaking out of the national/international duality that previously dominated. The first international smash format hit, *Who Wants to Be a Millionaire?*, originated in the United Kingdom in 1998 and quickly spread around the globe, followed by hundreds of others. Since then scholarship on international television formats has flourished, as has the genre, allowing an approach based more on transnational negotiations of content than on circulation of national productions.

The last decade has produced several works key to the current project. Jeanette Steemers's *Selling Television: British Television in the Global Marketplace* revealed how the British television industry, second only to the United States in terms of television exportation, distributes content to key markets in the United States, Europe, Australia, New Zealand, and East Asia. It specifically examines the ways in which companies such as BBC Worldwide and Granada International (now absorbed by ITV Studios) export programs and formats and participate in coproductions.[37] In 2012, two books appeared that focused directly on the US-UK reciprocal relationship: Hilmes's *Network Nations*, which traces the history of transatlantic exchange between Britain and the United States from the 1920s through the 1970s,[38] and Elke Weissmann's *Transnational Television Drama: Special Relations and Mutual Influence between the US and UK*. Weissmann picks up the story from the 1970s to the present, focusing on topics including the role of perceived cultural difference in importation, the influence of UK programs upon US broadcasters, the activities of transnational audiences in online spaces, and the growing importance of coproduction.[39]

But in television time, 2012 is an eon ago. Since then, the international expansion of mostly US-based digital subscription services such as Netflix, Amazon Prime, and HBO, as well as more regional "subscription video on demand" (SVOD) platforms has radically rearranged relationships between audiences and ways of viewing television, and between traditional terrestrial and cable broadcasters and the way that programs are made, distributed, and promoted. Largely (though not entirely) removing the element of scheduled weekly broadcasts so basic to the television experience across the twentieth century, SVOD services have created a new concept, more similar to a library than to a broadcast service, into which viewers can dip according to their own tastes and schedules. Though advertiser-supported television still remains strong, as do many (but not all) public broadcasters, the subscription model has become a vital adjunct to the contemporary television universe, to which terrestrial broadcasters and cable channels have had to adjust.

As a result, scripted drama has even more firmly established itself as the most valuable commodity in the international television trade, and the US and UK television industries direct more and more of their finances and efforts into its production and international distribution. Steemers, in a 2016 article updating her earlier book, observes that in the "increasingly volatile environment" of an industry coping with the massive disruption of streaming television, "drama continues to drive the sales of the larger [UK production] companies."[40] A recent report on the "impressive" growth of UK television exports stated that "investment in premium content for scripted and non-scripted programmes was believed to be central to future export growth."[41] Indeed drama now makes up around half of BBC Worldwide's total investment, as a result of a "deliberate rebalancing" from other genres.[42] The second-ranked UK international distributor, ITV Studios, estimates that

> the global content market is growing at about 5% per annum, with some genres such as drama growing more rapidly than others. To capitalise on this, our strategy remains to develop, own and manage content rights in genres that return and travel internationally—namely drama, entertainment and factual entertainment.[43]

Drama, says the distributor, has particular value as "standout, original content becomes brand defining for both broadcasters and OTT [over-the-top] players."[44]

As each company strives to find the hits that strengthen the brand and attract new subscribers both at home and abroad—*House of Cards, Man in the High Castle, Game of Thrones*—their rivalry, argues Gillian Doyle,

> has significantly boosted demand for one particular category of content: high-end drama. The impetus for SVODs to build recognition through investment in "big statement" drama content has encouraged a retaliatory response from incumbent pay-TV services that can afford it such as, in the United Kingdom, BSkyB.

As Saul Venit, chief operating officer of Lookout Point, a leading UK independent production and distribution company, told Doyle,

> There has been a knock-on effect to other services so it's not just the SVOD services who are now looking for [high-end drama]. . . . There is a *House of Cards* effect across the industry. When you look at just the scale of the investment Netflix made—and other networks that are competing for space, like Sky, feel they need to match that with really big commissions like *Fortitude* in the same way.[45]

The essays in this volume, then, aim to contribute to our understanding of the role that television drama plays in this radically changed media universe, especially prominent in the relationship between two of its largest and most deeply intertwined producing and consuming nations. Doing so means reflecting on audience practices and fan identities as much as industrial and textual structures. Historically, the study of transatlantic flows of capital and meaning, along with strong and weak variants of transnationalism or "marked"/ "unmarked" textualities, hasn't always considered how audiences contribute to these factors. But third-wave research has tended to be more attentive to the role of audiences and fans within such processes. For instance, the previously mentioned *Transnational Television Drama* by Elke Weissmann includes a chapter specifically exploring how transnational audiences for forensic science drama (*Silent Witness, Waking the Dead*, and *CSI*) use other imports, as well as texts sharing the country of origin, as evaluative points of comparison. Despite a strong transatlantic awareness and contextualization, "supposed national differences are constantly reiterated" in these audiences' online reviews.[46] This raises the question of how contemporary television drama has not only been *consumed* as variously (trans)national, but also potentially *(co)created as transatlantic* by its digital fans, reinforcing or contesting transnational discourses circulating officially in and around US/UK television dramas.

TRANSATLANTIC FANDOM

As waves of transnational scholarship have developed, so too have cultural and media-technological contexts altered, reframing how transatlantic TV audiences tend to make sense of their viewing practices. The first wave of scholarship, marked by a focus on US cultural imperialism, positioned emblematic programs such as *Dallas* as a problematic "disturbance," likely looming large "only in the ivory towers of the policy-makers and other guardians of the 'national culture.' In the millions of living rooms where the TV set is switched on to *Dallas*, the issue is rather one of pleasure," argued Ien Ang in *Watching "Dallas"*, thereby instead exemplifying second-wave scholarship's turn to cultural and audience studies.[47] However, in first and second wave theorizing there was a pronounced asymmetry in approaches to—and in the discourses and experiences of—transatlantic audiences. Whereas the United Kingdom's mass audiences for popular US dramas had to be distanced from accusations of cultural imperialism, a situation that resulted in Ien Ang's 1980s account of *Dallas* and its "emotional realism"[48] being altogether disarticulated from national identity, by contrast US audiences for selected public service productions from Britain were positioned as part of an elite taste culture. *Masterpiece Theatre* had been very deliberately branded as non-American via its UK-English spelling from its origination in 1971, after its working title, *The Best of the BBC*, was superseded.[49] Unlike transatlantic audiences on the UK side, who were presumed to be under threat from American influence and subjected to a cultural lowering in taste, in this pre-HBO era, US audiences were assumed to be elevated and distinguished via their consumption of "quality" British TV, often adaptations of literary classics or historical dramas, as marked by the name of its emblematic show: not television, but "theatre."

The more recent third-wave of transnational scholarship confronts a very different world of transatlantic fans and audiences, with this asymmetry having given way to a relative convergence of US and UK audience discourses. Today, UK fans of quality US TV drama can make just as much claim to affirming their "place as a cultural elite" distinguished from the national-cultural mainstream as can their US counterparts who embrace the best of British TV imports.[50] Conversely, US fans can enjoy British drama on different levels, including genres and formats that *Masterpiece* would never consider, sci-fi and fantasy in particular. Transatlantic difference has readily and pervasively become a marker of audience distinction on both sides of the Atlantic, it would seem, with the Reading Contemporary Television book series published by I.B. Tauris involving audience study in relation to the likes of *Sex and the City*, *CSI*, and *Doctor Who*.[51] Herbert Schwaab has argued that the book series belongs "to a new genre of books that could be called fan/ scholar literature,"[52] but he views this as a negative development in certain ways:

> What is at stake reading *The Sopranos, Sex and the City* or *Desperate Housewives*? Everybody knows that Tony Soprano is a complex character, everybody notes the ironies involved in the construction of Carrie Bradshaw or in the nostalgia driven suburbia of Wisteria Lane. It is an extension of a pleasure already granted by the object. . . . This easy to read television . . . puts the television scholar in a very stable position of repeating exactly what the authors and producers intended to achieve.[53]

Here, contemporary television drama's "readability," and its construction as quality TV addressing, if not interpellating, an educated fan audience possessing high levels of cultural capital, suggest that the (transatlantic) audience pleasures of these US TV dramas are somehow preprogrammed as matters of distinction. Even scholarship is seemingly caught up in this process, no longer challenging and transgressing the meanings and values of TV drama, and thus no longer being akin to Ien Ang's defense of the pleasures of *Dallas*, which operated contra discourses of cultural imperialism.

But to dismiss third-wave scholarship on transnational TV drama's audiences and fans (often itself produced by scholar-fans) as simply having been assimilated into the TV industry misses the range of different ways that transatlantic fandom can be performed, and the forms of distinction that are associated with them. In *Reading "Lost"*, Will Brooker muses on his experience of watching "television out of time," following *Lost* as a weekly series of downloads close to the US broadcast, where "by the time a show . . . reaches DVD, the season is complete, a finished text. The case is closed, the detection is over."[54]

Audiences coming along at this later point, whether they are academics wanting to study *Lost*, or fans who are late to the party, cannot easily join the community of devotees puzzling over the program: "The *Lost* follower . . . may find him or herself isolated and out of time, with no obvious place within an online community that, perhaps quaintly, remains structured around traditional broadcast schedules and global geography."[55]

Accordingly, transatlantic audiences continue to face difficulties caused by time differences, even if broadcast schedules have become less relevant as a result of full-season "drops," and because different US/UK broadcasters have moved their transmission of specific episodes closer together in order to try and minimize piracy and illegal downloading or streaming. *Lost*'s 2010 finale was shown on Sky1 in the United Kingdom at 5:00 a.m.—simultaneous with its West Coast American broadcast—meaning that hardcore fans in Britain could stay up or get up early to watch. Similarly, new weekly episodes of *Twin Peaks: The Return* have been simulcast with the United States on Sky Atlantic, airing at times such as 3:20 a.m. And US fans of *Doctor Who* shared in BBC America's social media simulcasting of the thirteenth Doctor announcement after ESPN had broadcast the 2017 men's Wimbledon final (which started at 9:00 a.m. ET on Sunday, July 16, in the United States). At such moments, fandom renders the United States and United Kingdom as part of a singular "zone of consumption."[56] But at other points, when there is less hyped-up news or less-anticipated new content, fans may wait a day or two to catch up with programs from across the Atlantic, or they may—as Brooker points out—discover and binge a program some appreciable time after it was current in TV and social media terms. Audiences are therefore called upon to navigate a series of transatlantic temporalities; neither fans nor academics constitute a singular bloc "reading" TV in the same way, nor encountering it at the same time. The different time zones of the United States and United Kingdom, along with variations in broadcast schedules, mean that some fans will do their very best to integrate into nonnational times, using whatever means they can to access a TV program.

In *Rogue Archives: Digital Cultural Memory and Media Fandom*, Abigail De Kosnik refers to this as "media time," defining it "as consisting of the schedules mandated by the culture industries' production and sales cycles: the time of broadcasting in the network television industry, the time of "drop dates" . . . in the online streaming industry."[57] De Kosnik argues that, given the analysis and criticism of what's been termed by Matt Hills in *Fan Cultures* "just-in-time fandom,"[58] whereby fans begin posting online as soon as they can after TV transmission—live-tweeting during broadcast would be another version of this—we "can read in . . . [this work] a wish for fan time to be different from media time, for fans to have their own performance times, that is, their own schedules for making and sharing performances, that are not so tied to media time."[59] This is a fair commentary on arguments from *Fan Cultures*, which suggested that fans were in danger of becoming overly enmeshed within industrial rhythms and temporalities.

However, the transnational, and specifically transatlantic, disavowal of time zones in favor of simulcasting (however odd the national time it leads to) creates an unusual and rather different industrial position. Here, media time is adjusted in favor of De Kosnik's "fan time," just as midnight screenings or midnight shop openings recognize fans' desire to gain immediate access to their fan object, as well as operating at least partly outside of "mainstream" norms of consumption as a marker of fan distinction. Transatlantic simulcasts therefore facilitate a fannish zone of consumption (staying up until 3:00 a.m., Greenwich Mean Time +1, to watch *Twin Peaks* is undoubtedly a performance of fan dedication) as well as combating online piracy. In *Time Passing: Modernity and Nostalgia*, Sylvanie Agacinski argues that "we live . . . *in the time of the media*, and their programs,"[60] but rather than generalizing a mediatized time, contemporary transnational fandom demonstrates that a temporary slippage between time zones can be promoted for transatlantic "event" TV.

Where US or UK media industries do not recognize and validate fans' desires to switch between different time zones, then fandom can take the matter into its own hands, of course. For example, there were lengthy delays between *Sherlock*'s UK and US broadcast dates prior to "The Abominable Bride" special, which aired in both countries on January 1, 2016. As a result, series 1 to 3 were accessible to US fans only via illegal downloads immediately after their UK premieres. This situation, which licensing broadcasters such as the BBC have increasingly sought to avoid, gives rise to "user-led transnationalism"[61] where fans refuse to accept the limitations of official industrial circulations of texts. And as fans discuss TV programs online, they often "state where they are from in the course of any substantial interchange with other users, and this locative aspect of self-presentation remains . . . important to the meanings being drawn out by others." Adrian Athique goes on to argue that fans are able to enact and observe "the operation of grassroots 'international relations' in real time."[62] But these audiences are more than international, that is, where a national audience consumes TV drama from a different country of origin. Instead, these are necessarily transnational fans, not only combining national identities within their grouping, but also going beyond national identity in their constitution of a fan affinity and collective. It is because of this "trans" capacity, this going beyond the nation-state as a marker of identity, that some have argued that border-crossing fandoms should properly be thought of as transcultural, setting to one side the question of national affiliations and their imagined communities:

> Fans become fans of border-crossing texts or objects not necessarily because of where they are produced, but because they may recognise a subjective moment of affinity

regardless of origin. This is not to say that the nation is unimportant, but rather that it is but one of a constellation of possible points of affinity upon which transcultural fandom may be predicated. Nation-based differences or similarities may well appeal to people across borders; but so, too, might affective investments in characters, stories, and even fan subjectivities that exceed any national orientation.[63]

However, even when viewed as transcultural, fandom has a tendency to fall back into aspects of national difference, evaluation, and distinction, following well-established patterns of meaning-making. Sandra Annett characterizes this process of transcultural fandom as one built "through flow but also through friction."[64] That is, transcultural fandoms involve fans setting aside national differences in favor of shared "affective investments" in storyworlds at the same time that conflict accompanies this conjunction, precisely as a result of fans' interconnection across (national and other) differences. Graeme Turner has argued along related lines, suggesting that far from convergence culture and transnational Web 2.0 networks rendering the nation-based analysis of television as a "zombie category,"[65] for both scholars and audiences-users alike, it has instead resulted in a reconfiguration of trans/national identities. The transnational can represent less of an intrusion or disruption for contemporary (fan) audiences than a possibility to explore and perform newly emergent cultural distinctions.

In this sense, transatlantic TV may be experienced very differently by audiences as compared to national institutions, for whom transnational, OTT industry players can instead represent both an economic and a cultural threat. Piers Wenger, the BBC's current controller of drama, has strongly contrasted the BBC's expertise-driven culture of drama production to Netflix's allegedly algorithm-driven commissioning, suggesting that only the former can deliver genuine originality and innovation.[66] Likewise, the director of BBC Arts, Jonty Claypole, has argued that while "You can go to Netflix for a wonderful snack or a wonderful feast of a single thing, . . . I think the BBC's role as an arts provider is going to become more and more unique." By this he means that the BBC can offer cross-platform themed programming, with specific TV dramas being scheduled within "moments of national interest," such as 2016's pan-BBC, online and broadcast Shakespeare festival.[67] Russell T. Davies's reworking of *A Midsummer Night's Dream* formed part of this commemoration of the four hundredth anniversary of Shakespeare's death, while 2017 involved a less stereotyped view of "national interest" via the BBC's "Gay Britannia" season, this time commemorating the fiftieth anniversary of the 1967 decriminalization of homosexuality in the United Kingdom.

But if the current reconfigurations of national and transnational dimensions of cultural identity can be productive for (fan) audiences and yet rather more threatening to national broadcasters, how might these industrial and audience discourses intersect and interact? National broadcasters need to engage with globalized markets, to be sure, and thus it comes as little surprise to see an increase in BBC-Netflix coproductions; nation-based producers also need to draw on national meanings and brandings that can circulate successfully on a transatlantic and a global stage—something that a big hit show such as *Sherlock* has done extremely well. But as transatlantic articulations of TV drama arguably become more visible and more clearly "marked," in Hjort's terms, then audience discourses can, in turn, work to affectively cocreate the category of transatlantic TV drama by amplifying and validating these textual markers of transnationalism, whether through blogged reviews, Tumblr expressions of emotion, or tweeted sentiments of transcultural fandom.

As should be apparent through our focus thus far on transnational theory, television markets, transatlantic scholarship, and fandom, many topics and approaches are covered across this collection. Despite such diversity, or perhaps thanks to it, a few central issues and themes emerge. Many of these are no doubt applicable beyond the US/UK context, and as similar disruptions and rearrangements take place around the globe. We will close by summarizing a number of these themes—transnational coproduction, partnerships, and representations—at the same time as introducing the chapters to follow.

STRUCTURING ISSUES

Given the many tensions and innovations that mark the long-standing relationship between US and UK broadcasters and producers—not to mention their shared audiences—it is not surprising that several of the chapters focus on an old practice in a new setting: *transnational coproduction*. Coproduction has become a bigger factor in television drama than ever before, and several chapters discuss its permutations and dominant trends, cutting across industries, texts, and fan activity. While Michele Hilmes places US public television's longest-running dramatic showcase, *Masterpiece*, in historical perspective, she also lays out some of the ways that the economic and decision-making relationship between its British and American coproduction partners has shifted over the last few decades, to the benefit, she argues, of both. Eva Redvall's chapter picks up the case of one of *Masterpiece*'s greatest hits, *Downton Abbey*, to examine the incentives for both British and American production partners to break out of traditional dramatic modes, combining elements of both "popular" and "quality" texts to create a transnationally successful hybrid. Robin Nelson looks at a different set of creative relationships in his chapter on *Rome* and *Parade's End*, both involving a partnership between the US pay-cable giant HBO and the BBC. In tracing how "residual tensions" still exist in the practice of coproduction—between public service and commercial entertainment, between "quality" and popular programs—Nelson illuminates the motivations of each partner in an increasingly competitive business. And on the audience side, Matt Hills focus on the Channel 4–originated, Netflix-continued anthology drama *Black Mirror*, arguing that that "fandom has become distinctively *multi-discursive* within the current contexts of transatlantic television flow." Building on his work in *Crossing Fandoms*,[68] Paul Booth examines a transatlantic fan community organized around three distinct TV dramas—WB and CW's *Supernatural* and the BBC's *Sherlock* and *Doctor Who*—which are playfully amalgamated by these fans into *SuperWhoLock*. Though it is stretching the term "coproduction" a bit to extend it to the production of fan spaces and narratives, these authors show that, through the discursive spaces created by fans around these programs, meanings and interpretations are effectively coproduced—and disputed—in a transatlantic space. Overall, this thematic thread demonstrates that while the old policy-grounded mandates for emphasizing national culture over more culturally hybrid approaches have been largely overturned, nationally specific tensions still exist and are being played out in different terms and over different terrains.

Related to coproduction, but going beyond specific programs to examine larger entities, a second theme recurs around *new transnational relationships* and how they require us to adjust our thinking about incentives, traditions, and proximities. On the industry side, Christine Becker looks at the transformation of the cable channel BBC America from a UK-owned outreach to the US cable market based on British programs, to a half-US-owned high-profile space for both imported and original productions from all over, whose breakout show was the Canadian-produced sci-fi drama *Orphan Black*. She argues that BBC America's "Britishness" now serves as a form of "transnational coding" whose value lies in its role as a "key node in the transnational networked relationship between BBC Worldwide, the BBC, and AMC Networks." Tracing a similar shift in her chapter, Roberta Pearson argues that the concept of "cultural proximity," as developed by Straubhaar and others in the 1990s, needs to be expanded in the contemporary transatlantic context to allow for more flexible relationships between industries, texts, and audiences. She proposes a "cultural proximity index" that recognizes that there is "a spectrum ranging from the negative to the positive—cultural discount to cultural accessibility to cultural premium," illustrating its markers and effects in a comparison of *Elementary* in the United Kingdom and *Sherlock* in the United States.

Likewise, Lincoln Geraghty's examination of the transformation of the San Diego Comic-Con from a US-based comic and sci-fi-oriented convention to a place where a wide range of international media meet and mingle shows how important the "British brand" promoted through such shows as *Doctor Who* has become for both fans and industry. Lori Morimoto expands further into the space of transatlantic audiences by looking at the online relationships between British and American fans, contrasting the tension between cultural specificity and "American monoculture" in transnationally popular programs with the practices of *Coronation Street* fans in Canada, where cultural differences are valued as part of the transnational experience.

Amid these changing relationships and practices, new ways of *representing and framing*—or, as we might say, "marking"—transnationalism have begun to emerge. Karen Petruska and Faye Woods interrogate the use of the word "original" to describe international programs on Netflix and its competitors, arguing that it has lost its traditional meaning linking texts to a specific site of production or commissioning. Instead, they conclude, such discursive framings "advance a consistent narrative that SVOD services are global, innovative, and productive, and that their programs transcend national identities and cultures." Jonathan Bignell demonstrates that one such program, HBO's series *Episodes*, in fact represents an extended inquiry into just such contentious conceptual shifts: the show "makes transatlantic relationships visible and reflexively plays them out" as it tells the story of British television writers transported to Hollywood. "It is a self-reflexive discourse about discourses that are already highly caricatured," working out the dislocations of transnational television. In their chapter focused on acting in *Game of Thrones*, Simone Knox and Gary Cassidy—one a media studies scholar, one a professional actor turned academic—explore the basis for the long-standing "binary" that associates British acting with technique and American acting with spontaneity. Noting the increasing transnational mobility of British actors appearing in US-based productions, they provide an in-depth analysis of two scenes in the series and show how two British-trained actors have adapted their technique to the demands of transnational serial production. On the industry side, Sam Ward investigates the ways that the Sky Atlantic channel represents its transnational identity as a pipeline for "quality" American programs through its exclusive rights to HBO and Showtime dramas. Using a strategy and imagery of "transnational bridging," on screen and off, Sky Atlantic seeks to make "transnational brand integration" visible on the screen. And Paul Rixon turns to critical reception analysis in his chapter on one key site of reception discourse in the United Kingdom, the *Guardian*'s television blogs, to discover the terms in which UK critics discuss "quality" US programs and what that can tell us about the role of television criticism today in the transnational context.

Through this exploration of contemporary transatlantic drama industries, texts, and audiences, linked by common themes around coproduction, relationships, and representations, we hope that these chapters not only illuminate a significant sector of the transatlantic US/UK television phenomenon, but provide some insights that can be applied to other sites of transnational exchange. What other long-standing circuits of coproduction have been transformed by digital streaming platforms in the same—or different—ways? What other new transnational relationships have arisen or will arise as platforms like Netflix extend globally, expanding the collision and interaction of national televisual cultures—and what new platforms will arise out of such partnerships? Crucially, how will the resulting cultural collisions be represented to their audiences of critics, viewers, and fans alike—will they be acknowledged or obscured, clearly or falsely marked, provide productive or disruptive experiences, stimulate creativity or create antagonism? And what kinds of representations, uses, and meanings will audiences themselves create? Although we have flagged it up here, this new phase of scholarship has only begun.

NOTES

1. See, for example, Paolo Russo and Lindsay Steenberg, "Imagining the Post-forensic Landscape: The Crime Drama on Transnational Television," *New Review of Film and Television Studies* 14:3 (2016): 299–303; Jesse Ferreras, "32 New TV Shows from Other Countries You Should Be Watching Right Now," *HuffPost*, November 19, 2015, http://www.huffingtonpost.ca/2015/11/19/new-tv-shows_n_8587028.html; Mary Kay Schilling, "In Praise of International Crime Dramas," *New York Times*, May 9, 2017, https://www.nytimes.com/2017/05/09/t-magazine/entertainment/best-international-crime-dramas-tv.html.
2. See Michele Hilmes, *Network Nations: A Transnational History of British and American Broadcasting* (New York: Routledge, 2012) for an extended analysis of this history. For more on the concept of the "national" in television studies see Andrea Esser, "Defining 'the Local' in Localization or 'Adapting for Whom?,'" in *Media across Borders: Localising TV, Film and Video Games*, ed. Andrea Esser, Iain Robert Smith, and Miguel A. Bernal-Merino (London: Routledge, 2016), 19–35.
3. See Paul Rixon, "American Programmes on British Screens: A Revaluation," *Critical Studies in Television* 2:2 (2013): 96–112.
4. See Janet McCabe and Kim Akass, eds., *TV's Betty Goes Global* (London: I.B. Taurus, 2013).
5. However, this does not take into account the growing number of Spanish-language broadcasters and cable channels that began to flourish in the 1980s, alongside a profusion of satellite channels from around the world available on cable systems starting in the 1990s—most of them linguistically inaccessible to the English-speaking audience.
6. Pierre-Yves Saunier, "Transnational," in *The Palgrave Dictionary of Transnational History*, ed. Akira Iriye and Pierre-Yves Saunier (Basingstoke: Palgrave Macmillan, 2009), 1047–1055.
7. Quoted in Saunier, "Transnational," 1048.
8. Compiled in Arjun Appadurai, *Modernity at Large: Cultural Dimensions of Globalization* (Minneapolis: University of Minnesota Press, 1996).
9. Saunier, "Transnational," 1054.
10. Michael Curtin, "Media Capital: Towards the Study of Spatial Flows," *International Journal of Cultural Studies* 6:2 (2003): 202–228.
11. Mette Hjort, "On the Plurality of Cinematic Transnationalism," in *World Cinemas, Transnational Perspectives* (New York: Routledge, 2010), 12–33.
12. Jeanette Steemers, "Selling Television," *Media Industries Journal* 1:1 (2014): 44.
13. *ITV Plc Annual Report and Accounts 2016*, 26.
14. TBI reporter, "Drama Data: Europe Challenges the US," April 21, 2014.
15. Edward Jay Epstein, "Hollywood's Profits, Demystified," *Hollywood Economist*, August 8, 2005, http://www.slate.com/articles/arts/the_hollywood_economist/2005/08/hollywoods_profits_demystified.html.

16. "Those Economic Storms Are Not Sinking Sales; Despite Eurozone crisis, Streaming Video Services among Factors Buoying Studios," *Broadcasting and Cable*, September 24, 2012 (no. 142), 37.

17. Shawn Shimpach, *Television in Transition* (Oxford: Wiley-Blackwell, 2010), 24.

18. CBS Corporation, Annual Report Pursuant to Section 13 or 15(d) of the Securities Exchange Act of 1934 for the fiscal year ended December 31, 2016, I-1.

19. CBS Corporation, Annual Report, I-4.

20. CBS Corporation, Annual Report, I-4.

21. CBS Corporation, Annual Report, II-20, 24.

22. CBS Corporation, Annual Report, II-10.

23. TRP Research, *UK Television Exports 2015–16*.

24. PACT, "Impressive Growth in UK Television Exports, up 10% to £1,326m," February 3, 2017, http://www.pact.co.uk/news-detail.html?id=impressive-growth-in-uk-television-exports-up-10-to-1-326m.

25. *BBC Worldwide Annual Report 15/16*, 3.

26. *BBC Worldwide Annual Report 15/16*, 3.

27. Key works include Kaarle Nordenstreng and Tapio Varis, "Television Traffic: A One-Way Street," in *UNESCO Reports and Papers on Mass Communication 70* (Paris: UNESCO, 1974); Herbert Schiller, *Communication and Cultural Domination* (New York: International Arts and Sciences Press, 1976); Jeremy Tunstall, *The Media Are American* (New York: Columbia University Press, 1977).

28. Key works include Jay Blumler, "The New Television Marketplace: Imperatives, Implications, Issues," in *Mass Media and Society*, ed. James Curran and Michael Gurevich (London: Arnold, 1991), 194–215; Richard Collins, "Wall to Wall Dallas? The US-UK Trade in Television," *Screen* 27:5 (1986): 66–76; James Curran, "Mass Media and Democracy: A Reappraisal," in Curran and Gurevich, *Mass Media and Society*, 82–117; and Nicholas Garnham, "Public Service versus the Market," *Screen* 24:1 (1983): 6–27.

29. Representative works include Ien Ang, *Desperately Seeking the Audience* (London: Routledge, 2001); David Morley and Kevin Robbins, *Spaces of Identity* (London: Routledge, 1995); John Sinclair, Elizabeth Jacka, and Stuart Cunningham, eds., *New Patterns in Global Television* (Oxford: Oxford University Press, 1996); Michael Skovmand and Kim Christian Schroder, *Media Cultures: Reappraising Transnational Media* (London: Routledge, 1992).

30. Appadurai, *Modernity at Large*; Homi K. Bhabha, *The Location of Culture* (London: Routledge, 2004); Nestor Garcia Canclini, *Consumers and Citizens: Globalization and Multicultural Conflict* (Minneapolis: University of Minnesota Press, 2001).

31. Denise Bielby and Lee Harrington, *Global TV: Exporting Television and Culture in the World Market* (New York: New York University Press, 2008); Timothy Havens, *Global Television Marketplace* (London: BFI, 2006).

32. Havens, *Global Television Marketplace*, 3.

33. Barbara J. Selznick, *Global Television: Co-producing Culture* (Philadelphia: Temple University Press, 2008).

34. Paul Rixon, *American Television on British Screens: A Story of Cultural Interaction* (Houndmills, Basingstoke: Palgrave Macmillan, 2006).

35. Jean K. Chalaby, "At the Origin of a Global Industry: The TV Format Trade as an Anglo-American Invention," *Media, Culture and Society* 34:1 (2012): 36–52.

36. Chalaby, "At the Origin," 36.

37. Jeanette Steemers, *Selling Television: British Television in the Global Marketplace* (London: BFI, 2004).

38. Hilmes, *Network Nations*.

39. Elke Weissmann, *Transnational Television Drama: Special Relations and Mutual Influence between the US and the UK* (Basingstoke: Palgrave Macmillan, 2012).

40. Jeanette Steemers, "International Sales of U.K. Television Content: Change and Continuity in 'the Space in between' Production and Consumption," *Television & New Media* 17:8 (2016): 734–753.

41. PACT, "Impressive Growth."

42. *BBC Worldwide Annual Report 15/16*, 9.

43. *ITV Plc Annual Report and Accounts 2016*, 26.

44. *ITV Plc Annual Report*, 27.

45. Gillian Doyle, "Digitization and Changing Windowing Strategies in the Television Industry: Negotiating New Windows on the World," *Television & New Media* 17:7 (2016): 638.

46. Weissmann, *Transnational Television Drama*, 139.

47. Ien Ang, *Watching "Dallas"* (London: Methuen, 1985), 3.

48. Ang, *Watching Dallas*, 41.

49. Rebecca Eaton, *Making "Masterpiece"* (New York: Viking, 2013), 14.

50. Jeffrey S. Miller, *Something Completely Different: British Television and American Culture* (Minneapolis: University of Minnesota Press, 2000), 178.

51. Deborah Jermyn, "In Love with Sarah Jessica Parker: Celebrating Female Fandom and Friendship in Sex and the City," in *Reading Sex and the City*, ed. Kim Akass and Janet McCabe (London: I.B. Tauris, 2004), 201–218; Matt Hills and Amy Luther, "Investigating 'CSI Television Fandom': Fans' Textual Paths through the Franchise," in *Reading "CSI": Crime TV under the Microscope*, ed. Michael Allen (London: I.B. Tauris, 2007), 208–221; Rebecca Williams, "Tweeting the TARDIS: Interaction, Liveness and Social Media in *Doctor Who* Fandom," in *New Dimensions of "Doctor Who": Adventures in Space, Time and Television*, ed. Matt Hills (London: I.B. Tauris, 2013), 154–173.

52. Herbert Schwaab, "'Unreading' Contemporary Television," in *After the Break: Television Theory Today*, ed. Marijke de Valck and Jan Teurlings (Amsterdam: Amsterdam University Press, 2013), 23.

53. Schwaab, "Unreading Contemporary Television," 24.

54. Will Brooker, "Television Out of Time: Watching Cult Shows on Download," in *Reading "Lost"*, ed. Roberta Pearson (London: I.B. Tauris, 2009), 52.

55. Brooker, "Television Out of Time," 58.

56. Anna Pertierra and Graeme Turner, *Locating Television: Zones of Consumption* (New York: Routledge, 2013).

57. Abigail De Kosnik, *Rogue Archives: Digital Cultural Memory and Media Fandom* (Cambridge, MA: MIT Press, 2016), 157.

58. Matt Hills, *Fan Cultures* (London: Routledge, 2002), 179.

59. De Kosnik, *Rogue Archives*, 157.

60. Sylvanie Agacinski, *Time Passing: Modernity and Nostalgia* (New York: Columbia University Press, 2003), 46.

61. Adrian Athique, *Transnational Audiences* (Cambridge: Polity, 2016), 149.

62. Athique, *Transnational Audiences*, 150.

63. Bertha Chin and Lori Hitchcock Morimoto, "Towards a Theory of Transcultural Fandom," *Participations* 10:1 (2013): 99.

64. Sandra Annett, *Anime Fan Communities: Transcultural Flows and Frictions* (Basingstoke: Palgrave Macmillan, 2014), 131.

65. Graeme Turner, *Re-inventing the Media* (London: Routledge, 2016), 61.

66. In Georg Szalai, "BBC Drama Chief Vows to Back Britishness and the 'Unexpected' over Algorithms," *Hollywood Reporter*, May 5, 2017, http://www.hollywoodreporter.com/news/bbc-drama-chief-vows-back-britishness-unexpected-algorithms-1000476.

67. In Bryan Appleyard, "Is This the Saviour of BBC Arts?," *Sunday Times Culture*, August 13, 2017, 9.

68. Paul Booth, *Crossing Fandoms: SuperWhoLock and the Contemporary Fan Audience* (Basingstoke: Palgrave Macmillan, 2016).

Transatlantic Industries

INTRODUCTION

This part of the book looks primarily at recent developments in the media industry that underlie the rise of transatlantic television drama—keeping in mind that, although the UK-US exchange has been a particularly lively and important one, these trends are occurring around the world. The chapters define "media industry" broadly, as encompassing the sweep of practices concerned with the production and distribution of television drama in today's digital environment, covering contemporary television's major platforms: traditional broadcast or terrestrial TV, cable and satellite television channels, and digital streaming services. Thus, in these four essays, concerns as diverse as political and cultural contexts, policy and regulation, economics, marketing, and technological infrastructure are examined—the framework behind creative conditions in television drama that produce contemporary texts and their audiences.

The first chapter, "Making *Masterpiece* Matter: The Transnational Cultural Work of America's Longest-Running Drama Program," by Michele Hilmes, focuses on the history behind the transatlantic trade: the forces and conditions that at first limited the scope of the US-UK "special relationship" but later began to drive its expansion. In particular, the practice of transnational coproduction between Britain and the United States is traced through the lens of one particular program, *Masterpiece Theatre*—or simply *Masterpiece*, as it is now known—on the American public broadcasting network PBS. One of the first concerted efforts to distribute primarily BBC-produced television drama to American audiences in the 1970s, it contributed to the growth of the "heritage drama" genre in the United Kingdom, drawing from a broader range of producers. Along the way, the coproduction relationship forged between *Masterpiece* and British broadcasters sparked a host of transatlantic tensions around the touchy area of television's role as a producer of national culture as well as an avenue for foreign influences, still resonant today. Thanks in no small part to its British connection, PBS has expanded from a small, primarily educational channel to one that competes with the largest commercial networks in the United States.

Complicating the transatlantic picture further, in chapter 2, "Traveling without a Passport: 'Original' Streaming Content in the Transatlantic Distribution Ecosystem," Karen Petruska and Faye Woods challenge one of the basic concepts underlying the transnational TV trade. From a historical context in which terms like "original" link cultural products with a situated authorship rooted in national identity—a British show is one produced in Britain, by British creators who have taken a primary hand in its production—today's digital streaming services such as Netflix and Amazon muddy those waters by, in many cases, attempting to sever the traditional link between production and location and to rearticulate it as a dislocated business practice. Thus a "Netflix Original" may have nothing to do with any originating creative effort on the part of Netflix but instead denote a program's first appearance in a new market: an erasure of authorship and identity and an example of the kind of strategic "false marking" of identity that is as old as television itself, but is given far more power and reach by today's global streaming platforms.

In chapter 3, Christine Becker, who has previously written on the rise of another pioneering transatlantic venture, the US-based but BBC Worldwide–owned cable channel BBC America, focuses here on its transformation from a UK service presenting British programs on US cable to a US-dominated outlet not just for British TV per se but for what she calls "British-branded" television. "BBC America: Cloning Drama for a Transnational Network" argues that, in the wake of the its partial acquisition by US-based AMC Networks in 2004, the channel shifted away from an emphasis on its British roots toward a schedule built on high-quality, auteur-driven drama that might come from anywhere in terms of corporate ownership, but still holds onto key aspects of "Britishness" built up by the transatlantic (now global) trade since the 1970s. This is a quite different "Britishness" than that promulgated by *Masterpiece*, instead using shows like the Canada-produced drama *Orphan Black* to link the network to a more youthful, edgy identity built up by other British imports like *Doctor Who* and *Top Gear*. Becker details the forces operating on AMC's business strategies both transnationally and domestically, specifically in the hypercharged competition for cable carriage in the United States, as well as BBC Worldwide's ambitions to build its reputation as a global brand, despite the increasingly US-dominated face presented by BBC America.

Chapter 4 turns to the case of Sky Atlantic, a satellite channel launched in 2011 by Sky, the United Kingdom's largest subscription television provider. In his chapter, "Branding Bridges: Sky Atlantic, 'Quality' Imports, and Brand Integration," Sam Ward explores both the business and the promotional strategies used by Sky to mark its place as the leading provider of American "quality television" in Britain. He develops the concept of "transnational bridging" as both an industrial practice and a discursive device used to position Sky Atlantic as a bridge between British and American television culture. Focusing on a series of initial idents put out by the network itself that quite literally juxtapose scenes associated with the United States with others from the United Kingdom, he argues that such narratives work not only to create a new way for British audiences to understand the American drama beamed into their midst, but to craft an identity for Sky TV as a purveyor of a brand of "quality" that reflects the changing status of US-produced drama in Britain.

This part's four chapters set up a historically based framework for understanding the industrial and technological shifts that inform contemporary transnational television drama, specifically between the United States and United Kingdom but by implication around the world. In the next part, transatlantic texts themselves are explored for the ways in which negotiations of national culture and identity play out within the programs and in the ways that we might understand them and the increasingly prolific culture work they perform.

/// 1 /// MAKING *MASTERPIECE* MATTER

The Transnational Cultural Work of America's
Longest-Running Drama Program

MICHELE HILMES

After decades of derision and critical neglect, the fortunes of *Masterpiece*—formerly *Masterpiece Theatre*, the United States' longest-running prime-time drama program—are on the rise. Making its debut on the nascent Public Broadcasting Service (PBS) in 1971, the anthology-style drama showcase quickly became PBS's top-rated prime-time program, its Sunday night slot a fixture in a small but dedicated subset of homes across the United States.[1] A transnational enterprise from the very beginning, in its early years it relied on serial drama productions imported from Britain, both literary adaptations and original drama, during a time in which funding pressures drove the BBC to expand its international markets.[2] Yet due to PBS's relatively small ratings (1–3 percent of the audience, at a time when commercial networks reliably drew 20–25 percent) for many years its status as a "highbrow" niche program, a "market failure" outlet for types of drama not likely to succeed commercially, relegated it to cultural neglect and dismissive criticism from those who had hoped that American public television might provide something with more teeth than "safely splendid" period dramas in British accents.

All of that began to change in the program's fourth decade, under the onslaught of multiplying channels, on-demand viewing, and the new respectability of serial drama on prime-time schedules. Suddenly, the whole "postnetwork" American television industry found itself shifting to what PBS and *Masterpiece* had been doing all along: delivering niche programming to small but devoted audiences, via crowdsourced funding, extended fictional franchises, well-developed digital platforms, and the use of transnational talent and buzz to create addictive, high-production-value serialized drama and documentary.[3] With the breakout success of *Downton Abbey* in 2011, exactly forty years after *Masterpiece Theatre*'s debut, PBS and its most emblematic prime-time program achieved heights of audience share and publicity never before reached. PBS became the fifth-ranked national US network, outdoing commercial rivals and far outstripping critical darlings like HBO and Showtime. It quickly followed up *Downton Abbey*'s success with another younger crowd-pleaser, *Sherlock*. *Masterpiece*, television's Cinderella, finally got its reputation makeover—marked by the 2013 publication of *Making Masterpiece*, the book whose title this chapter references, written by the show's longtime executive producer, Rebecca Eaton.[4]

With *Masterpiece*'s new prominence, transatlantic television coproduction, for almost fifty years a public relations minefield for public broadcasters on both sides of the Atlantic, has come out into the open—into an environment quite different from the one that sparked the show. There can be no doubt that the transatlantic "special relationship" has helped to keep alive high-end drama (and documentary) production in both countries, giving British public service-oriented broadcasters the additional funds and markets that they need to continue to produce it, and giving American public television a type of drama that suits not only its "educational" mission but also its relatively feeble production infrastructure. Yet it remains a contested, touchy, and often hidden history, full of concerns about national priorities, cultural identity, and public broadcasting's often difficult balancing act between public service and financial stability. This chapter will trace out some of that long-obscured history, examine the shifting complex of tensions over time, and attempt to tease out the way that transatlantic coproduction has worked in the case of *Masterpiece*.

TOUCHY TRANSNATIONALISMS

The relationship between the national and the transnational in media culture has always been a contested one. Broadcasting arose out of the ashes of World War I to become the preferred instrument of nation-building, a means to bind up the ragged edges of postwar nations (and empires), with most states forming centralized national broadcasting systems responsive in some way to government regulation and imperatives, if not actually owned and operated by the government itself. And, as that other iconic twentieth-century medium, film, began to pour out of Hollywood across the world, radio was called into use as a counterweight to protect and preserve national cultures and identities, staving off cinema's denationalizing effects.[5] Interwar nations expended a considerable amount of effort to keep outsiders from invading their airspace, and to ensure that radio content supported and protected the national culture—or at least those aspects deemed desirable by the parties in charge.

Nationalizing pressures affected the film industry as well. As a counterbalance to the tide of American films engulfing theaters across much of the interwar world, many nations put in place a system of quotas and incentives that worked to boost domestic production while limiting the number of Hollywood films that could be shown in local theaters. After World War II, due to currency restrictions, emphasis shifted to subsidizing domestic film production through a system of official, or "treaty," coproduction agreements that allowed national film studios to join with international partners on strictly negotiated terms that stipulated what elements of each film would come from each partner (so many lead actors from one country, so many from the other), how much financial and technical support would be provided by each partner (filming in one location, postproduction in another), and divided up revenues by geography and participation formulas.[6] Though the United States lacked the public funding structure of most nations, its commercial studios could and did actively partner around the globe, often by purchasing a share of an existing foreign studio, or by setting up a London or Paris or Rome subsidiary that qualified as a domestic producer.

Into these arrangements wandered television. Despite Marshall McLuhan's rhapsodic vision of television's "global village" and the "window on the world" rhetoric that surrounded that medium as it emerged in the 1950s, US dominance in filmed television exports launched new waves of protectionism. National public broadcasters set quotas on imported programs to restrict American influence and wrote television charters mandating original production that reflected and promoted national cultures. Britain felt these tensions acutely, in light of a new commercial competitor to the BBC, Independent Television (ITV), initiated in 1955; a shared language that made American "invasion" easier and more attractive; and a pressing need to compete in the world television market. Meantime, in the United States, a struggling and underfunded National Educational Television (NET) network, attempting to establish itself as an alternative to commercial television, desperately sought a source of high-quality programs that could attract larger audiences.

However, many factors inhibited an active coproduction relationship between American and British public broadcasters from the start. First of all, expectations on both sides required that a national broadcaster produce programs originated in the home country that reflected and strengthened domestic national identity, not someone else's.

Second, in Britain in particular, the idea of making programs primarily or even partly for non-British viewers was anathema to a large sector of the British public, who were required to support the BBC through an annual license fee. Finally, the debates over ITV had exacerbated a long-standing suspicion of American culture and its incursions, not least because of US television's commercial priorities that, many argued, degraded the "quality" tradition to which the BBC was required by national mandate to aspire. These barriers made US/UK television coproduction controversial and conspired to keep it "dark"—rarely acknowledged and in fact hidden or downplayed whenever possible—for the next five decades, even as the practice grew exponentially.[7]

On the American side, PBS's roots in educational broadcasting, and its formation as an alternative to commercial networks, resulted in a mandate that prioritized public affairs and documentary programming. Drama was entertainment, something the commercial networks did all too well. While British drama and documentary were valued by many in the US cultural landscape—symbolizing, as Laurie Ouellette puts it, "public television's distinction from mass culture and its promise to cultivate learnedness and taste"—they also spoke of snobbishness and a slavish attitude toward the superiority of European culture.[8] Had America built its first national public network to provide a showcase for British television? Couldn't American public television produce its own quality drama? These are questions that continue to haunt PBS today. While it might be permissible for American public broadcasting to expend a small amount of its budget to import British stage drama—as indeed it did on *NET Playhouse* without controversy[9]—investing large sums in joint, but primarily British, coproductions was another matter entirely. This is the thin line that *Masterpiece* had to tread for its first four decades, but within which transatlantic coproduction would eventually emerge and flourish—under a cover of deniability—until the digital era altered the television landscape.

THE RELATIONSHIP BEGINS

By the 1960s, both the BBC and its ITV competitors were feeling the pinch of competition with American popular television, both at home and abroad. As one early promoter of a more popular and competitive British television culture put it in a BBC memo, referring to a potential coproduction deal with a commercial US company:

> We need some of their money and we need some of their skills. To adjust and lengthen a well-worn phrase, then, "if you can't beat 'em, join 'em, learn from 'em and then beat 'em at their own game." This simple, even crude method is, of course, "dignified" by the resounding name of "co-production."[10]

To challenge US dominance in the global market and to reap the profits that could support its domestic production, the BBC formed a Television Enterprises unit in 1961—parent of BBC Worldwide—and sought American sales and American coproduction partners. Though, as Jeffrey Miller writes, this strategy saw some success in the 1960s with shows like *The Avengers* and *The Prisoner* on commercial networks, in the long term first NET, then PBS, became Britain's best outlets.[11]

Contracting with Time-Life Films as its American distributor, the BBC found lucrative sales and won international accolades not only with popular series but also with genres now associated with PBS. Serial Shakespeare adaptations like *An Age of Kings* (BBC, 1960; NET, 1962) electrified American audiences; American publicity and awards resonated around the world, enhancing sales. High-budget documentary series like *Civilisation* (BBC, 1969; NET, 1970), *The Search for the Nile* (BBC, 1971; NBC, 1972), and *Alistair Cooke's America* (BBC, 1972–1973; NBC, 1972–1973; PBS, 1974), were aired on both public and commercial networks during this era of "redeeming the wasteland," in Michael Curtin's phrase.[12] Most of these were not really coproductions but at the most "coventures," a term describing a program or series produced primarily for one national audience—in this case Britain's—but with a preproduction sales and marketing agreement with an international partner, in return for an agreed amount of financial participation up front. By 1973, roughly 50 percent of BBC Television's coproduction income came from its partnership with Time-Life.[13]

The term "coproduction" itself has loaded connotations that became a subject of increasing debate within the BBC in 1970s, as the transatlantic partnership expanded. Many in the BBC preferred the term "cofinancing," indicating an arrangement by which the American partner agreed simply to contribute a percentage of the production budget, with a minimum amount of influence or oversight. The advantage of this kind of "up-front" financial commitment, as opposed to postproduction sale of rights for US broadcast, was that rather than go into general Television Enterprises coffers, US cofinancing dollars went directly into the individual production, which could be budgeted accordingly. In the words of one BBC report:

> The advantages to the BBC were obvious. To give one example: the BBC was determined to make Tolstoy's "War and Peace" for television. On our own we would probably have shot it on location in Scotland (and prayed for snow). With [US] co-finance it was possible to shoot it in Yugoslavia and to make use of a large part of the Yugoslav Army.[14]

It was understood from the beginning that US partners could choose to alter the original production in certain ways, by breaking it up into shorter segments to fit American time restrictions or to add an introduction by an American commentator, along with other small adaptations to US audience expectations. However, as US financing became more important, American television partners increasingly negotiated the right to weigh in at key points in the process, from commissioning decisions to script review to postproduction.

As the relationship continued, some in the BBC began to push back against what they saw as inappropriate pressure from their Time-Life partners. As one unit head put it succinctly, using the far more loaded term, "coproduction":

> The BBC cannot embark on the lowering of standards implicit in "Mid Atlantic" production . . . [O]ur programmes are designed for British audiences, the majority of the money in co-productions is British licence holders' money, and the editorial thrust must therefore be aimed at the British audience and not between both audiences.[15]

And as the BBC realized early on, "The typical BBC production, which is generally not in commercially exploitable series, nor tuned to the taste of the American mass audience, is much more acceptable to [NET] than to any other American organization."[16] And then a new player entered the scene.

MASTERPIECE DEBUTS

Under Cold War pressure, Lyndon Johnson's "Great Society" programs of the 1960s introduced a host of new cultural agencies of a kind the United States had previously shunned, most notably the National Endowment for the Humanities (NEH) and the National Endowment for the Arts (NEA). As a national showcase for works produced by this funding and to provide a place for the kind of educational and public affairs programs commercial broadcasting did not offer, Congress passed the Public Broadcasting Act of 1967, creating the Corporation for Public Broadcasting (CPB). This nonprofit corporation was tasked with channeling congressional and private funding toward the establishment of national public networks for both radio and television—America's first. A primary stipulation of the act, however, was that CPB and its television arm, PBS, could not themselves produce programs; instead, the bulk of CPB's funding would go directly to individual public broadcasting stations around the nation, which in turn would produce the programs distributed over PBS. This arrangement was intended to prevent the rise of a powerful centralized national broadcaster, like the BBC, and to keep American public television firmly grounded in the local (or, as some would argue, to keep it weak and divided). However, a few stations soon emerged as powerful national production centers: WGBH-Boston, WNET/Thirteen–New York, and WETA–Washington, DC, primary among them.

As PBS began to organize its institutional structure, NET was gradually sidelined. Yet it was NET that brought *The Forsyte Saga* (BBC, 1967) to American screens just before PBS's debut in 1969, the program that became American public television's first serial drama blockbuster: a British import.[17] "*Masterpiece Theatre* would never have been born without the 1969 broadcast of *The Forsyte Saga*," Rebecca Eaton claims; "*The Forsyte Saga*'s success among 'the intelligent audience' proved that you could show compelling long-form drama" on educational television.[18] Racking up the highest ratings ever achieved by an NET program, *The Forsyte Saga* exemplified the contradictions faced by imported drama: NET's major backer, the Ford Foundation, did not contribute to the series' purchase since it funded only "original" production. As NET president James Day put it, "Not even the *Forsyte Saga* had claim on Ford dollars; special funds had to be raised to acquire it."[19] And despite its audience appeal, the new masters of PBS did not rush to embrace *Forsyte*'s example. CPB's new president, John Macy, reported that "some of us gagged at its advance billing as 'a British Victorian soap opera'" and balked at pursuing further drama programs, even though *Forsyte* had attracted the largest audiences that US public television had ever experienced.[20]

Thus it was left to powerful Boston station WGBH to pick up the imported drama torch and run with it. Accounts of the origins of *Masterpiece Theatre* differ; some give primary credit to Stanford Calderwood, former Polaroid executive and new president of WGBH; others credit two British staff members with bringing the potential of imported British drama to Calderwood's attention: Frank Gillard (formerly of the BBC) and Christopher Sarson (formerly with Granada, a British ITV company), who became the show's executive producer.[21] But clearly the magic combination of inexpensive imported British drama and the selection of Alistair Cooke as host, along with PBS's drama deficit, worked to launch the show—considerably aided by Calderwood's ability to attract ongoing sponsorship by the Mobil Oil Corporation. Though Time-Life still held US distribution rights for BBC drama, Calderwood was able to convince the company to give WGBH access to dramatic productions too literary or too highbrow for commercial networks at a reduced price that the BBC, anxious to boost foreign sales, agreed on. So tightly tied to the BBC was the initial venture that one named considered for the series was "The Best of the BBC." Selecting the less specific *Masterpiece Theatre* was a good choice, since other British producers soon began to contribute to the show.[22]

Masterpiece Theatre debuted on January 10, 1971, with *The First Churchills* (BBC, 1969), an original BBC series featuring Susan Hampshire, star of *The Forsyte Saga*, in the lead role. Some thought it a poor choice, but PBS hoped Hampshire's presence would build on *Forsyte*'s popularity. First-season offerings drew heavily on adaptations of classic literature, including Hardy's *Jude the Obscure*, Balzac's *Père Goriot*, James's *The Spoils of Poynton*, Dostoevsky's *The Possessed*, and Tolstoy's *Resurrection*. Others were adapted from more popular novels: Stella Gibbon's *Cold Comfort Farm* and James Fenimore Cooper's *The Last of the Mohicans*.

The two most successful shows that season, however, were original dramas produced by the BBC: *The Six Wives of Henry VIII* and *Elizabeth R.*, which won an Emmy for Best Drama Series in 1972. Subsequent seasons would show a similar mix, with adaptations of classic British mystery novels gaining ground; this would lead to the spin-off of a separate series on PBS, *Mystery!*, in 1980. And despite the overall emphasis on literary adaptations, it was often original dramas written for television that sparked the most enthusiasm and buzz, from *Upstairs, Downstairs* to *Prime Suspect* to *Downton Abbey*. All were what was beginning to be called "miniseries," running from two to eight episodes in length; this was something truly different for American television, accustomed either to endless episodic series or the one-off made-for-TV movie.

INTROS AND "EXTROS"

In format, *Masterpiece Theatre* presented something of a throwback to an earlier era of anthology drama, when program "hosts" like Ronald Reagan and Loretta Young welcomed audiences to this week's drama and returned during breaks and at the end of the show to chat directly to the audience. WGBH decided to reinvent this tradition in the person of Alistair Cooke, who became the show's congenial and quite satisfactorily British host for its first twenty-one years, from 1971 to 1992. Cooke was known to American audiences as the suave host of *Omnibus*, an influential early experiment in "quality" television funded by the Ford Foundation that the three major commercial networks took turns airing from 1952 to 1961. *Masterpiece*'s first producer, Christopher Sarson, claims to have thought of Cooke for host immediately, "because he was transatlantic—an Englishman living in America."[23]

Like earlier TV hosts, Cooke's primary function was to become the show's public persona, the regular, recurring element that linked diverse dramas together, creating a coherent identity for the parent program. Described as "warm, witty, and eternally hospitable," Cooke's transatlantic experience gave him both an emblematic and a real expertise in translating between two cultures, putting British literature and history into a context that Americans could understand. Sitting in a leather armchair, surrounded by books and dark paneling, Cooke spoke directly into the camera at both the beginning and end of the program—its "intros" and "extros," as they were known on the *Masterpiece* set. Produced

FIGURE 1.1 Alistair Cooke, host of *Masterpiece Theatre* from 1971 to 1992

by WGBH, they may seem like an archaic affectation today, but the work they performed was key to the coproduction relationship.

For PBS, Cooke's introductions marked the program as "ours," detaching it from its British origins and placing it firmly within the American cultural context. They allowed WGBH to imprint its own creative efforts onto a collaboration that was disavowed at one end, dismissed at the other, and provided that element of "educational" value so important to US public television. They also provided details of British history and geography with which Americans might well not have been familiar—for instance, Cooke's introduction of the 1977 *Poldark* series has him drawing a map of England on a slate to show where Cornwall is located, giving a brief historical overview of the period in which the drama takes place, highlighting the importance of Cornwall's copper-mining industry, and introducing the main characters and plot line—all in four minutes (cut down to two minutes in later years).[24]

The other recurring element, subject of much later criticism, was the opening sequence with its now iconic theme music. Elements from Mouret's "Rondeau" are still used today, providing a continuity of mood in its portentous yet sprightly pavane of strings and brass, but the classic opening sequence was jettisoned forcefully in the show's 2008 makeover (discussed below). It consisted of a slow tracking shot across a series of tabletops in a cluttered Victorian-style parlor, traveling across a landscape of leather-covered books and silver-framed photos featuring *Masterpiece* productions, ending on a book cover opening to reveal the title page: *Masterpiece Theatre*. A stronger insistence on the connection between "quality" literature and television could hardly be devised: not just drama, but classy *literary* drama, done by Brits!

From Cofinancing to Coproduction

In its first years *Masterpiece Theatre* was able to make selections from a backlog of "off the shelf," already-produced British drama, with very little involvement in ongoing production. Joan Wilson succeeded Sarson as producer in 1975 and continued his hands-off role with British partners, describing her role as "the single biggest customer" of British television, one who might "make casting suggestions and editing suggestions," and perhaps very occasionally "cut the already-produced material," usually for reasons of cultural suitability.[25] When Wilson died suddenly in 1985, a young producer named Rebecca Eaton stepped into the role, one that she would play for the next thirty-plus years.

Eaton had gained some exposure to British life and culture through a college exchange internship with the BBC World Service in 1969. This led to a post with WGBH on her return, eventually as a producer in its very active documentary unit. When WGBH president Henry Becton offered her Wilson's former position as executive producer of *Masterpiece*, the idea of giving up production for what was at the time primarily a management position did not immediately appeal. But as she writes, by the early 1980s,

> *Masterpiece Theatre* had aired the backlog of great British programs, and the shelves at the BBC were thinning out. The British broadcasters were now asking [WGBH] to commit to programs by not only watching finished shows on cassette but also by reading scripts of proposed programs, or even treatments. The job of executive producer of *Masterpiece Theatre* had undergone an evolutionary change.[26]

By this time, too, the BBC's relationship with Time-Life Television had ended, and a new, partially owned partner, Lionheart Television International, took over American distribution of BBC programs. Even more significant was the expansion of the BBC Television Enterprises division into the more aggressive BBC Enterprises in 1979 (to become BBC Worldwide in 1994), not only distributing programs but actively seeking out coproduction opportunities.

The number of customers for British television expanded in the 1980s too, as US cable television grew. The Arts and Entertainment network, now A&E, debuted in 1984 with a mission to become a "commercial PBS" and immediately turned to coproduction deals with British producers. Over the next few years, A&E would give PBS a run for its money in the mystery category, partnering with both the BBC and ITV companies like Granada for classic and contemporary mystery novel adaptations, from Agatha Christie to P. D. James. Soon other cable and pay TV channels like Bravo, HBO, Showtime, SciFi (now SyFy), and FX would join them, looking for British coproducers who could bring distinctive programs to their lineups. At the same time, British television was changing. In the late 1980s and early 1990s, the BBC would go through one of the biggest shake-ups in its history, adjusting to a new system of downsizing in-house production and increasing "outsourcing" of programs—creating dozens of new, independent production companies that were eager and willing to work with producers both British and international.[27] Costume dramas were out, hard-hitting contemporary drama series were in, and "the classic drama pipeline was down to a trickle."[28] British producers learned that American commercial coproduction partners could drive a very hard bargain indeed, in terms of intervening in productions and asserting American preferences.

Now even the relatively small amount of funding that *Masterpiece* could put into a production—usually around 10 percent of the total budget—became an important contribution to expenses as well as a way to attract additional backers. In Eaton's words,

> They needed partners up front, and ones with real money, not just postproduction license fees. I realized that I was going to have to change from a show picker into a real co-producer and take risks on programs in the idea stage, long before the proof was in the pudding . . . in so many ways, our co-productions became forced marriages.[29]

Thus, in the mid-1990s, with its supply of historical drama drying up and competition at home increasing, *Masterpiece* went on the offensive and began to propose coproduction ventures to British producers.

Lining up Carnival Films, one of Britain's new independents, as producers, and bringing in Andrew Davies, soon to become one of the United Kingdom's top writers, Eaton persuaded the BBC to commission a six-part dramatization of George Eliot's *Middlemarch* (WGBH/BBC, 1993). Its success in both the United States and Britain prompted yet another WGBH proposal to British partners, this time an American property, Edith Wharton's unfinished novel *The Buccaneers* (WGBH/BBC, 1995)—a story oddly predictive of later blockbuster *Downton Abbey*, focusing on American heiresses marrying into British aristocracy. The BBC even agreed to shoot part of the series in the United States, a first. Its ratings, according to Eaton, were the highest ever achieved by *Masterpiece* until *Downton Abbey* (also with Carnival Films). By 1997, a British trade journal quoted Eaton as saying, "Whereas everything used to be acquisition, now it is 50 per cent co-production and only half is with the BBC."[30] Yet forces were at work that would precipitate a reconsideration of the transatlantic coproduction, straining the public broadcasting relationship on the eve of the digital era.

From the beginning, *Masterpiece* had been criticized for its Britishness. It had always been the intention of WGBH to produce American literary adaptation as well, but tight budgets—and Mobile Oil's fondness for noncontroversial British fare—held back original production. In 1999, with a strong mandate from PBS's new president, Pat Mitchell, and a special pot of money to back it up, *Masterpiece* launched its "American Collection," a series of seven dramas based on American literature that ran between 2000 and 2003. Though rarely voiced openly, it was an attempt not only to rebut Britishness but to add diversity to a series dominated by classic (read white, European, male) literature. *Masterpiece* launched into original production with an emphasis on American history and the American minority experience, with productions based on *Cora Unashamed* by Langston Hughes, Esmeralda Santiago's *Almost a Woman*, Willa Cather's *Song of the Lark*, and Eudora Welty's *The Ponder Heart*. In a separate arrangement, *Mystery!* partnered with Robert Redford Productions in a three-part series based on Tony Hillerman's Detective Jim Chee novels set on the Navajo and Hopi reservations of the US Southwest.

Despite generally favorable reviews, this experiment was short-lived. For one thing, WGBH had hoped to be able to sell its productions in Britain, to its former partners. But as Eaton writes, "I hadn't realized how strongly British broadcasters felt that adaptations of American classics, or dramas about American history, just would not be of interest to their audiences . . . pouring millions of dollars into British drama creates *no* obligation for the British to pour it back into ours."[31] And, in a further blow, in 2002 Mobil Oil announced that it would discontinue funding *Masterpiece* by 2004, after more than forty years. This created a crisis not only at WGBH but throughout PBS. A significant rebranding effort ensued, resulting in the expanded tripartite structure we see today: *Theatre* was dropped in favor of a division by focus into *Masterpiece Classics, Masterpiece Mystery,* and *Masterpiece Contemporary*, all launched in 2008. One major goal of the makeover was to reach out to younger audiences; the demographics of the program had been growing older for years. But by this time a new era had arrived: thanks to digital streaming and new television outlets like BBC America, Britishness now added just one more ingredient to a newly opened global universe of drama.

FIGURE 1.2 *Masterpiece Theatre*'s "American Collection," 2000–2003

NEW DIRECTIONS AND DRAMAS

With the 2008 reboot, the old coziness was out, a new hipness was in: instead of Alistair Cooke (or his successor Russell Baker), younger, sexier hosts gave breezily short intros of a minute or less: Gillian Anderson, Laura Linney, Alan Cumming, David Tennant. New opening sequences kept the literary allusions but dispensed with the Victorian clutter. While *Masterpiece Contemporary* has faltered a bit, the other two have gone from strength to strength, and have now largely dispensed with hosts altogether.[32] *Masterpiece Classic* launched with a rousing series, "The Complete Jane Austen," featuring all six of Austen's novels back to back from January to March 2008.[33] This brought in the long-desired but rarely achieved "'smart girls' demographic of women eighteen to forty nine,"[34] whose audience numbers increased by 125 percent. Then came the astonishing success of *Downton Abbey* in 2010, and the backing not only of new underwriters—notably Viking River Cruises and Ralph Lauren—but of a whole new concept in financing: the program-specific trust. The Masterpiece Trust, initiated in 2011, is "a collaborative initiative between MASTERPIECE's producing station WGBH Boston and PBS stations nationwide" that "provides the opportunity for individual donors and families who care deeply about the series to help provide for its future in a substantial way while also supporting their local PBS stations." A lengthy list of major donors, led by the names and photos of a few especially prominent individuals, today appear during the program's onscreen credits. Its success—over $10 million in donations since 2011—has sparked several such initiatives for other PBS programs.[35]

Not only has PBS's prominence in the US television universe risen, thanks to holding firm while other networks faltered, but changes in the structure of the television industry worldwide have made the steadiness and security of *Masterpiece* funding ever more attractive to the hundreds of independent production companies now seeking partners with money and clout. In 2015, the *Guardian* could still write dismissively, "Although [Eaton]'s cagey about details, the traditional Masterpiece co-production model is to put up 10% of the budget. . . . Masterpiece's 10% earns it the right to be consulted on casting and other creative decisions, though not control."[36] Yet years before this, industry trade publications knew the reality was different: "If there was a would-like-to-meet list for British TV drama producers, Rebecca Eaton of Boston, Massachusetts would be at the top of it. . . . She doesn't just buy: she pays upfront—investing anything from 5% to 30% of the budget." In this same article, Eaton herself goes on to explain, "I often hear about a project from [an independent producer]—particularly if we've worked together before—and they will attempt to gauge my interest and parlay that into a deal with the UK broadcaster. The broadcaster then phones me and finds out if it's real, and that closes the loop."[37] This is important clout, in the increasingly cluttered and competitive British television landscape.

In today's environment, where the former production monopolies of central public broadcasters have been broken apart, with independent production flourishing, and

FIGURE 1.3 *Masterpiece*'s new look

as transnational acquisitions have made it hard to determine who or what constitutes "British" or "American " production any longer, *Masterpiece* has established a secure and prescient niche at the intersection of television and a certain kind of literate if not always literary drama, a field others have entered but in which few have persisted with comparable impact. For its British coproducers, WGBH constitutes a familiar partner, attuned to public service ideals and idiosyncrasies, whose light but essential touch on the controls and huge ability to publicize a production globally become more and more desirable in the globalized networks of the present.

Recently, with distinctions between national and transnational programs fading,[38] the *Masterpiece* model has begun to expand. In an effort to give PBS "more influence in shaping programs" and in maintaining high production values, the network itself purchased a number of independently produced series from British partners in recent years, including *Call the Midwife* (BBC / Neale Street Productions), *Last Tango in Halifax* (BBC / Red Production Company), and *The Bletchley Circle* (ITV / World Productions), scheduling them in prime-time slots. Though these were simple cofinance agreements and not full coproductions per se, the remarkable element is that PBS, often critical of the WGBH "special relationship" with British producers, has now embraced its model and in fact gone over *Masterpiece*'s head to do business with independent British producers directly. Even more alarming to many, it marks an abrogation of one of the founding principles of American public television: that PBS stay out of the program production and acquisition business and confine itself to backing local station initiatives.[39] Yet the strategy has proven highly successful, both with audiences and with public television stations, boosting both ratings and membership support. It seems that what was once a "forced marriage" is now a nonexclusive consensual relationship, with US suitors lining up for the chance to court British partners, and vice versa. Clearly, more drama awaits!

NOTES

1. For more on the *Masterpiece* audience, see Simone Knox, "Masterpiece Theatre and British Television Drama," *Critical Studies in Television* 7:1 (2012): 29–48.
2. Elke Weissmann, "Paying for Fewer Imports? The BBC Licence Fee Negotiations (1975–1981) and Attitudes towards American Imports," *Television and New Media* 10:6 (2009): 482–500.
3. For an extended version of this argument, see Michele Hilmes, "PBS: Crowdsourcing Culture since 1969," in *From Networks to Netflix: A Guide to Changing Channels*, ed. Derek Johnson (New York: Routledge, 2017), 55–65.
4. Rebecca Eaton, *Making "Masterpiece"* (New York: Viking, 2013).
5. Mark Glancy, "Temporary American Citizens? British Audiences, Hollywood Films, and the threat of Americanization in the 1920s," *Historical Journal of Film, Radio and Television* 26:4 (2006): 461–84; see also Michele Hilmes, *Network Nations: A Transnational History of British and American Broadcasting* (New York: Routledge, 2012).

6. See Barbara J. Selznick, *Global Television: Co-producing Culture* (Philadelphia: Temple University Press, 2008).

7. See Hilmes, *Network Nations* for an extended history of these tensions. Also see Sheron Neves, "'Running a Brothel from Inside a Monastery': Drama Co-productions at the BBC and the Trade Relationship with America from the 1970s to the 1990s," PhD diss., Birkbeck University of London, 2013.

8. Laurie Ouellette, *Viewers Like You? How Public TV Failed the People* (New York: Columbia University Press, 2002).

9. *NET Playhouse* (later *PBS Playhouse*) ran from 1966 to 1972 and relied heavily on BBC productions of British stage drama. It was revived in 1982 as *American Playhouse*, a clear rebuke to its former British emphasis.

10. Ronnie Waldman to D. Tel., October 12, 1961, "Memo," R125/1/1/, BBC Written Archives Center (WAC), Caversham Park, United Kingdom.

11. Jeffrey Miller, *Something Completely Different: British Television and American Culture* (Minneapolis: University of Minnesota Press, 2000).

12. Michael Curtin, *Redeeming the Wasteland: Television Documentary and Cold War Politics* (New Brunswick, NJ: Rutgers University Press, 1995).

13. BBC, "Synopsis for General Advisory Council paper on Co-productions," June 4, 1979, R125/1, 002/1, WAC.

14. BBC, "Synopsis."

15. Aubrey Singer to David Attenborough, "Memo to DPTEL," March 22, 1974, T42/110/2, BBC, WAC.

16. Jack White, letter to Del Strother, March 21, 1961, National Educational Television Papers, Series 9, Box 7, Folder 6, Wisconsin Historical Society, Madison, WI.

17. David Stewart, "How Should Public TV Follow Up the *Forsyte Saga* Success?," *Current*, April 14, 1997, http://current.org/1997/04/how-should-public-tv-follow-up-the-forsyte-saga-success-2/.

18. Eaton, *Making Masterpiece*, 19. She goes on to point out that, although derided by traditional educational broadcasters as a jumped-up soap opera, it had an impact on commercial television too, with the advent of the miniseries based on literary properties.

19. James Day, *The Vanishing Vision* (Berkeley: University of California Press, 1995), 385.

20. John Macy, *To Irrigate a Wasteland: The Struggle to Shape a Public Television System in the United States* (Berkeley: University of California Press, 1974), 58.

21. Stewart, "How Should."

22. Sarson is also credited with coming up with the program's iconic theme music, Mouret's "Rondeau" (which he had heard at a Palermo Club Med) as well as recruiting Cooke as host; see Stewart, "How Should." And, for many years, it was his British-accented voice that delivered *Masterpiece Theatre*'s opening credit announcement.

23. O'Flaherty, "Interview with Christopher Sarson," 7.

24. *Masterpiece Theatre*, "Poldark," Alistair Cooke introduction (PBS 1977) https://www.youtube.com/watch?v=oIniCqfJOKM.

25. Most notoriously, she eliminated thirteen of the original twenty-six episodes from *Upstairs, Downstairs* because "the plots were repetitious and the performances not strong enough." A recurring theme in US/UK cooperation was the degree of leeway for nudity and obscene language given to British television that was not permissible in the United States. Along these lines, Wilson also cut a controversial five minutes out the orgy scenes in *I, Claudius*. Peter W. Kaplan, "Joan Wilson, Masterpiece Theatre production," *New York Times*, July 9, 1985, http://www.nytimes.com/1985/07/09/arts/joan-wilson-masterpiece-theater-producer.html.

26. Eaton, *Making Masterpiece*, 50.

27. Jonathan Bignell, "Conditions of Possibility: Docudrama, Television and Change since 1990," paper delivered at the NECS conference "Locating Media," Lund, Sweden, June 2009.

28. Eaton, *Making Masterpiece*, 117.

29. Eaton, *Making Masterpiece*, 136.

30. Greg Truman, "Helping Hand," *Broadcast*, September 26, 1997, 23.

31. Eaton, *Making Masterpiece*, 177.
32. Nancy West and Karen E. Laird have argued that the 2008 strategy marks not just a superficial change but "nothing less than an effort to redefine adaptation itself." See Nancy West and Karen E. Laird, "Prequels, Sequels, and Pop Stars: *Masterpiece* and the New Culture of Classic Adaptation," *Literature Film Quarterly* 39:4 (2011): 306–30.
33. *Pride and Prejudice* (BBC, 1995) and *Emma* (BBC, 1996) were existing adaptations, but WGBH coproduced *Northanger Abbey* (ITV/Granada, 2007), *Sense and Sensibility* (BBC, 2008), *Persuasion* (ITV / Clerkenwell Films, 2007), and *Mansfield Park* (BBC / Company Pictures, 2007), as well as an original drama based on Austen's letters, *Miss Austen Regrets* (BBC, 2008). Andrew Davies, author of the 1995 *Pride and Prejudice* film, served as writer for *Northanger, Persuasion,* and *Sense and Sensibility*.
34. Eaton, *Making Masterpiece*, 203.
35. *Masterpiece*, "Masterpiece Trust," http://www.pbs.org/wgbh/masterpiece/about-masterpiece/masterpiece-trust/.
36. Maggie Brown, "Rebecca Eaton: *Masterpiece* Is the 'Little Black Dress of British Drama,'" *Guardian*, March 1, 2015, https://www.theguardian.com/media/2015/mar/01/dowton-abbey-sherlock-rebecca-eaton-masterpiece.
37. Rachel Murrell, "US Drama Queen," *Televisual*, April 2004, 47–48.
38. Or being actively erased; see Petruska and Woods in this volume.
39. "Stations Fear Exclusion from Show Production as PBS Shifts Strategy," *Current*, June 13, 2013, http://current.org/2013/06/shift-in-strategy-at-pbs/.

2

TRAVELING WITHOUT A PASSPORT

"Original" Streaming Content in the Transatlantic Distribution Ecosystem

KAREN PETRUSKA AND FAYE WOODS

INTRODUCTION: TRANSATLANTIC DISTRIBUTION BUILT UPON THE "FALSE ORIGINAL"

"Original" content is hawked by streaming video on demand (SVOD) services like Netflix, Amazon, and Hulu as distinctive and special, but application of the term "original" to specific programs is complex, often inconsistent, and sometimes even objectionable.[1] Some programs are funded or commissioned by the SVOD service itself, including, for example, *Transparent* (Amazon, 2014–) and *House of Cards* (Netflix, 2013–). Labeling these programs "originals" is consistent with traditional uses of the term, which suggest a financial investment by the distribution network (cum SVOD) or, importantly, a distinctive national origin and identity. However, these are not the only programs deemed original by Netflix and Amazon, two SVOD services eager to develop and refine their brand identities. For instance, a British viewer will find programming originating on the US cable channel AMC under the label of "Netflix Original," while a similar viewer in the United States will find programming produced for the BBC and Channel 4, British public service broadcasters, also under the label of "Netflix Original." These programs— produced to air or stream in one country and distributed abroad as well—have traditionally been understood as imports. Yet here we see them marked distinctively as "originals," while other US, UK, European, and Korean content also acquired by Netflix does not bear this marker. To identify these programs as Netflix original content communicates exclusivity and freshness, but when this identification is used falsely, it erases the production and exhibition histories of the shows in their originating countries. Netflix did not produce AMC's *Breaking Bad* (2008–2013), NBC's *The Good Place* (2016–), BBC1's *Happy Valley* (BBC1, 2014–), or E4's *Chewing Gum* (2015–2017), yet the "original" framing suggests it did. Such practices dislocate the term "original" from its former association with national specificity, a key component of the regulatory apparatus of television in many countries, and rearticulate it to signal commercial licensing interests.[2] We argue that Netflix claiming an import as an original series rather than an "exclusive" import is one facet of a broader assimilation and contextualizing at play in the transnational streaming media distribution ecosystem. This signals the 2010s as a transitional televisual moment, as SVOD services entered and negotiated their place in the international television ecosystem.

A number of scholars have called for more work about global distribution patterns and the reception of international content within the United States and abroad. For example, Jeanette Steemers has noted that while film scholars have conducted extensive research into the distribution patterns of cinema, less work of this kind has been applied to the television market.[3] Steemers's own work has sought to close this gap through industrial ethnography and has recently begun to sketch the influence of SVOD on the international market for television rights, while Michael L Wayne has considered SVOD services' acquisition of US network and cable programming.[4] Michele Hilmes has also urged scholars to consider how the increase in international television content circulation in the United States may be shaping audience reception and industry practices, including coproduction deals.[5] Both scholars describe a need to reconsider content flows and consumption patterns, to explore distribution, what Alisa Perren describes as the "space in between" production and consumption.[6] In their own discussion of global media distribution flows, Jinna Tay and Graeme Turner urge caution to avoid an oversimplification of power in content flows, noting that the US model tends to be normalized when in fact global practices may be quite distinct in different regions.[7] Our study, therefore, concentrates its focus on a comparative study of international SVOD services' practices within the United States and the United Kingdom. Through this approach, we have identified a distinct, and likely transitional, historical moment in the continued maturation of streaming media platforms. This moment spotlights the presentation of imported programs streaming in both countries on SVOD services, focusing on the international brands of Netflix and Amazon and the US SVOD service Hulu.

The disjuncture between traditional and emerging designations of original content lies at the heart of a confusing and evolving set of distribution practices regarding circulation of transnational content by multinational SVOD services. In the 2010s these SVOD services inserted themselves definitively into the television distribution landscape and the trade in programming rights. Labels such as "original" and "exclusive," which serve as markers and categorizations akin to genre on these platforms, also reinforce branding and thus indicate the importance of imports and exclusivity to the growth of these services. At present, Amazon correctly terms its licensed content—either imports that were produced elsewhere for which it holds regional first-run rights, or second-window streaming rights for local content—as "exclusive" and reserves the term "original" for self-produced content. However, Netflix is less transparent, labeling both self-produced programs and certain imports to which it holds exclusive local rights as "Netflix Originals." This causes some definitional trickiness in analysis, so we distinguish between what we call the "false original" and the "self-produced original." The former refers to mislabeled licensed content in fact produced by another network or channel, and the latter refers to content commissioned and funded in part or whole by an SVOD service. The "self-produced original," therefore, is the only *true* original content. All this wordplay is meaningful beyond semantic debates, as it signals a distinctive shift from long-standing practices surrounding imports on both sides of the Atlantic, an instability produced by the paratextual framing practices of particular SVOD services.

There are many examples of this intentional discursive confusion, on both sides of the Atlantic. Netflix made a splash in 2016 with the debut of its first drama commissioned from a British independent production company: *The Crown*, made by Left Bank Pictures (partly owned by Sony), with a much-publicized £100 million budget for its first two series.[8] *The Crown* is a self-produced Original, distributed across all Netflix's global territories. It is distinct from *The Fall*, which Netflix claims as an Original in the United States but we dub a "false original." *The Fall* (2013–) was produced by British-based independent production companies Fables and Artist Studio (the latter owned by superindie Endemol Shine) for BBC Two and Irish channel RTE. It is a program in which Netflix has no ownership stake, but merely has first-run rights in the United States. *The Fall*, therefore, does not originate with Netflix and thus is a false original.

A similar distinction can be made in the United Kingdom, where *Orange Is the New Black* (2013–), produced by the American company Lionsgate for Netflix, is labeled a Netflix Original, but so is *Breaking Bad*, produced by Sony for US cable channel AMC, and *Scream* (2015–), produced by Dimension Television for US cable channel MTV. Looking at these examples, one might suggest that "Original" refers to having first-run UK rights to a Netflix import, yet not all first-run imported programming is bestowed

FIGURE 2.1 CW's *Riverdale* as "Netflix Original"

with the moniker. For example, in 2016 Netflix acquired British first-run rights to two programs that originally aired on the CW network in the United States, *iZombie* (2015–) and *Crazy Ex-Girlfriend* (2016–), yet neither was labeled a Netflix Original. But in 2017 it acquired *Riverdale* (2017–), which also originally aired on the CW, which it labels a Netflix Original in the United Kingdom. This irregular labeling leads to the question, when is an import not an import? The answer would seem to be, "When it's a Netflix Original."

Over the past ten years, the volume of global television and the speed with which it crosses borders have been increased by legal web-delivered platforms (joining the often illegal peer-to-peer circulations that flow beneath the surface).[9] In the space of a few years these SVOD services—Netflix and Amazon Video internationally, Hulu in the United States—have matured from providing valuable outlets for distribution companies' underutilized library content to competing in the international television market for the highest-profile content, inflating budgets and the cost of rights in land grabs for programming, particularly drama.[10] Importantly, these global distribution practices have impacted established practices of windowing[11] and threatened the parceling of regional rights that has long been central to the funding models of the European television industry, which operates without the deep pockets of the US studios that support the US industry.[12] Imports have therefore played a profound role in helping SVOD services expand across the Atlantic and beyond. Amazon's international expansion of its Prime Video platform has been built upon a self-produced original, *The Grand Tour*, although arguably this program was built on the back of the globally successful brand of *Top Gear* built by the BBC. Netflix began pushing for exclusive international rights deals with limited hold-back windows as it expanded globally. FOX's *Gotham* (2014–) was the first such deal. In 2014, Hulu in the United States promoted forty-one programs as originals, with more than half of them being international content, originating in countries such as the United Kingdom, Australia, Canada, France, and Israel. During this period, self-produced content remained relatively limited across these SVOD services, and, as a result, rights to prized US network and cable shows were an essential part of drawing subscribers in new territories. Now, as the SVOD services ramp up their programming budgets for original content and acquisitions to billions of dollars, these exclusive rights remain part of their arsenal in the international quest for new subscribers.[13]

Television has always been an expensive business in which producers and distributors must sell and resell their programming repeatedly to recoup their investments, both internationally and in local syndication markets. In turn, reframing texts is a long-standing process, with programs "acquired by broadcasters and then shaped, changed, assimilated and used by and within a schedule."[14] These texts have always been recognized as imports, yet certain SVOD services' appropriation of foreign content as original obscures the complex economics of the industry. By claiming others' work as their own, certain SVOD services engage in a form of production plagiarism, denying producers who take on the bulk of the risk the visibility of their success in order to build the creative capital of their own brands. The increased circulation of international content is a boon for audiences, but when removed from their national contexts and subsumed into multinational SVOD brands, these programs are made less "foreign": they lose their distinctive national meaning, and audiences lose global media literacy.

CASE STUDY: *HAPPY VALLEY* AND TRANSATLANTIC TRANSLATION

Digital distribution technologies have made it easier for international content to reach transatlantic audiences, but this does not necessarily mean that these original series are unadapted or rendered less foreign or lack a process of translation. As we will explore in more detail below, there are a variety of occlusions supporting this system, some that continue well-recognized historical practices and some that signal new issues for media scholars to untangle. First there is a question of the hegemony of American media companies, which have long enjoyed primacy in international sales markets. SVOD services like Netflix, Amazon, and Hulu appropriate and decontextualize successful foreign content as an extension of their emerging producing prowess by claiming them as original rather than exclusive acquisitions. This practice of "false originals" bolsters the critical reputation and subscription value of emerging SVOD services, obscuring the fact that libraries of self-produced and coproduced originals at this point remain a small percentage of their content. Such false originals enable these companies to boost their libraries at relatively low cost, developing an image of incredible productivity that supports a discourse of "disruption," a celebratory term that suggests new entrants to the media industry have the potential to rewrite the rules and upend traditional operations.[15] While standing on the shoulders of a range of traditional media producers and distributors, SVOD services nevertheless earn accolades for their transformative potential and impressive growth. Previous acquisition deals have showcased international origins as prestige markers, as with Sky Atlantic's promotion of itself as the exclusive home for all HBO content in the United Kingdom. The British and European satellite broadcaster Sky debuted this new pay channel 2011 in order to draw high-earning demographics to its imported US prestige drama, showcasing the channel as the British "home of HBO."[16] But an SVOD service's "false original" appellation, rather than the more accurate "exclusive," confers the prestige on itself by blurring such origination.

Take as an example *Happy Valley*, which was produced for the BBC by British independent production company Red, airing on BBC1 in the United Kingdom, but claimed by Netflix as an original in the United States and other markets. In some ways, *Happy Valley* is an unlikely candidate for US import from the United Kingdom. Made up of six episodes per season, the series is set in a town in West Yorkshire and features heavy regional accents. It is distinctively a British production in its genre of the detective serial, in which the BBC and ITV have developed a reputation for specialization, from *Prime Suspect* (ITV, 1991–2006) to *Messiah* (BBC1, 2001–2004) and *Luther* (2010–).[17] *Happy Valley* producer Nicola Shindler commented that the program "felt quite local and specific" to its UK context, confirming that the program was not made with international distribution in mind.[18] But *Happy Valley* also fits comfortably within an American concept of "prestige television," focused on a strong antihero(ine) operating within the dark and emotionally complex world featured in the program.[19] (Notably, its key prestige marker in the United Kingdom—creator and sole writer Sally Wainwright—has little international value.) Netflix US had previously licensed and then taken over funding the US adaptation of the Danish drama *The Killing* (2011–2014) from AMC, but lacked a self-produced, prestige, female-led crime drama of its own. Thus *Happy Valley* filled this gap and asserted a prestige claim that reinforced the value of a Netflix subscription package. *Happy Valley* can not only target a niche audience interested in British series but also may appeal to fans of US prestige "difficult men" series like *The Shield* (FX, 2002–2008) and *Breaking Bad.*

A trailer promoting the arrival of *Happy Valley* season 2 on Netflix in 2014 constructs a national collage in its complex promotional messaging.[20] The trailer serves as a visual metaphor for the process of usurpation some international programs experience as they

FIGURE 2.2 The BBC's *Happy Valley* as "Netflix Original"

cross the Atlantic to reach a new audience. First, the trailer is framed by a stark white screen that features the "Netflix" ident as a wipe effect shifts to the program content. A voice-over at the conclusion of the trailer speaks with a northern British accent (consistent with the regional accents featured throughout the program) while a wipe transition returns to the white screen, now featuring the words, "Only on Netflix." As the program content plays, the Netflix brand appears on every single frame of the trailer in the lower right corner—the assertion of ownership is thorough and constant. And yet Netflix did not make this trailer. In fact, its core is the exact same trailer as produced by the BBC to advertise the series in the United Kingdom.[21] The new brand is slapped onto existing material like a vinyl sticker with slightly peeling edges. The difference between the two trailers is uncanny, for they seem familiar and strange all at once. Confusions abound for audiences, as we see with website comments from American fans of *Happy Valley* who wonder if Netflix will be renewing the series, missing the fact that it is the BBC who will make renewal decisions.[22] While audiences—outside of the knowledgeable circles of fandom, and their campaigns against cancellation—have always been somewhat removed from such industrial decisions, foreign audiences who enjoy an international series are doubly removed from that process.

Trailers for SVOD programming function as spreadable media but are also embedded on the platforms, adding to the logos, genre tags, and other program-specific promotions that surround the program's imagery on the interface. These paratextual elements help organize content for SVOD services that carry deep and diverse libraries, shaping the identity and meaning of these programs by establishing the "frames and filters through which we look at, listen to, and interpret" the program.[23] The ways in which these services have deployed imports on their interactive home pages demonstrate the continual importance and influence of contextual framing. Paul Rixon highlights how imported US programs have long been reshaped and framed as they are assimilated into British linear television flows.[24] SVOD services lack the contextual frame of a linear channel, with its time-bound schedule and the inserted paratextual interstitial elements by which an import is actively assimilated into a national television broadcast.[25] Yet in deploying an "original" or "exclusive" marker, an SVOD service also provides metatextual frames, in service of the construction of its own brand and its appeal to potential subscribers. The practice of affixing a marker of originality to an imported text through the surrounding paratextual frame —the "Netflix Original" logo layered over a program's menu image, or the categorization under which it is generically grouped on the digital interface—plays a fundamentally more disruptive role than the shift of an ad break or the genre adjustment suggested by a newly commissioned trailer.[26] This creates what John Ellis terms a "narrative image," one that removes a text's national origin and the commissioning broadcaster's identity.[27] Such false originals bolstered Netflix's critical reputation and value to subscribers at a time when its roster of self-produced and coproduced originals was still being built.

The paratextual frames used to categorize programming within SVOD services create slippages and blurrings. An imported international program may not be described as international.[28] It may not bear the brand of the network that first aired it, nor the company that produced it. If it won awards granted by an international organization, the SVOD service is unlikely to hawk that honor, instead privileging honors received in the nation of the streaming company. In short, international content can appear as if it were a domestic production—in its production history, its content, and its appeal. This can lead to a streaming site that played no role in the development or production of a series claiming it as an original program. This discursive application of "original"—claiming ownership over a series created entirely by a different channel in a different nation—homogenizes international productions under the ever-encroaching spread of Netflix, with Amazon in hot pursuit. The diversity of global content depends upon the continued success of a broad range of producers, and false originals potentially threaten their viability, as SVOD services subsume distinctive national broadcasters and their brands into production funnels that feed a monopolistic, global "Netflix nation."

MARKETPLACE DYNAMICS: DISCOURSES OF "DISRUPTION"

Our analysis brings a consideration of content flows and assimilation to scholarship that has largely been built around analysis of SVOD services' "self-produced original" programming and surrounding promotional discourse.[29] We agree with Chuck Tryon's warning that care must be taken around the "disruptor" discourse—of both viewing and distribution practices, as well as television itself—that circulates in both journalistic and scholarly work. There is arguably more continuity than change at play with the ways SVOD services are interacting with traditional and emerging producers and distributors.[30] Our own analysis adds a consideration of SVOD services' promotion of imports to the preexisting work on linear channels' assimilation of US and UK imports.[31] This highlights SVOD services' continuity within—rather than entire disruption of—international distribution flows (both unscripted and scripted formats and completed programming) and their contribution to existing transatlantic flows of programming and influence.[32]

The tension between discourses of disruption and continuity emerge in the financial arrangements underpinning the promotional strategies that catalyzed our study. Historically, US television networks and British channels have participated (to varying degrees) in the development, commissioning, financing, and production of programs that they broadcast. Referring to programming as original, therefore, carries particular weight in the world of television, because it suggests that (1) a network or channel has the financial resources and potential audience to invest in the production of new content, and (2) they can potentially profit from the resale of that content in secondary markets, domestic and international. As emerging SVOD services sought to increase subscribers and industry esteem, they asserted their brands' value through the presentation of "original" content alongside licensed "exclusives."

A channel's maturation from a predominance of licensed content toward the production of original drama is an established journey in both the United States and the United Kingdom. For example, Home Box Office was born as a subscription, satellite-delivered, pay-TV channel and built its brand in the 1970s and 1980s on acquired film alongside live comedy and sports specials. Its first foray into original content came with made-for-TV movies, but it was during the 1990s that HBO began to assert itself as a new kind of television network, with original series like *Sex and the City* (1998–2004) and *The Sopranos* (1999–2007).[33] It took decades, then, for HBO to become a powerhouse producer of its own original series, having built its reputation with recycled film content. In turn, British digital channel E4 relied on reality TV and US imports to build its target youth audience, until it was sufficiently established and budgeted by its parent corporation Channel 4 to produce original British youth comedy and drama in *Skins* (2007–2013), *The Inbetweeners* (2008–2010), and *Misfits* (2009–2013).[34] The production of original content generally suggests the maturation of a new channel or a reworking of a channel brand, serving as a declaration of arrival and a deepening of brand identity.

For streaming sites, the historical process of moving from licensed to original content has progressed on an intensified timeline. Building their brands on libraries of licensed content, SVOD services have helped perpetuate what industry press termed a veritable "arms race" for television drama on the international market, conditions that perpetuate what in 2015 FX executive John Landgraf termed "peak TV," a calculation that content production in the United States had increased to its highest historical level ever.[35] This phenomenon—the idea that new television outlets meant an increase in television *production*, rather than a mere increase in content *circulation* internationally—was driven by both original and imported high-profile US and UK television dramas and their value to home and international markets.

In a crowded market, SVOD services have sought to differentiate themselves with exclusive tent-pole content, both self-produced and imported, aggressively pursuing first-run international licensing deals for high-profile US programming. Licenses to stream this acquired content are temporary and region-specific; thus the best way for SVOD services to stabilize content availability and drive aggressive international expansion is to produce original content in which the streaming company has an ownership stake and licensing authority. Yet while the growth of these SVOD services is signaled by their increased investment in and touting of "original" content, the extent to which the SVOD service deserves any creative credit as producer for some of this content is at times a promotional illusion, building a prestige brand on false foundations.

UNSTABLE FRAMING PRACTICES

The second half of the 2010s have seen SVOD services solidify their brands through increasing investment in self-produced content, with Hulu becoming the first streaming service to win the Emmy for Outstanding Drama Series with *The Handmaid's Tale* in 2017. Yet its journey to prestige purveyor of original programming saw it engage in assertions of ownership similar to Netflix's own claims. Hulu's framing of E4's British youth telefantasy *Misfits* illustrates practices of fuzzy, random, or downright perplexing framing during the first half of the 2010s. Produced by Clerkenwell Films for E4 (a digital channel owned by public service broadcaster Channel 4) and distributed by BBC Worldwide, the series began streaming in the United States on Hulu two years after its UK debut in 2009. This occurred at a time when Hulu was competing with US cable networks to license British programming, with the SVOD service eagerly investing in British imports as a way to differentiate itself in the US industry. One British distribution executive noted the platform was willing to sign exclusive deals and pay licensing fees that were far higher than usual.[36] At the time of *Misfits'* premiere on Hulu during the summer of 2011, the service promoted it as a first-run exclusive within the United States.[37] Both its creator and Channel 4 executives had sought to accentuate the program's

Britishness when commissioning the program in the United Kingdom, in part to distinguish it from *Heroes* (NBC, 2006–2010) and the raft of imported US teen drama TV airing on E4.[38] Yet national identity was absent when Hulu framed its acquisition, with the SVOD service's senior vice president of content acquisition, Andy Forssell, citing as Hulu's motivation the program's "rabid fan base online," rather than its British audience or even its BAFTA award. This online audience, in Forssell's phrasing, lacks any national identity, suggesting the program's appeal overcomes any potential barriers resulting from national origin, including accents and the particularities of British youth television. Thus a show that was marketed as a distinctively British series at the time of its development in the United Kingdom became the product of an American company, sold to its American audience absent any markers of its national past.

Hulu licensed *Misfits* due to its fit with the Hulu brand, owing to its similarities to American programs carried by the service, including *Heroes* and *Flash Forward* (ABC, 2009–2010), both produced by subdivisions of conglomerate owners of Hulu.[39] Grouping *Misfits* as part of a broader set of American programs, Forssell is playing the role of "mediator" that Steemers and Rixon describe, playing up the way that an imported program continues or extends preexisting practices, rather than disrupts them.[40] Like the British executives Rixon interviews, Forssell is framing an import through local cultural discourse in order to assimilate and "nationalize" it within American programming. Thoroughly Americanized, *Misfits* became Hulu's most viewed program.[41] This is where the story of *Misfits'* national identity crisis becomes even more complicated.

Two years into its run, Hulu began labeling (and coding) *Misfits* as an "original series," one of many British series then claimed by Hulu as an original.[42] This marker is perplexing not only because it demonstrates a change in how Hulu promoted the series to its viewers but also because the term implies an ownership stake. Operating as an international licensee, Hulu nevertheless claimed *Misfits* as its own. Discussing the Hulu licensing deal, Gary Woolf, vice president of business development and digital media, commented, "There's value in those rights, and we intend to capture the value."[43] Hulu also extracted value in terms of brand identity by entwining distinctive British programming inextricably with its own emerging brand in order to distinguish itself from competitors. Moreover, the financial costs of these types of international licensing deals remained "pretty modest," according to *Variety*, allowing a relatively new distribution enterprise to build its library of content without the heavy expenditures of production and development.[44] There is something odd here in a program's brand value coming from its Britishness—as is seen in Hulu's use of British content as a marker of distinction—yet this distinction not being asserted in its Hulu branding, which instead asserts ownership and origination through the "original" tag. Time and again we see this peculiar

FIGURE 2.3 Channel 4's *Misfits* as "Hulu Original"

intertwining of distinction and prestige brought by an import, with an attempted erasure of its status as import through its categorization as a false original. Here SVOD services piggyback prestige at a cut-price rate, although as the arms race for content increases, some of this acquired prestige can come at a much higher price tag.

Programs that travel internationally can undergo a process of translation and assimilation that potentially distances local audiences from the series' original contexts and meanings, as their mediators construct a paratextual frame that "blend[s] them to become part of the output of that channel."[45] Some imports have their origins foregrounded, such as UK cable channel Sky Atlantic's marketing of itself as the "home of HBO." Chris Becker has illustrated how US cable channel BBC America built its brand identity of "hip quality" around clearly labeled imports from the BBC and Channel 4.[46] On Hulu, however, *Misfits* appeared as a program with no past. The SVOD service's distinctiveness in comic programming in the early 2010s was built on a British foundation, yet this British foundation, the acclaim and prestige of its originating content, was erased in its branding.

Another case in point is *Breaking Bad*, which arguably helped Netflix break into the UK market, where LoveFilm, a combination DVD subscription and streaming service (acquired by Amazon in 2011, with the streaming service ultimately assimilated into Amazon Prime Video), had an established market hold. The program's first two seasons saw faltering success on linear television (on the pay-cable channel FOX in 2009 and on free-to-air digital channel 5USA the following year), and its sales rights languished by 2011. Netflix acquired first-run rights in 2012 and claimed it as a Netflix Original. Its fourth season "broke viewing records . . . across the board" at Netflix, with creator Vince Gilligan suggesting that the SVOD service had been instrumental in the show's ascension to the status of phenomenon in the United Kingdom.[47] A day-and-date release of each episode of part 2 of season 5 in 2013, with episodes uploaded the day after the US broadcast, linked Netflix closely with the patterns of linear television distribution and made it indistinguishable from AMC as the program's author within this UK televisual frame. Like Hulu and *Misfits*, here we can see how such false originals contributed to Netflix's bid to present itself as content producer with a significant cultural footprint rather than merely a library of imported and syndicated content.

CONCLUSION

In late 2016, Netflix laid out its plan to move toward 50 percent of its content being made up of "original productions," a statement that asserted its cultural and industrial validity through the value of original content. *Variety* noted that Netflix CFO David Wells framed this designation of "original" as made up of "a mix of content owned and produced by Netflix, as well as co-productions and acquisitions."[48] Wells's categorization of acquisitions as originals rather than the licensed content they actually were went unchallenged in the trade press. This suggests that Netflix had normalized its appropriation of selected imported content as branded originals and was using this to bolster its claims of cultural validity. With this continual pursuit, Netflix seemingly sought to change the definition of "original"—was it the new "exclusive"? Yet not all the SVOD service's exclusive first-run imports were given the Netflix Original marker, so no clear definition can be made.

False originals certainly assist Netflix's building of its brand as not just a library, but a streaming channel with buzzworthy content and awards potential, at a cost lower than original production. But as unacknowledged acquisitions, the programs lose their national specificity and their sociocultural context, subsumed to the international brand of Netflix. SVOD services do not service local markets (as networks have done in the United States through their owned-and-operated stations), and they fall under limited regulatory control. Will indigenous channels ultimately serve as unacknowledged content farms for monolithic international SVOD services whose power and spread is only limited by the depth of their pockets and the penetration of broadband? Or will rights-holders push back against these practices as part of their sale of licensing rights?

Originating producers have begun to assert their ownership in this landscape of cloudy attribution and appropriated authorship. Beginning in 2015, licensing rights deals have begun to include network and studio branding as markers layered onto the library image. This is seen in US streaming second-run rights deals in which producing networks have negotiated branding rights. For example, ABC's logo appears on *How to Get Away with Murder* (2014–) streaming through Netflix, and Fox's logo appears on its content streaming through Hulu.[49] On the import front, Amazon UK features the AMC logo on *Halt and Catch Fire*'s (2014–) library image, yet notably the USA and Starz logos are absent from season 2 of its highest-profile acquisitions, *Mr. Robot* (2015–) and *Outlander* (2014–), with "Amazon Exclusive" taking pride of place. *Call the Midwife* (2012–) was originally produced by British indie Neal Street Productions for BBC1 and aired in the United States on PBS. Netflix acquired second-window rights from the BBC's commercial arm, BBC Worldwide, which handled the international rights sales; thus the program appears on Netflix with a BBC logo on its menu image, as do other BBC Worldwide–sold programs.

Such tags can also offer up interesting clashes of ownership. For instance, on US Amazon, *Poldark* (2015–), which is produced by British indie Mammoth Pictures for BBC1 and airs on PBS in the United States, appears with a PBS banner affixed. However, on Amazon UK, it is affixed with an ITV logo, as Mammoth Pictures is owned by ITV studios (which is the production arm of the British channel ITV). Netflix chief content officer Ted Sarandos ostensibly dismissed the need for such claims, on the basis that "in the pay-television world . . . the channel brand equity means a lot, and in our world, it really doesn't."[50] Yet blurring or disguising the origins of its library content through paratextual framing certainly benefits the Netflix brand, one that is built just as much on acquisitions as it is on "originals." If origin and brand equity really did not matter, then Netflix Originals, of all shades, would not exist.

In a potential shift away from the false-original stage, SVOD services—like many US cable channels—have begun increasing their involvement in coproductions.[51] This allows involvement and ownership at the ground floor, rather than potentially costly fights for global licensing rights for finished products. Coproduction allows smaller or new channels to fight for space within "peak TV" by obtaining potential prestige drama at a cut-price rate with no need to invest in development costs. Coproduction is facilitated by UK and European broadcasters, for whom coproduction is an increasing necessity in the drama "arms race," both to offset the increasing costs of drama production needed to compete in the global marketplace and to avoid losing creative personnel to the deep pockets and tales of creative freedom that surround SVOD services. The latter risk was recently exemplified by the case of *The Crown*, which was pitched to both the BBC and ITV but snatched up by Netflix.

Sky and French broadcaster Canal+ partnered on *The Tunnel* (2013–) and *The Smoke* (2014–), while Channel 4 and Kudos worked with US cable channel AMC on *Humans* (2015–). AMC recently took an ownership stake in BBC Worldwide, a move that built on its strategic forays into British content coproduction, servicing its prestige brand. Amazon,

Hulu, and Netflix have also moved into coproduction deals. Amazon coproduced *Fleabag* (BBC Three, 2016) with the BBC to much critical acclaim on both sides of the Atlantic. This strongly authored comedy with an acerbic edge and a sharp female protagonist fit handily alongside *Transparent*, Amazon's award-winning, self-produced original. Hulu paired with the BBC on the farcical accidental-action comedy *The Wrong Mans* (2013–2014), continuing the platform's success with British imports. In the first half of 2016 alone, Netflix came onboard with a string of British programming in development, including BBC1's new adaptation of *Watership Down* (produced with British indie 42) and E4's first-ever coproductions, teen dramas *Kiss Me First* (Channel 4, 2018) (from indie Balloon and Kindle Entertainment) and *Crazy Face* (E4, 2017) (produced by Urban Myth Films).

These deals gave the British channels ownership on home soil, with the SVOD partner taking over in US and international distribution. Such coproductions blur the "sharp distinctions between home-grown and imported product, and between the local and the global."[52] In turn, the national distinction of homegrown content is potentially at stake. The rise of coproduction drives the market toward glossy international thrillers such as *The Night Manager* (BBC1/AMC, 2016), with their £2 million plus per episode price tags. What does the increasing necessity of coproduction, with SVOD services and beyond, mean for the development of smaller, intimate, nationally specific drama? How is the state of the nation articulated with one eye across the sea? As discussed in more detail by Michele Hilmes in this volume, programming driven by a national mission has struggled for decades to fulfill that mission, and this challenge has only been heightened by digital streaming and the "TV arms race" it has precipitated.

Our study has focused on the shifting lexicon guiding SVOD services' paratextual framing and promotion of selected international content in the national contexts of the United States and the United Kingdom, but its broader themes address larger patterns and debates within transnational television content distribution. While American audiences are accessing more international content than ever before, that content often flaunts only the imprimatur of the brand of the US-based SVOD service, effectively lessening its foreignness and appropriating its distinction. False originals help Netflix bolster its reputation as a producer of original content, which helps solidify its status as a creative producer rather than a library of programs produced by others. These falsely attributed programs advance a consistent narrative that SVOD services are global, innovative, and *productive*, and that their programs transcend national identities and cultures. Meanwhile those same US-based SVOD services are inflating costs within the international marketplace for licensing rights, leading the financial benefits drawn from US television to remain in US hands, rather than serving as tent poles that help draw audiences and advertising money to local channels and support their indigenous programming.

The slipperiness of the term "original" conveys a vernacular in development, a labeling of industrial practices for which the rules have not yet been established. The contradictions behind these labels reveal contestations about ownership, distribution, corporate branding, national identity, technological shifts, and audience reception. Digital distribution technologies may have made it easier for international content to reach foreign audiences, but this does not necessarily mean that they fit seamlessly into their new environment.[53] The programs may travel, but they are doing so without a passport.

NOTES

1. While SVOD services are distinguished by their distribution technology (streaming), the term also references their business model, subscription. We focus upon Netflix, Hulu, and Amazon Prime Instant Video, but other SVOD services, some connected to linear channels, include CBS All Access, BBC iPlayer, YouTube Red, Playstation Vue, HBO Now, Now TV, and many others.

2. In 2011 the BBC deployed "original" as a marker of its production of and investment in British drama, in response to the high-profile launch of Sky Atlantic by Sky plc. This satellite channel was built around prestige US imports, most notably an exclusive deal for HBO content in the United Kingdom, which it foregrounded in its marketing. The BBC's promotional campaign foregrounded BBC2's "Original British Drama," a brand that expanded to cover all the broadcaster's drama content. This asserted originality and national specificity as a marker of the public service broadcaster's value. Tara Conlan, "BBC2: Putting the British in Drama," *The Guardian*, April 13, 2011, https://www.theguardian.com/media/organgrinder/2011/apr/13/bbc2-drama.

3. Jeannette Steemers, "Selling Television: Addressing Transformations in the International Distribution of Television Content," *Media Industries* 1:1 (2014), http://www.mediaindustriesjournal.org/index.php/mij/article/view/16.

4. Jeanette Steemers, *Selling Television: British Television in the Global Marketplace* (London: BFI, 2004); Steemers, "International Sales of U.K. Television Content Change and Continuity in 'the Space in between' Production and Consumption," *Television & New Media*, published online before print, June 21, 2016, doi:10.1177/1527476416653481; Michael L. Wayne, "Netflix, Amazon, and Branded Television Content in Subscription Video On-Demand Portals," *Media, Culture & Society*, published online before print, October 13, 2017, https://doi.org/10.1177/0163443717736118.

5. Michele Hilmes, "Transnational TV: What Do We Mean by 'Coproduction' Anymore?," *Media Industries Journal* 1:2 (2014): 1–8.

6. Alisa Perren, "Rethinking Distribution for the Future of Media Industry Studies," *Cinema Journal* 52:3 (2013): 165–171.

7. Jinna Tay and Graeme Turner, "Not the Apocalypse: Television Futures in the Digital Age," *International Journal of Digital Television* 1:1 (2010): 31–50.

8. John Plunkett, "Netflix Plans £100m Epic on the Queen," *The Guardian*, May 23, 2016, https://www.theguardian.com/media/2014/may/23/netflix-epic-the-queen-crown-peter-morgan.

9. By January 2016 Netflix had expanded into two hundred territories, while Amazon, not to be overlooked, used *The Grand Tour* to expand its video service into two hundred territories by December 2016. Peter White, "Netflix Expands into 130 Countries," *Broadcast*, January 7, 2016, http://www.broadcastnow.co.uk/news/netflix-expands-into-130-countries/5098600.article; Jane Martinson, "Amazon to Stream *The Grand Tour* in 200 Countries and Territories," November 16, 2016, https://www.theguardian.com/tv-and-radio/2016/nov/16/amazon-stream-the-grand-tour-200-countries-december. For more on piracy studies, see also Patrick Vonderau, "Beyond Piracy: Understanding Digital Markets," in *Connected Viewing: Selling, Streaming, and Sharing Media in the Digital Era*, ed. Jennifer Holt and Kevin Sanson

(New York: Routledge, 2014): 99–123; Ramon Lobato, *Shadow Economies of Cinema: Mapping Informal Film Distribution* (London: Palgrave Macmillan, 2012).

10. Kate Bulkey, "The Price Is Right for VoD," *Broadcast*, March 15, 2012, http://m.broadcastnow.co.uk/5039298.article.

11. Windowing refers to designated periods when an acquired program can air that are established contractually in a deal for its rights, such as "first run" or "second run" rights in a particular country, or holding back a program until the completion of the broadcast of a full season in the originating country.

12. Steemers, "International Sales," 4.

13. As part of a *Variety* report that tracked the impact of expanding budgets in the era of "peak TV," Mo Ryan identified that in 2017 "Apple already has a TV budget of at least $1 billion. Disney, Time Warner, NBC Universal and CBS spent $36 billion on TV last year—a third more than just seven years ago. Hulu will part with $2.5 billion this year, which tops HBO's annual $2 billion budget. Netflix is upping its ante to $7 billion in 2018. Amazon spent $4.5 billion this year." "Taking the Wrong Lessons from the Success of 'Game of Thrones,'" *Variety*, September 26, 2017, http://variety.com/2017/tv/opinion/game-of-thrones-success-hbo-money-wrong-lessons-1202573525/.

14. Paul Rixon, *American Television on British Screens: A Story of Cultural Interaction* (London: Palgrave Macmillan, 2006), 184–185.

15. For just a small sample of these types of awe-filled articles, see also Josef Adalian, "How Amazon Became a Major Player in Half-Hour Television," *Vulture*, October 6, 2016, http://www.vulture.com/2016/10/amazon-became-a-major-player-in-half-hour-tv.html; Tara Conlan, "Netflix's Breaking Good: From DVD Mail-Order Firm to UK's Top Streaming Service," *The Guardian*, March 28, 2016, https://www.theguardian.com/business/2016/mar/28/netflix-hits-5m-subscribers-become-uk-top-streaming-service; Tim Wu, "Netflix's War on Mass Culture," *New Republic*, December 4, 2013, https://newrepublic.com/article/115687/netflixs-war-mass-culture.

16. John Plunkett, "Sky Atlantic to Launch Next Month with Scorsese Drama," *The Guardian*, January 5, 2011, https://www.theguardian.com/media/2011/jan/05/sky-atlantic-launch-boardwalk-empire.

17. Arguably Nordic noir's popularization of Danish and Swedish serialized detective stories in *The Killing* (*Forbrydelsen*) (DR1, 2007–12) and *The Bridge* (*Bron/Broen*) (SVT1/DR1, 2011–) developed from these British traditions.

18. Alex Ritman, "'Happy Valley' Producer: TV Opening Up to 'Less Posh British Drama,'" *Hollywood Reporter*, March 16, 2016, http://www.hollywoodreporter.com/news/happy-valley-producer-posh-british-876104.

19. Brett Martin, *Difficult Men: Behind the Scenes of a Creative Revolution: From "The Sopranos" and "The Wire" to "Mad Men" and "Breaking Bad"* (New York: Penguin, 2013).

20. "*Happy Valley* Season 2 Trailer Netflix," accessible on *YouTube*, March 10, 2016, posted by Netflix US & Canada, https://www.youtube.com/watch?v=p-XeH76o4xQ.

21. "*Happy Valley* Season 2 Trailer BBC One," accessible on *YouTube*, February 1, 2016, posted by the BBC, https://www.youtube.com/watch?v=QrFBNcLuSgY&list=FLZ1_qi7AEsxPlvJwibOEfzQ&index=1.

22. Kasey Moore, "Doubts Surround Season 3 of Netflix Original *Happy Valley*," *What's on Netflix*, April 15, 2016, http://www.whats-on-netflix.com/news/doubts-surround-season-3-netflix-original-happy-valley/.

23. Jonathan Gray, *Show Sold Separately: Promos, Spoilers, and Other Media Paratexts* (New York: New York University Press, 2010), 3.

24. Rixon, *American Television*, 184–185.

25. Imports can be edited for content due to a move to an earlier time slot or to accommodate differently timed commercial breaks, while continuity announcements and presenters, bumpers, and promotional trailers frame the audience's reading of a program. Paul Grainge, "Lost Logos: Channel 4 and the Branding of American Event Television," in *Reading "Lost": Perspectives on a Hit Television Show*, ed. Roberta Pearson (London: I.B. Tauris, 2009); Faye Woods, "Teen TV Meets T4: Assimilating The OC into British Youth Television," *Critical Studies in Television* 8:1 (2013) 14–35.

26. Grainge, "Lost Logos," 102–105.

27. John Ellis, *Visible Fictions: Cinema, Television, Video* (London: Routledge, 1982), 24–25.

28. In contrast to the nation-erasing tendencies of Netflix, the SVOD service of British broadcaster Channel 4, All4, groups and heavily markets its foreign-language imports under the "Walter Presents" brand.

29. See also Cory Barker, "'Great Shows, Thanks to You': From Participatory Culture to 'Quality TV' in Amazon's Pilot Season," *Television & New Media*, published online before print, September 15, 2016, doi:10.1177/1527476416667817; Amanda Lotz, *Portals: A Treatise on Internet-Distributed Television* (n.p.: Michigan Publishing, 2017); Mareike Jenner, "Is This TVIV: On Netflix, TVIII, and Binge-Watching," *New Media & Society* 18:2 (2016) 257–273; Nick Marx, "Industry Lore and Algorithmic Programming on Netflix," *Flow* 21:6 (April 22, 2015) http://www.flowjournal.org/2015/04/industry-lore-and-algorithmic-programming-on-netflix/; and the special issue edited by Sarah Art and Anne Schwan, "Screening Women's Imprisonment: Agency and Exploitation in *Orange Is the New Black*," *Television and New Media*, published online before print, May 23, 2016, doi:10.1177/1527476416647499.

30. Chuck Tryon, "TV Got Better: Netflix's Original Programming Strategies and Binge Viewing," *Media Industries* 2:2 (2015), http://www.mediaindustriesjournal.org/index.php/mij/article/view/126.

31. Rixon, *American Television*; Simone Knox, "*Masterpiece Theatre* and British Drama Imports on US Television: Discourses of Tension," *Critical Studies in Television* 7:1 (2012) 29–48; Christine Becker, "From High Culture to Hip Culture: Transforming the BBC into BBC America," in *Anglo-American Media Interactions, 1850–2000*, ed. Joel H. Wiener and Mark Hampton (Basingstoke: Palgrave Macmillan, 2007), 275–294.

32. Michelle Hilmes, *Network Nations: A Transnational History of British and American Broadcasting* (New York: Routledge, 2012); Jean K. Chalaby, "Drama without Drama: The Late Rise of Scripted TV Formats," *Television & New Media* 17:1 (2016) 3–20; Faye Woods, *British Youth Television: Transnational Teens, Industry, Genre* (London: Palgrave Macmillan, 2016), 107–142; Steemers, *Selling Television*.

33. Avi Santo, "Para-television and Discourses of Distinction: The Culture of Production at HBO," in *It's Not TV: Watching HBO in the Post-television Era*, ed. Marc Leverette, Brian L. Ott, and Cara Louise Buckley (New York: Routledge, 2008), 31-57.

34. Woods, *British Youth Television*, 39–41.

35. Chris Curtis, "The Scripted Arms Race Escalates," *Broadcast*, April 21, 2016, http://www.broadcastnow.co.uk/opinion/the-scripted-arms-race-escalates/5102849.article; Mo Ryan and Cynthia Littleton, "TV Series Budgets Hit the Breaking Point as Costs Skyrocket in Peak TV Era," *Variety*, September 26, 2017, http://variety.com/2017/tv/news/tv-series-budgets-costs-rising-peak-tv-1202570158/; Cynthia Littleton, "FX Networks Chief John Landgraf: 'There Is Simply Too Much Television,'" *Variety*, August 7, 2015, http://variety.com/2015/tv/news/tca-fx-networks-john-landgraf-wall-street-1201559191.

36. Bulkey, "Price Is Right."

37. "Brit Skeins Set U.S. Bows on Hulu," *Daily Variety*, June 13, 2011, 6.

38. Woods, *British Youth Television*, 72.

39. Paul Bond, "Hulu to Roll Out Episodes of Three Hit U.K. Series," *Hollywood Reporter*, June 13, 2011, http://www.hollywoodreporter.com/news/hulu-roll-episodes-three-hit-197041.

40. Rixon, *American Television*; Steemers, *Selling Television*, 17–20.

41. Leo Barraclough, "Time-Shifts Lift Drama Karma," *Variety*, October 17, 2011, TV, 1.

42. Examples of other British series promoted by Hulu as original series at this time included structured reality program *The Only Way Is Essex* (ITV2, 2010–) and BBC sitcoms *Pramface* (BBC Three, 2012–2014), *The Thick of It* (BBC Four / BBC Two, 2005–2012), and *Rev* (BBC Two, 2010–2014); Bulkey, "Price Is Right."

43. Barraclough, "Time-Shifts."

44. Cynthia Littleton, "Hulu Draws New Lines with 'Battleground,'" *Daily Variety*, January 24, 2012, TV, 2.

45. Rixon, *American Television*, 105.

46. Becker, "From High Culture," 284.

47. Jeffrey Morgan, "*Breaking Bad* Fifth Season Gets Netflix Premiere Date," *Digital Spy*, October 16, 2012, http://www.digitalspy.com/tv/breaking-bad/news/a430335/

breaking-bad-fifth-season-gets-netflix-uk-premiere-date/; Todd Spangler, "Netflix Lands First-Run Rights for 'Breaking Bad' Final Season in U.K., Ireland," *Variety*, July 26, 2013, http://variety.com/2013/digital/news/netflix-lands-first-run-rights-for-breaking-bad-final-season-in-u-k-ireland-1200568547/.

48. Todd Spangler, "Netflix Targeting 50% of Content to Be Original Programming, CFO Says," *Variety*, September 20, 2016, http://variety.com/2016/digital/news/netflix-50-percent-content-original-programming-cfo-1201865902.

49. Joe Flint, "TV Programmers Push Netflix for Promotions, Branding," *Wall Street Journal*, November 13, 2015, http://www.wsj.com/articles/tv-programmers-push-netflix-for-promotions-branding-1447433281; Keach Hagey and Shalini Ramachandran, "Hulu Steps Up Its Fight against Netflix," *Wall Street Journal*, June 16, 2015, http://www.wsj.com/articles/hulu-steps-up-its-fight-against-netflix-1434497311.

50. Hagey and Ramachandran, "Hulu Steps Up."

51. Hilmes, "Transnational TV."

52. Paul Torre, "Reversal of Fortune? Hollywood Faces New Competition in Global Media Trade," in *Global Television Formats*, ed. Tasha Oren and Sharon Shahaf (London: Routledge, 2012), 178–200.

53. UK Netflix currently claims as Netflix Originals programs that originate on channels in the United States (*Designated Survivor*, ABC, 2016–), France (*A Very Secret Service*, Arte, 2015–), and Argentina (*El Marginal*, Public TV, 2016), while US Netflix claims as original series from broadcasters in the United Kingdom (many, from *Chewing Gum* to *Marcella*, ITV, 2016), Israel (*Fauda*, Yes, 2015), Colombia (*La Niña*, Caracol, 2015), France (*No Second Chance*, TF1, 2016), and Italy (*Call Me Francis*, Mediaset, 2015).

3

BBC AMERICA

Cloning Drama for a Transnational Network

CHRISTINE BECKER

No outlet better represents the state of transatlantic television in 2016 than BBC America, which is co-owned by a British and an American company and airs British imports, US-UK coproductions, and American originals, while its most acclaimed series is a Canadian production. In my 2007 essay "From High Culture to Hip Culture: Transforming the BBC into BBC America," I discussed the evolution of BBC America in the early 2000s into a cable channel that both stood out as distinctive within the US cable lineup and served a key branding role for the BBC back in the United Kingdom, as the corporation fought to retain its public funding. In the decade following that publication, the goals of BBC America and those of its British parent BBC Worldwide have shifted, particularly in the wake of AMC Networks' purchase of a 49.9 percent stake in the channel. These developments illustrate how transatlantic corporate partnerships have become central to global distribution trends, underscoring the complex interdependency of public service and commercial economic models in today's transnational and multiplatform TV ecosystem. For the new BBC America, the linchpin to success in this ecosystem is primarily scripted drama that draws on branding elements of the BBC and Britishness, which is driven by the overarching goal to connect with upscale, engaged viewers on linear TV and video-on-demand platforms, in line with the aspirations of its American corporate parent AMC Networks. This chapter will outline the industry mandates and conditions that led to this economic and programming evolution at BBC

America, as the channel shifted from independent outlet to interdependent node in a transnational network.

FROM HIP CULTURE TO *ORPHAN BLACK*

In "From High Culture to Hip Culture," I argued that BBC America's programming brand was based upon parroting genres that were successful across the cable lineup while pitching them as higher-culture versions of their American counterparts, particularly drawing on connotations of risk, realism, and refinement that British culture embodied for American audiences. BBC America's mid-aughts "cool but high quality" programs included distinctly British versions of "HBO-style edginess, TLC's lifestyle reality, FX's gritty police dramas, and USA's light-hearted ones, Comedy Central's topical sketch comedy, and CNN-style news."[1] The architect of this programming approach, CEO Paul Lee, was successful enough to be poached away in 2004 to run ABC Family. However, he left behind a channel with limited reach, as by 2006 BBC America was in only about 50 million pay television homes (out of about 94 million possible) while earning a tiny 0.1 household rating.[2] BBC America had carved out a distinctive niche under Lee, but it was not a very visible one.

Beginning in 2007, the channel began to significantly transform under the guidance of Garth Ancier, who was named president of BBC Worldwide's American division and also assigned the task of running BBC America. Drawing on his expertise in American television as only the second person to have run three separate network entertainment divisions (NBC, Fox, and The WB), Ancier saw the key to greater carriage in programming prime-time dramas targeting upscale audiences who could in turn be touted as valuable assets to cable and satellite operators. A rise in coproductions with the BBC with shows like *Jekyll* (2007) was the result. Ancier told *Variety* that British fare like this would attract the "intellectually curious" viewer, which is another way of describing the college-educated elite at the heart of the upscale demographic.[3] To help raise ratings and ad rates, Ancier also saw the importance of attracting younger audiences, hence the 2007 move to begin importing the popular motoring series *Top Gear* and, the next year, to poach the BBC's cult science fiction hit *Doctor Who* from Syfy. Ancier scheduled *Doctor Who* for Saturday nights, perceived as a slow night for American TV but matching its traditional BBC slot.

While these developments tied the channel to its British roots, a new marketing campaign strove to highlight the "America" in BBC America more fully. Starting in 2007, the new channel taglines were "A little Brit different" and "A bit of Britishness in the American landscape," while a new logo dropped the familiar Union Jack design and instead placed a large A in the center of concentric circles to draw attention to the America in the channel's title. General manager Kathryn Mitchell said the channel's market research discovered that audiences who had never watched assumed BBC America was "all about red buses and bowler hats," and this campaign strove to signal that the channel instead represented common ground between the United States and the United Kingdom.[4]

By 2009, BBC America was moving in the right direction, as it had expanded to 68 million homes and had apparently found many of those "intellectually curious" viewers Ancier desired. *Multichannel News* reported that the channel had "the most affluent and educated audience in cable, combining the highest percentage of viewers with household income of more than $100,000 and four years or more of college," while the median viewer age had also dropped.[5] However, *Deadline*'s Nellie Andreeva noted in 2009 that "despite its growth in the past three years, BBC America is yet to branch out beyond a niche following." She also observed that BBC Worldwide's production studio had yet to develop a hit show under Ancier.[6]

That may have helped prompt the exit of Ancier and the 2010 appointment of Herb Scannell to replace him. Scannell had previously made his mark in cable television as the president of Nickelodeon and TV Land and was happy to take over a channel drawing an upscale demographic, but BBC America's overall ratings were still unimpressive, as prime time averaged just 136,000 viewers from 2009 to 2010.[7] Therefore, Scannell set out to increase the programming budget and expand the prime-time lineup beyond just British offerings, expressing his intent to develop "some made-in-America shows that will be of the kind of smart, irreverent innovative spirit that the BBC has had."[8] In 2011, BBC Worldwide America's general manager, Perry Simon, similarly described the development goals of BBC America as needing to "maintain the British connectivity that's crucial to everything we do, but do it with more of a focus on the US audience."[9]

The channel's first original solo-produced series, *Copper* (2012–2013), unfortunately never found enough of any audience, nor did it have much British connectivity. Set during the time of the American Civil War, *Copper* focused on an Irish immigrant policeman in New York City and was produced by heavyweights Tom Fontana and Barry Levinson. *Copper* debuted on a Sunday night to record premiere viewership for BBC America, but ratings declined from there. Perhaps more importantly, the series never garnered much buzz, and it was cancelled in 2013 following its second season, failing to have broken out as either a ratings or a critical hit.[10]

What finally did connect with devoted audiences and critics was the Canadian import *Orphan Black* (2013–present), a science fiction series produced by Temple Street Productions in Toronto that began airing on BBC America in March 2013. Strikingly, *Orphan Black* earned lower ratings than *Copper* but far outstripped it in terms of critical attention and a committed fan following, with fervent appreciation garnered around star Tatiana Maslany's virtuosic performance as multiple clone characters. For a channel fighting to grow its presence beyond a niche in a saturated cable lineup, critical attention and headlines held more value than just individual eyeballs. TV critic Tim Goodman wrote of *Orphan Black*'s higher profile following Maslany's 2013 Best Actress Emmy nomination: "Often critics are the first to champion low-profile but high-quality shows on channels viewers struggle to find or identify with. In the exploding world of scripted program across countless channels, this can be a valuable consumer service—not to mention giving a much needed boost to the host channel, in this instance BBC America."[11]

Orphan Black also embodied greater connectivity to BBC America's British brand than *Copper*, despite its Canadian roots, New York setting, and fantastical world of proliferating clones. It offered a natural pairing with *Doctor Who*—and in fact premiered along with a new half-season of *Doctor Who* as part of a "Supernatural Saturday" themed block—due to its science fiction genre trappings with an undertone of camp and its twisting narrative, not to mention that the show's primary clone is meant to be a British woman, living in New York. *Orphan Black*'s ambitious creative qualities also connote the innovation that Scannell believed was at the heart of the Britishness in BBC America's brand, an aspect later echoed by his successor at the channel, Sarah Barnett: "There's something very interesting in the original content we're developing that isn't necessarily about being British but about this idea of being a little outside the mainstream that, I think, is a really exciting access point for this brand." Barnett added further that shows like *Orphan Black* represent "creative courage and risk-taking," which "are true BBC qualities."[12] That in turn makes the show valuable in global markets, including Great Britain, as BBC Worldwide acquired international distribution rights and placed *Orphan Black* on BBC Three. Such transnational coding is therefore an invaluable economic asset, as Serra Tinic writes:

> Although *Orphan Black* is not "British," despite being acquired by BBC America, the fact that it may be perceived as such aligns with BBC Worldwide's current objective to build the BBC brand globally through investing in and developing coproductions with culturally proximate industry partners. Canadian producers have long been seen as favorable international coproduction partners due to the perception that they are cultural intermediaries who are conversant with the American television industry yet bring a slightly "European sensibility" to their projects. Moreover, *Orphan Black* fulfilled the channel's goal to purchase content that would complement and expand its genre-based brand recognition in the US market beyond the landmark *Doctor Who*.[13]

By 2014, BBC America was available in over 80 million pay television households and, thanks especially to *Orphan Black*, it could tout resonant brand recognition that drew upon but still distinguished itself from the BBC brand.[14] But in broader industry economic terms, BBC America's and BBC Worldwide's revenue prospects were still limited due to the channel's status as an independent outlet in a sea of conglomerate partnerships and consolidating pay TV outlets. Therefore, one could argue that the biggest return on the *Orphan Black* investment was in how it helped position the channel to be acquired by a larger media entity.

AMC NETWORKS' BBC AMERICA

In October 2014, AMC purchased 49.9 percent of BBC America for $200 million, with BBC Worldwide retaining majority ownership but AMC Networks granted full operational control, including advertising and distribution sales. BBC America thus became the fifth channel in the AMC Networks portfolio, alongside AMC, IFC, Sundance TV, and WEtv. The BBC and AMC Networks had enjoyed a coproduction relationship oriented around prestige dramas in the years leading up to the deal, with their most prominent successes being the BBC Two / Sundance Channel airings of *Top of the Lake* (2013–present) and *The Honourable Woman* (2014). But there were numerous incentives on both sides to take this partnership to the next level via joint ownership of BBC America.

While BBC America had finally achieved a level of brand awareness in the wake of *Orphan Black*'s success, it was vulnerable as an independent cable channel in a time of shrinking pay television bundles, with no leverage other than its own value come carriage negotiation time, when cable channels jockey for inclusion and placement on US cable systems. Rather than individually, cable carriage is typically negotiated as a combined portfolio, with the most valuable channel in a group owned by a media corporation helping to lift the value of the least valuable as a result. BBC America could not get this benefit as a stand-alone channel. As a growing number of households either choose smaller channel bundles or threaten to cut the cable cord altogether, independent and narrowcast channels become expendable, and a number of independent channels

FIGURE 3.1 AMC Networks portfolio

have disappeared in recent years as a result, including Pivot and Al Jazeera America.[15] *Deadline*'s David Lieberman identified this as a crucial factor justifying the deal for BBC Worldwide: "The combination with AMC should help BBC America at a time when the business landscape is becoming precarious for independent cable channels. Many distributors, eager to cut their programming outlays, are looking to drop networks that appeal to relatively narrow or niche audiences."[16]

Not only did BBC America previously have to take on carriage negotiations independently, but advertising sales were also individually negotiated. As AMC Networks' CEO, Josh Sapan, explained at a media summit, this meant that even popular series like *Orphan Black, Top Gear,* and *Planet Earth* likely sold short of their potential value: "It is probably the case that they were not being rewarded appropriately in advertising pricing for that material. And it was tough to be—to run one channel and not have a group when you are out selling."[17] *Orphan Black* premiered its third season simultaneously across all five of the AMC-owned channels, which AMC Networks COO Ed Carroll says was intended to signal to advertisers that the show and the channel's brands were compatible with their other channels, which would be relevant come upfronts negotiation time, the annual gathering where television executives pitch their channel offerings to advertisers.[18] BBC Worldwide CEO Tim Davie had lamented months before the AMC Networks' deal that "in the U.S., we remain a small business, which in terms of scale needs to grow."[19] AMC Networks' part ownership of BBC America offered exactly such scale and growth potential.

The benefits of this venture accordingly have the potential to trickle back up to BBC Worldwide and the BBC itself. Beyond the $200 million check that came in from the acquisition purchase, AMC Networks has taken over more programming and labor costs at a time when the BBC is fighting significant budget cuts.[20] BBC Director-General Tony Hall has explained the importance of outside investment gained via BBC Worldwide: "That puts more money on screen for the British public and helps take the best British content to global audiences. But this model only works if BBC Worldwide is thriving. It is an indivisible part of the BBC."[21] Accordingly, the BBC has pushed to make BBC Worldwide "a more internationally-facing business, focused on improving appreciation of the BBC and UK creative industries abroad"[22] and on being more active "in the global marketplace developing the BBC's international profile and maximising returns to licence payers."[23] The AMC Networks acquisition is proof of successful efforts in those areas.

For AMC Networks' part, it too was looking to expand its industry positioning and boost revenue, as well as gain greater access to international programming and platforms. Cable analysts speculated that the timing of the BBC America acquisition was linked to the merger of Comcast and Time Warner Cable earlier in 2014.[24] Josh Sapan confirmed in a 2015 earnings call that he did feel the company needed more leverage than the four channels it already had in its portfolio to negotiate for better carriage deals for the group, given increasing consolidation of pay TV ownership.[25] Even just one prominent show on one channel can lift all rates. As Michael O'Connell describes, "BBC America's *Orphan Black* delivers tiny ratings, but its rave reviews lifted the network's profile—one reason why AMC paid $200 million for a 49.9 percent stake in October."[26]

Profile is especially important at a time when viewers have more choice than ever before and are increasingly likely to watch via video-on-demand outlets rather than on linear television. This makes shows that can breed a strong, committed following beyond their original airing crucial. To clarify this point, it is worth quoting at length from Josh Sapan's commentary on a 2015 earnings call:

> First, as consumers exert more choice over what they watch, they are moving away from TV shows they are indifferent to and are favoring shows that speak to them in some particularly meaningful way; and our shows do just that. Our content orientation and development has over the past decade been toward developing and creating high-engagement, high-quality programming that targets select audiences and resonates with those audiences, with brands, shows, and talent that are among the very favorites of those who watch them. Shows like IFC's *Portlandia*, SundanceTV's *The Honourable Woman*, WE tv's *Braxton Family Values*, and AMC's *Mad Men, Better Call Saul*, and *The Walking Dead*. It is in no small part why we acquired a stake in BBC America. You take a look at the enormous fan communities around *Orphan Black* and *Doctor Who*, and we think it's clear those shows matter quite a lot to the people who watch them. So our shows are not just the show that's on that 10:00, that's after the show that's on at 9:00, that's hoping to pick up whatever random audience happens to have hung around. We think that approach is less effective in a world in which the viewer exerts greater intention, choice, and control. When viewers have flexibility and choice, our shows are among those that they actively select.[27]

Herb Scannell said something similar in 2015 when he remarked that considerable programming development effort would have to go into "deepening the attachments between fans and the shows they watch."[28]

This is also where program ownership, not just channel ownership, becomes central, as a series can be sold to other platforms, both in the United States and globally, and this can be particularly lucrative when the shows are produced and owned by partner studios within the corporate network. AMC Networks' deal with BBC Worldwide does grant profit participation rights to "shows that are sold to digital platforms in the US that air on BBC America."[29] Another investment made in the year prior to the BBC America deal will help spread this benefit around the globe. In February 2014, AMC Networks announced it had completed the acquisition of Chellomedia, a company that operates global cable networks across 138 countries. The company was subsequently renamed AMC International and has given the company an outlet for worldwide distribution of its programming.[30]

Finally, the BBC America acquisition was logical for AMC Networks from a branding perspective. COO Ed Carroll described in 2014 the qualities that united the original programming on the channels that AMC Networks already owned: "smarter shows that tell slightly complicated stories and have outsize appeal to an upscale audience."[31] One could easily mistake this for a Garth Ancier or Herb Scannell quotation. With the exception of WEtv, AMC Networks' channels also draw upon rhetoric of quality television tied to connotations of independent cinema, directly so in the case of IFC and Sundance, and this is naturally extended to the quality rhetoric so often tied to the BBC and British television. Josh Sapan expressed this idea at a media summit in saying that the BBC is "arguably one of if not the highest-quality television studio[s] in the planet in terms of television quality production. Now, that's a relative term. It doesn't mean necessarily everything rates high. I think their quality is spectacular."[32] As this indicates, impressions now carry as much value as individual viewers. The BBC America deal includes continued commitment to BBC Worldwide coproduction and distribution partnerships, and this can be exploited across the AMC Networks portfolio, as has been evidenced from prestigious dramas like *The Night Manager* (2016) on AMC and *The A Word* (2016) on Sundance.

Scripted drama in particular currently reigns supreme from the national to the global scene. It has been quite apparent that the BBC is favoring prestige drama in its fight to retain license fee funding. While budgets are being slashed in nearly every sector to satisfy demands for a leaner corporation, scripted drama is being disproportionately protected. For instance, the recent shift of youth-oriented channel BBC Three from broadcast to online only was intended to save 30 million pounds that would then be shifted over expressly to fund drama on BBC One.[33] Tony Hall has defended this weighted focus on drama, stating, "The public associates the BBC with great drama. It's something that's in the lifeblood of the BBC. It's just crucial to us as a creative and cultural organization."[34] It also helps that this investment is simultaneously paying off financially in the international marketplace, as dramas are thriving as an import and coproduction commodity across the globe. The BBC's controller of drama, Polly Hill, in 2015 even identified this as "a perfect storm," saying, "In all the years I've been working in drama I don't think there been a time where there's been such an incredible appetite for it."[35] For its part, BBC

Worldwide reported record spending in 2013, with most earmarked for drama funding.[36] BBC Worldwide CEO Tim Davie said in February 2014, "When you look at those people in the U.S. who have transformed their channel businesses, it's been through high-quality programming; big scripted drama transforms businesses."[37] Not surprisingly, this drive for drama is evident at BBC America.

GENRE AND PRESTIGE DRAMA AT BBC AMERICA

The current architect of BBC America is president and general manager Sarah Barnett, who came over in December 2014 from within the AMC Networks' stable as president and general manager of SundanceTV. While helming Sundance prepared her for the new job, Barnett remarked to *Variety* that the industry had changed considerably in the brief six years since she had started the previous one. Most importantly, she clarified that an understanding of how and where audiences watched TV hadn't been on the table when she began at Sundance; now it would be fundamental. As a result, programming decisions at BBC America would have to be made not just on the basis of program quality or channel branding but on assumptions of audiences' viewing behavior and their use of viewing technologies. Barnett explained what she saw as central for BBC America's approach in this regard: "Every network is challenged with monetizing content, and we want to cut through with shows that still have urgency in the linear environment. But the changing patterns of consumption really create a long tail for smart, serialized programming. It has currency on many different platforms, it does well internationally, which is great for a network like BBC America."[38]

Echoing her predecessors, Barnett argued that BBC America has a "high-production-value, brainy identity" and, like Herb Scannell, believes that the programming it showcases need not be strictly British but rather "very energetic, vital and relevant to an American pop-culture audience."[39] Notably, she told *Variety* of talking with the BBC America development team after she arrived, "We spent a lot of time thinking about what the 'A' stood for in BBCA."[40] It somehow stands for Canadian imports, because Barnett sees *Orphan Black* as the model show for the network to build around: "I think all the values within the DNA of that show are probably things that will propel us forward from a brand, marketing and programming perspective. It's a fun, splashy, entertaining, thrilling ride. It's truly serious about some feminist issues but never wears that heavily. It excites me to think about how we build on that. How do we do more of that, creating relevant, electric and urgent noise around this brand?"[41]

The impression of *Orphan Black* as equally fun and serious, splashy and relevant, echoes the new BBC America brand. In a time of programming and channel saturation, as well as greater transnational and multiplatform spread, the channel has moved away from the genre range programming model of the early 2000s and now more narrowly focuses on headline-grabbing scripted drama, with two primary areas of focus in cult genre drama and high-end prestige drama. This is similar to AMC's approach on its original channel, with genre shows like *The Walking Dead* and *Hell on Wheels* and prestige dramas like *Mad Men* and *Breaking Bad* helping to distinguish that channel, and it has the benefit of attracting audiences that are upscale, engaged and committed, and vocal on social media about their fandom and cultural tastes. Barnett says the key to both is engaging passionate audiences in a saturated landscape, and, as a result, it ultimately doesn't matter whether the dramas are even British or not: "We're agnostic as to where it comes from. We'd love it to come from the UK but I want those shows that are really going to define the brand, speak to that audience and create a reason for people to continue to come to what is a medium-sized cable network. They're not going to come unless there's a real fresh pipeline."[42]

The roots of the genre drama strategy precede the AMC Networks' stewardship and go back to the *Doctor Who* acquisition, which helped to secure BBC America's place in the cult television world, as signaled by the show's first official appearance at Comic-Con in 2008. This focus was ramped up with *Orphan Black*'s March 2013 premiere, which was followed in the "Supernatural Saturday" schedule by a ten-episode run of the pop-culture talk show *The Nerdist*, hosted by Chris Hardwick. An adaptation of the popular American podcast, *The Nerdist* did not focus primarily on British programming, but was heavily oriented toward "geek culture" and science fiction shows like *Star Trek* and *Doctor Who*. The episode that aired following *Orphan Black*'s series premiere was entitled "The BBC Extravaganza" and included guest actors from *Doctor Who* and *Orphan Black*. Hardwick described the scheduling logic: "I want this weekly show to feel like, 'You've watched *Doctor Who*, you've watched *Orphan Black*, now welcome to our show.' . . . We want this to be a nice, little, fun kind of nerdy hangout session at the end of your sci-fi night."[43] This fits with the logic of creating shows that have "urgency in the linear environment" while also breeding the social media talk that could push viewers to subsequently follow the "long tail for smart, serialized programming" to video-on-demand platforms.

Barnett has continued this strategy, as evidenced by the first original production greenlit under her tenure, *Dirk Gently's Holistic Detective Agency*, which premiered its first of eight episodes in October 2016. BBC America's corporate sibling AMC Studios is a coproducer of the series, offering a profit participation benefit as the series moves to additional platforms. Another coproducer, Netflix, represents one of those additional platforms, as the series will be available to audiences outside the United States on Netflix's streaming service worldwide. Inspired by science fiction novels from British author Douglas Adams, *Dirk Gently's Holistic Detective Agency*, quite like *Doctor Who*, features a charismatic, eccentric man taking a companion on metaphysical adventures of investigation. The program was promoted at New York Comic-Con alongside *Doctor Who* and the upcoming import *Class*, a *Doctor Who* youth spinoff from BBC Three. *Ad Week* described the convention as "a whirlwind of fandom," and Barnett told the publication that BBC America was there to connect with "the most pop-culture literate groups of people" and to send the message that BBC America is "superfans" of its viewers.[44] Barnett is developing other such series she hopes will inspire "crazy love" in viewers, including a remake of the British science fiction classic *Quatermass* and a series called *Memoria* from *Orphan Black*'s Temple Street Productions, which will depict the unraveling of a man's life as he struggles to cope with technology.[45]

At the same time, BBC America has also showcased dramas more likely to appear at the Emmys than at Comic-Con, including imports like ITV's *Broadchurch* and the BBC's *Luther*. These programs serve to garner critical praise and attract upscale audiences, and while this could be viewed as parroting the AMC strategy, the precedent for this wider movement in American cable and streaming television is arguably found in British television, as Barnett herself identifies: "Auteur TV used to be a Brit thing, with individual geniuses creating six or eight episodes before they would tire of it or maybe have a nervous breakdown. Now the auteur or limited series are hallmarks of prestige drama in the U.S. on all or every platform, and the business model finds new ways to sustain that."[46]

The Last Kingdom, with its eight-episode first season created by an acclaimed producer, is an example. Made with co-production investment from the BBC and BBC

FIGURE 3.2 BBC America's 2016 New York Comic-Con promotion

America and produced by Carnival Films, the NBC-Universal-owned British production company best known for *Downton Abbey, The Last Kingdom* was created by Gareth Neame, whose production credits include *Downton Abbey, Spooks* (called *MI-5* in the United States), and *State of Play*. The series is an adaptation of an acclaimed historical fiction book series set in the late ninth century that chronicles what could be considered the true establishment of England, as the Saxons battle Viking invaders and witness the collapse of nearly all of their kingdoms save one, Wessex, from which King Alfred then turned the tide and ultimately unified England for good. Some TV critics speculated that *The Last Kingdom* was the BBC's attempt to match HBO's *Game of Thrones* in epic drama prominence, but the show's representatives continually deflect those comparisons, particularly to draw on connotations of greater prestige in regard to realism over fantasy. At the 2015 summer Television Critics Association press tour, Neame insisted, "This is not *Game of Thrones*. Brilliant though that show is, ours is a historical drama based on the real events around the foundation of England."[47] Using traditional code words for quality realism, star Alexander Dreymon described *The Last Kingdom* as "a lot less glossy and more gritty" than *Game of Thrones*.[48] Critics obliged in perpetuating these themes, with an *Independent* reviewer called the series more "earthy" and "less silly" than *Game of Thrones*, and *Telegraph* reviewer Charlotte Runcie handing the show's marketing team a gift by calling the show "the thinking person's *Game of Thrones*."[49]

As if to counter any fears that this meant the series was pretentious or plodding, Sarah Barnett insisted to *Multichannel News* that *The Last Kingdom* shared a sensibility with BBC America's more campy genre programs:

> Our shows have depth in writing but they are characterized by not taking themselves too seriously—there's a certain kind of cheekiness or wit with *Doctor Who* and *Orphan Black* that you see in *The Last Kingdom*, despite a genre that is not characterized by cheeky wit. So I think there are some things that we are starting to realize that our fans . . . really love about us, and *The Last Kingdom* is absolutely within that wheelhouse.[50]

Barnett is clearly pushing for shows that foster passion and produce buzz. In an unusual scheduling practice, *The Last Kingdom* premiered on BBC America in early October 2015, two weeks before its BBC Two run started, and the second episode was made available online immediately after the first episode aired. Barnett explains, "The thinking was to get people hooked. We eroded the second week numbers but then it built to a bigger number in week three. We're constantly trying to think of ways to cut through."[51] Unfortunately, the show did not cut through for BBC America, despite doing well in its BBC Two airing, and Barnett declined to pick up its second season. Barnett hopes for better success from other prestige dramas in the pipeline, including the BBC–BBC America coproduction *Undercover*, a political thriller starring Sophie Okonedo and Dennis Haysbert, and *Trip*, a reimagined adaptation of the classic Chinese novel *Monkey: Journey to the West*, which is being produced by the company that made *Top of the Lake*. Beyond the prime-time originals, the rest of the BBC America schedule clearly reflects the stewardship of AMC Networks. Barnett describes her strategy as simplifying the schedule via stripping nonscripted shows and scripted reruns in daytime and focusing on original drama and movies in prime time.[52] Gone are all of the lifestyle shows that defined BBC America's Paul Lee–era lineup, *BBC World News America* left the channel in 2011, and there is little focus on comedy in any part of the day. There is some British reality fare in daytime, like *Dragon's Den* and *Man vs. Wild*, but the morning and prime-time schedules are frequently made up of marathons of American dramas, including *Star Trek: The Next Generation* and *CSI: Miami*. *CSI: Miami* has also aired on AMC and WEtv, and indeed, looking at the daily schedule, one would be hard-pressed to recognize it as belonging to BBC America, except for when the showcase dramas and nature documentaries like *The Hunt* are airing. Ad breaks also regularly feature promos for shows on other AMC Networks channels, and on many evenings, one could even mistake the lineup for AMC itself, with its regular offerings of American movies from the 1980s and 1990s plus the airing of two AMC series, *Into the Badlands* and *Humans*, on Saturday nights in weeks leading up to *Dirk Gently*'s airing. Perhaps the *Orphan Black* influence extends to cloning the programming schedule. But one can see the AMC Networks' era strategies for BBC America as adapting to the realities of viewing habits and American cable television today. The comfort-food reruns and movies are designed to grab those still surfing on linear TV, while the showcase genre and prestige dramas encourage appointment viewing but also breed engagement for the committed time-shifter. And the strategy is working; according to BBC Worldwide Annual Report 2015–16, BBC America had its best year ever in total viewers in the 2015–2016 season.[53] It's striking to note that this growth happened as the channel became more like any other AMC Networks channel and less distinctively British.

CONCLUSION

AMC Networks has brought together linear channels with compatible brands, financial partnerships with international outlets and producers, and production studios that own the content to be spread across those channels, platforms, and partners. As a result, BBC

America itself is now positioned as a vital transnational network particularly oriented around the lucrative value of prime-time drama in the international and multiplatform landscape. In "Communication Business Networks in an Era of Convergence," Amelia Arsenault remarks upon the economic power embedded in such networks: "A corporation may amass hierarchical control over a stable of media properties, but its ability to do so successfully is predicated upon its ability to leverage the larger network within which it is embedded. Power is thus not necessarily concentrated within any single company but embedded in the processes of association between key nodes in the network."[54] BBC America is no longer an independent in the American cable lineup. It is now a key node in the transnational networked relationship between BBC Worldwide, the BBC, and AMC Networks. Notably, this seems to have resulted in a push to make the "America" in BBC America more prominent, with the BBC operating more as a brand than a direct presence. However, the value of a cable channel is no longer just in the individual brand, as it might have been a decade ago. Now its value lies in the larger corporate network of program ownership and access to platforms, and therein lies the transatlantic advantage of BBC America. In her 2012 book *Transnational Television Drama*, Elke Weissmann predicted that "US television will increasingly incorporate transnational television in order to sustain its dominance in the global market," as opposed to power shifting more to the international margins.[55] BBC America's evolution is consistent with this prediction. One can witness it back in the United Kingdom too, with Viacom's ownership of Channel 5 plus frequently swirling rumors of an American conglomerate purchasing ITV or Channel 4. Nor does it appear that the flow of imports to the United States will slow down, not only on linear channels, but also on the streaming services. Hulu and Netflix have augmented their libraries with numerous British programs, and in fact, Netflix picked up the second season of *The Last Kingdom* that BBC America rejected. These fluid distribution relationships reflect significant changes in the worldwide structure of the television industry, as Michele Hilmes explores elsewhere in this collection. Hilmes pinpoints tensions that developed among transatlantic players across *Masterpiece*'s evolution, and one wonders how BBC Worldwide executives feel about the transformation of BBC America into a channel that is ultimately more AMC than BBC. One such executive, Paul Dempsey, president of global markets for BBC Worldwide, at least says he does not see a problem with foreign partnerships influencing national strategies: "With these top shows, what's good for the UK is also good for the international market. For the BBC to be the best it can for the licence-fee payer, it has to think of itself as a global player. That's the nature of media now."[56] And that's the also nature of BBC America now.

NOTES

1. Christine Becker, "From High Culture to Hip Culture: Transforming the BBC into BBC America," in *Anglo-American Media Interactions, 1850–2000*, ed. Mark Hampton and Joel Wiener (New York: Palgrave Macmillan, 2007), 284.

2. R. Thomas Umstead, "Ancier Sits Atop BBC in U.S.," *Multichannel News*, February 19, 2007, 9. Expanded Academic ASAP (GALE A159538394).

3. Jon Weisman, "BBC America Captures Saturdays," *Variety*, May 2, 2008, http://variety.com/2008/scene/features/bbc-america-captures-saturdays-1117985054.

4. Linda Haugsted, "'Brit Different" Image for BBCA," *Multichannel News*, January 8, 2007, 8. Expanded Academic ASAP, GALE A157030984.

5. Kent Gibbons, "BBCA: Our Viewers Have Money," *Multichannel News*, March 16, 2009, 2. Expanded Academic ASAP, GALE A195652762.

6. Nellie Andreeva, "Garth Ancier Exiting BBC Worldwide America," *Hollywood Reporter*, November 19, 2009, http://www.hollywoodreporter.com/news/garth-ancier-exiting-bbc-worldwide-91552.

7. Kent Gibbons, Mike Reynolds, and Todd Spangler, "New Presidential Views at BBCA, Sportsman, Bravo," *Multichannel News*, June 7, 2010, 6. Expanded Academic ASAP, GALE A230958349.

8. Gibbons, Reynolds, and Spangler, "New Presidential Views."

9. R. Thomas Umstead, "BBC America Kicks Off Development Slate with Three Series," *Multichannel News*, August 1, 2011, 14. Expanded Academic ASAP, GALE A265195642.

10. Michael O'Connell, "BBC America Cancels *Copper* after Two Seasons," *Hollywood Reporter*, September 19, 2013, http://www.hollywoodreporter.com/live-feed/bbc-america-cancels-copper-two-631830.

11. Tim Goodman, "BBC America on the Rise with *Orphan Black*, Standout Dramas," *Hollywood Reporter*, July 25, 2013, http://www.hollywoodreporter.com/bastard-machine/bbc-america-rise-orphan-black-593426.

12. "BBCA Seeks 'Rarified' Air: New Chief BARNETT Aims outside Mainstream," *Multichannel News*, April 20, 2015, 10. Expanded Academic ASAP, GALE A412728178.

13. Serra Tinic, "Where in the World Is *Orphan Black*? Change and Continuity in Global TV Production and Distribution," *Media Industries Journal* 1:3 (2015), http://www.mediaindustriesjournal.org/index.php/mij/article/view/106/151.

14. Katherine Rushton, "BBC America Now Almost Half-Owned by US Cable Company AMC," *Daily Telegraph*, October 24, 2014, http://www.telegraph.co.uk/finance/newsbysector/mediatechnologyandtelecoms/11184252/BBC-America-now-almost-half-owned-by-US-cable-company-AMC.html.

15. Nellie Andreeva and David Lieberman, "Pivot's Demise: Death by Skinny Bundle, Millennials Fleeing TV or No Must-See Programming?," *Deadline*, August 18, 2016, http://deadline.com/2016/08/pivot-tv-shut-down-reasons-skinny-bundles-millennials-1201805108.

16. David Lieberman, "AMC Networks Pays $200M For 49.9% of BBC America," *Deadline*, October 23, 2014, http://deadline.com/2014/10/amc-networks-pays-200m-49-9-bbc-america-859244.

17. "AMC Networks Inc at Moffettnathanson Media & Communications Summit—Final," *Fair Disclosure Wire*, May 19, 2016. ABI/INFORM Trade & Industry, doi:1793666666.

18. "Q1 2015 AMC Networks Inc Earnings Call—Final," *Fair Disclosure Wire*, May 4, 2015. ABI/INFORM Trade & Industry, doi:1681923471.

19. Steve Clarke, "BBC Worldwide CEO Hunts for Big Game," *Variety*, February 21, 2014, http://variety.com/2014/tv/global/bbc-worldwide-exec-hunts-for-big-game-1201111429.

20. Rushton, "BBC America."

21. Ben Kendall, "Privatization 'Risk' to BBC Worldwide," *Glasgow Herald*, September 18, 2015, 7. Lexis Nexis Academic.

22. BBC Trust, "BBC Commercial Review 2009," BBC.co.uk, 2, http://downloads.bbc.co.uk/bbctrust/assets/files/pdf/our_work/commercial/commercial_review.pdf.

23. Steve Hewett, "BBC Worldwide: Smoke and Mirrors," *The Guardian*, July 27, 2014, https://www.theguardian.com/media/2014/jul/27/bbc-worldwide-annual-report-results.
24. Daniel Frankel, "AMC Pays $200M for 49.9 Percent Share of BBC America," *FierceCable*, October 24, 2014, http://www.fiercecable.com/cable/amc-pays-200m-for-49-9-percent-share-bbc-america.
25. "Q1 2015 AMC Networks Inc Earnings Call—Final."
26. Michael O'Connell, "Prestige Often Outweighs Performance in Cable's Scripted Push," *Hollywood Reporter*, December 26, 2014, http://www.hollywoodreporter.com/news/prestige-outweighs-performance-cables-scripted-759119.
27. "Q1 2015 AMC Networks Inc Earnings Call – Final."
28. Jon Lafayette, "All this TV: too much of a good thing? Surplus of originals poses stiff challenges to nets and threatens to take some shine off current Golden Age," *Broadcasting & Cable*, July 13, 2015, 6. Expanded Academic ASAP, GALE A422061120).
29. "Q4 2014 AMC Networks Inc Earnings Call—Final," *Fair Disclosure Wire*, February 26, 2015. ABI/INFORM Trade & Industry, doi:1662469591.
30. Georg Szalai, "AMC Networks Completes $1 Billion Acquisition of Liberty Global's Chellomedia," *Hollywood Reporter*, February 3, 2014, http://www.hollywoodreporter.com/news/amc-networks-completes-1-billion-676601.
31. "Q4 2014 AMC Networks Inc Earnings Call—Final."
32. "AMC Networks Inc at Moffettnathanson Media & Communications Summit—Final."
33. "BBC One to Get £30m from Three Closure," BBC News, March 6, 2014, http://www.bbc.com/news/entertainment-arts-26464007.
34. Patrick Foster, "BBC Director-General Lord Hall: We Can't Win against Deep Pockets of Netflix," *The Telegraph*, March 19, 2016, http://www.telegraph.co.uk/news/bbc/12198280/BBC-director-general-Lord-Hall-We-cant-win-against-deep-pockets-of-Netflix.html.
35. Jon Creamer, "The *Televisual* Drama Report," *Televisual*, December 7, 2015, http://www.televisual.com/blog-detail/The-Televisual-Drama-Report_bid-838.html
36. Georg Szalai, "BBC Worldwide Eyes Record Spending on U.K. Content," *Hollywood Reporter*, September 5, 2013, http://www.hollywoodreporter.com/news/bbc-worldwide-eyes-record-spending-622238.
37. Steve Clarke, "BBC Worldwide CEO Hunts for Big Game," *Variety*, February 21, 2014, http://variety.com/2014/tv/global/bbc-worldwide-exec-hunts-for-big-game-1201111429.
38. T. L. Stanley, "How BBC America Is Building Buzz," *Advertising Age*, April 5, 2015, http://www.adweek.com/news/television/beeb-creates-buzz-splashy-thrillers-163898.
39. Michael Pickard, "Getting Engaged: Sarah Barnett of BBC America," *Drama Quarterly*, March 1, 2016, http://dramaquarterly.com/highlights/getting-engaged.
40. Cynthia Littleton, "BBC America Developing Projects with Amy Poehler, 'Orphan Black' Producers," *Variety*, May 31, 2016, http://variety.com/2016/tv/news/amc-rejuvenates-bbc-america-1201785334.
41. Stanley, "BBC America Building Buzz."
42. Pickard, "Getting Engaged."
43. Alex Strechen, "Geek Fanboy Culture Drives *The Nerdist*," *Leader-Post*, March 20, 2013. Lexis Nexis Academic. The future AMC Networks–BBC America marriage was foreshadowed by the fact that Hardwick previously made his mark on AMC hosting the *Walking Dead* discussion show *Talking Dead*, starting in 2011. *Orphan Black* also had its own dedicated talk show called *After the Black*.
44. Sami Main, "BBC America Teases 2 New Shows (and the Return of *Doctor Who*) at New York Comic-Con," *Ad Week*, October 7, 2016, http://www.adweek.com/news/television/bbc-america-teases-2-new-shows-and-return-doctor-who-new-york-comic-con-173938.
45. Littleton, "BBC America Developing Projects."
46. Debra Birnbaum, "BBC America President Sarah Burnett Talks Limited Series, 'Uber' Fans," *Variety*, January 10, 2015, http://variety.com/2015/tv/news/bbc-america-president-sarah-barnett-talks-limited-series-uber-fans-1201399707.

47. Ben Dowell, "BBC2 Evokes *Game of Thrones* Vibe with New Anglo Saxon Epic *The Last Kingdom*," *Radio Times*, July 9, 2014, http://www.radiotimes.com/news/2014-07-09/bbc2-evokes-game-of-thrones-vibe-with-new-anglo-saxon-epic-the-last-kingdom.

48. Bryn Elise Sandberg, "*The Last Kingdom* Boss Shoots Down *Game of Thrones* Comparisons," *Hollywood Reporter*, July 31, 2015, http://www.hollywoodreporter.com/live-feed/last-kingdom-boss-shoots-down-812451.

49. Sean O'Grady, "*The Last Kingdom*: TV Review," *The Independent*, October 22, 2015, http://www.independent.co.uk/arts-entertainment/tv/reviews/the-last-kingdom-tv-review-this-viking-saga-is-less-silly-than-game-of-thrones-and-less-exciting-too-a6705071.html; Charlotte Runcie, "*The Last Kingdom*, BBC Two, Review," *The Telegraph*, October 23, 2015, http://www.telegraph.co.uk/culture/tvandradio/tv-and-radio-reviews/11948970/The-Last-Kingdom-BBC-One-review.html.

50. R. Thomas Umstead, "What Sarah Barnett Wants You to Know about *The Last Kingdom*," *Multichannel News*, October 9, 2015, http://www.multichannel.com/blog/picture/what-sarah-barnett-wants-you-know-about-last-kingdom/394448.

51. Pickard, "Getting Engaged."

52. Pickard, "Getting Engaged."

53. "North America: Building Global Brands," *BBC Worldwide Annual Review 2015–2016*, https://www.bbcworldwide.com/media/1999/bbcw_usmarket.pdf.

54. Amelia Arsenault, "Communication Business Networks in an Era of Convergence," in *The Political Economies of Media: The Transformation of the Global Media Industries*, ed. Dwayne Winseck and Dal Yong Jin, Ebook ed. (n.p.: Bloomsbury Publishing, 2011), 55.

55. Elke Weissmann, *Transnational Television Drama* (New York: Palgrave Macmillan, 2012), 192.

56. Benji Wilson, "Made in Britain; How Do Our TV Shows Fare Abroad?," *Sunday Times*, February 15, 2015, http://www.thesundaytimes.co.uk/sto/culture/film_and_tv/article1517434.ece.

/// 4 /// BRANDING BRIDGES

Sky Atlantic, "Quality" Imports, and Brand Integration

SAM WARD

In January 2011 Tony Soprano appeared glowering from billboards and bus stops across the United Kingdom. This was despite James Gandolfini's anti-hero having made his final appearance in the last episode of *The Sopranos* (HBO, 1999–2007) some four years previously. Rather than advertising the show itself, the posters announced the arrival of a new channel from Sky, the country's leading subscription television provider. Sky Atlantic would be exclusively available to Sky customers, included as standard in all of its subscription packages, and as such would be positioned as a crucial asset for the company in its bid to turn viewers of free-to-air terrestrial television (funded by advertising or the universal license fee) into subscribers. As suggested by its name (and the prominent role played by the New Jersey kingpin in the early marketing), the key selling point offered by the channel was exclusive access to imported drama from the United States; and these were not any old American imports, but series that were distinguished as "quality."

As a precursor to the channel's launch, in July 2010 Sky secured exclusive rights to all of the past and future drama output of Home Box Office (HBO). The deal with the renowned producer of big-budget and critically acclaimed series covered the next five years, at a reported cost of £150 million.[1] Besides the content itself, this bought Sky Atlantic the right to use the slogan "The Home of HBO in the UK." While HBO content was to make up around 40 percent of the channel's programming, Sky also sought life-of-series deals for several Showtime dramas, with *Dexter* (2006–2013) and *Nurse Jackie* (2009–2015) among its early offerings. It also bought a package of content from the distribution company Lionsgate that included *Mad Men* (AMC, 2007–2015), poaching the series from BBC Four, which had aired the first four seasons. With this aggressive approach the channel was positioned as a clear challenge to its public service broadcaster rivals—especially the BBC and Channel 4—and central in efforts to expand the demographic makeup of Sky's customer base to a "quality" audience that, in the United Kingdom, had historically been the domain of the free-to-air sector.

While transatlantic flows of content have been important in British television culture for several decades,[2] Sky Atlantic represents a shift within this history in that the transnational industrial activities underpinning its existence have formed a defining theme for the channel's branding. On one level, we might treat this as a symptom of the dissolution of the media industries' traditional nation-centric organization, as scholars have observed since the late twentieth century. Discussing transnational corporate groups that have launched channels across numerous countries since the late 1990s, Jean K. Chalaby concludes that "the semiotics of television has become global. National TV cultures remain different but they are increasingly like dialects of a universal language. All TV markets have strong connections to the homogenized culture of world television."[3] However, in this chapter I will demonstrate how that very different-ness—far from being eroded or diluted—is itself objectified and commodified in the promotional discourse around Sky Atlantic, suggesting that a more complex definition of transnationality is required than one of homogenization. The channel's basic concept and early development dramatize Michele Hilmes's assertion that "the transnational in fact produces and stimulates the national, and conversely . . . a sense of cultural borders is extremely important in encouraging and promoting transnationality."[4] I will demonstrate how the very interpenetration between the national and the transnational industrial spheres has been channeled in Sky Atlantic's domestic consumer-facing identity as a means not just of sourcing content but, more importantly, of generating discursive value in pursuit of a business aim that is specific to the national market.

First I will define the central concept of *transnational bridging* through which I want to approach Sky Atlantic, and identify how this promotional strategy prompts a reassessment of previous theorizations of importation by taking into account the way transnational industrial operations can themselves be promotionally objectified in order to shape the consumer's understanding of a domestic television brand. I will then describe how this was achieved in practice through Sky Atlantic's on-screen identity, in the construction of an overarching narrative of transnational bridging as its founding rationale. This metaphorical projection of the channel as a "bridge" was given a concrete signifier in the coexistence of the HBO and Sky Atlantic brands on the channel, and the chapter will finish by considering this hitherto rare phenomenon of transnational brand integration. Rather than simply being an incidental contractual obligation, HBO's presence in fact instigated a set of value associations around the channel, suggesting that in the contemporary television landscape the dynamic flow of brand values and cultural capital is more important than any basic commercial advantage secured in importing this or that particular piece of content.

My concern here, then, is with the way in which promotional discourse *represents* content importation—that is, the discursive co-opting of the interplay between global and national within what Chalaby calls the "semiotics of television." Nonetheless, my argument builds on work that has emerged since the turn of the century studying importation itself. The role played by professional-cultural factors in determining how programs move across borders has been an especially fruitful question.[5] (That is not to mention the issues raised by coproductions, remakes, and format sales, which are picked up on by other authors in this volume and elsewhere.) Fundamental to Sky Atlantic's promotional workings is the fact made clear through this work that importation is a far more dynamic and unpredictable process than one of discrete financial transactions. Before imported programs can become part of the national television ecology, they are circulated at a global level in textual form at trade fair screenings and in commodity form via negotiations between distributors and buyers. In his book *Global Television Marketplace* Timothy Havens describes the complex dynamics of the transnational professional communities that facilitate this circulation. As well as hard financial and commercial concerns, the individual buyer's personal tastes and skills of negotiation combine to form the highly contingent basis on which the discursive economy underlying content trade is defined. As Havens argues, this means that the "business-people who populate the global television marketplace function as gatekeepers, mediating between the economic imperatives of transnational media conglomerates and the fickle viewing pleasures of audiences worldwide."[6] The professional standing of the acquisitions executives relies on their status as "privileged interpreters of national tastes, thereby securing their clout in an industry that is predicated upon catering to those tastes."[7]

At the same time, the process of importation cannot simply be understood as a matter of behind-the-scenes intracorporate negotiations and professional kudos. In his study of the history of imports on British channels, Paul Rixon shows how the perceived value of imports continues to be shaped through the paratextual framing imposed upon their arrival in a new national market: the scheduling decisions and "secondary text such as press releases, websites, videos sent to critics, trailers and advertisements," through which broadcasters "try to marry the image and understanding of American programmes to their needs."[8] Echoing Havens's image of the global marketplace populated by mediatory gatekeepers, Rixon conceptualizes the importing channel's personnel as "active mediators, buying and assimilating such programmes into the British output."[9] Instead of incidental "filler" packing out an otherwise domestic schedule of content, Rixon makes clear how imports can become a valued and "naturalized" part of the national culture. With Sky Atlantic (which was only in the early stages of planning when Rixon was writing his book) we find this mode of active mediation finessed into something of a textbook case—the careful allocation of spending power on the global content marketplace matched by focused promotional framing of the resultant purchases as a defining feature of the domestic broadcaster's offering.[10]

More than this, though, the channel's use of importation requires us to rethink some of the assumptions behind the models of assimilation and mediation offered by Havens and Rixon. Such concepts offer a usefully nuanced picture of the balance of agency between transnational and national industrial forces, supporting the broader argument that global media trade "is not reducible to the dynamic of dominant versus peripheral nations, especially because an array of individuals and organizations have collectively constructed a transnational system that moves programming from one nation to another."[11] However, Havens and Rixon both frame their analysis in terms of a unidirectional flow of content from source (producer/distributor) via mediation (buyers, schedulers, press, and so on) to consumption (viewer). In particular, "assimilation" suggests a process in which any excessive signs of transnationality are removed or obscured in order that the program in question will play better to the domestic audience. By contrast, with Sky Atlantic we have a domestic channel in effect working the middle stage of this process *into* its promotional identity, presenting the channel itself primarily as a nationally oriented curator of the transnational marketplace.

An underlying argument of this chapter is that this projection of the channel as "curator" of the global marketplace situates it as surrogate to the kind of cosmopolitan consumer that has been the subject of wider discussion across sociology and media and cultural studies in recent decades.[12] In the context of technological and industrial changes in how content is distributed and consumed, scholars have observed various ways in which the consumption of "foreign" media content has been undertaken as part of a self-conscious and affirmative formation of a specific audience identity. As they have become both more common and more fast-moving in the digital age, media flows across national borders do not so much produce *either* unthinkingly receptive *or* culturally isolationist responses among indigenous audiences. Instead, the cultural formation of these flows is negotiated through a combination of commercial strategy and grass-roots audience engagement, with the movement of content often multidirectional and unpredictable in terms of both the meanings ascribed to it and its commercial success. There are numerous implications and complications to the workings of this phenomenon, but key for our purposes here is how this complex negotiation makes possible—even necessitates—a form of knowing transnational engagement on the part of audiences, what Henry Jenkins terms a "pop cosmopolitanism."[13] At the same time, the personnel responsible for the acquisition of content from the global marketplace have developed a large and sophisticated professional community that in many ways mirrors the cosmopolitanism of audiences. Giselinde Kuipers describes this community as a "cosmopolitan tribe" who, on a personal level, identify more readily with the transnational culture embodied by their professional circles than with the national audiences for whom they are selecting content.[14] What I want to explore here is how, in turn, this industrial cosmopolitanism is ripe to be reincorporated into brand discourses in order to reaffirm and thus commodify the consumer's sense of transnational connectedness and awareness. In the following section, through a close reading of key texts that established the Sky Atlantic brand at its launch, I will demonstrate how this can be achieved in the specific confines of one channel brand—not just in the persona of the buyer but, more powerfully, in the narratives that the channel tells about itself.

NARRATIVES OF TRANSATLANTIC BRIDGING: IDENTS AND MARKETING

From the outset, Sky Atlantic's on-screen identity was defined by a *narrative of bridging* between America and Britain. Its onscreen idents (sequences between programs displaying the channel logo and allowing for continuity announcements) communicated this clearly, as described by the then creative director of the agency behind the new channel's branding:

> The idents are inspired by the thought that Sky Atlantic is the channel that bridges the best of US and UK culture, shown visually by splicing together British and American locations and seeing them exist on screen at the same moment in time.[15]

For example, one of the five idents, entitled "Bridge," blended shots of the Tyne Bridge in Newcastle in the northeast of England with the Manhattan skyline as viewed from Brooklyn Bridge.[16] In "Café" an all-American diner where a waitress takes an order from a cowboy transitions into an upmarket London café overlooking St Paul's Cathedral. In each sequence the metaphorical suggestion of bridging was sustained by visual fluidity between the two settings. Scenes from one side of the Atlantic were visually segued with the other via objects that could be common to both settings, appearing out of focus in the extreme foreground (girders, ketchup bottles, and so forth). Consolidating this idea of uncanny continuity, the "City Cab" ident alternated between two busy city scenes— New York being signaled by a yellow taxi and London by a black hackney carriage—with several narrative echoes: a woman drops her papers in the wind as a cyclist passes on the New York street, whose line of movement is then picked up precisely by another cyclist in the London scene where we see another woman picking up papers.

The subtle editing together of these various parallel moments deploys transnational connectedness as a shorthand narrative for the channel's basic business rationale. Rather than taking the foreignness of its content per se as its brand theme (or even American-ness more broadly, as with competitor channels like 5USA), the channel itself was presented as a dynamic point of cultural bridging in the form of a televisual environment. Of course, this narrative was the broad basis for the channel's name, drawing on the symbolic association of the Atlantic as a physical interface between the two countries. As one member of Sky's marketing team explained, "The creative thought 'Bringing Cultures Together' plays off the Atlantic as the membrane between the US and UK. The idents explore and celebrate the similarities and differences between the UK and the US."[17] Most of them also presented *travel* of some sort, with two other examples centering on trains and buses. Enhancing the dramatic nature of this proposition, the idents coded the channel's act of bridging as, on the one hand, fast, modern, and industrial (the trains were seen speeding across the contrasting countryside of the two countries), while on the other, epic and aesthetically refined (those speeding trains were, in fact, shown in slow motion, as were all the idents' footage, with lush orchestral strings forming the soundtrack).

Marketing for the channel around the time of its launch made use of similar metaphors of geographical and physical transition, drawn from the programming that was to form its schedules. In prelaunch trailers, lines of dialogue from several shows were spliced into sequences that collectively emphasized the channel's provision of exclusive access to an expansive choice of content. One closed with clips from HBO's television movie *Temple Grandin* (HBO, 2010), a biopic of the American scientist. The voice of one of the film's characters, Dr. Carlock (David Strathairn), is heard issuing the instruction to "think of it as a door—a door that's going to open up on to a whole new world for you." We then see a shot from the film of an actual door, which opens as the camera moves toward it, followed by another of Temple (Claire Danes) herself, dressed in a graduation gown and climbing a ladder upward toward the camera. This fades into the channel logo, with its caption "The Home of HBO."[18] Another slightly shorter trailer for the channel ended with a line of dialogue from Nucky Thompson (Steve Buscemi), the lead character in *Boardwalk Empire* (HBO, 2010–2014), stating, "Everything you see here is yours." It then cut to a shot of Nucky looking out on a wide-open Atlantic Ocean (the show being set in Atlantic

City). Superimposed on this image was the launch slogan "Let the stories begin," which was then replaced by the same logo and HBO caption.[19]

In this way, the channel's early marketing fused the narrative images of its flagship shows with messages of connectedness, mobility, and access. This was tied specifically to the theme of transatlantic exchange that underpinned the channel's industrial purpose by the localities on show in the idents and in particular by the geographically liminal setting of *Boardwalk Empire*, which was the first show to air on the channel and a key flagship in its first few years. But while the promotional texts described above were designed to turn the channel's use of imports into a general narrative theme, the way in which it has integrated the globally familiar HBO brand with its identity requires particular attention.

PACKAGING "QUALITY": BRAND INTEGRATION

Sky Atlantic was not the first British channel that had incorporated HBO content into its own promotional identity. Most notably, since the 1990s the public service broadcaster (PSB) Channel 4 had nurtured a reputation as "the home of top US drama" in Britain, with HBO productions—most notably *The Sopranos* and *Six Feet Under* (HBO, 2001–2005)—forming key assets in what Janet McCabe describes as the channel's "discursive negotiat[ion]" of its projected demographic as "aspiring" and up-market.[20] Similarly, Elke Weissmann describes how "Channel 4's publicity after 1990 actively negotiated the brand of 'quality dramas' for its own marketing and branding exercises."[21] These descriptions compare closely with the strategy undertaken by Sky Atlantic: to court a cosmopolitan, "quality" audience segment by positioning the channel as a reliable, discerning selector of the best offerings of US drama production. Indeed, Channel 4's airings of early HBO hits (along with healthy DVD sales in Britain over the same period) was instrumental in securing the association between HBO and "quality" among the domestic audience on which Sky Atlantic would later capitalize.

The key difference, though, is that the provision of prestigious access offered by Sky Atlantic to imported "quality" drama has been encapsulated specifically via the direct merging of the HBO brand within the fabric of the channel. For Channel 4, individual HBO shows contributed to its general positioning as "the channel that brings world-class television to the UK marketplace."[22] While the "quality" association of the HBO brand in particular was certainly important for Channel 4, the shows functioned as only one strand in a diverse and changeable mix of imports, as well as (quota fulfilling) domestic programing.[23] Indeed, both McCabe and Weissmann also discuss the channel's historical association with NBC content. Equally, the general attraction of a "quality" drama audience was not the sole target of its importation approach. For example, teen dramas like *Dawson's Creek* (The WB, 1998–2003) and *The O.C.* (US, Fox, 2003–2007) were arguably more definitive of Channel 4's overall brand status during the same period, providing the backbone for the high-profile, youth-oriented Saturday daytime strand T4 (on air between 1998 and 2012).[24] Ultimately, the specific demographic and discursive functions served by its American imports had to be evaluated against Channel 4's multifaceted public service remit "which encourages diversity, innovation and experimentation."[25] The prestige of the HBO brand was less important than the textual specifics of particular programs.

The importance of this assimilation of the imports with Channel 4's broader needs is underlined by the fact that any exposure enjoyed by the HBO brand would generally be limited to the programs themselves, with the familiar fuzzy screen logo sequence appearing momentarily at the beginning and end of each episode (something outside the control of the "assimilators"). By contrast, as reflected in the trademarked phrase "the home of HBO in the UK" in the trailers described above, the integration of HBO within Sky Atlantic was proactively pursued *beyond* the confines of the content, in order that the two brand names collectively constitute, rather than compete for, the focus of the audience.[26] With this non-PSB channel, the discursive potential of the exporter brand itself functioned as the primary commercial asset, rather than any specific textual or even generic compatibility of the individual programs with the importer's brand.

So what made HBO suitable to being explicitly conjoined with Sky's new channel-brand, rather than simply supplying some of its content? As many scholars have observed, the industrial function of HBO's association with textual "quality" is tied to the mode of distinction articulated by its position as a premium cable channel.[27] Outside the influence of advertisers, and with a comparative lack of regulatory restriction, the definition of "quality" in this instance hinges on HBO's distinction from the "trash TV" perception associated with the "least objectionable" approach historically taken by the American networks.[28] The famous HBO slogan—"It's Not TV. It's HBO"—draws a valuable association between the industrial status of premium paid-for content and its cultural consecration as distinct from the popular commercialism of "ordinary" free-to-air television:

> Safely quarantined from the distractions and interruptions of commercial television, the viewers of HBO dramas are permitted to detach themselves from typical modes of television viewing, to approach the state of disinterested contemplation idealized in Kantian aesthetics, a disposition instantly adopted by patrons in a museum gallery or a symphony concert hall, but one seldom achieved in the family room.[29]

This brand narrative encodes HBO's subscription-based business model as an *aesthetic* position, drawing on the historical tendency for television to be deemed "quality" precisely through reference to other, more legitimate art-forms. The slow-burning and well-made story arcs of HBO series recall the extensiveness and complexity of a nineteenth-century novel, while innovative camerawork and expensive, authentic-looking mise en scènes put the series in the same visual bracket as cinema.[30]

The HBO brand therefore offered a discrete signifier of a specific kind of cultural value, based on a correlation between the financial investment represented by subscription-based viewing and the cultural capital offered by contradistinction with "ordinary" TV. In fact, unlike HBO, Sky's revenue is split between subscriptions and advertising sales (although increasingly reliant on the former). Nevertheless, on a *discursive* level, HBO's globally nurtured reputation could be fairly seamlessly and efficiently deployed as the driving force of Sky Atlantic's own brand identity.

This was an important shift in Sky's historical outlook, having been known since its launch in the late 1980s for its mass "commercial" appeal, largely based around exclusive sports coverage and Hollywood blockbuster premieres. With the HBO partnership, Sky Atlantic was billed as courting "the generally more upmarket viewers who have so far resisted the siren call of live Premiership football and cinema-fresh movie releases. . . . The chattering classes, if you like."[31] Stuart Murphy, Sky's director of programs at the time, summed up the intention thus: "We want them, Freeview viewers, to reappraise Sky."[32]

The channel's encouragement of such reappraisal was not limited to the simple appearance of the HBO logo in its idents and on its posters but instead extended to a powerful set of discursive signposts. From the outset, the rhetoric surrounding the channel's launch tapped the association that HBO represents with high production values, merging them with the idea of the acquisition deal itself being expensive, exclusive, and unprecedented in British television history (notwithstanding the compatibility of several *non*-HBO imports, such as *Mad Men*, with this overall message). Press coverage of the channel's launch emphasized these themes. *Hollywood Reporter* announced that "British viewers in search of the cream of 'epic and immersive' television can tune into Sky's lavish new entertainment channel,"[33] while the British press roundly described the deal as "audacious" and a "cultural game-changer."[34] This idea of the channel as a challenge to the status quo of British television was driven home by the heavily trailed launch night of the channel itself on February 1, 2011, introduced by journalist and television presenter Mariella Frostrup (known for her high-brow arts programming). Against a backdrop of what seemed to be the Hollywood hills, Frostrup announced to viewers across all of Sky's channels: "Tonight . . . television history will be made with the launch of a brand new TV channel: Sky Atlantic HD, the home of HBO in Britain."[35] *Let the Stories Begin*, an hour-long preview program narrated by Frostrup and featuring interviews with celebrity fans of the shows as well as HBO cast and crew, was then shown (again, across the whole Sky portfolio).

The presentation of the launch as a significant event in British television history, transcending the audience's normal expectations, was sustained by the content that formed the schedule for the opening night and those that followed. As mentioned above, a common definition of HBO's "quality" status is in the association with art forms that are more legitimated than television. Accordingly, besides clips of Danes in *Temple Grandin*, several other prestigious cinematic stars also underpinned the launch of the channel. The channel started its first evening with the feature-length pilot episode of *Boardwalk Empire* (repeating it twice that night), which was directed by Martin Scorsese. This was followed by HBO's other new television movie, *You Don't Know Jack* (2010), starring two more Academy Award winners, Al Pacino and Susan Sarandon. Scorsese had not worked in television since 1986 and, despite the fact that, beyond the pilot, he only played an advisory role as executive producer on *Boardwalk Empire*, the show was routinely announced in the British press as "the Martin Scorsese prohibition-set drama."[36] *Boardwalk Empire* provided an effective focus for the range of associations drawn by HBO's historical output to be repeated in discussions of Sky Atlantic's arrival. Reviews spoke of the "big-screen values" of the pilot, which was the world's most expensive to date, as well as Scorsese's "signature cinematography—extravagant tracking shots, colorful close-ups and lavish period detail."[37] Previews of the show quoted creator Terence Winter describing the premise, drawn loosely from a nonfiction book of the same name, as "lend[ing] itself to a really long narrative. It's an epic novel."[38]

These links with cinematic and literary artistry in the *programming* were readily transferred into the promotion of Sky Atlantic as a whole. A prelaunch trailer for the channel featured Hollywood veteran Dustin Hoffman, seen standing on a balcony overlooking the New York skyline, giving a speech on the theme of the slogan "Let the stories begin."[39] He muses over the universal value of storytelling. It is not specified as televisual but is given more abstract associations with longevity and distinction from the ordinary: "Stories? We all spend our lives telling them. About this, about that, about people. But some stories are so good we wish they'd never end . . .—stories that are so powerful, they really are with us forever." The camerawork is subtly stylized, panning fluidly across Hoffman's closely framed face, which is partially obscured by lens flare from the sun, suggestive of an art-house cinema style (and perhaps directly reminiscent, for more cinephile viewers, of the swimming pool scene in one of Hoffman's most famous films, *The Graduate* [1967]). Hoffman's appearance was in anticipation of his leading role in the forthcoming HBO series *Luck* (2011), which would be one of Sky Atlantic's flagship shows after *Boardwalk Empire*. Similarly to Scorsese, it was the first time Hoffman had appeared in a television series other than for occasional cameos, being better known as a stage and film actor, as was made clear in publicity surrounding the series:

> Dustin Hoffman is as surprised as anyone to see himself—after five decades on the stage and big screen—showing up on television. When he mentioned his interest in the show "Luck," the David Milch–Michael Mann horse-racing series on HBO, his friends and colleagues were not optimistic. People said, "Oh, no, you're into television!' he recalls. . . . "It causes divorce, it maims people physically; you knock out so many pages a day." . . . When Hoffman, now 74, started out as an actor in the '50s, he had no way of knowing how sophisticated television would eventually get.[40]

With the "not-TV" connotations cued by both the HBO content and the star names attached, combined with the aesthetic register of cultural prestige struck by the channel's promotional discourse, this was a television channel that would apparently bring British viewers something different to the mass-produced procedurals (in which "you knock out so many pages a day") that had previously been associated with American imports on multichannel television.

BUYING BUZZ: RATINGS AND THE NEW GATEKEEPER

Not all press coverage was so congratulatory as that quoted above. While the "quality" found in the content lent the channel a valuable image of distinction, the hard numbers into which such "niche" appeal inevitably translates was framed in more negative terms as the novelty of the channel's launch wore off. Given the fact that Sky Atlantic was only received by the portion of the population that subscribed to Sky, the potential audience was already limited, and several series saw the channel's numbers dip to potentially embarrassing levels. Having debuted with 438,000, *Boardwalk Empire* shed viewers as the episodes of its first two series progressed, with national and trade press making much of the decline. The trend was particularly noticeable with programs that had been taken from British channels in the free-to-air listings. While Sky had reportedly bid at least 25 percent higher than the BBC to take the fifth series of *Mad Men*, it struggled to command comparable audience numbers in its new home.[41] Compared with 355,000 viewers and a 1.9 percent share of the audience for the opening of the fourth season on BBC Four fifteen months previously (and several times that number when it was repeated on BBC Two), the opening episode of the show's fifth season in March 2012 on Sky Atlantic was watched by only 98,000, amounting to a 0.4 percent share of the overall audience.[42]

This sank to 47,000 for the third episode, prompting a *Daily Mail* article to estimate that the acquisition was costing Sky £5 for every viewer.[43] Numbers continued to fall for the sixth season, the opening episode in April 2013 drawing 58,000 viewers.[44] Through the channel's first few years, audiences continued to remain relatively small, including for HBO series, with only *Game of Thrones* bucking the trend. A particular low was reached in January 2014 when the first episode of comedy drama *Looking* (HBO, 2014–) aired to just 8,000 viewers.[45]

Notably, such numbers invited criticism to be leveled at the channel rather than the content itself. Richard Desmond, chairman of Channel 5's then-owners Northern & Shell, made the following dig in a speech to the Royal Television Society Convention in September 2013: "Channel 5 really gets behind U.S. acquisitions, and we support them across our whole portfolio. We don't perform Sky Atlantic–style magic on them—and make the audience disappear."[46] Analysis of Sky Atlantic's early ratings in industry magazine *Broadcast* blamed the channel's concentration on content made for the "chattering classes": "Shows like Boardwalk and Mad Men get talked about a lot, but rarely achieve the ratings the volume of noise suggests."[47] However, as Sky spokespeople were quick to insist, such commentary missed the point of Sky Atlantic's purpose as part of Sky's portfolio. The *Guardian* paraphrased Sky's chief operating officer Mike Darcey's argument that, rather than viewing figures, "it is buzz, or 'column inches,' about Sky Atlantic that is much more important at the moment as it is about making the overall Sky channels portfolio attractive to subscribers."[48] The loss of viewers suffered by imports like *Mad Men* as they "made the crossing" (as several headlines punned) from free-to-air channels to Sky Atlantic links to the association between the "quality" American drama epitomized by HBO and a "minority" audience share, with the value represented by the content not accounted for by crude mass-market logic but rather to be found in the "soft" ratings of critical acclaim and awards. Having previously been associated with commercial entertainment, with its new channel, coming as it did with HBO built in, Sky aimed to attract a demographic more readily associated with niche (rather than mass) appeal. This new turn in Sky's approach was gradually picked up by journalists and affirmed as having broader cultural benefits:

> Do low ratings really matter, though? Such shows aren't intended to appeal to everyone. Instead they're a benchmark of quality for the rest to aspire to. They will endure, stand up to repeated viewings, inspire analysis and discussion. . . . They also perform a valuable function of raising the reputation of television, meaning the medium continues to attract the finest creative talent and isn't seen as a poor relation of film or theatre.[49]

Ultimately, then, in being seen to *avoid* the rush for ratings (while, in reality, steadily increasing subscription rates kept the balance sheet more than healthy), Sky's role as a platform was framed in terms of the cultural kudos associated with hard-won broadcast rights that brought high financial costs and relatively low audience draw. In setting Sky apart from the overabundance of content that characterizes the digital media environment, the channel has served to position Sky as cultural custodian, championing the "gems" of the transnational content market and arranging them in one place for the British viewer. The company effectively imported the *discursive* value associated with HBO's identity as a purveyor of "quality" drama as well as the imports themselves, challenging its historical association with "commercial," mass-appeal fare.

CONCLUSION

By analyzing the promotion of Sky Atlantic as it was introduced to the British television landscape, I have shown how the cross-border, intercorporate activities that make up importation have been reframed as a consumer-facing evaluative discourse. I have necessarily limited my view to the channel's early months. As new rivals have appeared in the form of the streaming services Netflix and Amazon Prime, its position as a distinguished "bridge" into the global content market has come under increased pressure. In turn, Sky Atlantic's mix of content has been diversified in ways that further complicate its status as a "quality" importer and the workings of transnational brand integration (including several investments in foreign language drama and trans-European coproductions). At the same time, as I have discussed elsewhere, the channel's drama content eventually came to form a key aspect of Sky's on-demand services, which have taken an increasingly central place in its appeal to would-be subscribers, further underlining arguments made in defense of Sky Atlantic's small but dedicated linear broadcast audiences.[50] Expensive investment in its transatlantic partnership, and the explicit and aggressive translation of its acquisition strategy into the branding discourse around Sky Atlantic, have thus formed just one important part of Sky's negotiation of the significant shifts that have taken place within television's industrial and technological formation in recent years. Indeed, it remains to be seen how the planned takeover of Sky's controlling stakeholder, 21st Century Fox, by the Walt Disney Company will impact the HBO partnership specifically, given that the latter is a prized possession of Disney's competitor corporation WarnerMedia (previously Time Warner).

Against this changing landscape, however, "quality" American drama has remained firmly at the center of the Sky Atlantic brand. The HBO deal was renewed in January 2014, reportedly costing £275 million to extend the exclusive rights until 2020.[51] Nearly doubling what Sky had paid for the catalog of shows, this confirmed just how important an asset they had become for the channel—and how inseparable from its brand identity. In fact, besides continuing the supply of content, the new deal was announced with the promise that the partnership between the companies would be expanded to involve coproductions. At the time of going to press (January 2018) the results of the deal were yet to be seen in earnest, with only one miniseries—*The Young Pope* (HBO / Sky Atlantic, 2016–)—having come to fruition, followed by an announcement in April 2017 that several high-end dramas would begin airing from 2018.[52] However, given that HBO had previously only entered into transatlantic coproductions with the BBC, this extension of Sky's brand integration strategy to production rather than just acquisition reflects its importance in the company's increased dominance of British television culture in recent years. With a similar deal agreed with CBSs Corporation in 2016 for exclusive rights to all of Showtime's drama, it is clear that the Sky Atlantic's transnational positioning is both evolving and well financed. The decisions taken more recently to deepen—and perhaps complicate—Sky Atlantic's brand claim as a transnational bridge build on a discursive foundation that has defined the transatlantic flow of content as itself a potent form of promotional currency.

NOTES

1. James Robinson, "Sky Buys Complete HBO TV Catalogue," *The Guardian*, July 29, 2010, http://www.theguardian.com/media/2010/jul/29/bskyb-buys-hbo-tv-catalogue.
2. Several authors have discussed the historical use of American imports by various British channels, some of which are cited below. For a good overview and bibliography, see Paul Rixon, *American Television on British Screens: A Story of Cultural Interaction* (Houndmills, Basingstoke: Palgrave Macmillan, 2006).
3. Jean K. Chalaby, "Broadcasting in a Post-national Environment: The Rise of Transnational TV Groups," *Critical Studies in Television* 4 (2009): 39–64, doi:10.7227/CST.4.1.5.
4. Michele Hilmes, "Whose Text Is It Anyway? Creativity, Authorship and the Transnational in Television," *Critical Studies in Television* 3 (2008): 101, doi:10.7227/CST.3.2.8.
5. For example, see Jeanette Steemers, *Selling Television: British Television in the Global Marketplace* (London: BFI, 2004); Timothy Havens, *Global Television Marketplace* (London: BFI, 2006); and Giselinde Kuipers, "The Cosmopolitan Tribe of Television Buyers: Professional Ethos, Personal Taste and Cosmopolitan Capital in Transnational Cultural Mediation," *European Journal of Cultural Studies* 15 (2012): 581–603.
6. Havens, *Global Television Marketplace*, 1.
7. Havens, *Global Television Marketplace*, 9.
8. Rixon, *American Television*, 107–108.
9. Rixon, *American Television*, 105.
10. In the year of Sky Atlantic's launch, Sky spent £1.22 billion on marketing, an increase of £105 million from the previous year, which, as Sky's annual report stated, "primarily reflect[ed] the successful above-the-line marketing campaigns surrounding the launch of Sky Atlantic" (BSkyB, Annual Report 2011, http://annualreview2011.sky.com/_assets/downloads/PDF/SKY-AnnRep2011/Full_Annual_Report_2011.pdf, 32).
11. Timothy J. Dowd and Susanne Janssen, "Globalization and Diversity in Cultural Fields: Comparative Perspectives on Television, Music, and Literature," *American Behavioral Scientist* 55 (2011): 520.

12. See, for example, Don Weenink, "Cosmopolitanism as a Form of Capital: Parents Preparing Their Children for a Globalizing World," *Sociology* 42 (2008): 1089–1106; Denise D. Bielby, "Staking Claims: Conveying Transnational Cultural Value in a Creative Industry," *American Behavioral Scientist* 55 (2011): 525–540, doi:10.1177/0002764211398077.

13. Henry Jenkins, "Pop Cosmopolitanism: Mapping Cultural Flows in an Age of Media Convergence," in *Globalization: Culture and Education in the New Millennium,* ed. Marcelo M. Suárez-Orozco and Desirée Baolian Qin-Hilliard (London: University of California Press, 2004).

14. Kuipers, "Cosmopolitan Tribe," 596.

15. Quoted in "Heavenly Makes Waves with Sky Atlantic Launch," Heavenly, February 1, 2011, 8http://heavenly.co.uk/brand-agency-news/heavenly-makes-waves-with-sky-atlantic-launch/.

16. All the 2011 idents can be viewed at https://theident.gallery/skyatlantic-2011.php.

17. Denny Tu, "Sky Atlantic Takes Flight with Brand New Identity," *Art and Business of Motion* (blog), February 2, 2011, http://dennytu.wordpress.com/2011/02/02/sky-atlantic-takes-flight-with-new-brand-identity/.

18. The trailer is available to view at http://www.youtube.com/watch?v=aFhUM8E_ivg.

19. The trailer is available to view at http://www.youtube.com/watch?v=EowzgpAtQ-g. The montage of the Atlantic horizon shot and the slogan was also used for billboard posters as part of the launch campaign.

20. Janet McCabe, "Diagnosing the Alien: Producing Identities, American 'Quality' Drama and British Television Culture in the 1990s," in *Frames and Fictions on Television: The Politics of Identity within Drama,* ed. Bruce Carson and Margaret Llewellyn-Jones (Exeter: Intellect, 2000), 141.

21. Elke Weissmann, "Negotiating American Quality: The NBC Brand in Britain," *Critical Studies in Television* 3 (2008): 53, doi:10.7227/CST.3.2.5; also see Rixon, *American Television,* 98.

22. Weissmann, "Negotiating American Quality," 51.

23. Since Sky Atlantic's exclusivity deal with HBO, Channel 4 has invested more and more heavily in drama imports from Europe, more recently packaged within its Walter Presents strand and forming a central part of its on-demand offerings. A similar shift had also taken place previously on BBC Four, after it lost *Mad Men* to Sky Atlantic in 2011.

24. See Faye Woods, "Teen TV Meets T4: Assimilating *The O.C.* into British Youth Television," *Critical Studies in Television* 8 (2013): 14–35, doi:10.7227/CST.8.1.4.

25. Janet McCabe, "Creating 'Quality' Audiences for ER on Channel 4," in *The Contemporary Television Series,* ed. Michael Hammond and Lucy Mazdon (Edinburgh: Edinburgh University Press, 2005), 212.

26. In his recent article, Michael L. Wayne discusses a slightly different form of brand integration in the case of network television content bought by on-demand services Amazon Prime and Netflix ("Netflix, Amazon, and Branded Television Content in Subscription Video On-Demand Portals," *Media, Culture & Society,* forthcoming, doi:10.1177/0163443717736118). While Wayne's focus is on shifting industrial priorities *within* the US national market, it is important to note his observation that such interpenetration between a program's original brand environment and that of a distributor who is buying it is as likely to be *resisted* (as in the case of Netflix) as it is cultivated (as with Amazon Prime) in the dynamic world of multiformat, intensely fragmented digital television industries.

27. HBO's "quality" drama has been studied from too wide a variety of perspectives to cover fully here. On the specific question of the relationship between its branding and distinction, see Jane Feuer, "HBO and the Concept of Quality TV," in *Quality TV: Contemporary American Television and Beyond,* ed. Janet McCabe and Kim Akass (London: I.B. Tauris, 2007), 145–157; and Christopher Anderson, "Producing an Aristocracy of Culture in American Television," in *The Essential HBO Reader,* ed. Gary R. Edgerton and Jeffrey P. Jones (Lexington: University Press of Kentucky, 2008), 23–41.

28. It is important to note that any straightforward delineation of HBO's "quality" drama in opposition to "ordinary" TV is complicated by claims for quality across basic cable and network television, not least more recently as a result of HBO's influence (see Anthony N. Smith, "Putting the Premium into Basic: Slow-Burn Narratives and the Loss-Leader Function of AMC's Original Drama Series," *Television and New Media* 14 [2013]: 150–166, doi:10.1177/1527476411418537).

29. Anderson, "Producing an Aristocracy," 25.
30. Feuer, "HBO," 150–151.
31. Gerard Gilbert, "Choppy Waters for the Atlantic Crossing," *The Independent*, March 19, 2011, 20.
32. Quoted in Maggie Brown, "Sky Atlantic to Signal a Sea Change for Viewers," *The Guardian*, January 11, 2011, http://www.theguardian.com/media/organgrinder/2011/jan/11/sky-atlantic-x-factor. Freeview is the primary platform for accessing free-to-air digital terrestrial channels in the United Kingdom (in other words, those not behind the paywall of a subscription service), including all of the public service channels.
33. Mimi Turner, "Sky Atlantic Launches in February with 'Mad Men,' 'Boardwalk Empire,'" *Hollywood Reporter*, January 5, 2011, http://www.hollywoodreporter.com/news/sky-atlantic-launches-february-mad-68710.
34. Mark Sweney, "BSkyB to Launch Sky Atlantic," *The Guardian*, October 1, 2010, http://www.theguardian.com/media/2010/oct/01/bskyb-sky-atlantic-mad-men; Stephen Price, "Recording the Boardwalk," *Broadcast*, February 11, 2011, http://www.broadcastnow.co.uk/recording-the-boardwalk/5023599.article.
35. The launch can be viewed at http://tinyurl.com/o3gsv4k.
36. John Plunkett, "Boardwalk Empire: 438,000 Walk over to Sky Atlantic," *The Guardian*, February 2, 2011, http://www.theguardian.com/media/2011/feb/02/tv-ratings-boardwalk-empire.
37. Mark Sweney, "Boardwalk Empire," *The Guardian*, n.d., https://www.theguardian.com/tv-and-radio/tvandradioblog/2011/feb/01/boardwalk-empire-season-one-episode-one.
38. Quoted in Christina Radish, "Martin Scorsese and Terence Winter Interview: Boardwalk Empire," *Collider*, September 15, 2010, http://collider.com/boardwalk-empire-interview-martin-scorsese-terrence-winter/.
39. The trailer is available to view at http://www.campaignlive.co.uk/article/dustin-hoffman-stars-sky-atlantic-ad/1048319#.
40. Scott Timberg, "Big Screen or Small, Dustin Hoffman Feels 'Luck'-y," *Los Angeles Times*, February 17, 2012, http://articles.latimes.com/2012/feb/17/entertainment/la-et-dustin-hoffman-20120217.
41. Tara Conlan, "BSkyB Poised to Snatch Mad Men from BBC," *The Guardian*, October 1, 2010, 9.
42. Jason Deans, "*Mad Men* Series 5 Opener Attracts Nearly 100,000," *The Guardian*, March 28, 2012, http://www.theguardian.com/media/2012/mar/28/mad-men-series-5-tv-ratings.
43. Paul Revoir, "Mad Men Costing Sky £5 for Every Viewer as Audience Shrinks to Just 47,000," *Mail Online*, April 5, 2012, http://www.dailymail.co.uk/news/article-2125827/Mad-Men-costing-Sky-5-for-viewer-audience-drops-just-47-000.html.
44. John Plunkett, "*Mad Men*'s Sky Atlantic Return Proves a Hard Sell with Just 58,000 Viewers," *The Guardian*, April 11, 2013, https://www.theguardian.com/media/2013/apr/11/mad-men-sky-atlantic-tv-ratings.
45. Peter White, "Analysis: Sky and HBO Co-pro Deal," *Broadcast*, February 6, 2014, http://www.broadcastnow.co.uk/news/international/analysis-sky-and-hbo-co-pro-deal/5066251.article.
46. Quoted in George Szalai, "U.K.'s Channel 5 Committed to U.S. Dramas," *Hollywood Reporter*, September 12, 2013, http://www.hollywoodreporter.com/news/uks-channel-5-committed-us-628232.
47. Price, "Recording the Boardwalk."
48. Mark Sweney, "Sky Atlantic's Entourage Gathers Posse of 18,000," *The Guardian*, February 4, 2011, http://www.theguardian.com/media/2011/feb/04/entourage-sky-atlantic-tv-ratings.
49. Michael Hogan, "Do *Mad Men*'s Low Ratings Really Matter?" *The Telegraph*, March 28, 2012, http://www.telegraph.co.uk/culture/tvandradio/9171775/Do-Mad-Mens-low-ratings-really-matter.html.
50. Sam Ward, "Box Sets on the Set-Top Box: The Promotion of On Demand Television in Britain," in *DVD, Blu-ray and Beyond: Navigating Formats and Platforms with Media Consumption*, ed. Jonathan Wroot and Andy Willis (Houndmills, Basingstoke: Palgrave Macmillan, 2017), 177–196.
51. Mark Sweney, "BSkyB Signs New Five-year Deal for Exclusive Rights to HBO TV Catalogue," *The Guardian*, January 20, 2014, 27.
52. BBC, "Sky Announces HBO Co-production deal," BBC News, April 20, 2017, http://www.bbc.co.uk/news/business-39651301.

Transatlantic Programs

INTRODUCTION

The book's first part examined the ways in which television producers and distributors—both traditional broadcasters and digital streaming services—participate in and benefit from the transatlantic television trade. This part switches the focus from institutions to individual programs. Chapters 5, 6, and 7 explore the functions that the selected case study programs serve for specific broadcasting institutions (PBS, Sky, ITV, HBO, and the BBC) that partner in one form or another with their transatlantic counterparts. These chapters also explore the themes of national identity, heritage, and channel branding touched upon in the first part, highlighting their importance to the relationship of transatlantic partners and to specific programs' placement within their import markets. Chapters 8 and 9 investigate the ways in which two programs, *Episodes* and *Game of Thrones*, textually encode some of the problematics of the transatlantic relationship—widespread assumptions about the differences between US and UK production contexts and acting styles.

Roberta Pearson's chapter, "*Sherlock* and *Elementary*: The Cultural and Temporal Value of High-End and Routine Transatlantic Television Drama," argues for two broad distinctions between types of imported content. Some programs, like *Sherlock, Downton Abbey*, and *Game of Thrones*, are high end; they are often coproduced, have large budgets, high production values, and complex narratives, and engender large global fandoms. These are also the programs that television studies scholars tend to favor in their research. Yet, despite content producers' commitment to high-end drama flagged in the book's introduction, much of the transnational and transatlantic television trade consists of routine drama such as *Elementary, NCIS*, and *Midsomer Murders*. Even with their relatively low budgets and production values and the absence of a large and fervent fan base, these programs generate reliable revenue streams for their producers and distributors, perhaps through their sustained appeal to casual viewers unwilling to commit to the often-complex seriality of the high-end content. Both high-end and routine dramas are essential components of transatlantic trade, but their relative points on what Pearson terms the cultural and temporal proximity indices determine their value to their importers and their positioning in their import markets.

Eva N. Redvall's chapter, "Mainstream Trends and Masterpiece Traditions: ITV's *Downton Abbey* as a Hit Heritage Drama for *Masterpiece* in the United States," details the ways in which the program successfully negotiated the different broadcasting cultures and storytelling traditions of the United Kingdom and the United States. In so doing, the creators produced a "postheritage" drama marked by the UK tradition of heritage drama, a European "auteur" sensibility, the quickly moving narratives of quality US television, and the ensemble storytelling structures and recognizable personal dramas character-istic of ITV soap operas. Drawing upon trade press sources, paratexts, and qualitative interviews, the chapter details the collaboration between ITV and *Masterpiece*, which from the beginning intended to create a transatlantic hit that would have great value to both its producers and its importers through strengthening audience perceptions of quality brands.

Just as Redvall emphasizes the importance of negotiation and a resultant hybridity in transatlantic content, so does Robin Nelson in his chapter, "Boundary Collisions in HBO-BBC Transnational Coproduction: *Rome* and *Parade's End*." Both programs fell well short of *Downton Abbey*'s breakout success; the reasons for their comparative failure may lie in a greater mismatch of brands than that between ITV and PBS. As Nelson points out, HBO and the BBC do not seem like "natural bedfellows," the former an inde-pendent subscription channel appealing to niche audiences and the other the most his-toric of all public service broadcasters. This distinction resulted in tensions between the two institutions' perceptions of production strategies and audience reception. However, as Nelson argues, such distinctions become more porous and flexible in the production of transatlantic content. The chapter seeks to explain why HBO chose to coproduce the two programs with the BBC despite their probable lack of appeal to an American audi-ence. Nelson concludes that the programs succeeded in boosting both partners' prestige brands but failed to build audiences for either HBO or the BBC.

In chapter 8, "Metacommentary and Mythology: *Episodes* as a Performance of Transatlantic TV," Jonathan Bignell continues the part's exploration of national identity, examining a program that bases its fundamental narrative premise upon the oft-perceived superiority of British to American television culture. However, argues Bignell, discursive differences may drive the plots, but they must also be minimized in order for the pro-gram to appeal to viewers, since for Showtime's audience, *Episodes* is American and for BBC audiences it is British. *Episodes* thus textually encodes the traces of the extratextual negotiations that characterize all transatlantic coproductions. Bignell analyzes the ways in which national distinctions are played out in the text from conceptions of authorship and quality to acting styles.

Chapter 9, "*Game of Thrones*: Investigating British Acting," is an in-depth exploration of the apparent distinctions between the "theatricality" of British acting and the "naturalness" of American acting, or as Simone Knox and Gary Cassidy put it, the difference between the disciplined use of technique and an organic "shooting from the hip." The authors argue that this frequent discursive trope acts to disguise the nuances and complexities of British actors' backgrounds and their acting styles. They take as their case study a program that features a number of established and emerging Irish and British actors and conduct a close textual analysis of two scenes, one featuring Irish actor Liam Cunningham and the other British actor Conleth Hill. Knox and Cassidy focus on the actors' vocal performance, since British actors have often been lauded for their strong vocal technique. This analysis serves to counter the conventional discursive assumptions about and binary distinctions between British and American acting, underlying, as do many of this part's chapters, the national hybridity of transatlantic texts.

/// 5 /// *SHERLOCK* AND *ELEMENTARY*

The Cultural and Temporal Value of High-End and Routine Transatlantic Television Drama

ROBERTA PEARSON

This chapter explores the emergence of two tiers of international television programs, high end and routine, and argues that the two types of content serve different functions in their import markets. The content's cultural and temporal proximity to the import market determines the uses made of it by broadcasters as they attempt to appeal to their domestic audiences. But understanding these different functions requires complicating and nuancing the long-established concept of cultural proximity and developing the concept of temporal proximity. In the case studies, *Sherlock* and *Elementary* are used as exemplars of the high end and the routine.

The first section establishes the distinction between high-end and routine drama and justifies the choice of *Sherlock* and *Elementary* as case studies. The second section establishes the concept of the cultural proximity index and explores the ways in which *Sherlock*'s cultural premium, stemming from the textual encoding of British national identity, made it valuable to the US importer, PBS. The third section argues that *Elementary* is characterized by cultural accessibility, stemming from its generic identification as a procedural; this determines the uses made of the show by its importer, Sky Living. The fourth section establishes the concept of the temporal proximity index in relation to high-end and routine television, arguing that the high-end *Sherlock* can suffer a temporal discount, while the routine *Elementary* cannot, a factor that once again determines the programs' position in their respective import markets.

SHERLOCK, ELEMENTARY, AND HIGH-END AND ROUTINE TELEVISION

Over the last few years, British television critics have celebrated the ascendance of *Sherlock* (BBC / Hartswood Films, 2010–) to the rarefied ranks of global event television. According to Richard Beech in the *Mirror Online*, "Television shows such as *Sherlock, Doctor Who, Game of Thrones* . . . *Breaking Bad* and *Homeland* are worldwide events now, . . . on a par with FA Cup finals and breaking news events."[1] A few months later, the *Guardian*'s John Plunkett and Jason Deans made a similar point. "*Sherlock* aside . . . BBC1 is arguably lacking breakout hits that got the nation talking in a way that ITV's *Broadchurch* did last year. The bar has been raised in the era of Netflix and global drama hits; less *Midsomer Murders*, more *House of Cards*."[2] Anticipating the 2016 one-off special "The Abominable Bride," *Guardian* journalist David Batty wrote that *Sherlock* looked set to "cement its reputation as a global phenomenon" and had "joined the ranks of event television alongside the likes of *Game of Thrones, Breaking Bad* and *Mad Men*."[3] Writing before the premiere of the fourth series, Batty's colleague, Julia Raeside, declared that the program was now indisputably a global phenomenon. "*Sherlock* now has a global popularity that's too intense to comprehend."[4] Almost simultaneously, the *Independent*'s James Rampton asserted that *Sherlock* could "now be described as the most popular drama in the world."[5]

Distribution figures confirm the journalists' assertions. *Sherlock*'s third series was licensed to 224 territories and "The Abominable Bride" to 216; both the third series and the one-off special were distributor BBC Worldwide's top-selling programs in their respective years.[6] *Sherlock*'s impressive performance on the international market boosted the overall profile of its distributor. Said Matt Forde, executive vice president of sales and coproductions at BBC Worldwide Americas, "The success of *Sherlock* means there are more people picking up the phone to talk about new opportunities. . . . In the US, there is a renewed respect for British programming and they want to work with UK content creators."[7]

Sherlock's global phenomenon status suggests the emergence of a two-tiered international distribution system, the first tier consisting of high-end programs like *Sherlock* and the second of routine programs like *Midsomer Murders*, a British mystery-of-the-week broadcast on ITV since 1997. Like *Sherlock, Midsomer Murders* airs in over two hundred territories,[8] is a reliable source of revenue for its producer and distributor, and is viewed by millions worldwide; indeed, in 2004 the program was one of the three best-selling UK exports.[9] In the United States, the program airs on the public broadcasting network (PBS) and on the streaming services Netflix and Acorn TV, all of these windows producing more profits and drawing additional viewers. *Midsomer Murders* is undeniably successful measured by profits and audience numbers, but unlike *Sherlock*, the program has not generated critical acclaim, intense media coverage, or a vast and avid fandom that breathlessly awaits the next series. *Sherlock* is event television; *Midsomer Murders* is not.

Elementary (CBS, 2011 to present), the US television adaptation of the Sherlock Holmes tales, is more *Midsomer Murders* than *Sherlock*. It too performs well in the international market, attracting significant revenues and sizable audiences. Indeed, as the program's ratings flagged in the United States, international sales helped to secure its renewal for seasons 5 and 6. Since CBS produces as well as airs the show, revenues from off-network, SVOD, and international sales totaled $80 million during the show's first four seasons.[10] CNN reported that "CBS's long-running *Hawaii Five-O* and *Elementary* . . . aren't huge hits on the network, but amass more than $3 million per episode from international deals."[11] But, like *Midsomer Murders, Elementary* is neither event television nor critically acclaimed and, in contrast to its UK counterpart, has failed to attract significant media or fan buzz.

Sherlock's and *Elementary*'s presence in multiple international territories is at least partially attributable to the power of their respective sales agents. As of 2014, CBS Studios International was the top-ranked global television distributor.[12] It describes itself as "the leading supplier of programming to the international television marketplace, licensing to more than 200 markets in more than 60 languages across multiple media platforms."[13] With the exception of the powerful US studios, BBC Worldwide is the most successful international distributor of television content. Writing before *Sherlock*'s 2010 debut, *Variety* reporter Steve Clarke noted that a distributor's size is critical to international success. "As Hartswood knows to its benefit, having a big backer like BBC Worldwide onboard . . . helps enormously."[14]

Sherlock and *Elementary* both appeal to international audiences, both are sold by top international distributors, and both adapt the same source text but update the character to the twenty-first century. And, as we shall see below, both programs contributed to the successful rebrands of their respective US and UK importers. Despite these similarities, however, *Elementary* has not achieved *Sherlock*'s must-see status or media buzz. Said Ben Stephenson, the BBC's head of drama commissioning, "*Elementary* is a good show, but it's week-in-week-out, story-of-the-week—it's there to do a job and it does it really, really well. . . . *Sherlock* is there to be a special event, it's there to be like a big movie that comes out every so often, and is explosive when it does—they're very different beasts."[15] Different beasts indeed—*Sherlock* is high-end television and *Elementary* is routine television.

As long-form drama has established itself as the most valuable commodity in the international market, the term "high-end television" has become increasingly common in industrial and academic discourse.[16] Drawing on the work of Robin Nelson and Trisha

Dunleavy, Audun Engelstad argues that high-end television drama is distinguished by the following characteristics:

> high budget, visible in the cinematic production values (budgets per produced hour are close to that of a medium-budget movie); a must-see allure that promotes of [*sic*] a kind of essential viewing experience; authorial input that promises creative innovation . . . a narrative complexity based on systematic cutting between different subplots; and a genre-based story, which often showcases a radical mixing of genres.[17]

Sherlock's feature-length episodes compare well to theatrically released films. Indeed, both "The Abominable Bride" and the first episode of series 4 were screened in cinemas in the United States and the United Kingdom. *Sherlock* is insistently and widely promoted as essential viewing on both sides of the Atlantic. As audiences endure the agonizing wait between its brief series, their narrative speculations and fan-produced paratexts generate valuable promotional buzz. *Sherlock* benefits from the authorial input of showrunners Steven Moffat and Mark Gatiss, both well-known from their previous television work, especially *Doctor Who*. *Sherlock*'s narrative complexity derives both from individual episode subplots ultimately revealed as interconnecting and from the narrative arc that links all episodes in a series.

Generically, *Sherlock* is an intertextual mash-up– part Conan Doyle, part *Doctor Who*, part British heritage television, and more. Tom Steward's and Elizabeth Evans's respective chapters in Louisa Stein and Kristina Busse's *Sherlock and Transmedia Fandom* both address *Sherlock*'s dense web of intertextuality.[18] Steward's chapter on the program's employment of television conventions enumerates a number of these. There is the Conan Doyle canon: "For public service . . . broadcasters, the literary source . . . serves their remit for quality television and producing programs with cultural and artistic value."[19] Then there are the many previous television versions of that canon: "The program . . . can often be read as a response to and reappropriation of many of the established tendencies of TV adaptations."[20] Several of these adaptations took comedic form, in the United Kingdom drawing on "the national cultural traditions" of "situation comedy and political satire."[21] "Steven Moffat and Mark Gatiss, both former situation comedy writers, reenvision Sherlock and John's shared flat as a 'domestic difficulty' comedy," while satire takes the form of occasional sarcastic mentions of contemporary events, such as the banking crisis.[22] The program "treads a fine line generically between period literary adaptation and the police-detective program."[23] It adopts the "narrative style of contemporaneous U.S. police/detective series" but also has "elements of the UK mystery drama."[24] Evans argues that *Sherlock* meets the needs of the BBC as a "global public service broadcaster" by combining "the US quality tradition and the UK prestige tradition of television drama."[25] "The series may recreate the aesthetic and narrative characteristics of highly-praised U.S. quality drama, but the deliberate emphasis on the character's literary provenance and Victorian origins allows it to call on the literary pedigree of Holmes and so maintain a clear place within British cultural history."[26]

Sherlock also resembles many internationally distributed high-end dramas in being a coproduction, the result of a partnership brokered by BBC Worldwide between the US Public Broadcasting Service's *Masterpiece* and UK independent producer Hartswood Films.

> With the expansion of the independent broadcasting sector in Europe in the 1990s, followed by the advent of digital platforms in recent decades, coproduction has exploded to become the "new normal" in high-end drama and documentary, in particular. The United States and the United Kingdom became not only the two largest global exporters of television programs but also each other's biggest customers and most frequent coproduction partners.[27]

Sherlock is one manifestation of BBC Worldwide's increasing commitment to coproduction in the face of the rising costs of developing high-end dramas. The *Australian Financial Review* spoke with Worldwide's Tim Davie and reported that "the BBC is more likely to partner with other production companies and distributors to defray costs and ensure programs will perform well in their target markets." Said Davie, "We've moved from being in pure distribution to co-production. . . . I think you are seeing more and more decisions being made further up the development process."[28]

Made by CBS Studios with no foreign investment, *Elementary* is not a coproduction. In this and other respects, *Elementary* is *Sherlock*'s mirror image; if the latter exemplifies high-end drama, then the former exemplifies routine drama. The program lacks the cinematic aesthetics of such high-end US dramas as *The Handmaid's Tale* and the narrative complexity of others such as *Fargo*. *Elementary* is so far from essential viewing that potential fans may not have heard of it, as the following anecdotal evidence suggests. Responding to a favorable *Guardian* review, reader Notfamousanymore commented, "Found it a bit by accident when there was not a thing on TV, and we were mooching about through box sets."[29] *Elementary* showrunner Rob Doherty, previously associated with *The Ringer* (CW, 2011–2012) and *The Medium* (NBC, 2005–2009) lacks Moffat and Gatiss's auteur aura and high media profile.

Generically, *Elementary* clones the procedural genome, adding a bit of Sherlock Holmes DNA to the sequence in an attempt to distinguish the program from the similarly cloned procedurals that CBS schedules to appeal to its older-skewing audience. Many US critics' reviews of the pilot episode explicitly linked the program to this CBS brand. *The Los Angeles Times* said that the program was set in "the land of the CBS procedural, where instead of pursuing egghead-y cases about purloined letters, Holmes tracks serial killers, sex offenders and other villains of the prime-time grotesque. This is Sherlock Holmes, Les Moonves [CBS president] style."[30] According to Alan Sepinwall, *Elementary* is "essentially, a traditional CBS procedural mystery with a famous literary hero at the center."[31] While British critics praised *Sherlock* for cleverly updating the original stories, US critics asserted that *Elementary*'s CBS house style almost completely overwrote the Conan Doyle canon. The *Hollywood Reporter* noted, "The procedural structure of the pilot is more like current CBS shows like *The Mentalist* than the classic Holmes stories."[32] The *Houston Examiner*'s Allison Nichols also made comparison to *The Mentalist.* "Standing out will be the challenge for this show, and not just from *Sherlock.* Right now there are quite a few shows that feature an eccentric male lead who notices things that most people don't, to name a few: *Psych, Perception,* and *The Mentalist. Elementary* needs to work on making itself stand apart."[33] In other words, *Elementary* had failed to achieve the right balance between the standardization and differentiation required of all texts that rely upon generic formulas. Indeed, the program's seemingly most radical divergence from the Conan Doyle texts, transforming Watson into a woman, could be seen as conformance to procedurals' frequent pairing of an "eccentric male lead" with a more grounded female costar, as in *Perception* and *The Mentalist* but also *Monk* and *Castle,* in a trope that dates back to *The X-Files* Mulder and Scully.

High-end drama now dominates industry discourse concerning the international distribution market. Noting that fourteen of BBC Worldwide's top twenty best-selling programs were dramas, Tim Davie said, "I think this reflects quite significant changes in the industry. With the emergence of subscription VOD players, people are clearly looking for content that is 'must-have.' . . . There's no room for the average. I think the market can be quite brutal on programs that don't deliver."[34] By contrast, this chapter asserts that there is still room for average or routine programs such as *Elementary.* Routine television drama may not deliver prestige or buzz or avid fandoms, but it does consistently deliver audiences and revenues in multiple territories. Nonetheless, imported routine television serves different functions than imported high-end television within the foreign broadcast context.

This chapter argues that the different functions result from broadcasters' assessments of the imported contents' cultural and temporal proximity. Broadcasters do not assess programs with reference to what Andrea Esser terms the "national imaginary"—an imagined nationwide, homogeneous audience. As Esser says about adapting formats:

> Adaptation includes considerations to modify content in ways that take into account the specific audiences targeted by the broadcasters with the programs in question.

Additionally, we need to consider: the overall channel identity . . . and the specific aims and enabling or constraining forces the broadcaster has to contend with at the time of the format acquisition and adaptation.[35]

Imported scripted content cannot be modified or adapted; rather, broadcasters insert foreign programs into the domestic schedule based upon assessments of their cultural and temporal value to specific audience segments and to channel identity. High-end and routine content has different cultural and temporal value to distinct audience segments and to specific channels' identity; broadcasters thus manage the high-end differently from the routine.

SHERLOCK AND THE CULTURAL PROXIMITY INDEX

At the LA Screenings, an annual event held in Los Angeles at which the US studios pitch their content to foreign buyers, CBS Studios International distributed a questionnaire seeking to ascertain acquisition personnel's criteria for acquiring US content. The questionnaire asked respondents to rank genre, length, cast recognition, setting (location/era), target demographic, and cultural relevance in order of importance to their decision-making.[36] Academics also consider cultural relevance but refer to it as cultural proximity. In their home markets, television programs benefit from proximity to viewers' culturally formed expectations. As Joseph Straubhaar says, "Cultural capital, identity, and language tend to favor an audience desire for cultural proximity, which leads audiences to prefer local and national productions over those that are globalized and/or American."[37] The degree to which a television program encodes nationally specific signifiers can affect its worth in the global market. According to McFayden, Hoskins, and Finn, programs "suffer a cultural discount, or loss in value, as they cross national boundaries in international trade." As they explain,

> A particular television program (or other cultural good) rooted in one culture, and thus attractive in the home market where viewers share a common knowledge and way of life, will have a diminished appeal elsewhere as viewers find it difficult to identify with the style, values, beliefs, history, myths, institutions, physical environment, and behavioral patterns.[38]

The industry speaks of "relevance," while academics speak of "cultural proximity" and "cultural discount" but understanding the decisions made by broadcasters with regard to audience segments and channel branding requires a more nuanced formulation. Cultural proximity involves not just cultural discount but also "cultural premium" and "cultural accessibility." British television dramas may perform well on the international market precisely because of the cultural premium derived from strong textual codes of national identity. By contrast, the US industry's century-long dominance of the global screen trade has rendered audiences familiar with Hollywood's textual codes, such as genres and narrative structures as well as with US "style, values, beliefs, history, myths, institutions, physical environment, and behavioral patterns." US television dramas thus have a degree of cultural accessibility around the globe, although this may vary in correlation with the extent to which the text presumes specific knowledge of the national context. For example, *The Sopranos* (HBO, 1999–2007) and *Godless* (Netflix, 2017), respectively, reworkings of the classic American gangster and Western genres, may have a greater degree of accessibility than the political drama *Designated Survivor* (ABC, 2016–18) or the legal drama *The Good Fight* (CBS, 2017-present), which may suffer a cultural discount by virtue of requiring knowledge of US government or laws. What I term the "cultural proximity index" is a spectrum ranging from the negative to the positive—cultural discount to cultural accessibility to cultural premium.

I hypothesize that the cultural proximity index distinguishes the high-end *Sherlock* from the routine *Elementary*, with the former appealing to its transatlantic audience through cultural premium and the latter through cultural accessibility. But both programs initially derived a similar market advantage from the Sherlock Holmes character's long-established global brand. Speaking to *Variety* in 2009, Sue Vertue, chairwoman of Hartswood Films, expressed confidence that the proposed *Sherlock* series would attract coproduction funding since "there aren't many characters that possess the universal appeal of Sherlock Holmes."[39] The hundreds of adaptations produced in all media and in numerous countries since the character's first appearance in 1887 attest to this "universal appeal." Paradoxically, however, the character's ability to transcend national boundaries stems at least in part from the cultural premium of his defining Englishness. Since the advent of sound, screen adaptations have featured young Sherlocks or old Sherlocks, nineteenth- or tw   enty-second-century   Sherlocks, human or animal Sherlocks, London-, Sussex-, or New York City–based Sherlocks, deerstalker-wearing and deerstalker-shunning Sherlocks, but in every case the character is English and in the majority of cases is played or, in the case of animation, voiced by an English actor. But while almost all adaptations encode the character as English, other textual codes necessarily reflect their specific production circumstances. For example, in the Warner Bros. *Sherlock Holmes* and *Sherlock Holmes: A Game of Shadows*, Robert Downey, one of the few non-Englishmen to play the character since the silent film era, adopts an English accent, but this Holmes's extreme physicality and participation in several extended action sequences makes him an appropriate hero for an American film intended as a global blockbuster.[40]

Warner Bros. produced a "Hollywoodized" version of the character, while Hartswood Films and the BBC produced a very British version, exploiting the cultural premium of the character's essential Englishness. *Sherlock* showrunner Steven Moffatt has spoken of the program's encoding of markers of British national identity. When asked how to attract global audiences, he said, "I think the way you appeal to other cultures is to be your own culture, just to be yourself. Americans like British shows; they want it to be British. . . . The shows are British because they are made by British people. It's just natural, isn't it."[41] Responding to CBS's request to license a US remake, Moffatt characterized *Sherlock* as so "definitively" and "obtrusively" British that the idea of an American remake was "insane." *Sherlock* is "about as British as it gets."[42] Moffatt's assertions concerning *Sherlock*'s national identity follow a long-established strategy for international distribution. From silent cinema in the 1920s to twenty-first-century television, UK film and television producers have exploited Britishness to gain a competitive advantage in the global screen trade. As Eva Redvall says in her chapter in this volume, "Whereas most European countries have produced few historical drama series with a wider transnational appeal, Britain has a long tradition of exporting costume drama—or what scholars such as Andrew Higson have discussed as heritage drama—to the rest of the world."[43] *Sherlock* is not costume drama, but it is, in some respects, heritage drama.

Barbara Selznick argues that exported UK television has frequently encoded a Britishness consisting of traditional and "mod" versions of the heritage brand. [44] The first, relying primarily on the country's past, associates Britain with high culture and classic literature, as in the numerous BBC Jane Austen and Charles Dickens adaptations. The Holmes stories, firmly rooted in nineteenth-century popular culture, are neither high culture nor classic literature, but their longevity and ubiquity have bestowed an aura of canonicity upon them. While *Sherlock*'s updating of the character to the twenty-first century might seem to reject the past, the producers nonetheless consistently foreground the canonical source texts and their author. Paratextually, Moffat and Gatiss characterize themselves as Sherlockian fanboys and express their admiration for Arthur Conan Doyle. Textually, the producers have incorporated numerous citations of the original stories, such as variant titles—"A Study in Pink" (*A Study in Scarlet*), "A Scandal in Belgravia" ("A Scandal in Bohemia"), "His Last Vow" ("His Last Bow")—and updated references— "a three-patch problem" for "a three-pipe problem," an iPhone for a pocket watch. The one-off episode "The Abominable Bride" not only returns the characters to their original Victorian setting but also alludes to the stories' initial appearances in the *Strand Magazine* and to those stories' illustrator, Sidney Paget. To use Matt Hill's term, *Sherlock*'s "heretical fidelity," the simultaneous invocation and reworking of the original texts, links the program to the traditional heritage brand.[45] The program's London setting reinforces the brand, showcasing iconic sites such as Buckingham Palace, Trafalgar Square, and New Scotland Yard. Says Moffatt, "We amp up the London-ness of *Sherlock* as we make it in Cardiff."[46]

Selznick describes the "mod" heritage brand as "decidedly contemporary, highlighting the current and modern elements of British culture," and incorporating "sexuality, fashion, style, pop culture, and irreverence."[47] The mod brand is consistently encoded into *Sherlock* throughout the series' four seasons. To cite just a few examples, in "A Scandal in Belgravia," Sherlock appears naked in Buckingham Palace, the Victorian-set "The Abominable Bride" reflects twenty-first-century sensibilities concerning female equality, and Sherlock's trendy and fashionable Belfast overcoat became so iconic that it featured in the Museum of London's exhibit about the character. The mod brand also manifests in aesthetics: "Often these texts are expected to offer something alternative in terms of style (such as fast-paced editing, low key lighting, or handheld camera work)."[48] Here too *Sherlock* conforms to the brand with textual practices such as the on-screen imposition of text messages and the rapid and disorienting editing of the mind-palace sequences.

Sherlock's paratextual invocations and textual encodings of aspects of the traditional and "mod" heritage brands results in the Britishness of which Moffatt speaks. This bestows a cultural premium on the program that enhances its profitability in the international market. A BBC Worldwide executive told Jeanette Steemers, Sherlock is "deeply British" but also "translates worldwide."[49] In 2014 the *Telegraph*'s Josie Ensor reported,

> Industry experts say Americans have finally got a taste for British television and record numbers are tuning in. . . . Broadcasters have been enjoying record success with the three most popular imported dramas—*Downton Abbey*, *Doctor Who* and *Sherlock*. . . . The quintessentially British detective show *Sherlock* . . . reaches up to four million viewers an episode.[50]

In his chapter in this volume, Paul Booth confirms that *Sherlock*'s appeal to its American fans stems from its cultural premium: their "love of *Sherlock* and *Doctor Who* was precisely that Britishness which Dylan Morris hails as 'Young American nerds appropriat[ing] Britain as a second heritage.'"[51]

Sherlock's cultural premium made it especially attractive to its US broadcaster, which employed the program in the successful culmination of *Masterpiece's* rebranding for younger audiences. Beginning in 1971, *Masterpiece Theatre*, produced by Boston station WGBH and airing on the PBS network, programmed content that frequently if not always conformed to the British heritage brand; the premiere season included *Elizabeth R*, *The First Churchills* and *The Six Wives of Henry VIII*. These and subsequently aired heritage programs successfully appealed to a small niche audience of older, educated and relatively affluent viewers—precisely those likely to pledge financial support to their local PBS station. During the 1970s, *Masterpiece Theatre* benefited from a unique brand and business model predicated on British content and became PBS's top rated program. But, as Simone Knox says, competitors soon arose; in the 1980s, other channels, most notably A&E, began featuring British content and in 1998 BBC America began drawing a younger audience with contemporary dramas like *Torchwood*. These developments threatened *Masterpiece Theatre*'s business model and brand. It looked "more staid, 'starchy' and 'fusty by comparison" and came to be seen as a "lower budget alternative for US audiences, available without having to pay for cable." [52]

Masterpiece Theatre's executive producer Rebecca Eaton agreed, saying that the brand was "iconic but fading."[53] Seeking to refresh the brand, she split *Masterpiece Theatre* into three separate but complementary strands: *Masterpiece Classic*, *Masterpiece Mystery!* and *Masterpiece Contemporary*. According to Knox, this strategy afforded the opportunities of the "integrated brand clustering" of "vertically-integrated commercial television" and gave greater prominence to contemporary drama.[54] Two years later, in 2010, according to Redvall's chapter in this volume, PBS and BBC renewed their co-production partnership, announcing that *Masterpiece* would mark its 40th anniversary by becoming involved in the BBC's new production of *Sherlock* and two other programs. By 2011, says Hilmes in her chapter in this volume, "PBS and its most emblematic prime-time program achieved heights of audience share and publicity never before reached. PBS became the fifth-ranked national US network, outdoing commercial rivals and far outstripping critical darlings like HBO and Showtime." Much of PBS's new commercial and critical success was attributable to *Downton Abbey* and "another younger crowd-pleaser, *Sherlock*."

Indeed, *Sherlock*, together with *Downton*, played a significant role in the *Masterpiece* rebrand that brought an influx of younger viewers and higher ratings. *Sherlock*'s 2010 premiere drew 6.5 million viewers, making it the highest-rated *Masterpiece* program in thirteen years, while the three episodes of the 2014 third season averaged 6.6 million per episode, much higher than the average ratings of previous programs scheduled in the 10:00–11.30 Sunday nighttime slot.[55] *Sherlock* was aired following *Downton* in the 9:00–10:00 p.m. slot. Said Beth Hoppe, chief programming executive and general manager, general audience programming, PBS, "The pairing of 'Downton Abbey' and 'Sherlock' was a winning blueprint this year, helping both series reach record audiences on PBS member stations."[56] Among those record audiences were the coveted younger viewers that Eaton had hoped the rebrand would attract. Speaking in front of a live audience, sixty-seven-year-old Eaton said that PBS's traditional audience "tends to look like me." Answering a question from a teenager about *Sherlock*, she responded that the program "has been wonderful for us, it has been great for us to get people like you to watch *Masterpiece*."[57] Eaton told the *Guardian* that *Downton* and *Sherlock* had helped refresh *Masterpiece*'s aging audience, attracting college-educated twenty-five- to thirty-four-year-olds.[58] Both the refreshed brand and the refreshed audience testify to the market power of *Sherlock*'s and *Downton*'s cultural premium. Both programs encoded the traditional British heritage brand, but both also updated it: both *Sherlock* and *Downton* adopted some of the narrative strategies of US quality content (see Redvall in this volume on the latter), while *Sherlock* blended traditional and "mod" heritage. The cultural premium of Britishness evolves over time, as producers reconfigure the heritage genre in response to changing social and cultural conditions, textual signifiers, and audience expectations.

ELEMENTARY AND THE CULTURAL PROXIMITY INDEX

I hypothesized above that US television dramas benefit globally from cultural accessibility, since audiences have been trained for the past century in the comprehension of American narrative, generic, social and cultural codes. But audiences in the English-speaking geolinguistic region should find US programs more culturally accessible than audiences elsewhere.[59] McFadyen, Hoskins, and Finn say that "regional television markets, where producers based in a country within the region dominate trade, have flourished because the cultural discount is less for foreign products from within a region than for foreign products from outside the region."[60] However, the specific context of a particular national market within a regional market needs to be accounted for in judging cultural proximity. In the United Kingdom the inevitable contrasts between *Elementary* and the phenomenally successful *Sherlock* subjected the former to a cultural discount unique to the national market.

Writing in the *Guardian* at the time of *Elementary*'s third-season UK premiere, Phelim O'Neill said that the program "has been largely ignored here, and it doesn't take strong sleuthing powers to see why. How dare they try to beat us at our own game."[61] The *Times*' Caitlin Moran, an "out" *Sherlock* fan, facetiously protested the appearance of *Elementary*'s first season on British television, calling it a "terrible national insult."

> It's hard, as a Briton, not to feel a little piqued by the arrival of *Elementary*. As the US Sherlock Holmes reboot—commissioned after the success of *Sherlock* in the UK— the very existence of *Elementary* feels a little . . . rude, to be honest. Surely, in insisting on their own 21st century TV Sherlock—rather than just accepting our smashing,

pre-existing one—the Americans have breached a whole slew of etiquette guidelines. Why was our Sherlock not good enough for them?[62]

Moran wrote with tongue firmly embedded in cheek, but many of *Elementary*'s initial UK reviewers made similar derogatory comparisons to the homegrown product. From *Metro*: "The trouble is, when stacked up against the BBC's *Sherlock*, *Elementary* feels a little. . . elementary."[63] From the *Times*: "America's translation of Sherlock Holmes to the present day is superior to our *Sherlock* in only one respect: its title, *Elementary*."[64] And finally from the *Guardian*: "Almost certainly the second best modern-day Sherlock Holmes to currently grace the small screen. In almost certainly the second best modern-day Sherlock Holmes show."[65]

Importantly, however, the *Guardian*'s reviewer pointed out that *Elementary* shares more with US programs than it does with its UK rival; he spoke of the program as "basically . . . any number of American cop shows, just with a couple of characters plucked from the past and the other side of the Atlantic dropped in. As if Holmes and Watson got a ride in Moffat's TARDIS [the space-time machine in *Doctor Who*], and ended up wandering into CSI:NY."[66] The UK reviewer here echoes the opinions of his transatlantic counterparts as seen above. Despite the unique cultural discount *Elementary* experienced in the United Kingdom, the program's industrial classification as a procedural most significantly determined its cultural proximity and its insertion into the UK broadcast context. US procedurals, the epitome of routine television, dominate the international market, their familiar and formulaic narrative structures rendering them accessible in both English- and non-English-speaking geolinguistic regions. In 2013, the best-performing US series in fifteen major territories were the NCIS and CSI franchises, together with *Criminal Minds*, *Castle*, *The Mentalist*, and *Bones*.[67] Foreign acquisitions personnel responded favorably to *Elementary*'s arrival at the 2012 international trade fairs, recognizing it as yet another potentially successful procedural. Reviewing the "7 Hot Shows at MIPCOM," the *Hollywood Reporter* said that *Elementary* was "arguably the only sure-fire hit among the studios' crop of new fall dramas" because the program "ticks all the right boxes for international buyers: It's a crime procedural (the world's best-selling genre), is based on a tested franchise with a built-in fan base and features in Liu an internationally recognizable star."[68] Reporting on the LA Screenings, *Deadline Hollywood* wrote that "of the procedurals, CBS/CBS Studios' Sherlock Holmes reboot *Elementary* is getting very strong reviews across the board."[69]

The year 2012 was a good one for the international sales of US drama; Armando Nuñez, president of CBS Studios International, said, "The business is really quite robust." But he pointed out that "not every American show will play on primetime on a big terrestrial network in each European market. . . . Some will not be on primetime and some will be on cable or satellite."[70] In the United Kingdom, *Elementary* was acquired not by one of the big terrestrial broadcasters but by Sky UK, a subscription satellite service comprised of a portfolio of entertainment, news, and sports channels, three of which, Sky Atlantic, Sky One, and Sky Living (which became the program's UK home) air original and imported drama. Sky Atlantic, which negotiated an exclusive deal for HBO content, has established a distinctive brand as the place for high-end US drama, but Sky One and Sky Living have struggled to construct an individual identity. But just as *Sherlock* contributed to the successful *Masterpiece* rebrand, so did *Elementary* to the successful Sky Living rebrand.

Sky Living initially targeted a female demographic, but in 2013 then director Antonia Hurford-Jones announced that she had decided to "de-pink" the channel, transforming the pink logo and interstitials to a blue and silver palette intended to appeal to men as well as women. Said Hurford-Jones, "We keep being told that women like watching television with their partners. They don't want to sit alone in their pink fluffy bedroom, wearing their pink fluffy negligee, watching shows on their own. It's all about watching with their partners. So shared viewing is extremely important."[71] Prior to the official shared-viewing rebrand symbolized by the switch from pink to blue and silver, Sky Living had already been airing a suite of US procedurals, known to appeal to both sexes. *Broadcast* reported on the strategy's success. "Sky Living's bid to move away from niche programming towards shared viewing of US and homegrown drama is paying dividends." *Elementary* played an important role in encouraging this shared viewing.

> So far this year, twice as many programmes have rated above 300,000 as in 2012, while 16 rated above 800,000, up from just three in the same period last year. Most of these were episodes of US contemporary Sherlock Holmes series *Elementary*, which was launched on Sky Living in October 2012, *Hannibal* and *Criminal Minds*, with a few scattered *Bones*. US dramas such as these have already provided the shared viewing experience for Sky Living and help to explain the increase in share of men. The top programme for 16–34 males this year was *Elementary*.[72]

In 2014, *Broadcast* noted that the US dramas were performing much better than Sky Living's original content. "Shows such as *The Blacklist, Elementary, Criminal Minds* and *Bones* regularly dwarf original commissions with consolidated ratings frequently over 1 million."[73] The following year the magazine reported Sky Living would no longer originate content but would instead consolidate the channel brand around the US dramas. Stuart Murphy, director of Sky entertainment channels, told his staff, "The majority of home-grown shows on Sky Living will move over to [Sky One] from next fiscal, with Sky Living focusing almost exclusively on US dramas going forward."[74]

Catherine Johnson argues that the individual channel authors the experience of watching television. "It does this in a number of ways: through the commissioning and scheduling of programs, through the use of interstitials, logos, and idents, and through promotion and branding. All of these strategies function to create an experience over and above watching an individual program that can be attributed back to the channel itself."[75] Sky Living used acquisitions, scheduling, interstitials, logos, and idents to promote and brand the experience of the shared viewing of US procedurals that, partially by virtue of their cultural accessibility, appeal to both male and female audiences. Like *Sherlock*, *Elementary* contributed significantly to the rebrand of its transatlantic channel, but with an important difference. *Sherlock*'s contribution to the *Masterpiece* rebrand was predicated upon the cultural premium of its textually encoded Britishness. By contrast, *Elementary*'s contribution to the Sky Living rebrand resulted from the channel's paratextual association of the program with culturally accessible US procedurals, not from a cultural premium of textually encoded national identity. In both cases, however, the programs' position on the cultural proximity index, which may be related to their status as high-end or routine television, helps to explain their insertion into their foreign broadcast contexts. As discussed in the brief final section, temporal proximity also explains the ways in which broadcasters manage their imported content.

SHERLOCK, ELEMENTARY, AND THE TEMPORAL PROXIMITY INDEX

A program's position on the temporal proximity index, which is related to its high-end or routine status, contributes to foreign broadcasters' scheduling decisions. Timothy Havens observes that, in addition to cultural discount, "programs typically encounter a 'temporal discount' in windows far removed from their original production date."[76] Just as the concept of cultural discount requires nuancing, so does the concept of temporal discount. In this case I propose a temporal proximity index comprising temporal discount, temporal neutrality, and temporal premium, hypothesizing that high-end television can benefit from temporal premium or suffer from temporal discount, while routine television tends toward temporal neutrality.

Distributors and foreign broadcasters have incentives to circulate high-end television as rapidly as possible in order to discourage piracy and synchronize transmedia storytelling and promotional materials. In 2015, Rebecca Eaton said that illegal downloads of *Sherlock* had impacted PBS's audience share. "It airs in England and they get it before we broadcast it, it's hugely hard on us, because it diminishes our audience, and it's difficult for the future of PBS because they're not PBS members, they're not paying."[77] Illegal downloading may have been diminishing precisely the younger audience segment that Eaton aspired to attract; in contrast to PBS's traditional older-skewing audience, many younger viewers would have the technological knowledge to acquire content illegally. Rapid circulation can also intensify audience engagement, as fans from around the globe congregate on the internet to criticize, engage in forensic analysis, and produce memes, gifs, fan fiction, and other texts; all these activities augment the distributors' and broadcasters' own promotional efforts. Decreasing the window between the domestic and foreign distribution of high-end content fits the viewing habits of the younger audience segment, whose technological skills and fannish inclinations predispose them to both illegal downloading and to participation in global fan forums such as Reddit.

By contrast, delayed distribution results in the nonsynchronization of ancillary texts, the exclusion of fans from the conversation, and the proliferation of spoilers, all of which contribute to a temporal discount. *Sherlock* fan Samantha Suchland complained about "an ambush of Internet spoilers after BBC aired the season two finale of 'Sherlock' in Britain last week. It's baffling that British broadcasters delay the airing of new seasons of shows that are already popular in America. This delay has become a familiar issue for American fans of British television."[78] BBC Worldwide and Masterpiece eventually addressed Suchland's complaint, with simultaneous transatlantic transmission of the one-off special "The Abominable Bride" and of the fourth season. Speaking of the former, *Targeted News Service* said, " 'Bride' breaks interesting new ground for the *Sherlock* series and is a sign of the changing nature of international television. Up until now, episodes of British series like this one or *Downton Abbey* completed their runs in the U.K. before airing in the United States. . . . 'Bride' debuts today in both countries, a television first."[79]

Distributors and foreign broadcasters lack incentives for the rapid circulation of routine television; generally such programs are not subject to piracy and lack both transmedia extensions and the large fan communities that augment promotion. The chief determinant of *Elementary*'s UK broadcast dates has been Sky Living's attempt to deal with the problem of the US midseason hiatus. In the TV1 and TV2 periods, during which television content was predominantly consumed at the time of transmission, US series ran consecutively over a period of months between the autumn and the spring. But among the developments of TV3 was the reconfiguration of the nature of the television season, as technological convergence enabled new viewing practices. As part of this reconfiguration, the US networks have increasingly broken a season into two halves, taking a series off air for an extended break over the Christmas and New Year's holiday season. However, in the United Kingdom the many fewer episodes of a series are aired consecutively over a few weeks. In scheduling *Elementary*, Sky Living was caught between US broadcasting practices and UK viewer expectations. The channel could choose to premiere the new season a few weeks after its US debut and take a midseason break, as it did with the first four series, or delay the new season for months after its US broadcast and not take a break, as it did with the fifth series. I've not been able to find any data on *Elementary*'s season 5 ratings, but clearly Sky Living's programmers had no concerns about the longer delay negatively impacting the program's performance since there is not a large and avid fandom eager to download the program before its airing nor to engage in global forums with fans who have already seen the episodes. This tends to substantiate my hypothesis concerning *Elementary*'s position on the temporal proximity index; the delayed broadcast of a routine program should not impose a temporal discount.

CONCLUSION

The different ways in which their US and UK importers managed *Sherlock* and *Elementary* do provide some initial confirmation of the chapter's fundamental hypothesis concerning the relationship among high-end and routine content and the cultural and temporal proximity indices. *Masterpiece*'s rebrand specifically benefited from the strong textual and paratextual encoding of national identity that gives *Sherlock* its cultural premium among a specific audience segment. By contrast, Sky Living's rebrand was predicated upon *Elementary* and other US procedurals' cultural accessibility to a specific UK audience segment, the shared viewing one. However, *Elementary*'s unique cultural discount in the United Kingdom points to the importance of accounting for the specificities of national markets. Evidence also points to the importance of the temporal proximity index and suggests that high-end content suffers from temporal discount. Delayed distribution results in the nonsynchronization of ancillary texts, the exclusion of fans from the conversation, and the proliferation of spoilers, all of which contribute to a temporal discount among a technologically savvy and fannishly inclined younger audience. By contrast, simultaneous distribution results in a temporal premium; for the broadcasters, it decreases illegal downloading and for the viewers increases their pleasure in engaging in global fan forums. Routine content, however, is temporally neutral since it does not engage viewers to the extent that they employ illegal downloading or participate in global fan forums. As we have seen, *Sherlock*'s scheduling is determined by its temporal premium and *Elementary*'s by its temporal neutrality.

How generalizable are these findings from a mere two case studies? Is national identity always strongly encoded in high-end drama? Does routine television drama always display fewer markers of national identity than its high-end equivalent? Will schedulers increasingly decrease the delay between the domestic and foreign broadcasts of high-end programs? These and other questions need to be posed and answered as television studies comes to grips with the increasing importance and complexity of the international distribution system in which cultural and temporal proximity are such significant determinants of imported content's insertion into the foreign context. As Sherlock Holmes demanded, "Data! Data! Data! I can't make bricks without clay."

ACKNOWLEDGMENTS

My thanks to Gabriel Paletz for a very helpful discussion of the concept of cultural proximity, to Andrea Esser for providing me with a copy of her essay, and to Michele Hilmes for very valuable editorial feedback.

NOTES

1. Richard Beech, "Sherlock Spoilers Are the Same as Football Results—Look Away If You Don't Want to Know the Score," *Mirror Online*, January 13, 2014.
2. John Plunkett and Jason Deans, "Saving BBC3 'Would Have Meant Cutting Funds for Dramas Such as Sherlock,'" *Guardian*, March 7, 2014, http://www.theguardian.com/media/2014/mar/07/saving-bbc3-cutting-funds-dramas-sherlock.
3. David Batty, "Sherlock Enters New Year as Global TV Phenomenon," *Guardian*, December 30, 2015, https://www.theguardian.com/tv-and-radio/2015/dec/30/sherlock-enters-new-year-as-global-tv-phenomenon?CMP=Share_iOSApp_Other.
4. Julia Raeside, "The Return of Sherlock: 'Being a Hero Isn't about Being Bigger, Richer, More Powerful,'" *Guardian*, December 17, 2016, https://www.theguardian.com/tv-and-radio/2016/dec/17/benedict-cumberbatch-sherlock-series-four?CMP=Share_iOSApp_Other.
5. James Rampton, "On the Set of Sherlock—Why Has This Version of Conan Doyle Chimed with Audiences Everywhere?," *The Independent*, December 29, 2016, http://www.independent.co.uk/arts-entertainment/tv/on-the-set-of-sherlock-the-most-popular-drama-in-the-world-why-has-this-version-of-conan-doyle-a7497571.html.
6. *BBC Worldwide Annual Review 2013/14*, 10.
7. "Scripted Sales Soar at BBCW," *Broadcast*, March 3, 2011.
8. Adam Sherwin, "Not Bad for a Small Island That No One Listens To: British TV Exports Hit £1.2bn," *The Independent*, October 7, 2013, http://www.independent.co.uk/arts-entertainment/tv/news/not-bad-for-a-small-island-that-no-one-listens-to-british-tv-exports-hit-12bn-8864779.html.
9. Department for Digital, Culture, Media & Sport, "Strong DVD Market Boosts UK TV Export Revenues," May 2005.
10. Nellie Adreeva, "Elementary Creator Rob Doherty Inks New Overall Deal with CBS TV Studios," *Deadline Hollywood*, June 10, 2016, http://deadline.com/2016/06/elementary-creator-rob-doherty-inks-overall-deal-cbs-tv-studios-1201770308/.
11. Brian Lowry, "Ratings No Longer Tell Whole Story in TV Show Survival Odds," CNN Media, September 13, 2016, http://money.cnn.com/2016/09/13/media/tv-ratings-new-season/index.html?linkId=28798709.
12. TBI reporter, "Drama Data: Europe Challenges the US," *Television Business International*, April 21 2014, http://tbivision.com/news/2014/04/drama-data-europe-challenges-the-us/262962/.
13. CBS Corporation, "CBS Studios International," https://www.cbscorporation.com/portfolio/cbs-studios-international/.

14. Steve Clarke, "Global Mystery," *Variety*, October 5–11, 2009.

15. Neil Midgley, "*Sherlock, Downton Abbey*: What the US Can Learn from Our TV Exports," *The Guardian*, August 31, 2014. http://www.theguardian.com/media/media-blog/2014/aug/31/sherlock-downton-call-midwife-television-drama-america.

16. See, for example, Leo Barraclough, "Film Companies Fight to Get a Piece of Drama Action," *Variety*, April 3, 2017, http://variety.com/2017/tv/spotlight/film-companies-tv-drama-babylon-berlin-top-of-the-lake-1202019915/.

17. Audun Engelstad, "Sensation in Serial Form: High-End Television Drama and Trigger Plots," *Kosmorama* #263 (2016) (www.kosmorama.org). See also Trisha Dunleavy, *Television Drama: Form, Agency, Innovation* (Basingstoke: Palgrave-Macmillan, 2009) and Robin Nelson, *State of Play: Contemporary "High-End" TV Drama* (Manchester: Manchester University Press, 2007).

18. Kristina Busse and Louisa Stein, eds., *"Sherlock" and Transmedia Fandom: Essays on the BBC Series* (Jefferson, NC: McFarland, 2012).

19. Tom Steward, "Holmes in the Small Screen: The Television Contexts of *Sherlock*," in Busse and Stein, *Sherlock and Transmedia Fandom*, 137, 135.

20. Steward, "Holmes," 136.

21. Steward, "Holmes," 137–138.

22. Steward, "Holmes," 138.

23. Steward, "Holmes," 143.

24. Steward, "Holmes," 144, 145.

25. Elizabeth Evans, "Shaping Sherlocks: Institutional Practice and the Adaptation of Character," in Busse and Stein, *Sherlock and Transmedia Fandom*, 112, 114–115.

26. Evans, "Shaping Sherlocks," 115.

27. Michele Hilmes, "Transnational TV: What Do We Mean by 'Coproduction' Anymore?," *Media Industries Journal* 1:2 (2014): 11.

28. James Chessell, "Streaming Brings BBC 'Golden Age,'" *Australian Financial Review*, March 14, 2016, 31.

29. Notfamousanymore, comment on Stuart Heritage, "Sick of Sherlock? *Elementary* Has All the Holmes Comforts You Need," *The Guardian*, January 14, 2017, https://www.theguardian.com/tv-and-radio/2017/jan/14/elementary-jonny-lee-miller.

30. Steven Zeitchik, "Fall TV Preview: The Sherlock Holmes of 'Elementary' Is on the Trail of a New Idea," *Los Angeles Times*, September 8, 2012, http://www.latimes.com/entertainment/tv/showtracker/la-et-st-fall-tv-preview-elementary-20120909,0,5190834.story.

31. Alan Sepinwall, "Review: 'Elementary' Makes Sherlock Holmes a Part of the CBS Brand," *Hitfix*, September 26, 2012, http://www.hitfix.com/whats-alan-watching/review-elementary-makes-sherlock-holmes-a-part-of-the-cbs-brand.

32. Andy Lewis, "Fall TV Pilot Preview: CBS' 'Elementary,'" *Hollywood Reporter*, July 10, 2012, http://www.hollywoodreporter.com/live-feed/elementary-cbs-pilot-preview-lucy-liu-jonny-lee-miller-347179.

33. Allison Nichols, "New Fall TV Drama: CBS's 'Elementary,'" September 4, 2012, *AXS Entertainment*, http://www.examiner.com/article/new-fall-tv-drama-cbs-s-elementary.

34. Chessell, "Streaming."

35. Andrea Esser, "Defining 'the Local' in Localization or 'Adapting for Whom?,'" in *Media across Borders: Localising TV, Film and Video Games*, ed. Andrea Esser, Iain Robert Smith, and Miguel A. Bernal-Merino, eds. (London: Routledge, 2016), 30.

36. CBS Studios International, CBSSI 2012 LA Screenings, https://www.surveymonkey.com/r/CBSSIScreenings2012?sm=fjjjPJ7Cof0IAC09UjX2cTbyATgJDAYH1cjyaNwThAs%3d.

37. Joseph Straubhaar "Choosing National TV: Cultural Capital, Language, and Cultural Proximity in Brazil," in *The Impact of International Television: A Paradigm Shift*, ed. Michael G. Elanmar (New York: Routledge 2003), 78.

38. Stuart McFadyen, Colin Hoskins, and Adam Finn, "Measuring the Cultural Discount in the Price of Exported U.S. Television Programs," in *Economics of Art and Culture: Invited Papers at the 12th*

International Conference of the Association of Cultural Economics International, ed. Victor A. Ginsburgh (Bingley: Emerald Publishing Group, March 2015), 50.

39. "Can Holmes Solve Co-prod Mystery?" *Variety,* October 1, 2009, http://variety.com/2009/film/news/can-holmes-solve-co-prod-mystery-1118009441/.

40. For more on the Holmes character's adaptation to different texts, see Evans, "Shaping Sherlocks," and Stephanie Sommerfield, "Guy Ritchie's Sherlock Bond: The Deerstalker and Remediation," in *Film Remakes, Adaptations and Fan Productions,* ed. Kathleen Loock and Constantine Verevis (Basingstoke: Palgrave Macmillan, 2012), 45–66.

41. *Guardian* video, "Steven Moffat: *Sherlock* and *Doctor Who* Are Successful in the US Because They Are Quintessentially British," *The Guardian,* June 20, 2014, http://www.theguardian.com/media/video/2014/jun/20/steven-moffat-sherlock-doctor-who-cannes-lions-video.

42. Adam Miller, "Steven Moffat Does NOT Want to See Any Foreign Remakes of 'Definitively British' *Doctor Who* or *Sherlock,*" *Entertainmentwise,* February 27, 2014, http://www.entertainmentwise.com/news/142148/Steven-Moffat-Does-NOT-Want-To-See-Any-Foreign-Remakes-Of-Definitively-British-Doctor-Who-Or-Sherlock.

43. See, for example, Andrew Higson, *English Heritage, English Cinema: Costume Drama since 1980* (New York: Oxford University Press, 2003).

44. Barbara Selznick, *Global Television: Co-producing Culture* (Philadelphia: Temple University Press, 2008), 77, 84.

45. Matt Hills, "*Sherlock's* Epistemological Economy and the Value of 'Fan' Knowledge: How Producer-Fans Play the (Great) Game of Fandom," in Busse and Louisa Stein, *Sherlock and Transmedia Fandom,* 27–40.

46. *Guardian* video, "Steven Moffat."

47. Selznick, *Global Television,* 82.

48. Selznick, *Global Television,* 84.

49. Jeanette Steemers, "International Sales of U.K. Television Content: Change and Continuity in 'the Space in between' Production and Consumption," *Television and New Media* 17:8 (2016): 748.

50. Josie Ensor, "How America Fell in Love with British TV," *Telegraph,* July 19, 2014, http://www.telegraph.co.uk/news/worldnews/northamerica/usa/10978139/How-America-fell-in-love-with-British-TV.html.

51. Dylan Morris, "Britain as Fantasy: New Series *Doctor Who* in Young American Nerd Culture," in *Fan Phenomena: "Doctor Who",* ed. Paul Booth (Bristol: Intellect, 2013), 51.

52. Simone Knox, "*Masterpiece Theatre* and British Drama Imports on US Television: Discourses of Tension," *Critical Studies in Television* 7:1 (2012): 33.

53. "Love of Literature, England Come Together in Ideal Job; Eaton Attracts New Viewers to PBS' *Masterpiece,*" *Broadcasting and Cable,* December 17, 2012.

54. Knox, "*Masterpiece Theatre,*" 38.

55. Michael Rosser, "Sherlock Smashes Ratings Record in US," *Broadcast,* November 17, 2010, http://www.broadcastnow.co.uk/sherlock-smashes-ratings-record-in-us/5020635.article; PBS press release, "Sundays on PBS Remain TV's Top Destination for Drama," March 26, 2014,http://www.pbs.org/about/news/archive/2014/downton-sherlock-national-ratings/.

56. "Sundays on PBS Remain TV's Top Destination for Drama; Ratings for 'Downton Abbey' and 'Sherlock' on MASTERPIECE up from Previous Seasons," *Business Wire,* March 26, 2014.

57. Martha Shanahan, "PBS Producer Gives an Inside Look at 'Masterpiece,'" *Keene Sentinel,* July 26, 2015.

58. Maggie Brown, "Rebecca Eaton: Masterpiece Is the 'Little Black Dress of British Drama,'" *The Guardian,* March 1, 2015, https://www.theguardian.com/media/2015/mar/01/dowton-abbey-sherlock-rebecca-eaton-masterpiece.

59. John Sinclair says that a "geolinguistic region is one united more by a common language than by geographical contiguity, and reflects very much the enduring influence of colonialism in the spread of languages around the world. Thus, Britain, Spain, Portugal and France each form a geolinguistic region with their respective former colonies." John Sinclair, "The De-centring of Cultural Flows, Audiences and their Access to Television," *Critical Studies in Television* 4.1 (2009): 28.

60. McFadyen, Hoskins and Finn, "Measuring the Cultural Discount," 50.

61. Phelim O'Neill, "*Elementary*—Box Set Review," *The Guardian*, January 17, 2014, https://www.theguardian.com/tv-and-radio/2014/jan/17/elementary-box-set-review.

62. Caitlin Moran, "A US Holmes Feels a Little Rude. Was Ours Not Good Enough?," *The Times*, October 27, 2012, https://www.thetimes.co.uk/article/caitlin-moran-on-tv-a-us-holmes-feels-rude-was-ours-not-good-enough-dzxjv7gq52r.

63. "Elementary Saw Jonny Lee Miller Score as an Oddly Boyish Brainbox," *Metro*, October 23, 2012, http://metro.co.uk/2012/10/23/elementary-series-1-episode-1-tv-review-606682/.

64. Andrew Billen, "Last Night's TV: *Elementary*," *The Times*, October 24, 2012, https://www.thetimes.co.uk/article/last-nights-tv-elementary-k9jzznnqlwn

65. Sam Wollaston, "TV Review: *Elementary*; George Clarke's Amazing Spaces; Tool Academy," *The Guardian*, October 23, 2012, https://www.theguardian.com/tv-and-radio/2012/oct/23/elementary-tool-academy-tv-review.

66. Wollaston, "TV Review."

67. TBI reporter, "Drama Data: Europe Challenges the US," *Television Business International*, April 21, 2014.

68. Scott Roxborough, "7 Hot Shows at MIPCOM," *Hollywood Reporter*, September 25, 2012, http://www.hollywoodreporter.com/news/7-hot-shows-at-mipcom-373899.

69. Nellie Andreeva, "Ghost of 2004 Hovers over L.A. Screenings as Int'l Buyers Lament Lack of Breakouts,|" *Deadline Hollywood*, May 24, 2012, http://deadline.com/2012/05/ghost-of-2004-hovers-over-l-a-screenings-as-intl-buyers-lament-lack-of-breakouts-277305/.

70. "Those Economic Storms Are Not Sinking Sales; Despite Eurozone Crisis, Streaming Video Services among Factors Buoying Studios," *Broadcasting and Cable*, September 24, 2012, 37.

71. Josh Halliday, "Sky Living Director: 'I Am De-pinking the Channel,'" *The Guardian*, August 24, 2013, https://www.theguardian.com/media/2013/aug/24/sky-living-channel-rebrand.

72. "Sky Living: Ratings Analysis," *Broadcast*, October 10, 2013.

73. "Antonia Hurford-Jones, Sky Living," *Broadcast*, September 11, 2014.

74. "Hurford Jones Exits as Sky Living Halts Originations," *Broadcast*, April 10, 2015.

75. Catherine Johnson, "The Authorial Function of the Television Channel: Augmentation and Identity," in *A Companion to Media Authorship*, ed. Jonathan Gray and Derek Johnson (Malden: Wiley-Blackwell, 2013), 275.

76. Timothy Havens, *Global Television Marketplace* (London: BFI Publishing, 2006), 15.

77. Shanahan, "PBS Producer."

78. Samantha Suchland, "TV Airing Delays from UK to US Make for a Baffling Case," *Daily Bruin*, January 24, 2012, 1.

79. "PBS Announces Mid-season Schedule," *Targeted News Service*, December 1, 2016.

6

MAINSTREAM TRENDS AND MASTERPIECE TRADITIONS

ITV's *Downton Abbey* as a Hit Heritage Drama for *Masterpiece* in the United States

EVA N. REDVALL

Britain has a long tradition of exporting costume, or heritage, drama to the rest of the world. The most successful recent example is *Downton Abbey* (2010–2015), produced by the NBC-owned but UK-based company Carnival Films for the British network ITV, with the Boston-based American PBS station WGBH and its *Masterpiece* series as coproducer in the United States.[1] This chapter explores the successful meeting of "mainstream trends" and "masterpiece traditions" in the commissioning and production of *Downton Abbey*, and the way in which its production marks a significant transatlantic encounter between different broadcasting cultures and storytelling traditions.

Downton Abbey has been analyzed as "post-heritage drama,"[2] or as a reinvention of the British costume drama through playing with the "quality components" of heritage drama.[3] *Downton*'s producer, Gareth Neame, has said that he is always looking for unique ideas in terms of "something we can do that the United States cannot."[4] This chapter argues that the series' production story illuminates the creation of "post-heritage drama" as a genre as well as revealing key aspects of the success of *Downton Abbey* around the world. *Downton*'s creators crafted a long-form narrative that tapped into the UK tradition of heritage drama and its European "auteur" sensibility, while drawing on the speed and storytelling style of

US television series to give the past a contemporary feel. It also represents an intriguing matchup between a commercial UK broadcaster and a US public broadcaster that were not looking for period drama content at the time of commissioning, but decided to take a chance on the material anyway. Drawing on recent research exploring the special relationship and mutual influence between the United Kingdom and the United States in television drama production,[5] the chapter analyzes *Downton Abbey* as a successful attempt to incorporate current US television trends into UK historical drama traditions. It closes with a discussion of the program's popularity in the United Kingdom, the United States, and beyond.

HERITAGE DRAMA AS A TRANSATLANTIC EXPORT

Whereas most European countries have produced few historical drama series with a wider transnational appeal, Britain has a long tradition of exporting costume drama—or what scholars such as Andrew Higson have discussed as heritage drama—to the rest of the world.[6] As an example, in Denmark between 2005 and 2014, UK historical drama productions represented 53 percent of all historical drama broadcast (based on first broadcast, not reruns). This was three times more than historical drama from the United States (16 percent), while historical drama from the neighboring Nordic countries took up only 8 percent and the rest of Europe 18 percent.[7] With legendary titles such as *The Forsyte Saga* (1967) and *Upstairs, Downstairs* (1971–1975), UK historical dramas have been traveling widely for many years, and mainstream European audiences have thus been brought up to have a taste for UK stories of the past.

In the United States, UK heritage productions have found a niche audience as part of the *Masterpiece* (formerly *Masterpiece Theatre*) anthology series that has been produced by WGBH Boston for PBS since 1971.[8] The series is America's longest running weekly prime-time slot for drama, whose content includes a great number of shows produced in the United Kingdom. As discussed by Simone Knox in her work on discourses of tension between *Masterpiece Theatre* and British drama imports on US screens, *Masterpiece* has always had a strong stamp of what she calls "British culturedness."[9] However, Knox argues that one should also understand *Masterpiece* in relation to US quality television drama traditions in the way that it started as an anthology television drama sponsored by a major corporation.[10]

As pointed out by television scholar Elke Weissmann, the PBS network lacks the funds to produce expensive television dramas of its own, and thus "*Masterpiece Theatre* can be understood as a transnational reaction to national challenges" in the way that its producers looked to UK productions when wanting to offer a certain kind of content to US audiences that they were unable to finance by themselves.[11] Its coproduced series were framed as quality television through such mechanisms as on-air hosts (most notably, British-born Alistair Cooke) who introduced the programs, emphasizing their historical relevance and educational value or their literary sources.[12]

Among US audiences, *Masterpiece* is generally perceived as representing quality TV. Terrence O'Flaherty's illustrated history of *Masterpiece* makes the case that *Masterpiece* has provided American audiences with "classic stories and classy performances" and should be regarded as an "enduring oasis of sophisticated substance and style" that "has set the standard for literate, quality television."[13] In an article about the complicated relations between television programs and corporate sponsorships, Laurence Jarvik defines *Masterpiece* as "a much-loved staple of élite television in America."[14] He argues that Mobil sponsored *Masterpiece* during its formative decades to add luster to the company brand, since association with the "cultural excellence" of the programming would establish the company as an example of "corporate excellence."[15]

There has been an established collaboration between the BBC and its much less dominant US counterpart for many years, with most of the heritage dramas on *Masterpiece* coming from the BBC. In the 1970s, the BBC and WGBH set up a long-term deal that ensured that the former "had a regular presence in a small but culturally important niche of the US broadcasting landscape."[16] Weissmann argues that in a time of general decline for UK dramas on US screens, the deal was important in terms of "facilitating and continuing discourses about the BBC and the UK more generally as a provider of quality content which it could later build on when UK producers developed more aggressive export strategies."[17]

In 2010, what was described as a "co-production partnership" between PBS and BBC was renewed with the announcement that *Masterpiece* would mark its fortieth anniversary by becoming involved in the BBC's new production of *Upstairs, Downstairs* (2010–2012), as well as *Sherlock* (2010–) and three Aurelio Zen mysteries.[18] At the time, *Masterpiece* executive producer Rebecca Eaton described these three series as "everything about what 'Masterpiece' aims to be: iconic, rich with wonderful actors, witty, literate, and timeless."[19] At the beginning of the 2010s, the historically robust transatlantic collaboration between *Masterpiece* and the BBC was moving steadily forward, but the greatest success of *Masterpiece* in the 2010s turned out to be *Downton Abbey*, coproduced with the commercial UK broadcaster ITV.

This chapter explores how this specific collaboration came about by tracing the series' production story based on trade press sources, paratexts, and qualitative interviews, as well as Rebecca Eaton's 2015 memoire *Making "Masterpiece"*.[20] To a large extent, this production study is based on texts that pose the danger of being marked by a retrospective justification of career choices or by "corporate scripts."[21] Similarly, the qualitative interviews with what can be understood as "exclusive informants" present methodological challenges in the way that such informants are inclined to present their past professional decisions in a favorable way.[22] Nonetheless, the valuable behind the scenes information that these sources offer is essential in production story research, particularly in terms of highlighting the importance of individual agency, personal tastes, and specific institutional outlooks at specific points in time to our understanding of the dynamics of particular transatlantic encounters.

COMMISSIONING AND COPRODUCTION: MAINSTREAM TV MEETS *MASTERPIECE*

The idea for *Downton Abbey* came from UK producer Gareth Neame at Carnival Films. Neame wanted to see writer Julian Fellowes return to the territory of his Academy Award–winning feature film *Gosford Park* (2001), but in a multiepisode television form with time to develop an ensemble story week after week. As mentioned above, Neame placed a high priority on ideas that are unique in doing something that UK creative industries can and that US industries cannot.[23] As examples, Neame highlights spy stories as a distinct British genre because of the James Bond films and Graham Greene's novels, along with the "country house" genre, which includes both Agatha Christie's whodunnits and Jane Austen's novels: "These houses are great big statements that don't really exist anywhere else in the world. And stories set in them travel very well; people find it a fascinating world. So I suppose I'd always thought it was a territory to go into."[24]

Neame's deliberate intention was to create a country house story with a distinct British profile and an international potential. Based on Fellowes's previous work, Neame thought that he was the right man for the job. Fellowes was attracted to the idea but worried about revisiting material that mirrored *Gosford Park*. However, he decided that he did want to write a long-form television story centered on a country house in the Edwardian era. A couple of months after Neame pitched the idea, Fellowes proposed the basic structure of the series with the main characters and the central overall conflict concerning the lack of a male heir.[25]

While *Masterpiece* has a long tradition of first acquisitioning BBC productions and later also coproducing a selection of these, there have also been transatlantic collaborations with other UK broadcasters over the years. Conceiving of the United Kingdom and the United States as "networked nations," Michele Hilmes has written about the long-standing relationship between the two countries in the field of television. Hilmes argues that this relationship has been deeply productive "providing a constant circuit of influence and adaptation that, while often resisted or even reviled, nonetheless worked powerfully to enliven and expand the cultural horizon of both nations."[26] Traditionally, this US-UK axis represents two different television cultures, with the US model as the world's primary commercial, market-driven system and the British model epitomizing the characteristics of European public service broadcasting. However, in the production of *Downton*, these roles were reversed. The series was commissioned by the UK broadcaster ITV, the oldest and biggest commercial broadcaster in Britain (still subject to certain public service obligations even though it is sustained by advertising). Although NBC-Universal owns Carnival Films, it passed on coproducing the series, as did HBO and all other commercial US networks, according to Rebecca Eaton.[27]

Neame went to ITV as part of his strategy to "reactivate a brand-new audience for this kind of show."[28] Following the success of the show, Neame has argued that *Downton* might not have been as groundbreaking had the BBC aired it; appearing on ITV garnered the series special attention. Furthermore, on the BBC *Downton* would have competed with a new version of *Upstairs, Downstairs*, a program also centered around an aristocratic house, albeit not a country one. According to my interview with ITV commissioner at the time, Laura Mackie, ITV was originally not the least interested in a period piece when Neame and Fellowes took the idea for *Downton* to her and to Sally Haynes at ITV, where it ended up moving into production in 2009. ITV was under pressure since the recession had led to an advertising downturn. According to Mackie, ITV had tried to target younger audiences, but the series designed for these audiences failed to find the desired success.[29] However, even if ITV did not envision a costume drama as the obvious choice of content at the time, Mackie and Haynes found *Downton* to be a strong project and provided what Neame has described as "enthusiastic backing" from ITV.[30]

Masterpiece's Rebecca Eaton argues that ITV took a significant risk in commissioning *Downton* in that it moved into the period drama domain normally dominated by the BBC.[31] However, one can argue that ITV also has a strong tradition of certain kinds of period drama, having produced popular historical fare such as *Upstairs, Downstairs*, and the 2000s saw the production of more upscale ITV period drama such as the Jane Austen TV movie adaptations *Mansfield Park* (2007) and *Northanger Abbey* (2007). The statements by Neame and Eaton on the special positioning of *Downton* at ITV versus BBC point to certain notions of these broadcasters' particular brands and how a new period drama would fit the profile of each.

Scholars such as Catherine Johnson have emphasized how branding—of broadcasters as well as channels and specific programs—has become still more important in a digital television landscape marked by abundance and fierce competition.[32] While *Downton* is of course a period drama, it is simultaneously a clear example of what Ross Garner has discussed as "flagship programming" in his analysis of ITV's 2013 rebranding.[33] Both original series and drama imports are an important part of building a "quality" brand, and production and commissioning considerations around new series will always address questions about how certain kinds of programming fit the identity and intended audience of a particular broadcaster. In the case of *Downton*, ITV got involved despite the initial sense that period drama was not the best content for appealing to younger demographics, and the series is now a cornerstone of the broadcaster's brand.

In the United States, Eaton originally turned down *Downton* for *Masterpiece*, since "it didn't look like something we needed."[34] Moreover, after what she describes as years of "vigorous attempts" to resurrect *Upstairs, Downstairs*—a huge hit for *Masterpiece* in its time—the decision to coproduce the new version with the BBC was a "no-brainer."[35] Her statement underlines the importance of network histories and the always essential issue of the timing of new coproduction proposals.

Given that *Masterpiece* had previously coproduced *The Buccaneers* (1995)—a series about American heiresses marrying British aristocracy—and was about to coproduce the new *Upstairs, Downstairs, Downton* seemed surplus to *Masterpiece*'s requirements. But Eaton eventually changed her mind, due both to the casting of Maggie Smith in one of the main roles and to personal connections, such as the actress Elizabeth McGovern (who was cast as Cora Crawley, Countess of Grantham), being enthusiastic about the project and recommending that she rethink her position.[36] In her writings on *Masterpiece*, Weissmann has argued that one should not underestimate the "transnational work experience" of specific producers and commissioners, such as Rebecca Eaton, in our understanding of specific programming strategies.[37] Transnational work experiences and networks are important in a "nobody knows" industry based on a large degree of trust, and in the case of *Downton* personal connections seem to have been influential in terms of Eaton's reassessment of the new series' potential. Eaton has had no reason to regret her decision to coproduce *Downton*, since the show went on to become the top PBS drama of all time, with the numbers peaking at a weekly average audience of 13.3 million viewers in season 4.[38]

According to television scholar Jeanette Steemers, *Downton* is a good example of the current challenges in the production of expensive dramas where the fragmentation of audiences and revenues calls for "more company consolidation and international coproduction to support the high costs of origination."[39] It is, however, notable that this transatlantic coproduction ended up not being with the US owner of Carnival, but with the PBS broadcaster and its *Masterpiece* series and not with the BBC but with ITV. Mackie argues that ITV always focuses primarily on the national audience, but will exploit the international appeal of certain programs.[40] In the press material for *Downton*,

Neame too insists that the domestic market has always been the priority.[41] However, as shown in his statements about deliberately focusing on a country house story, *Downton* was always conceived as having an international appeal, and Neame made great efforts to find an American coproduction partner to finance the expensive series with a budget of around £1 million per episode.

Once the coproduction decision had been made, the collaboration was quick and unproblematic, with the US partner not exerting much control over decision-making. According to Eaton, her role as a coproducer is to inject money at the outset and then give the series the best and biggest possible exposure in the United States when it airs. She has described her perception of coproducing with the United Kingdom as trying to give her collaborators' creativity free rein:

> My strong feeling about our British co-productions is that we're in business with some
> of the best drama producers in the world, and what they need most is to be left alone
> to do their work. Plenty of British network executives are watching them nervously,
> people who have an even bigger stake in the project, at least financially, than we do;
> and except for a few key casting, script, and editing moments, the last thing these
> producers need is noise from an executive who is three thousand miles from the set.[42]

Eaton's statement indicates her belief that her UK collaborators will deliver a product that works both for the *Masterpiece* and for the ITV audiences; she feels no need to have oversight of every decision made on the UK side. The production of the first season of *Downton* did seem to go rather smoothly. The series went swiftly from shooting in March 2010 to airing on ITV in September—ahead of the *Upstairs, Downstairs* competition in December. The series attracted large audiences from the very first episode, which had 11.6 million viewers on ITV, a 32 percent audience share. The commissioning process shows how Carnival Film successfully convinced two very different broadcasters originally looking for different material to come on board in what turned out to be a productive meeting between a mainstream commercial UK broadcaster and a US public service platform for "*Masterpiece* content."

GENRE AND AUTHORSHIP: HERITAGE SETTING
AND MAINSTREAM STORYTELLING

Downton represents a meeting between the heritage tradition of the British country house genre and the producers' desire to create a series with a more modern look. Neame has described the original idea as focused on having "the traditional setting of the Edwardian country house but the density of stories and pace of narrative that is more familiar in a contemporary series."[43] He sees this blend of influences as crucial to *Downton*'s success, which is predicated upon "a much-loved, familiar and expressly British genre, that of the English country house" reconfigured by the pace, energy, and accessibility of contemporary shows.[44] Mackie claims that producers envisioned the show in some respects as closer to a series like *The West Wing* (1999–2006) than to previous historical dramas.[45] Eaton has argued that both in Britain and in the United States *Downton* "rejuvenated the genre that has been *Masterpiece*'s meat and drink for forty years: high-end period drama."[46]

The country house setting can be compared to US workplace dramas, such as the "cop and doc shows" or *The West Wing*, that bring together many different characters in the same space but within the confines of social and professional hierarchies. *Downton* has around twenty main characters whose stories intertwine. *Upstairs, Downstairs* has often been compared to *Downton*, and Fellowes has explained how he was inspired by what he has called "the philosophical spirit" of *Upstairs, Downstairs*, but not by its narrative structure. When developing the series, he thought along the lines of what he describes as American storytelling structures, referring to series such as *E.R.* (1994–2009), *Chicago Hope* (1994–2000), and *thirtysomething* (1987–1991) as sources of inspiration.[47] In his opinion, many UK series are too slow, and the scripts for *Downton* were mandated to exceed normal script length, so that the action had to be squeezed into the running time, in order to create pace and energy.[48] Besides the pacing, the intention was to create a new look for the genre by going for a "rich feel" with really bold colors, which is not typical of costume dramas.[49]

Another thing that sets the series apart is its approach to the period genre. While most period drama can be categorized in the "high-end drama" territory, there are many competing notions of how to understand *Downton* in terms of genre. Mackie referred to the series as a "period saga."[50] Neame has argued that *Downton* is "unmistakably a drama series, but thanks to the wit of our screenwriter, directors and actors it is also at times extremely funny. You wouldn't describe the show as a comedy, yet humour is so much at the heart of it."[51] Fellowes agrees that there is more humor in the series than in most historical drama, but argues that they go for "chuckles" rather than the big laughs.[52]

While comedy is relatively unusual in a period drama, commentators have focused on the series' relationship to soap opera. Katherine Byrne has called the series a "soap-opera-style makeover of period drama."[53] Byrne and Charles Doyle define *Downton* as a series with soap-like plotting, but also note that it was "an important attempt to write the working classes back into history" that reminds audiences that "history can be about, and for, ordinary people too."[54] They argue that the series succeeded in "immersing us into history by entertaining us and making the past seem very close, very familiar and rather comforting."[55] *Downton* is a type of history that sets out to be "less intellectually demanding, and watchable and accessible to all."[56] This contrasts with other historical series such as *Parade's End* (2012–2013) that turn history into art and "problematise questions surrounding the representation of the past."[57] Acknowledging the soap elements of the series, other media scholars such as Ib Bondebjerg have argued that even if *Downton* can be characterized as "heritage soap," it is "much more than just a nostalgic look into a past world."[58]

The transatlantic producers do not reject *Downton*'s association with the traditionally less prestigious soap opera genre. As Neame states:

> If a soap is defined as a weekly drama with an ensemble of characters cohabiting in a specific environment with their myriad personal stories intertwined, then, dramatically speaking, *Downton* is a soap. I would suggest it is a soap of cinematic production values and the finest writing and acting, but a soap nonetheless.[59]

Eaton speaks of *Downton* as a "high-end soap opera" with a big cast whose lives are "tossed and turned weekly by dramatic life events."[60] She acknowledges that escapism is central to the show's appeal. But contrary to commentators who have linked this escapism to the recession and the longing for a stable society in which people knew their place, she stresses that the series appeals to the audience by telling stories about a community and people trying to do the right thing in difficult times. She believes that the series has morality at its core and that audiences have responded to warm-hearted material marked by a sense of "goodness" lacking in many contemporary series such as *Breaking Bad* (2008–2013), *Mad Men* (2007–2013), and *House of Cards* (2013–).[61] This "good-hearted" approach links *Downton* to mainstream fare that holds out the hope of happy endings. Byrne notes that *Downton* is "bookended with disasters," but also points to the series' insistence that "there is no tragedy that cannot be overcome with togetherness, loyalty and love. As a metaphor for contemporary Britain beset with economic and social difficulties, *Downton* acts as an idealised vehicle of reassurance for its audience."[62]

As these statements indicate, *Downton* can be regarded as a meeting between the high-end British historical drama genre, the pace of contemporary mainstream US drama series, and the ensemble storytelling structures and recognizable personal dramas familiar from popular ITV soaps such as *Coronation Street* (1960–) and *Emmerdale* (1972–). Historically, *Masterpiece* has aimed at an association with discourses of high art and deliberately excluded anything that too much resembled "afternoon soaps." Weissmann argues that for many years "conventions of melodrama and high emotion were perceived as not suitable for *Masterpiece Theatre* since the quality discourses around the anthology series meant that the generic term soap was used primarily as an evaluative term that stands for the lowbrow and bad."[63] *Downton* seems to have made soap elements acceptable to *Masterpiece* while its successful mix of mainstream and masterpiece traditions proved to work well for both UK and US audiences as well as in many other countries.

Important to this mix was the strong authorial voice of Julian Fellowes, both in the production process and in the promotional surround. Unlike most historical dramas adapted from classic novels, *Downton* was based on original screenplays by an acclaimed screenwriter. This associated the series with the single-auteur art house cinema rather than with the multiple authorship of the television writers' rooms that create most long-form US shows or soap operas. According to Mackie, the production experimented with additional writers during the first season but found that this did not work very well and reverted to having Fellowes write all the episodes.[64] Publicity clearly identified Fellowes as the author and showrunner of the series. While there is currently much talk about the virtues of collaboration and writers' rooms for European drama series, *Downton* is thus an example of a series created and penned by one writer who was also presented as its only maker to audiences.[65]

Fellowes has argued that *Downton*'s success comes from treating every character in terms of his or her narrative strength.[66] Neame identifies a major component of the series popularity as Fellowes's "extraordinary ability to write romance, hatred, rivalry, love, jealousy, laugh-out-comedy humour and tragedy."[67] Eaton calls Fellowes's writing style "commercial," saying that he manages to capture the particular world of the unique setting while writing what she calls "the most brilliant soap opera."[68] However, both journalists and academics have questioned *Downton*'s portrayal of the upstairs-downstairs characters and its approach to themes of class and conservatism.[69] This is due in part to Fellowes's status as a public figure in Britain who is not only a prolific writer but also sits as a Conservative member in the House of Lords. Fellowes happily acknowledges that he is "fascinated by the shaping effect of the random selection of class, and how, even today, it has a lasting influence on our aspirations and prospects" and has engaged in several debates over these topics. [70] This has generated serious discussions about *Downton*'s content and helped position it as the personal work of one "master" that should be taken seriously despite the fact that the series' mainstream appeal targets broader audiences than most classical historical dramas.

DOWNTON ABBEY AS A TRANSATLANTIC HERITAGE HIT

Downton has undeniably been a huge success. The program was originally commissioned as a one-off miniseries but turned into a six-season juggernaut that attracted large global

audiences. In the United Kingdom, it realized ITV's dream of a huge hit; the final episode established a record-setting highest gain in delayed viewership in British television
history, adding an extra 4 million viewers to achieve a final viewership of 10.9 million.[71]
In the United States, *Downton* was "a game changer" in stimulating interest in *Masterpiece*
and in PBS and in helping to ensure new sponsors.[72] *Downton* also set social media records
for PBS. When the series ended, *Forbes* magazine ran a feature celebrating the "cash cow
and critical darling for the public service broadcaster" that had not only revitalized PBS in
the United States but also found an estimated global audience of 120 million through sale
to over 220 countries.[73] Both UK and US broadcasters stress the series' ability to attract
the younger viewers who are not traditionally the core audience for historical drama but
whom both ITV and Masterpiece would like to see represented in their audience demographics. For ITV, younger viewers are important for securing advertising revenues, and
for PBS they are the donors of the future (indeed, contributions are PBS's single largest
source of funding).[74]

Hilmes has argued that the "transnational creative space" created by long-standing
US-UK collaboration in television drama has called into being

> a transnational public, not only composed of US and British audiences but assembling
> others from across the globe, whose members arguably have as much as or more in
> common with each other in terms of cultural affinities and shared affective experi-
> ence, across national boundaries, than they have with other audiences in their home
> countries.[75]

Downton's global success indicates that many different kinds of audiences have embraced
the series' approach to portraying the past. For example, *Downton* did very well on the
main Danish public service channel DR 1 in the Sunday night slot usually devoted to
domestic drama.[76] British series generally do well on Danish public service television,
but they don't normally appeal to younger audiences. However, series such as *Downton*
and *Sherlock* have attracted members of this crucial demographic, thereby persuading
the competing public service broadcaster, TV 2, to invest in more British drama at the
same time that it will no longer air US series in prime time because of their disappointing
performance. The head of acquisitions at TV 2, Ander Leifer, highlighted the success
of *Downton* as important to the new strategy of focusing more on UK than US series.[77]
While *Downton* has thus been a transatlantic success for its UK and US broadcasters, it
has also been a global hit and has had an impact on the perception of UK series and their
audience potential in smaller broadcasting nations.

CONCLUSIONS AND CLIFFHANGERS

This chapter has focused on how to understand *Downton Abbey* as a successful meeting between what can be regarded as mainstream elements and masterpiece traditions in a particular transatlantic coproduction. The series worked very well for its UK commercial broadcaster ITV as well as for its US PBS coproducer and has also found wide international success. The chapter argues that the series' production story points to some of the possible explanations behind *Downton*'s remarkable success. It was designed as a specifically UK country house story that built upon the traditional heritage dramas that have proven international appeal. However, it added storytelling traditions from contemporary US series, together with the comedy and soap opera not usually regarded as appropriate in the serious high-end UK quality drama that *Masterpiece* usually broadcasts. It also benefited from the strong authorial voice provided by Julian Fellowes. The analysis of *Downton* illustrates some of the many different ways in which individual agents, broadcasting histories, and creators' perceptions of the characteristics of transatlantic texts and audiences influence the choices made during the development, writing, and production of new series.

Weissmann has argued that the popularity of a series such as *Downton* means that "US producers more readily look to the UK for sources of inspiration."[78] However, Weissmann wrote before Brexit, the impact of which remains to be seen. Naturally, Brexit currently causes concern in terms of the many insecurities related to how future collaborations may look, not only across the Atlantic, but also across the English Channel.[79] Talking about *Masterpiece* as "the little black dress of British drama"—by being "always in fashion, elegant in style, reliable"—Rebecca Eaton has estimated that *Masterpiece* has in total "put half a billion dollars into British drama" by either financing it, by acquiring rights or publicity, or by flying over the casts to meet the American press.[80] That is a lot of money, and *Masterpiece* is still focusing on UK drama. However, the current television landscape is marked by more competition through new digital players as well as US cable broadcasters now being more interested in coproducing UK dramas. The Netflix original series *The Crown* (2016–) shows how global SVOD services are now also investing in UK historical drama as part of their flagship programming.

There are thus several changes challenging the traditions of the transatlantic collaborations between the United Kingdom and the United States, but one thing is certain. Producers and broadcasters in both countries would love to see more series with the popular appeal and global impact of *Downton Abbey*. The series concluded with "happy endings for virtually every single character," as the *Guardian* put it when reviewing the last episode of what was described as "one of Britain's most successful ever cultural exports in history and the strangest televisual phenomenon ever."[81] It will be interesting to see where the UK heritage drama goes from here and how the UK-US collaboration evolves in a post-Brexit world of global television platforms and changing audience patterns.

ACKNOWLEDGMENTS

The chapter is based on research conducted as part of the HERA-financed research project Mediating Cultural Encounters through European Screens (MeCETES.co.uk) and the FKK-financed research project What Makes Danish TV Series Travel? (http://danishtvdrama.au.dk/).

NOTES

1. *Downton Abbey*. Carnival Films. Written by Julian Fellowes. ITV (UK)/PBS (US). 2010–2015.
2. Katherine Byrne, "Adapting Heritage: Class and Conservatism in *Downton Abbey*," *Rethinking History* 18 (2014): 311–327.
3. James Chapman, "*Downton Abbey*: Reinventing the British Costume Drama," in *British Television Drama: Past, Present and Future*, 2nd ed, ed. Jonathan Bignell and Stephen Lacey (Basingstoke: Palgrave Macmillan, 2014), 131–142.
4. Neame in Rebecca Eaton, *Making "Masterpiece": 25 Years behind the Scenes at "Masterpiece Theatre" and "Mystery!" on PBS* (New York: Viking Adult, 2013), 232.
5. E.g., Michele Hilmes, *Network Nations: A Transnational History of British and American Broadcasting* (London: Routledge, 2011); Elke Weissmann, *Transnational Television Drama* (Basingstoke: Palgrave Macmillan, 2012).
6. Andrew Higson, *English Heritage, English Cinema: Costume Drama since 1980* (New York: Oxford University Press, 2003).
7. Ib Bondebjerg, "Transnational Europe: TV-Drama, Co-production Networks and Mediated Cultural Encounters," *Palgrave Communications*, June 14, 2016.
8. For more on *Masterpiece* and its transatlantic "coventures," see the chapter by Michele Hilmes in this collection.
9. Simone Knox, "*Masterpiece Theatre* and British Drama Imports on US Television: Discourses of Tension," *Critical Studies in Television* 7 (2012): 47.
10. Knox, "*Masterpiece Theatre*," 47.
11. Weissmann, *Transnational Television Drama*, 105.
12. Weissmann, *Transnational Television Drama*, 107–108.
13. Terrence O'Flaherty, *Masterpiece Theatre: A Celebration of 25 Years of Outstanding Television* (San Francisco: KQED Books, 1996), bc.
14. Laurence Jarvik, "PBS and the Politics of Quality: Mobil Oil's 'Masterpiece Theatre," *Historical Journal of Film, Radio and Television* 12 (1992): 271.
15. Jarvik, "PBS," 253.
16. Weissmann, *Transnational Television Drama*, 106.
17. Weissmann, *Transnational Television Drama*, 106.
18. Lisa Horowitz, "BBC, PBS Renew 'Masterpiece' Partnership," *The Wrap*, February 22, 2010, http://www.thewrap.com/bbc-pbs-renew-masterpiece-partnership-14482/.
19. Eaton in Horowitz, "BBC, PBS Renew Masterpiece."

20. Eaton, *Making Masterpiece*.

21. John Thornton Caldwell, *Production Culture: Industrial Reflexivity and Critical Practice in Film and Television* (Durham, NC: Duke University Press, 2008), 3.

22. Hanne Bruun, "The Qualitative Interview in Media Production Studies," in *Advancing Media Production Research: Shifting Sites, Methods and Politics*, ed. Chris Paterson, David Lee, Anamik Saha, and Anna Zoellner (Basingstoke: Palgrave Macmillan, 2016), 131–146.

23. Neame in Eaton, *Making Masterpiece*, 232.

24. Neame in Eaton, *Making Masterpiece*, 232.

25. Interestingly, at the time of the meeting with Neame, Fellowes was reading a book about the cultural phenomenon known as "buccaneers," referring to American heiresses—also known as "dollar duchesses"—who arrived in the United Kingdom in the 1880s and 1890s. This led to the development of the American character Cora, who thus apparently grew out of the interest and research in the times rather than being a creation with US audiences in mind (described in Eaton, *Making Masterpiece*, 237–238).

26. Hilmes, *Network Nations*, 3.

27. Eaton, *Making Masterpiece*, 243.

28. Neame in Eaton, *Making Masterpiece*, 234.

29. Telephone interview by the author with Laura Mackie, June 4, 2014.

30. Neame in Emma Rowley, *Behind the Scenes of "Downton Abbey"* (New York: St. Martin's Press, 2013), 11.

31. Eaton, *Making Masterpiece*, 234.

32. Catherine Johnson, *Branding Television* (London: Routledge, 2012).

33. Ross Garner, "Brand Reconciliation: A Case Study of ITV's 2013 Rebrand," *Critical Studies in Television* 10 (2015): 13.

34. Eaton in Patricia Treble, "Why I Turned Down *Downton Abbey*: Rebecca Eaton," Macleans.ca, December 20, 2013, http://www.macleans.ca/culture/masterpieces-rebecca-eaton-on-the-day-she-turned-down-downton-abbey/.

35. Eaton, *Making Masterpiece*, 229.

36. Eaton, *Making Masterpiece*, 243.

37. Weissmann, *Transnational Television Drama*, 105.

38. Hayley C. Cuccinello, "'Downton Abbey' by the Numbers: Farewell to a Multimillion-Dollar Dynasty," *Forbes*, March 6, 2016, http://www.forbes.com/sites/hayleycuccinello/2016/03/06/downton-abbey-by-the-numbers-farewell-to-a-multimillion-dollar-dynasty/#730f6bf73798.

39. Jeanette Steemers, "Selling Television: Addressing Transformations in the International Distribution of Television Content," *Media Industries Journal* 1 (2014): 46.

40. Mackie, interview.

41. ITV, "The *Downton Abbey* (Year 4) Press Pack."

42. Eaton, *Making Masterpiece*, 244.

43. Neame in Rowley, *Behind the Scenes*, 10.

44. Neame in Rowley, *Behind the Scenes*, 11.

45. Mackie, interview.

46. Eaton, *Making Masterpiece*, 269.

47. Fellowes in Eaton, *Making Masterpiece*, 239.

48. Rowley, *Behind the Scenes*, 29.

49. Rowley, *Behind the Scenes*, 30.

50. Mackie, interview.

51. Neame in Rowley, *Behind the Scenes*, 12.

52. Fellowes in Rowley, *Behind the Scenes*, 20.

53. Byrne, "Adapting Heritage," 326.

54. Katherine Byrne and Charles Doyle, *Edwardians on Screen: From "Downton Abbey" to "Parade's End"* (Basingstoke: Palgrave Macmillan, 2016), 9.

55. Byrne and Doyle, *Edwardians on Screen*, 11.

56. Byrne and Doyle, *Edwardians on Screen*, 13.

57. Byrne and Doyle, *Edwardians on Screen*, 13–14. See Nelson in this volume for more on the "difficulty" of *Parade's End*.

58. Ib Bondebjerg, "*Downton Abbey*—The UK Series That Conquered the World," MeCETES.co.uk, January 13, 2016.

59. Neame in Rowley, *Behind the Scenes*, 13.

60. Eaton, *Making Masterpiece*, 272.

61. Eaton, *Making Masterpiece*, 277. .

62. Byrne, "Adapting Heritage," 324.

63. Weissmann, *Transnational Television Drama*, 107.

64. Mackie, interview.

65. E.g., in relation to the making of Danish television drama: Eva N. Redvall, *Writing and Producing Television Drama in Denmark: From "The Kingdom" to "The Killing"* (Basingstoke: Palgrave Macmillan, 2013).

66. Fellowes in Jessica Fellowes and Matthew Sturgis, *The Chronicles of "Downton Abbey"* (New York: HarperCollins, 2012), 6.

67. Neame in Rowley, *Behind the Scenes*, 20.

68. In Eaton, *Making Masterpiece*, 232.

69. E.g. Byrne, "Adapting Heritage."

70. Fellowes in Fellowes and Sturgis, *Chronicles of Downton Abbey*, 8.

71. Cuccinello, "Downton Abbey."

72. Eaton, *Making Masterpiece*, 269.

73. Cuccinello, Downton Abbey."

74. Eaton, *Making Masterpiece*, 273.

75. Michele Hilmes, "Bollywood, Hollywood—Tollywood?," blog, February 21, 2014, http://blogs.nottingham.ac.uk/screenfocus/2014/02/21/tollywood/.

76. Interview by the author with Kaare Schmidt in Copenhagen, May 1, 2014.

77. Telephone interview by the author with Anders Leifer in Copenhagen, May 27, 2014.

78. Weissmann, *Transnational Television Drama*, 37.

79. E.g., Elsa Keslassy, "Can British-French Cooperation Survive Post-Brexit," *Variety*, June 29, 2016, http://variety.com/2016/tv/global/britain-france-tv-brexit-1201805014/.

80. Eaton in Maggie Brown, "Rebecca Eaton: *Masterpiece* Is the Little Black Dress of British Drama," *The Guardian*, March 1, 2015.

81. Viv Groskop, "*Downton Abbey*—the Finale: Happy Endings for Virtually Every Single Character," *The Guardian*, December 25, 2015.

7

BOUNDARY COLLISIONS IN HBO-BBC TRANSNATIONAL COPRODUCTION

Rome and *Parade's End*

ROBIN NELSON

Michele Hilmes remarks that "with the expansion of the independent broadcasting sector in Europe in the 1990s, followed by the advent of digital platforms in recent decades, [television] coproduction has exploded to become the 'new normal' in high-end drama and documentary, in particular."[1] This chapter responds to her advocacy of exploration of "the boundary collisions inherent in transnational coproduction."[2] *Rome* (HBO/BBC/ RaiDue, 2005–2007) and *Parade's End* (BBC/HBO/ VRT, 2012) are the first ever coproductions between HBO and the BBC (each with a third partner). *Rome* established a new relationship that eased the path for the more challenging *Parade's End* some seven years later. In any given instance of transnational cooperation, a key issue is the "fit" between product and partners. The BBC had previously been associated with HBO on the Emmy Award–winning series *Band of Brothers* (HBO, aired BBC2, rpt. BBC1, 2001) and the Emmy Award–winning TV film *The Gathering Storm* (HBO/BBC2, 2002), but their relationship had not extended to a coproduction. Indeed, the ethos of the two companies, one an independent narrowcaster channel born from cable and satellite in the United States, and the other the United Kingdom's historic national public service broadcaster, might suggest they are not natural bedfellows. Moreover, in the network era at least, US audiences had different expectations of TV drama than their UK counterparts—more glamorous spectacle/melodrama and less gritty realism.[3] Today, however, Hilmes imagines a transnational text that "encourages cross-cultural understanding," though she recognizes "the longstanding ethnocentric closures of American television."[4]

Indeed, in making the generalized distinctions above, it must be acknowledged that, under changed circumstances, many formerly discrete conceptual categories have been rendered increasingly porous. Hybrid texts mixing genres distinguish TV3. Historic public service broadcasters have been drawn into commercial competition, BBC Worldwide—the wholly owned subsidiary commercial arm of the BBC—being a case in point.[5] "Nation" is a contested category in a global market context where, as Elke Weissman summarizes, "the industries operate, consume, produce and think transnationally."[6] Indeed, beyond the mutual influence over decades of the national television cultures of the United Kingdom and the United States, some contemporary products are now clearly dubbed "transnational." Led particularly by Barbara Selznick, Hilmes, and Weissman in this context, scholars have effected a "transnational turn," viewing television culture through a global or transnational lens rather than emphasizing national differences.[7]

The case studies to follow illustrate aspects of what is currently at stake in transatlantic coproduction. Where the formats and remakes (of sitcoms and dramas, for example) allow for adjustments to take account of national audience disposition, transnational coproduction, in Hilmes's summary, "involves a creative partnership in which national interests must be combined and reconciled, differing audience tastes considered, and, often, the collision of public-service goals with commercial expectations negotiated."[8] The new disposition for the BBC and HBO to coproduce is tempered by some residual tensions of national cultural difference in respect of intentions, production strategies, textual variation, and audience reception (both actual and as perceived by producers). Selznick (referencing Taylor) suggests that "international co-productions exist within the borders between the two main ways of conceiving of the visual mass media: as a cultural industry and as an entertainment industry."[9] Though the BBC and HBO may have grown closer together in disposition, tensions pertaining to their different responsibilities remain in this regard.

The miniseries form has proved to have potential for transnational sales when it avoids national specificity and domestic issues.[10] Nevertheless, as Selznick observes, coproducers are "faced with the conflicting needs to represent a global (nationally nonspecific) universe while still appealing to individuals who live their lives on a local level."[11] The case studies below instance two attempts at such coproduction "fits" that might not be immediately apparent from their subject matter. Tapping into the British "heritage brand"—which, according to Selznick, evokes "qualities of elitism, high culture, classical literature and orderly society"[12]—both *Rome* and *Parade's End* are set in Europe. *Rome* takes a grand-scale approach to imperial history, while *Parade's End* offers a historical Edwardian cameo approached through a quirky romance narrative. Why then would HBO choose to coproduce these programs with the BBC, despite their obvious lack of "fit" with the American context?

The pursuit of prestige as a primary motive for international coproduction has largely been displaced by the aim to increase profits through accessing wider markets and the pooling of financial resources to disperse costs—particularly for very expensive "high-end" miniseries. As used here, "high-end" indicates the self-consciously stylistic programming that, according to Caldwell,[13] emerged in the US networks in the 1980s but is fully established with sophistication in HBO's serial output in the late 1990s and early in the next century.[14] In her book-length study of coproduction, Selznick argues that today "economic considerations outweigh the cultural" amid a range of motives.[15] In the cases of *Rome* and *Parade's End*, however, prestige branding and learning from one another may have significantly motivated the HBO-BBC alliance. The BBC has traditionally claimed the "quality" high ground in respect of both original TV drama and period adaptations. But, at the time of these coproductions, the institution sought to restake its claim under ever-increasing competition both from home and overseas. ITV, the BBC's main commercial rival, had achieved much success with the popular period dramas *Foyle's War* (ITV, 2002–2015) and *Downton Abbey* (coproduced Carnival Films and Masterpiece, 2010–2015) along with contemporary dramas such as *Broadchurch* (Kudos Film & TV with Shine America / Imaginary Friends, 2014–2015). Though very different products, *Rome* and *Parade's End* are marked by a brand aspiration to be known for distinctive, quality drama programming that would have the potential to build audiences worldwide. The BBC might thus be seen to be raising the "quality" bar in epic drama with *Rome* and in period drama with *Parade's End*.

From a very different commercial context in the United States, HBO established a reputation for original TV fiction that slowly developed over time. *The Economist* reflects that "in the late 1990s HBO pioneered an intelligent, patient style of storytelling that gloried in loose ends and morally ambiguous characters, a style 'The Sopranos' came to epitomize."[16] HBO distinguished itself, and transformed the television industry, in establishing a market for distinctive and aspirational TV series based on good writing under the creative freedom of a premium subscription channel not beholden to advertisers' sensibilities. Like the BBC, however, HBO has faced increasing competition as the pay-TV ecosystem in which it operates has become more complex and premium channel competitors have emerged. Showtime, a premium network owned by CBS, has found success with original shows such as *Dexter* (2006–2013), *Nurse Jackie* (2009–2015), and *Weeds* (2005–2012), while Starz—run by Chris Albrecht, HBO's former boss—intends to do likewise. Since 2000, Showtime and Starz have each added about 6.7 million subscribers in America, more than twice as many as HBO (overall they have between 18 million and 20 million subscribers each, compared with HBO's 28 million).[17]

It is in this context that HBO has extended its interest in good writing to established literary sources. Alexandra Alter reports that "as Hollywood has increasingly shied away from difficult literary works in favor of blockbuster comic-book reboots and sequels, a growing number of novels are coming to television instead."[18] In addition, HBO has shifted its policy away from exclusively owning all its original content and toward coproduction, but it has sustained—even extended—its ambition and risk-taking. The case studies bear this out. *Parade's End* is a lavish period piece, costing about $20 million, with features typical of classic British period drama. But the adaptation of Ford Madox Ford's notoriously difficult modernist tetralogy of novels was a risk even for the BBC. Beyond accessing the British heritage brand, its appeal for HBO is not clear (but see below). The epic scale of *Rome* offered a different coproduction "fit" drawing on historical events of global significance. It is the most ambitious coproduced series with Americans in the history of the BBC. On agreeing to coproduce just the first twelve one-hour episodes, HBO committed $85 million to the production, with the BBC committing $15 million. But, besides being a financial milestone, the coproduction may also mark a further shift on HBO's part toward "serious" historical drama.

Rome and *Parade's End* may appear to have little in common. But both involve the adaptation of material to reconstruct in televisual form moments of historical significance, namely the ends of empires. Had *Rome* achieved the five seasons initially conceived, it would have fully documented an epoch in Roman history—the end, as well as the rise, of, the Roman Empire—just as *Parade's End* marks the end of the Edwardian and colonial eras in British history. The approach of the writers in both instances is to adopt an unusual perspective on major historical events, deviating from official histories and iconographies. Each series will first be discussed separately in what follows with regard to production, text(s) and reception, prior to bringing out features that illuminate what's at stake in today's "high-end" drama transatlantic co-productions.

ROME

At a first meeting, Anne Thomopoulos, HBO executive producer, and Jane Tranter, BBC controller of drama commissioning, happened to discover a shared love of the landmark BBC series *I, Claudius* (BBC Television, 1976). That Thomopoulos presented Tranter with a draft script of *Rome* by Bruno Heller just a year later reveals that HBO had for some time been considering a foray into historical drama. But the enterprise would inevitably be of feature-film scale and demand a budget even bigger than HBO might afford. The BBC, however, had simultaneously been contemplating something Roman and accordingly it seemed possible that the two television giants might collaborate if there were a treatment "fit." As Tranter recalls, "It was clear from the outset that writer Bruno Heller's take on the world of ancient Rome was really interesting. It was very similar to our home-grown BBC pieces on historical drama."[19]

Paralleling the modern approach of the BBC to historical figures, Heller's script humanized "the great" through an element of caricature, and he used an additional device to afford audience access to grand public events. Heller had discovered, in the research source of Cicero, two legionnaires, Pullo and Vorenus, from whom he developed the characters of two ordinary Roman soldiers and their families to afford an everyday perspective on grand events. This generic mix of one narrative strand unfolding everyday life and another recounting the excesses of a power elite would not be unfamiliar to HBO since it is precisely the mix informing *The Sopranos'* (HBO, 1999–2007) interweaving of mafia gangster movie and TV soap.[20] The context also afforded (as in *The Sopranos*) ample opportunity for scenes of violence and sexuality along with the potential for complex parallelism in storytelling and psychologically compelling characters, evidencing features of both modern American and traditional British TV drama. As they developed, the two levels of Rome contrasted a radical change in political culture and shifts in the manners and morals of everyday life. On one level, an aggressive imperialism rides roughshod over a seminal and prized republic; on another level, a proud republic grounded in aestheticism and self-constraint slides into a city of millions of individuals on the make.

The early appointment as adviser on *Rome* of Jonathan Stamp, formerly of the BBC Specialist Factual department, demonstrates HBO's openness to the educative and informative dimensions of the BBC's famous remit. But from the outset the aim was for authenticity rather than historical accuracy.[21] A BBC2 audience would inevitably have expectations of historical epic in these terms, but, from an HBO point of view, such a disposition suggests a move toward BBC public service "seriousness." As Tranter notes, "It's the first deep period drama for HBO and I think they saw us as a natural partnership on Rome. The BBC brand does mean something in the US and also the HBO brand means something over here. We were able to bring to the project the BBC hallmarks of factual historical authenticity, integrity, class and quality."[22] But the "fit" also emerged from the BBC's period dramas aiming to attract younger viewers by adopting some of the conventions of popular TV genres and formats. *Bleak House* (2005) experimented with form in being divided into soap-length thirty-minute episodes as well as deploying innovative sound and visual techniques. Andrew Davies's BBC adaptations of "classic novels" have incorporated overt sexuality, from Mr. Darcy (Colin Firth) emerging from the lake in *Pride and Prejudice* (1995) through to Helene Karagina's (Tuppence Middleton) overt affair with Fedya Dolokhov (Tom Burke) in *War and Peace* (2016). The time was thus right for HBO and the BBC finally to come together on a coproduction since, despite their institutional differences, a "fit" had developed in respect of a shared approach to TV drama.

But the coproduction of *Rome* involved not just HBO and the BBC but also RAI, Italy's national broadcaster, which sits institutionally between HBO, a wholly commercial (subscription) channel, and the BBC, a publicly funded broadcaster. RAI gains half of its revenue by means of a license fee and the other half through advertising. Though it invested some €4.5 million (c. $5 million), RAI is typically not listed as a coproducer of *Rome*.[23] Beyond contributing to production development at Cinecittà Studios, RAI Fiction (RAI's development and production division) financed the reshooting of scenes for the Italian market (see below).

Adviser Stamp was hostile to what he calls "the Holly-Rome look" and wanted to create a fresh vision of Rome as a densely inhabited, vibrant metropolis, avoiding the marble-columned clichés of previous representations of the city. Joseph Bennett, production designer, created a vast squalid slum area as well as a city of magnificent Roman villas and the Forum. An international crew of 350 was involved in building an impressively detailed set across an area of five acres and six sound stages. The avoidance of glamour extended to casting and characterization. In stark contrast to most American TV series, the producers strove to make the cast look like everyday real Romans at a time of public communal toilets and without cosmetics, dental implants, and curling tongs.

Despite reservations, HBO agreed to a predominance of British actors in *Rome*, all the major roles being taken by Brits, with a cluster of Italians in relatively minor parts. Since, in the past, it was axiomatic that an American voice must be heard in the first thirty seconds of an opening episode of a US TV series, the absence of American stars is a remarkable departure for HBO. It might be explained by the European setting in which American viewers would expect to hear foreign accents and, since Italian would not be a lingua franca, British English might serve the twin needs of accessibility and unfamiliarity.

In sum, the coproduction of *Rome* was a departure for the two major financial investors and a huge realization challenge for RAI Fiction, which oversaw the filming in Italy. In accepting a disposition to gritty realism, HBO was perhaps following its reputation for innovative departures from standard TV fare, but it was nevertheless militating against its established high-glamour successes. The BBC appeared to take fewer risks in that a disposition to authenticity is in line with its reputation but, since HBO was the major investor and likely to call the shots, this first coproduction posed challenges. Tensions between the impulse to entertain (perhaps foregrounding sex and violence, sensationalism and special effects) and a wish also to educate and inform (by way of adherence to historical authenticity) were likely to surface in the production process. It is notable that all three partners reserved the rights to edit and present the final material.

Ultimately there were several texts of *Rome*, since variant versions were deemed necessary for different national markets. The Italian *Rome* first aired on RAI-Due in a sanitized version leaving more to the imagination in respect of graphic scenes of sex and violence. In *Corriere della Sera*, Agostino Saccà, director general of RAI Fiction, acknowledged "major editing," but in fact additional material had to be shot with, for example, male nudes being covered up.[24] Though some Italians were outraged by what they saw as censorship, even more were unhappy with the representation of a Rome inhabited by British voices. As Paola Masini, RAI drama executive, puts it, "Watching British actors playing Romans rubs a lot of people the wrong way and prompted the press to find fault with the historical accuracy."[25]

Ironically, full access to historical context was denied to British viewers by a BBC edit of Michael Apted's intended version of the text. The BBC re-edited the first three episodes (all directed by Apted), reducing them to two by cutting the history of Rome. Though the BBC claimed that a British audience was more familiar with historical context than its American counterpart, Apted counterclaimed that the purpose was to boost ratings by increasing the prominence of scenes of sex and violence. The effect, he argued, was to "reduce the vital politics" and "make Rome hard to follow."[26] It may be that, in the dialectics of institutional ethos, the BBC pulled back at the eleventh hour from a commitment to educate and inform and ceded to an HBO sense of entertainment.

Italy apart—where the first airing on RAI Due attracted just 10 percent of viewers—initial reception was generally positive in terms of both ratings and critical acclaim.[27] Following a public launch in the United States at the Wadsworth Theater, "Stolen Eagle," the pilot broadcast, was seen by 3.8 million viewers and achieved a 9.1 household rating for Sunday prime time. In US subscription channels' customary multiple airings, *Rome* achieved a total of 8.9 million viewers over the eleven showings on HBO and HBO2.[28] BBC Two's premiere of *Rome* in the United Kingdom attracted 6.6 million viewers (27 percent of audience), though figures subsequently declined for future episodes, with the season finale achieving only 3 million viewers (13 percent audience share).[29] *Rome* achieved numerous nominations and awards both in the United States and the United Kingdom, including four Emmys for the series itself and others for special effects, sound, and cinematography.

Ultimately the proposed five seasons were not completed, largely owing to costs. Announcing the termination after season 2, then-HBO chairman and CEO Chris

Albrecht pointed out that the notoriously expensive show was developed as a miniseries under a two-year contract with the BBC and RAI. Remarking that "this was a big bite for them," he seemed to imply that the partners could not match HBO's level of resource.[30] A rumored film version did not materialize and, beyond viewers' memories, the legacy of *Rome* is a DVD or Blu-ray recording now readily available.

PARADE'S END

Parade's End is an adaptation for television of Ford Madox Ford's difficult (in the sense of deep, complex, and oblique) modernist tetralogy of novels of the same name. Though not on the scale of *Rome* in respect of locations and cast, it is nevertheless an expensive period drama requiring much historical reconstruction and scenic sites. Like *Rome*, it is a coproduction between BBC and HBO with a third partner, in this instance VRT, the national public service broadcaster for the Flemish Region and Community of Belgium. Even though it required mock-up of aspects of the English countryside, much of the series was filmed in Belgium because of the substantial tax breaks afforded to TV drama production in Belgium and not available in the United Kingdom at the time. However, significant scenes were shot on locations in Kent and London. *Parade's End* features the key characteristics of a British period TV drama that to an American audience may have exotic appeal: fine stately homes with appropriate fixtures and fittings, narratives of class and the mores of other times, and strong character acting by a stellar (largely) British cast (Benedict Cumberbatch, Rebecca Hall) sporting accurately reproduced period costumes.[31] Textual intricacy apart (see below), it is clear why the BBC, with a renewed commitment to challenging drama, might commission such a piece, even though the source is less well known than those by canonical authors.[32]

HBO's less obvious attraction to the coproduction may have stemmed from the company's commitment to TV as a writers' medium. According to Alter, HBO had at the time "a handful of novels in development, including works by William Faulkner, Jeffrey Eugenides's multigenerational family drama 'Middlesex,' Neil Gaiman's fantasy epic 'American Gods' and Tom Perrotta's quiet dystopian novel 'The Leftovers.' "[33] Alter acknowledges that *Parade's End* might prove particularly challenging, but Hank Stuever was incredulous at the choice.

What, besides pedigree, enticed HBO to help produce "Parade's End"? Even in its worst recent movie projects (the dreadful "Hemingway & Gelhorn," say, or "The Girl"), the network still puts a primacy on plot and movement. Even Todd Haynes's lavishly long "Mildred Pierce" understood that momentum was key. "Parade's End" is radiant with class, but it has almost no sizzle and very little sauce.[34]

Part of the answer to Stuever's question lies in the involvement of writer Tom Stoppard, who quelled executives' doubts about material they found very challenging. HBO executive Kary Antholis remarked that, in Stoppard, "we had one of the great living writers of the English language who was passionate about a piece of material."[35] Moreover, HBO representatives were aware that other adaptations (including *Band of Brothers* and *Mildred Pierce* [HBO: 2010–2011]) had proved successful with viewers on DVD and on-demand, helping the network to attract new subscribers.[36]

The tax breaks offered by coproduction in Europe may also have been a factor, but the puzzle might most readily be explained by HBO's scheduling of *Parade's End* in February 2013 just after the hugely popular British series *Downton Abbey* (aired in the United States under the *Masterpiece* banner on PBS), had attracted some eight million viewers. Indeed, *Parade's End* came to be widely seen as the thinking person's *Downton Abbey*.[37] To those who admire it (see below), *Parade's End* is rewarding at the level of aesthetics and affect, factors increasingly important for sustaining interest in high-end TV drama series.[38] It raises the bar in respect of "quality" TV drama, and Stuever's puzzlement may be further illuminated by brief consideration of both source and TV adaptation of *Parade's End*.

The historical narrative of *Rome* is driven by the self-assertion of Caesar in conflict with other powerful individuals and in breach of the codes and conventions of the celebrated republic. It thus lends itself to traditional dramatic conflict and established narrative arcs. In marked contrast, the narrative of *Parade's End* is fragmented and, in Madox Ford's novel, is related as a stream of consciousness. Set in the waning years of Edwardian England, *Parade's End* relates the story of Christopher Tietjens, a solid Tory and heir to a large estate, who endures a fraught marriage with his unfaithful and alluringly venomous wife, Sylvia, while, because of his devotion to "parade," a code of honor whose moment is past, denying himself love and happiness with a young suffragette, Valentine Wannop. Tietjens is so bound by his adherence to parade that he is able only to react to circumstances and sustain a surface propriety that belies the depth of his feelings. Thus, as Stuever notes, there is no source "primacy on plot and movement"; the conflict between the characters results in inaction rather than action. In this respect—and unlike the nineteenth-century novels that serve as the basis for much British period drama—*Parade's End* is a questionable vehicle for the BBC, let alone HBO. However, a passion-filled love triangle across class lines is certainly a familiar trope in period drama. Stoppard's treatment focuses upon the love triangle but not entirely at the expense of World War I and the Edwardian England social context, which is seeing challenges to its values, such as the suffragette movement, and is also familiar from other film and TV vehicles. Thus a pitch may well have sounded very plausible in respect of potential audience.

But Madox Ford's modernist treatment, focusing on the experience rather than the action of the moment, proved challenging even to Tom Stoppard, who worked for more than a year on the adaptation. As he remarked, "The whole thing looked so complicated to me that I thought I'd go mad if I tried to work it all out."[39] Ultimately, he dropped the fourth volume and to an extent streamlined the narrative to foreground the love triangle. He found the need also to write a number of new scenes to afford at least a little "sauce and sizzle" to the TV version. Indeed, in the first of the five episodes, there are two quite graphic sex scenes, paralleling those in *Rome* but not explicit in the novel. Though perhaps considered highbrow even in theater, where his plays have drawn considerably on modern philosophy, Stoppard's early background in journalism has given him appreciation of the need to entertain and tell a clear story. As he remarks of his process in writing *Parade's End*: "I've never had any interest in trying to impress an audience with my ability to juggle time and space in an intriguing, modernistic way. . . . Whatever you're doing, you always want a script to be a page-turner. It's very important never, ever, to feel above that."[40]

However, in skillfully sustaining something of the modernist feel of the source novel by cutting swiftly back and forth through time, the opening episode is not a straightforward linear narrative.[41] Viewers need to concentrate and work hard at piecing together the fragments just to make sense of the time frame of events. Furthermore, the motives of the characters as the series progresses do not fit neatly into a sense-making frame of cause and effect but remain unexplained. It is not clear why Tietjens (Cumberbatch) is so fixated on decorum and so committed to denying himself happiness or why Sylvia (Hall) remains with her husband only to hurt him. Likewise, it is not obvious why Valentine Wannop (Adelaide Clemens), a modern and progressive young woman, would devote herself to an older man entrenched in outmoded values. Traditional drama viewers accustomed to the explicatory paradigm of much television may have become disorientated.

Nonetheless, the critical acclaim for the series was widespread. Emma Dibdin summarized:

> *Parade's End* has been a compelling, thematically rich and fiercely intelligent drama, as frequently moving as it was unexpectedly comedic. Adapting a tetralogy as sprawling and historically expansive as Ford Madox Ford's is close to a fool's errand, and Stoppard, director Susanna White, Cumberbatch et al have pulled it off with valiance and grace.[42]

Grace Dent, writing in the *Independent*, simply judged it to be "one of the finest things the BBC has ever made."[43] At the BAFTAs in the United Kingdom, *Parade's End* received six TV nominations, including Best Actress for Hall, and it won Best Costume Design. Cumberbatch and Hall won Broadcasting Press Guild awards respectively for Best Actor and Actress, while Stoppard achieved the Writer's Award and the series itself won Best Drama Series. In the United States, five Primetime Emmy Awards nominations included Best Adapted Screenplay for Stoppard and Best Actor for Cumberbatch.

A SPECIAL RELATIONSHIP?

In some respects, these two different HBO-BBC coproductions mark a fresh twist in the notion of a special US-UK production relationship, but they do not really reflect national affinities. Both institutions departed from their own self-imposed protocols for the perceived advantage of mutual reinforcement of brand reputation in respect of challenging "quality" drama production. The gamble to raise the prestige branding stakes paid off well in respect of critical acclaim, and the main aim of the partnership was thus achieved. Since neither *Rome* nor *Parade's End* created an industry-changing wow factor in the way *The Sopranos* has done, however, the project was less effective in terms of the secondary consideration, audience building. Both coproductions sought to benefit from the broad success other vehicles in the genres of historical and period drama, notably *Downton*, were achieving.

There have been no further HBO-BBC coproductions since *Rome* and *Parade's End*. In what may be a sign of the times, the former BBC executives involved have now moved to Hollywood to work with, or within, American companies. Since 2015, Ben Stephenson has worked with J. J. Abrams at Bad Robot, and Jane Tranter (with Julie Gardner) formed Bad Wolf to cement an anticipated privileged relation with HBO. The latter companies agreed to a nonexclusive first-look deal, and they sought a broader partnership to foster HBO's ties with the UK production community. Since then, however, the global marketplace has moved on again, and other possible BBC-HBO partnerships have been overtaken. While the relationship between particular executives may be special and significant in achieving specific projects, market considerations ultimately supersede personal loyalties.

As Ward notes (in chapter 4 in this volume), Sky Atlantic moved in 2010 to secure exclusive distribution rights to all HBO material, past and future, with a subsequent nod, on renewing the deal in 2015, to possible coproductions. Where the budgets of megacorporations streaming product worldwide is concerned, coproduction, though it remains key to many epic and period dramas, is not now a prerequisite. Since the two case study coproductions discussed above, *Game of Thrones* (HBO, 2011–2016) has been produced by HBO alone at a reputed cost of £4 million per episode, but distributed by Sky Atlantic. An additional transnational element is evident in that it was shot substantially in Ireland (among other European countries) to take advantage of tax breaks. Conversely, filmed on home soil in Maryland, again because of the huge tax breaks afforded, *House of Cards* (2013–2017) adopted a parallel funding, production, and distribution model, being both commissioned and streamed by Netflix. Indeed, financial incentives more than any special international affinities appear to determine who coproduces with whom and where programs are shot. In today's multiplatform, global market environment, it makes sense, as Hilmes indicates, to speak less of partnerships between nations or institutions and more of an environment that "frequently partners public-sector broadcasters with independents and large commercial companies from two or more nations."[44]

The case studies here suggest, however, that the production of that seemingly transnational text which "encourages cross-cultural understanding," as Hilmes describes it,[45] may not be easy to attain and the local may not be simply melded into the "glocal." Unlike *Downton*, there is no American dimension to *Parade's End*, and it departs from classic TV narrative form. Despite sustaining aspects of American popular culture such as pace and spectacle, *Rome* lacks American actors and context (other perhaps than a broad imperialism). It may be, then, that neither constitutes a mirror to "reflect the sensibilities of viewers around the world" as Hilmes (following Stanley) suggests *Downton* has done.[46] Indeed, a residual sense of national concerns in the production and reception contexts is evident in the initial BBC edit of *Rome* resented by director Apted, and in the reception in Italy, where the audience resented British voices speaking for Rome. The locational specificity, both geographical and cultural, of both *Rome* and *Parade's End* may be a factor here. Unless it appeals to a mythic imaginary, the historical drama genre may not lend itself so readily to "the sensibilities of viewers around the world," a conception suggesting a universalism much contested by theorists championing cultural specificity. But this debate is beyond the scope of this chapter.

Taking a broad view in the light of the worldwide success of many and varied drama series, the established trait of national audiences to prefer homegrown product may well remain when it pertains to locality but ultimately impact little upon transnational product.[47] The Italians resented British accents in respect of Rome perceived as locality but largely rejected the censored "Italian cut" and demanded the experience others were afforded internationally.

With production and online streaming by Sky Atlantic, Amazon Prime, and Netflix, the specific circumstances that informed the special coproduction relationship between

BBC TV and HBO may have passed. The epic *The Young Pope* (coproduced Sky/ HBO/Canal+; aired Sky, HBO, October 2016) and period drama *The Crown* (Netflix, aired November 2016) might well have been contenders for HBO-BBC coproduction follow-ups to *Rome* and *Parade's End* in respect of "fit" and brand aspiration. But the first, directed by Paolo Sorrentino, is a Sky-HBO-Canal+ coproduction, and the latter, "costing more money than any other series to date," is commissioned by Netflix.[48] Under game-changing circumstances that have extended budgets beyond those historically associated with even "high-end" television drama production, the stakes appear to have risen, as Albrecht hinted, beyond the means of a PSB national producer such as the BBC in respect of transnational coproduction partnership. But circumstances can change. The small—and in some instances significantly declining—audiences for drama streamed on Sky Atlantic (see Ward, chapter 4) may not matter in the short term if brand reputation and subscription build steadily. But in time the costs may outweigh the advantages, and opportunities for BBC-HBO coproduction may yet re-emerge, though at present it looks unlikely.

Meanwhile, viewers still have access to "quality" drama on their various domestic and mobile screens but, increasingly, at a premium.

NOTES

1. Michelle Hilmes, "Transnational TV: What Do We Mean by 'Coproduction' Anymore?," *Media Industries Journal* 1:2 (2014): 1–8.
2. Hilmes, "Transnational TV," 5.
3. For a discussion of the "network era" (TV1), TV2, and TV3, see Robin Nelson, *State of Play: Contemporary "High-End" TV Drama* (Manchester: Manchester University Press, 2007).
4. Hilmes, "Transnational TV," 4, 3.
5. See Nelson, *State of Play*.
6. Elke Weissman, *Transnational Television Drama: Special Relationships and Mutual Influences between the US and UK* (Basingstoke: Palgrave Macmillan, 2007), 6.
7. Barbara Selznick, *Global Television: Co-producing Culture* (Philadelphia: Temple University Press, 2007); Michelle Hilmes, *Networked Nations: A Transnational History of British and American Broadcasting* (New York: Routledge, 2010).
8. Hilmes, "Transnational TV," 4.
9. Selznick, *Global Television*, 6.
10. See Selznick, *Global Television*, 47.
11. Selznick, *Global Television*, 47.
12. Selznick, *Global Television*, 76.
13. John Caldwell, *Televisuality: Style, Crisis, and Authority in American Television* (New York: Rutgers University Press, 1995).
14. See Nelson, *State of Play*, 2ff.
15. Selznick, *Global Television*, 17.
16. "The Winning Streak," *The Economist*, August 20, 2011, http://www.economist.com/node/21526314.
17. "The Winning Streak."

18. Alexandra Alter, "TV's Novel Challenge: Literature on the Screen," *Wall Street Journal*, February 22, 2013, http://www.wsj.com/articles/SB10001424127887323478004578306400682079518.

19. BBC Press Pack *Rome*, http://www.bbc.co.uk/pressoffice/pressreleases/stories/2005/08_august/26/rome.shtml.

20. See Nelson, *State of Play*, 27–35.

21. Though a contested issue, "historical accuracy" might be defined as adhering to the facts that we have and "authenticity" as the way in which those living in the period might have viewed and experienced their world.

22. BBC Press Pack *Rome*.

23. Nick Vivarelli, "Irritated Italos Give HBO's 'Rome' the Thumbs Down," *Variety*, March 26, 2006, http://variety.com/2006/tv/news/irritated-italos-give-hbo-s-rome-the-thumbs-down-1117940324/.

24. Alessandra Vitali, "Sesso, violenza e istinti animali così l'Impero si racconta in tv," *La Repubblica*, March 17, 2006, http://www.repubblica.it/2005/k/sezioni/spettacoli_e_cultura/fictiontv5/roma/roma.html.

25. Cited in Vivarelli, "Sesso."

26. Richard Brooks, "They Sexed Up My Roman Orgy, Says Glum Director," *The Times*, November 6, 2005, https://www.thetimes.co.uk/article/they-sexed-up-my-roman-orgy-says-glum-director-sz38zp0qq8m.

27. In Italy, the second series was never broadcast on analogue TV. Starting in October 2009, RAI Quattro, a digital-only channel, broadcast the original uncut version of the first series and went on to broadcast the second series unaltered as well.

28. Ryan Parsons, "HBO Wants More Rome," *CanMag*, September 13, 2005, http://www.canmag.com/news/4/21/1963.

29. Jason Deans, "Rome's Bloody Climax Wins 3m," *The Guardian*, January 5, 2006, http://www.theguardian.com/media/2006/jan/05/overnights.

30. Cited in Anne Becker, "HBO to Sack Rome after Season 2," *Broadcasting & Cable*, July 12, 2006, http://www.broadcastingcable.com/news/programming/hbo-sack-rome-after-season-2/29208.

31. Adelaide Clemens is Australian, but the cast also featured Anne-Marie Duff, Rupert Everett, Stephen Graham, Janet McTeer, and Miranda Richardson.

32. Jana Bennett, BBC director of television, remarks that "forging such a strong creative partnership with HBO, one of the world's most respected drama producers, is part of the BBC's role as both a catalyst and an enabler for exciting new projects. . . . Audiences around the world can look forward to a landmark piece of great television." BBC Press Office, "Ciaran Hinds, Kevin McKidd and Lindsay Duncan Head the Cast of BBC/HBO Epic Series *Rome*," March 22, 2004, http://www.bbc.co.uk/pressoffice/pressreleases/stories/2004/03_march/22/rome.shtml.

33. Alter, "TV's Novel Challenge."

34. Hank Steuver, "HBO's 'Parade's End': All Dressed Up with Nowhere to Go," *Washington Post*, February 25, 2013, https://www.washingtonpost.com/entertainment/tv/hbos-parades-end-all-dressed-up-with-nowhere-to-go/2013/02/25/685e12cc-7d12-11e2-82e8-61a46c2cde3d_story.html.

35. Cited in Alter, "TV's Novel Challenge."

36. See Alter, "TV's Novel Challenge."

37. See, for example, Tim Goodman, "*Parade's End*: TV Review," *Hollywood Reporter*, February 22, 2013, http://www.hollywoodreporter.com/review/parades-end-tv-review-423406.

38. See Robin Nelson, "The Emergence of 'Affect' in Contemporary TV Fictions," in *Emotions in Contemporary TV Series*, ed. Alberto N. Garcia (Basingstoke: Palgrave Macmillan, 2016), 26–51.

39. Cited in Alter, "TV's Novel Challenge."

40. Cited in Ian Crouch, "Adaptation," *New Yorker*, February 26, 2013, http://www.newyorker.com/books/page-turner/adaptation.

41. For a discussion of the aesthetic of *Parade's End*, see Stella Hockenhull, "Experimentation and Postheritage in Contemporary TV Drama," in *Upstairs and Downstairs: British Costume Drama Television from the "Forsyte Saga" to "Downton Abbey"*, ed. James Leggatt and Julie Taddeo (Lanham, MD: Rowman & Littlefield, 2015), 191–213.

42. Emma Dibdin, "*Parade's End*, Series Finale, BBC Two," *Arts Desk*, September 22, 2012, http://www.theartsdesk.com/tv/parades-end-series-finale-bbc-two.

43. Grace Dent, "Grace Dent on Television," *Independent*, September 7, 2012, http://www.independent.co.uk/arts-entertainment/tv/reviews/grace-dent-on-television-parades-end-bbc2-8113316.html.

44. Hilmes, "Transnational TV," 4.

45. Hilmes, "Transnational TV," 4.

46. Hilmes, "Transnational TV," 5.

47. Despite the disposition toward transnational texts, Selznick affirms that "most national audiences continue to prefer local programming with domestic stars and languages" (*Global Television*, 3).

48. Peter Vine, *The Guardian*, September 10, 2016, 7.

/// 8 /// METACOMMENTARY AND MYTHOLOGY

Episodes as a Performance of Transatlantic TV

JONATHAN BIGNELL

The comedy drama Episodes (BBC/Showtime, 2011–2017) is a transatlantic coproduction, created and written by Americans Jeffrey Klarik and David Crane and made with the British production company Hat Trick. Its five seasons of half-hour episodes have been highly successful, with positive reviews and multiple award nominations for writing and acting. Its premise is that a British husband and wife duo of award-winning screenwriters, Sean (Stephen Mangan) and Beverly Lincoln (Tamsin Greig), are invited to work on a US network adaptation of their hit UK sitcom. Coming to LA, their scripts are "Americanized," and their main actor is replaced by Friends (NBC, 1994–2004) star Matt LeBlanc. They become embroiled in the politics of the American television industry, and a series of infidelities and affairs. The program is a commentary on the similarities and differences between American and British television cultures, taking transatlantic television as its subject and self-consciously performing it. This chapter uses this notion that the show "performs" its identity to denote that Episodes makes transatlantic relationships visible and reflexively plays them out.[1] It is as if there is a set of tropes or rhetorical positions about transatlantic television that the show works through, like a performer playing out a scripted role.

There is an added twist to Episodes' performance of transatlantic identity because it is done in the genre of situation comedy. Sitcom as a genre opens up issues that the form can then close down, and sitcom is characterized by stasis. On one hand, playing out national differences and cultural contrasts is the engine of *Episodes'* comedy and generates storylines and character conflicts. On the other hand, the sitcom genre is inhabited by forces that push toward closure, unification, resolution, and the abolition of differences. There is a tension between these two forces, and this chapter argues that what is interesting about *Episodes* is how it generates comedy out of difference but has to collapse differences in order to exist. As a coproduction broadcast on both British and US television, national differences must be minimized enough for *Episodes* to get made and shown. Moreover, because it is screened on BBC2 and on Showtime, *Episodes* has to suit different contexts around channel identity and channels' relationships with national dramatic traditions and ideologies. National differences have to be more a performance than a reality, or *Episodes* cannot exist. So rather than evaluating whether *Episodes* accurately portrays national differences, this chapter will argue that it is a metacommentary on deeply embedded myths about the television of each nation. It is a self-reflexive discourse about discourses that are already highly caricatured. As well as analysis of the show, the chapter draws on press releases and journalistic commentary on *Episodes* that refer to these caricature positions.

NATIONAL DISTINCTIONS

From the beginning of *Episodes*, British television is represented by the screenwriters Sean and Beverly, linking Britishness to individual authorship. This crucial decision channels the series' representation of American television institutions and industry through individuals' points of view so that they are expressed via characterization. The first episode opens at the annual BAFTA award ceremony in London, where Sean's and Beverly's celebrations of their sitcom's success are interrupted by Merc Lapidus (John Pankow), an American television network executive. He repeatedly expresses admiration for their sitcom, *Lyman's Boys*, and invites them to Los Angeles to remake it. The couple accept, and subsequent scenes at the network's offices are focalized through Sean's and Beverly's reactions, emphasizing their relative powerlessness and the divergent attitudes that the British and American characters have to program making. We learn with Sean and Beverly that Merc has never seen *Lyman's Boys*; the transatlantic remake is purely a business decision. Discussions of casting the US version are maneuvered so that *Friends* star Matt LeBlanc takes on the lead role, though he seems wildly inappropriate for the format's headmaster of British private school pupils. The network changes the show into *Pucks!*, about a US high school hockey team and their coach.

Episodes draws on widely held attitudes to the US television industry. It represents Merc's network as what cocreator Klarik called "television by committee."[2] Executives responsible for large financial investments need to justify themselves by intervening in the production process from commissioning to the details of scripts, casting, and costume. *Episodes* dramatizes the commissioning of Sean and Beverly's sitcom through its transformation into *Pucks!* and subsequent threats to the show. Beverly's dismay at this embodies Crane's and Klarik's attitudes, which led them to work with an overseas co-producer, BBC, and the cable channel Showtime rather than a US broadcast network. Klarik explained: "We couldn't believe that we'd found a place where the network doesn't sit on your head the whole time."[3] The first season of *Episodes* was shot in the United Kingdom, so Crane heard about American production from a distance: "We talked to friends who were doing pilots back home and hearing the horror stories. A friend developed a show that took place in Washington and apparently the note [from the network] came back after the show had been bought, read and shot: 'There's too much politics'!" In this press release ahead of *Episodes'* premiere, the US industry that the sitcom critiques is represented by a series of similar anecdotes, such as another from Klarik: "Several years ago, I did a pilot about a girls' boarding school and there were two notes from the studio. One was 'Can't there be boys at the school?' The second was, 'Can we get those girls into nighties?' . . . And these notes were coming in two days before I started filming!"[4] Discourses around *Episodes* persistently reference similar half-humorous, half-shocking characterizations of the US industry. This sense that nervous executives will try to increase the marketability of a program by lowering its aesthetic and moral standards causes a problem for the discourse about American television, however. If US television is so bad, can Crane's previous success as cocreator of *Friends*, and Klarik's hit sitcom *Mad about You* be explained? The answer is to set up the trope of the creative individual battling, occasionally successfully, against the network machine. Klarik explains: "You happen to have one executive who champions it and the best thing they do is to make everyone else leave you alone."[5] Sean and Beverly were modeled on writing partners and life partners Crane and Klarik themselves.[6] Just as Crane and Klarik portray themselves through discourses of individual authorship, battling network interference, Sean and Beverly experience the same in *Episodes*.

By contrast, the British television industry is almost entirely unseen in *Episodes* and gains moral superiority by its very absence; almost everything British is represented by likable ingenues Sean and Beverly. Crane's and Klarik's admiration for British television culture was frequently expressed before *Episodes'* premiere. Crane credits *The Office* (BBC, 2001–2003), *Extras* (BBC/HBO, 2005–2007), and *The Mighty Boosh* (BBC, 2004–2007) as influences on his work, and reports that "when we were writing Episodes, we happened to be watching the second season of Outnumbered. We had to turn it off. It was just too good."[7] This discourse about British television is quite common, and American television critic Matt Zoller Seitz attributes the higher quality he finds in some British programs (including *Episodes*) to the patience of executive producers and channel controllers.[8] It comes from allowing creative staff to develop an "attentive, handcrafted quality," he asserts. American networks prefer a season's worth of daily episodes for syndication, totaling at least one hundred installments, whereas Seitz praises the shorter runs of British series, such as *Episodes'* first season of seven shows, as a way to prioritize quality of writing. "I thought, 'That's an awkward number. Who the hell orders *seven* shows?' Then I read the presskit and saw it was co-produced by—ta-*DAH*!—the BBC."[9] What *Episodes* does is to actualize and dramatize these discursive tropes, without making a point of the series' status as a coproduction: it is an example of what Michele Hilmes calls "unmarked transnationalism" at the production level, while explicitly thematizing transnationalism in its narrative.[10]

For Showtime's audiences *Episodes* is American, and for BBC audiences it is British. In 2011, when *Episodes* reached the screen, there were several premieres of British formats remade for American viewers, such as *Being Human* (SyFy, 2011–2014), *Shameless* (Showtime, 2011–2017), and *Skins* (MTV, 2011).[11] Theories of national difference refer back to the concept of cultural proximity (for example, between the Anglophone neocapitalist societies of Britain and the United States) to account for success in export, adaptation, or remaking of a television format.[12] Proximity is assumed at the beginning of *Episodes*; Merc's desire to remake *Lyman's Boys* is not questioned, but assuming proximity is just the precondition for drawing attention to cultural differences. *Episodes* thematizes the process of adaptation and transferability while reflecting on the otherness that Sean and Beverly experience, drawing on widespread perceptions of national difference. All of this estranges British and American television production cultures from each other, setting them up as opposite poles. But it also estranges production cultures from themselves; they become exaggerated caricatures, on which *Episodes'* comedy is based. The program's satirical thrust relies on this doubled opposition, which both asserts and questions the "essence" of each national entity, in a similar way that the relatively successful *Torchwood* (BBC, 2006–2011, screened on BBC America, 2007–2009) had done with national differences between England, Wales, and the United States.[13] *Episodes* uses differences rather than trying to conceal them.

Evaluations of each television culture rely on difference, but the ways that their meanings shift reveal that these meanings are contingent and rhetorical, rather than actual. Arguments about the "essence" of national television cultures are moves in a discursive contest in which the two poles of British and American television depend on each other. These positions are reversible, and although *Episodes* relies on them as the premise of its comedy, the actuality of the series' own production is more complex. It is a hybrid in which BBC and Showtime are partners, the director is British, while the writers are American, and most of the principal cast are Americans who traveled to Britain to shoot the episodes.[14] The relatively few exterior sequences were shot in Los Angeles, but much of *Episodes* takes place indoors, on sets constructed on soundstages. Merc's impressive office at the network, later taken over by Carol Rance (Kathleen Rose Perkins) and other subsequent network heads in the perpetual jostle for power in the series, is an uncluttered space dominated by large windows looking out over the city below and has predominantly white decor that reflects the bright California sunshine. In fact, the exterior views were created with green screen and photographic cycloramas by the British designer Grenville Horner, using bright white lighting and a palette of pale colors and hard textures to convey the environment of Southern California. The office is actually in a British studio. Those sequences made on location, such as when Sean and Beverly are driving open-topped cars on the LA freeways, or the repeated motif in which Beverly goes jogging or walking with Carol in the Hollywood Hills in the evening, are shot in the "golden hour" that bathes the actors in warm light, and scenes are color graded in postproduction to emphasize an apparently unchanging summer climate. The large, luxurious house allocated to Sean and Beverly is in the style of the detached mansions of Bel Air and Beverly Hills, mixing contemporary concrete construction with references to Spanish adobe, but this location was actually in the London suburbs, as was LeBlanc's supposed Malibu beach-house.[15] Places and spaces in *Episodes* conform to conventional representations of domestic and working environments associated with Hollywood, as markers that signal familiar discourses and representations.

Sean's and Beverly's responses to the alien US culture individualize the different responses that it provokes. Sean is fundamentally optimistic, impressed by LeBlanc, and excited by the glamour and luxury of Los Angeles. LeBlanc lets Sean drive his sports car and takes Sean on his private jet to a sushi restaurant that LeBlanc has launched in Las Vegas (S1, E3). Beverly, on the other hand, is preoccupied by the deceptiveness of the network powerbrokers, including the star power of the manipulative LeBlanc himself, and this establishes tensions both between her and Sean and between both of them and LeBlanc. In parallel scenes later in the first season (S1, E5), LeBlanc takes Sean to a celebrity fundraising party for rape prevention at which LeBlanc callously talks through the speeches and drinks free champagne, while Beverly sits with Carol in the empty *Pucks!* studio smoking marijuana and deploring the affair she is having with her boss, Merc. The triangular relationships then lead to Beverly having an affair with LeBlanc in season 2, breaking up her marriage. In season 3, Sean and Beverly go into therapy, allowing Crane and Klarik to script scenes that make fun of supposed Californian preoccupations. The therapist asks Beverly what her vagina would say if it could talk, for example. By season 5, LeBlanc has become the host of a game show, *The Box*, produced by Merc, who makes his life hell because of their soured relationship, and Carol is unemployed. Sean and Beverly work for Sean's former writing partner and fellow émigré Briton Tim (Bruce Mackinnon), whom they both despise. In these and many other storylines, conventional tropes representing Hollywood's glamour and ruthlessness, corporatism and incestuousness, and luxury and sordidness are explored through the detail of the characters and their recombinant relationships, and the twists and turns of the network's day-to-day production culture.

SITCOM FORMATS AND CONVENTIONS

Episodes was shot with a single camera, out of story sequence, in soundstage sets and a few outside locations, whereas a traditional sitcom is performed in story sequence, in as few takes as possible, and shot with multiple cameras in front of an audience. Crane and Klarik wrote each episode rather than adopting the more usual American practice of a sitcom writing team, collectively and collaboratively producing scripts based on prescribed outlines and a story arc provided by a creator-showrunner.[16] Because of their long runs of episodes over multiple seasons, new episodes for traditional network sitcoms are written while completed scripts for earlier episodes are being shot, but Crane and Klarik finished all the scripts for the first seven-episode season of *Episodes* before any shooting began. They were therefore able to be on set each day, watching the shoot alongside the director and executive producer.[17] They claimed that this creative control gave them scope to hone character arcs and polish dialogue in a way that would be impossible with a screenwriting team in a writers' room struggling to keep to a shooting schedule. In various ways, *Episodes* is not a sitcom.

Crane and Klarik were habitually insistent that the actors deliver the words on the page.[18] Inasmuch as *Episodes* is driven by the scripts and is not a star vehicle, the roles allow for commutation between actors, and indeed two actors in major roles, Thomas Haden Church (Merc) and Claire Forlani (Beverly) were replaced during preproduction due to diary conflicts. The most reflexive casting choice is Matt LeBlanc in the role of himself, and he was attached to the project at Crane's suggestion (Crane having known LeBlanc since before they worked together in *Friends*): "The idea was that in the original British version of the show the part was played by an elderly Shakespearean actor. So we thought—what is the furthest you could get from him? And then we went beyond even that. It's the worst piece of casting in the world!"[19] The first episode devotes its central scene to this casting meeting, in which Merc, Carol, and other studio staff keep up a stream of encouraging, upbeat platitudes while the British actor Julian Bullard (Richard Griffiths) is humiliatingly required to audition twice for the role of Lyman, the second time in a poor imitation of an American accent, because his British reputation carries no weight in the United States. Casting is a means for *Episodes* to set up and critique parochial American assumptions about British and American actors (Pearson 2010).[20]

The representations of acting in *Episodes* and *Pucks!* draw on mythologies about a "theatrical" British mode of acting versus a "cinematic" American one that form part of the larger comparative project of the show. As Simone Knox and Gary Cassidy show in their chapter for this volume, theatricality has divergent and contrasting meanings in transatlantic television culture. British performers are acknowledged for the rigor of their professional training, their attention to the detail of the script, and their immersion in a distinguished tradition of theater performance. But on the other hand, American acting is regarded as more spontaneous and natural, especially in the ways actors use their bodies and gestural expression, seen as more fitting for cinema or television than the more speech-focused medium of theater.

Episodes' first episode gives the audience occasional glimpses of *Lyman's Boys*, a traditional half-hour sitcom shot in front of a live studio audience and performed in story sequence in long takes, like a theater play. Its lead actor, Julian Bullard, is established as a famous British theater actor, known for his large-than-life performances, hinted at metonymically by his physically large size. Richard Griffiths, playing Bullard, was indeed an actor in the Royal Shakespeare Company, known in the United Kingdom (and to some extent through international syndication) for his performance in *Pie in the Sky* (ITV, 1994–1997), in which he played an English chef and police detective, and also for supporting roles in the Harry Potter film franchise. But *Episodes* probably draws most from his lead role in the theater play (2004–2006) and film *The History Boys* (2006), playing an eccentric teacher, a role that he reprised in a sellout Broadway run in 2006. Griffiths is much better known to US audiences than Greig or Mangan, even for the small audience of PBS screenings of the British programs they featured in.[21] The casting of Griffiths alludes to a transatlantic theater play, its internationally distributed film adaptation, and ideas about Britishness that are referenced via *The History Boys'* character of the schoolteacher Douglas Hector, an inspiring intellectual who is also a repressed homosexual.

Episodes thematizes its difference from traditional sitcom by means of *Pucks!*, the show-within-the-show that the protagonists are making. The different aesthetic of *Pucks!* includes its format, performance style, and mise en scène, each of which hark back to network sitcoms like *Friends*. The director of *Episodes*, James Griffiths, noted the difference between the style of *Episodes* and that of *Pucks!*: "It has a very different, heightened style, and feels like a very American sitcom."[22] The features that give this impression include spatial restriction, for almost all of the *Pucks!* scenes are shot on a set of a high school locker room. The performances in the show-within-the-show leave pauses for audience laughter and are directed outward to the missing fourth wall where an audience would be. In production, Griffiths explains, "It was definitely seen as its own little show, with a Pucks! crew, who spent two weeks with us at Pinewood Studios working alongside us."[23] The hockey coach in *Pucks!* is modeled closely on Joey, the character LeBlanc played in *Friends*, and in *Episodes* LeBlanc shifts back and forth between two performance styles. Sometimes he adopts the catchphrase-driven persona that he is required to adopt professionally in *Pucks!* and when he is responding to other characters in *Episodes* who expect him to be like Joey in *Friends*. But he also plays the "real" LeBlanc, an actor making *Pucks!* While LeBlanc comments frequently when playing himself in *Episodes* on how tiresome this role-playing is, he also responds to criticism about its banality with, "Tell that to my house in Malibu!" Sitcom performance is represented as highly conventionalized, but also effective and lucrative as a product or commodity. LeBlanc commented, for example, that "making Friends was like being in a play. The audience is in the scene with you and you have to wait for the laughter to die down before you deliver your next line. But this [*Episodes*] is much more real and grounded in reality."[24]

The effect of showing *Pucks!* being made in *Episodes* is to enhance the appeal of *Episodes* to verisimilitude, and Griffiths, for example, publicly attested that making *Pucks!* reflected what US sitcom production is really like: "We've had similar conversations in wardrobe and in casting sessions."[25] *Pucks!* and the story of its production are set up as satirical exaggerations that contrast with the fictional world of *Episodes* that enfolds them. However, this enables *Episodes* to point up the supposed reality of the American television industry all the more. When Sean and Beverly are invited to dinner at Merc's house (S1, E2), Beverly thankfully agrees with Carol's comment that the women can eat the hors d'oeuvres because they don't need to compete with surgically enhanced young actresses. But then when Beverly puts her whole canape in her mouth, Carol skillfully removes anything fattening from her own before eating it. Throughout *Episodes*, the British outsiders are keen to conform but are never sure of the distinctions between performance and reality. Mangan commented: "Episodes is pretty realistic actually. I shot a pilot out in LA about three years ago. The whole process is bewildering, unsettling and exciting."[26] Mangan already held an opinion about working in the United States that matched the complex political and economic machinations represented in *Episodes*, and in turn he commends the sitcom because it confirmed his view. Verisimilitude, in this context, means reinforcement of national differences already circulating in discourse.

The publicity around *Episodes* frequently draws attention to the question of the distinction between actor and role. For example, the first BBC press pack in December 2010, shortly before *Episodes* premiered, included a quotation from LeBlanc: "I am really excited to be working with Showtime and the BBC. And I am also so glad I got the part; seeing someone else playing Matt LeBlanc would have been devastating."[27] LeBlanc won the Golden Globe for Best Actor for this work on the first season of *Episodes* in 2011, and was nominated for an Emmy as best leading actor in a comedy. Another BBC press release quotes LeBlanc explaining: "He is more Matt LeBlanc than Matt LeBlanc, just as the Larry David on Curb Your Enthusiasm is some evil twin approximation of the real one."[28] Having played Joey in *Friends* until 2004, LeBlanc was given the spin-off *Joey* (2004–2006), in which the character, who was an actor, was relocated from New York to Hollywood. The continuities with *Friends* loaded considerable expectation on LeBlanc and the show, which it failed to fulfill, and LeBlanc did not perform again until offered the role of himself in *Episodes*. BBC's promotional discourse discusses LeBlanc's casting and quotes him explaining that he had been burned out from playing Joey for twelve years, and was "a little afraid of being exposed as the scripts hadn't been written yet—I was pretty nervous about what they might be making fun of."[29] In the first season's trip to Las Vegas (S1, E3) where LeBlanc impresses Sean with his new restaurant, Crane and Klarik draw on popular myths about the real LeBlanc by having him invite Sean to follow him into the toilet so that Sean can see LeBlanc's proverbially large penis. "It was like a science fiction creature," Sean reports to Beverly.

Of course, *Episodes* makes fun of LeBlanc's fame and fortune resulting from his success in *Friends* but also makes fun of his inability to play any other role. In *Episodes* LeBlanc has to audition for the role of himself. "How could I not get it?" he asks his agent in some confusion. "Well, they're seeing some really good people," the agent replies. After LeBlanc's audition the casting director comments, "I think we've got [someone] better." The program repeatedly raises the question of authenticity, not only in the sense of LeBlanc's role as himself but also in the willful deceptions and self-deception that the LeBlanc character displays. The people surrounding him can rarely perceive that he is other than the unsophisticated Joey, and he, his agent, and the network executives use this to manipulate Sean and Beverly into making changes to *Pucks!*

A repeated series of crises pose threats to the ongoing production of *Pucks!*, but these short-term problems run alongside characters' relationship narratives that develop over several episodes, or over several seasons. Traditional sitcoms have little or no storyline progression from episode to episode and have free-standing plots in each episode. Settings and character relationships remain constant, and any disruption to them is resolved within an episode so they are back in place for the following episode. But distinctions between series and serials are being eroded in an era of what Jason Mittel calls "narrative complexity" in which programs "feature some episodic plotlines alongside multiepisodic arcs and ongoing relationship dramas," and *Episodes* combines serial storylines with the closure achieved by resolving short-term plot twists.[30] The most significant of these serial arcs is the marital back-and-forth between Sean and Beverly. According to executive producer Jimmy Mulville, the fact that *Episodes'* characters are "emotionally driven so that it's not just a series of jokes" was one of the reasons BBC2 commissioned the series.[31] The implication is that the channel would not have been interested in a conventional episodic sitcom but was interested in a comedy drama with serial elements.

CHANNEL BRANDING AND COPRODUCTION

Until the fifth season in 2017, *Episodes* was coproduced by Hat Trick, Showtime, and the BBC. In 2015, BBC announced that it was withdrawing, but retained a license to broadcast *Episodes*.[32] Showtime became the exclusive owner of broadcast and distribution rights to the program, and for BBC it became, in effect, an import despite its production in British studios and the mixed British and American cast. When *Episodes* was put into production in 2009, Showtime Networks was owned by CBS Corporation. It ran the Showtime network, the Movie Channel, and Flix, as well as a bundle of channels under the Showtime and Flix brands. It created original programs and offered pay-per-view television entertainment specials, pop music concerts, and sporting events. In common with the traditional broadcast networks and other paid cable providers, Showtime was also developing its HD, web-based, and on-demand services. The high unit cost of drama and the necessity to sustain production bases mean that networks and studios require long-running series with an infinitely extendable narrative. Cable channels, not being dependent on spot advertising, can produce more diverse drama formats. They concentrate on shorter drama that reinforces channel branding and that is more innovative than network dramas because constraints on language and behavior are looser than for free-to-air network programs. Innovation and appearing distinct from ordinary TV have become important to Showtime and other US cable channels like HBO and Bravo, and *Episodes'* thematic focus on the differences between British and American cultures seems calculated to deliver exactly this stimulating if rather self-congratulatory pleasure to its audiences. *Episodes* denigrates conventional network sitcom but benefits from intertextual references to it through the casting of LeBlanc. The casting of British actors in its lead roles also signals its offer of distinctiveness and quality.[33]

Pay cable channels are funded mainly by subscription, which is the closest model that the United States has to the British license fee system that pays for the BBC. Similar problems and opportunities to those leading to Showtime's role in US television emerged in Britain during the 1990s. New channels, cable, and satellite began to erode and segment traditional audiences. BBC2 shifted from a paternalistic address to minorities within a public service remit into an address to upmarket audience niches, which did not mean excluding US imports but scheduling them more selectively.[34] On the mass-audience broadcast channels BBC1 and ITV, the number of US dramas decreased significantly in prime time, so American drama became less visible and was more significant to the smaller traditional channels BBC2 and Channel 4. Their audiences were relatively young and middle class, and those audiences were attractive to Channel 4's potential advertisers and for BBC's differentiation of BBC2 from BBC1. Rebranding at Channel 4 was built around specific US imports, including *Frasier* (NBC, 1993–2004), *Friends*, and Hat Trick's British entertainment gameshow *Whose Line Is It Anyway?* (1988–1999).[35] It was Rick Rosen from Hat Trick's US agency WME, which had represented the company since its successful US export of the *Whose Line Is It Anyway?* format to ABC (1998–2007), who telephoned Mulville to suggest a meeting with Crane and Klarik when they had first created the idea for *Episodes*.[36] There was already a transatlantic relationship between channel brands, writers, and producers that made *Episodes* possible.

Crane and Klarik coexecutive produced *Episodes* as well as writing it, working with Mulville, Hat Trick's cofounder. Hat Trick has a long record of successes in British comedy programs such as *Father Ted* (Channel 4, 1995–1998) and *Outnumbered* (BBC, 2007–2014), but its efforts to sell programs and formats in the United States had met with limited success hitherto. The sitcom *The Worst Week of My Life* (BBC, 2004–2006) was made as a pilot by Fox (2005) but not picked up; then it ran as a local version titled *Worst Week* on CBS (2008–2009) but was canceled after one season. Hat Trick's ethnic minority comedy *The Kumars at No. 42* (BBC, 2001–2004, 2005–2006) was remade as *The Ortegas* by Fox in 2003, but the episodes were never screened. Mulville was involved in attempts to remake the BBC sitcom *Game On* for Fox, about an agoraphobic man sharing an apartment. He recalled that network executives asked, "'Can't he leave the house once, to go down to Foot Locker?' . . . Bit by bit it got eroded from being a distinctive, quirky, black comedy into being about three jolly people sharing an apartment and it never got made."[37] This assumption that British television is dark, quirky, and depressing and so needs to be changed to appeal to American tastes underlies *Episodes'* dramatization of US network executives' compulsion to remodel *Lyman's Boys* as *Pucks!* British and more generally European public service traditions have a double-edged status, as old-fashioned, middle class, and middlebrow, yet at the same time achieving standards of artistic quality that can lead to overseas format sales and remakes.[38] *Episodes* invites a comparative analysis of both institutional structures and program aesthetics, and debates questions of quality and value. The fact that *Episodes* is a BBC coproduction is especially relevant, since although the British commercial channels (especially the main commercial broadcaster ITV) generally share its public service ethos, the BBC is most associated with the principles of public service broadcasting as the United Kingdom's founding radio and television service.

British comedy export to the United States has been significant since the 1960s,[39] though adapted sitcoms for US networks have had varying fortunes. Very successful series in Britain have failed in the United States,[40] such as *Dad's Army* (BBC, 1968–1977), which never survived beyond its pilot, titled *Rear Guard* (ABC, 1976). *Fawlty Towers* (BBC, 1975, 1979) was remade for US audiences several times. The first version was *Snavely* (ABC, 1978), whose pilot did not lead to a series, and although *Amanda's* (ABC, 1983) ran for one season, the next remake, *Payne* (CBS, 1999), was dropped after only nine episodes. Rather more successfully, the prison sitcom *Porridge* (BBC, 1973–1977) was remade as *On the Rocks* (ABC, 1975–1976) and achieved twenty-two episodes before cancellation. *Butterflies* (BBC, 1978–1983) ran for four series in the United Kingdom, but only the pilot of its 1979 US version for NBC was broadcast. *Birds of a Feather* (BBC, 1989–1998) was screened for only eight episodes as *Stand by Your Man* (Fox, 1992). *The Fall and Rise of Reginald Perrin* (BBC, 1976–1979) was remade as *Reggie* (ABC, 1983) but only managed one season in its US form. Much more successful examples include *Keep It in the Family* (ITV, 1980–1983), which ran for five series in the United Kingdom and lasted 151 episodes when remade in the US as *Too Close for Comfort* (ABC, 1980–1986). Similarly, the two British series of *Dear John* (BBC, 1986–1987) were extended to ninety NBC episodes (1988–1990) under the same title. The five BBC series of *One Foot in the Grave* (1990–2000) were remade and retitled *Cosby* (1996–2000) as a vehicle for the veteran comedian Bill Cosby and ran for four seasons. Perhaps the best-known transfer is *The Office*, which had been made available to American audiences on BBC America, launched in 1998 as an outlet for programming controlled by BBC Worldwide (see Chris Becker's chapter in this volume). Worldwide's remit is to generate revenue by undertaking commercial activities incompatible with the BBC's domestic public service role. It built audiences for cult programs like *Fawlty Towers* that had previously been available only on PBS and showcased programs that BBC had not hitherto sold to the US market. Alongside home improvement and gardening programs that were picked up for US network versions, comedy was part of the offering, leading to *The Office: An American Workplace* (NBC, 2005–2013).

Transatlantic trading in comedy has often relied on personal effort by well-placed individuals. For example, the British Beryl Vertue began as an agent who sold comedy scripts and formats across Europe and in the United States. Her meetings with the US producer Norman Lear resulted in the transatlantic remake of *Till Death Us Do Part* (BBC, 1965–1975), initially as *Those Were the Days* (ABC, 1969) and two unbroadcast pilots, before achieving long-running success as *All in the Family* (CBS, 1971–1979). The format led to both British and US spin-offs, developing characters from the original series. These included *Maude* (CBS, 1972–1978), which was then remade in Britain as *Nobody's Perfect* (ITV, 1980, 1982), and CBS sitcoms *The Jeffersons* (1975–1985), *Archie Bunker's Place* (1979–1983), *Gloria* (1982–1983), *Good Times* (1974–1979), and *704 Hauser* (1994). Vertue also set up Lear's version of the long-running BBC sitcom *Steptoe and Son* (BBC, 1962–1965, 1970–1974), retitled *Sanford and Son* (NBC, 1972–1977), with NBC spin-offs *Grady* (1975–1976), *The Sanford Arms* (1977), and *Sanford* (1980–1981). Her independent production company, Hartswood Films, produced *Men Behaving Badly* (ITV, 1992; BBC, 1994–1998), which was then remade for NBC in 1997 with same title and lasted twenty-eight episodes. Hartswood also made *Coupling* (BBC, 2000–2004), which was remade for NBC in 2003, cocreated by Vertue's son-in-law Steven Moffat and produced by her daughter, Sue. The same team made the drama *Sherlock* (2010–) which is an international coproduction with the US public broadcaster WGBH Boston.

Networks of professional business relationships are means of reducing the inherent creative and financial risk in seeking new program ideas and commissioning pilots, especially when the individuals involved have extensive industry contacts and track record. One of the creative team working on *Three's Company* in Hollywood was Len Richmond, an American who moved to Britain and wrote *Agony* (ITV, 1979–1981), which was then remade as *The Lucie Arnaz Show* (CBS, 1985). Jeremy Lloyd, cocreator and cowriter of *Dad's Army* and other British successes, performed in *The Rowan and Martin Laugh-In* (NBC, 1968–1973) and on returning to the United Kingdom launched the idea for *Are You Being Served?* (BBC, 1972–1985), which was remade as *Beane's of Boston* (CBS, 1979). This kind of entrepreneurship was also undertaken by Don Taffner (succeeded by his son Don Taffner Jr.), who was behind the US remake of the British sitcom *Man about the House* (ITV, 1973–1976), which ran for six series in Britain and was remade as *Three's Company* (ABC, 1977–1984). Characters from the series featured in spin-offs that were remade in the United States; *George and Mildred* (ITV, 1976–1979) became *The Ropers* (ABC, 1979–1980) but only for a single season. A British sequel, *Robin's Nest* (ITV, 1977–1981) was remade as *Three's a Crowd* (ABC, 1984–1985). Taffner also sold the format of *Tom, Dick and Harriet* (ITV, 1982–1983) to CBS as *Foot in the Door* (1982–1983), and his sale of ITV's *Full House* (1985–1986) to CBS led to the pilot *No Place Like Home* (1985), but not a series. He sold *Miss Jones and Son* (ITV, 1977–1978) as *Miss Winslow and Son* (CBS, 1979), leading to a six-episode run. ITV's *Keep It in the Family* (1980–1983) was another of Taffner's sales, becoming *Too Close for Comfort*

(ABC, 1980–1987), and he coproduced the BBC's long-running sitcom *As Time Goes By* (1992–2002). The assumption of cultural specificity that *Episodes* trades on has always been in dialogue with the adaptation of television forms, formats, and genres transnationally, brokered by personal and institutional links.

Episodes was commissioned for BBC2 by Cheryl Taylor, who had led comedy commissioning for BBC in various roles since 2006.[41] Taylor had previously worked at Channel 4 and was responsible for commissioning comedies including *Spaced* (1999, 2001) and *Black Books* (2000–2004). She had also been head of comedy for Hat Trick, for whom she cocreated *Drop Dead Gorgeous* (BBC 2006–2007) and was executive producer of *The Worst Week of My Life*. Relationships among the creative staff at Hat Trick, BBC, and Showtime smoothed the way for *Episodes*' transatlantic identity for the channels screening it. In press statements ahead of its premiere, Mulville claimed that *Episodes* is "a classic BBC Two show. Who knows, but if you like shows like Extras, 30 Rock, The Office and Outnumbered, you'll probably like this."[42] In the USA, *Episodes* was given the desirable Sunday evening slot at 9:30 p.m., and Showtime's president of entertainment, Robert Greenblatt, claimed, "This show complements our eclectic and critically acclaimed line-up of half-hour comedies beautifully."[43] Genre manipulation in *Episodes* is a way of signaling quality by stressing both distinctiveness and consonance with other offerings. Like BBC's previous coproduction *Extras*, also set in the world of filmmaking with celebrities playing themselves, *Episodes* brands the channels that show it and the audiences that consume it, helping them to compete effectively and define themselves among their peers.

Television in Britain has been inhabited throughout its history by a concern for nationality and also a concern for global reach and connection, especially in Britain's acquisition of US programs and attempts to market British programs to the United States. This implicitly perpetuates a debate over the function of television as both reflective and also constitutive of ideas of national identity. Television has been a conduit for the representation of the external, other, and unfamiliar, as well as the shaping of domestic, national identities. In the academic arena, as Michele Hilmes notes: "Most histories of broadcasting have stayed within national boundaries. Comparative studies have been few, and largely confined to discussion of structures, laws and economies. The tricky business of comparative cultural studies of the media remains largely unexplored."[44] Discussions of international television exchanges in more recent times have gone beyond an initial focus on debates over media globalization,[45] because those debates tended to oscillate between generalizing theories of television's homogenization or national differentiation. There is a cadre of professionals in television distribution who identify and trade in formats and completed programs, with the aim of finding those creative products' place in new contexts beyond their territory of origination. The business culture and taste preferences of television traders guide the ways that ideas of transferability and distinctiveness circulate.[46] Once relocated, the local adaptation of programs may involve significant changes to the original, as in the case of *The Office*, for example, especially over the span of several seasons.[47] Rather than trading in completed programs, or formats for local remakes, coproduction like that undertaken by BBC and Showtime for *Episodes* shows that, once program making begins, national differences may be less significant than the discursive representation of those differences. Ideas about specificity and difference circulate within the production cultures organized around the making of programs as well as within the television programs themselves.[48] Place matters in television in terms of the location of the industries and institutions of production, and the representation of place as an aspect of the ways audiences can engage with local, regional, and national identities. *Episodes* negotiates between notions of "here" and "there" that take a wide variety of forms and are drawn from well-established ideas about transatlantic television relationships between the United Kingdom and the United States. These ideas of "here" and "there," familiar and alien, are deictic, meaning that they point to place in contingent ways that can change and even reverse their significance depending on where the user of the discourse is situated. If it could not perform difference and also erase it, *Episodes* could not run for five seasons on each side of the Atlantic. The achievement of *Episodes* is that it not only shows how national identities are deployed as rhetorical moves, but also plays out the question of transatlantic identity and holds it in suspension at the same time.

NOTES

1. The theoretical notion of performativity adopted in this chapter derives ultimately from the deconstruction of sexual identity as performance in Judith Butler, *Bodies That Matter: On the Discursive Limits of "Sex"* (London: Routledge, 1993).
2. BBC, "*Episodes*—an Interview with Writers David Crane and Jeffrey Klarik," December 17, 2010, http://www.bbc.co.uk/pressoffice/pressreleases/stories/2010/12_december/17/episodes9.shtml.
3. BBC, "*Episodes*—an Interview with Jimmy Mulville, Hat Trick Productions," December 17, 2010, http://www.bbc.co.uk/pressoffice/pressreleases/stories/2010/12_december/17/episodes8.shtml.
4. BBC, "Interview with Crane and Klarik."
5. BBC, "Interview with Crane and Klarik."
6. BBC, "Interview with Crane and Klarik."
7. BBC, "Interview with Crane and Klarik."
8. Matt Zoller Seitz, "The Problem with American Remakes of British Shows," *Salon*, February 9, 2011, http://www.salon.com/2011/02/09/prime_suspect_remake/.
9. Seitz, "American Remakes."
10. Michele Hilmes, *Network Nations: A Transnational History of British and American Broadcasting* (New York: Routledge, 2012), 257.
11. Matt Zoller Seitz, "What Makes Matt LeBlanc's New Show So Good," *Salon*, February 3, 2011, http://www.salon.com/2011/02/03/showtime_episodes.

12. Joseph Straubhaar, "Beyond Media Imperialism: Asymmetrical Interdependence and Cultural Proximity," *Critical Studies in Mass Communication* 8:1 (1991): 39–59.

13. See Gareth James, "'Cool but High Quality': *Torchwood*, BBC America and Transatlantic Branding, 1998–2011," in *"Torchwood" Declassified: Investigating Mainstream Cult Television*, ed. Rebecca Williams (London: I.B. Tauris, 2013), 33–50.

14. Stephen Armstrong, "*Episodes'* Matt LeBlanc, Tamsin Greig and Stephen Mangan on Making a TV Show about Making a TV Show," *Radio Times*, May 14, 2014, http://www.radiotimes.com/news/2014-05-14/episodes-matt-leblanc-tamsin-greig-and-stephen-mangan-on-making-a-tv-show-about-making-a-tv-show. In fact, the second series of *Episodes* had to be shot in Los Angeles due to a requirement for a quick turnaround, but all production had been intended to be based in Britain.

15. Armstrong, "Making a TV Show."

16. BBC, "Interview with Crane and Klarik."

17. BBC, "Episodes: Matt LeBlanc Plays Matt LeBlanc," December 17, 2010, http://www.bbc.co.uk/pressoffice/pressreleases/stories/2010/12_december/17/episodes3.shtml.

18. BBC, "Interview with Crane and Klarik."

19. BBC, "Interview with Crane and Klarik."

20. Roberta Pearson, "The Multiple Determinants of Television Acting," in *Genre and Performance: Film and Television*, ed. Christine Cornea (Manchester: Manchester University Press, 2010), 166–183.

21. Jeanette Steemers, "British Television in the American Marketplace," in *American Remakes of British Television: Transformations and Mistranslations*, ed. Carlen Lavigne and Heather Marcovitch (New York: Lexington, 2011), 1–16.

22. BBC, "*Episodes*—an Interview with Director James Griffiths," December 17, 2010, http://www.bbc.co.uk/pressoffice/pressreleases/stories/2010/12_december/17/episodes7.shtml.

23. BBC, "Interview with James Griffiths."

24. BBC, "Matt LeBlanc Plays Matt LeBlanc."

25. BBC, "Interview with James Griffiths."

26. BBC, "Episodes—Stephen Mangan Plays Sean," December 17, 2010, http://www.bbc.co.uk/pressoffice/pressreleases/stories/2010/12_december/17/episodes4.shtml

27. BBC, "Episodes Introduction," December 17, 2010, http://www.bbc.co.uk/pressoffice/pressreleases/stories/2010/12_december/17/episodes.shtml

28. BBC, "Matt LeBlanc Plays Matt LeBlanc."

29. BBC, "Matt LeBlanc Plays Matt LeBlanc."

30. Jason Mittel, "Narrative Complexity in Contemporary American Television," *Velvet Light Trap* 58 (2006): 32.

31. BBC, "Interview with Jimmy Mulville."

32. Nellie Andreeva and Nancy Tartaglione, "Showtime Takes Over Production of 'Episodes'; BBC2 Still Will Air Season 5," *Deadline Hollywood*, August 27, 2015, http://deadline.com/2015/08/episodes-showtime-takes-over-production-season-5-bbc-2-1201507801/.

33. Elke Weissmann, *Transnational Television Drama: Special Relations and Mutual Influence between the US and UK* (Basingstoke: Palgrave Macmillan, 2012), 170.

34. Elke Weissmann, "Drama Counts: Uncovering Channel 4's History with Quantitative Research Methods," *New Review of Film and Television Studies* 7:2 (2009): 189–207.

35. Catherine Johnson, "Tele-branding in TV III: The Network as Brand and Programme as Brand," *New Review of Television Studies* 5:1 (2007): 5–24.

36. BBC, "Interview with Jimmy Mulville."

37. BBC, "Interview with Jimmy Mulville."

38. Christopher Hogg, "Cracking the USA? Interpreting UK to US TV Drama Translations," *New Review of Film and Television Studies* 11:2 (2013): 111–132.

39. Jeffrey Miller, *Something Completely Different: British Television and American Culture* (Minneapolis: University of Minnesota Press, 2000), 111–138.

40. See, *Radio Times Guide to TV Comedy*, ed. Mark Lewisjohn (London: BBC, 2003), 856.

41. BBC, "Cheryl Taylor, Controller, CBBC," *Inside the BBC: Management Structure*, June 30, 2016, http://www.bbc.co.uk/corporate2/insidethebbc/managementstructure/biographies/taylor_cheryl.

42. BBC, "Interview with Jimmy Mulville."

43. BBC, "Interview with James Griffiths."

44. Michele Hilmes, "Introduction," in *The Television History Book*, ed. Michele Hilmes and Jason Jacobs (London: British Film Institute, 2003), 1.

45. John Sinclair, Elizabeth Jacka, and Stuart Cunningham, "New Patterns in Global Television," in *The Media* Reader, ed. Paul Marris and Sue Thornham (Edinburgh: Edinburgh University Press, 1999), 170–190.

46. See Denise Bielby and C. Lee Harrington, *Global TV: Exporting Television and Culture in the World Market* (New York: New York University Press, 2008); Giselinde Kuipers, "The Cosmopolitan Tribe of Television Buyers: Professional Ethos, Personal taste and Cosmopolitan Capital in Transnational Cultural Mediation," *European Journal of Cultural Studies* 15:5 (2012): 581–603.

47. Alexandra Breeden and Joost De Bruin, "*The Office*: Articulations of National Identity in Television Format Adaptation," *Television & New Media*, 11:1 (2010): 3–19.

48. Jean Chalaby, "The Making of an Entertainment Revolution: How the TV Format Trade Became a Global Industry," *European Journal of Communication* 26:4 (2011): 293–309; Timothy Havens, *Global Television Marketplace* (London: British Film Institute, 2006).

/// 9 /// *GAME OF THRONES*

Investigating British Acting

SIMONE KNOX AND GARY CASSIDY

In an often-repeated story, Sir Laurence Olivier, playing opposite Dustin Hoffman in the 1976 Marathon Man, *is said to have been astonished at the American actor's lengthy and exhausting Method-inspired preparation activities. Finally, Olivier decided to offer Hoffman some advice. "Why don't you try acting?" he suggested.[1]*

This much-mythologized encounter encapsulates long-standing notions of difference concerning the acting by British and by American actors, notions that have been articulated and referenced by industry practitioners, critics, and scholars on both sides of the Atlantic. For example, in Carole Zucker's 1995 *Figures of Light*, Lindsay Crouse is one of a number of US actors to express the belief that discipline and control are

> the biggest thing missing in American acting. We're great at is this kind of organic, shoot-from-the-hip, react-off-the-other-person, casual arena of acting. What we're not so good at is the control—voice work, interpretation, clarity, being able to use the text. . . . It's what the English are so good at, and also why we love their theater.[2]

There is a strong binary quality detectible in these views, which posit that where American acting is organic, inside out, "from the guts,"[3] concerned with "emotional truth"[4] and

181

more suitable for the screen, British acting is the inverse: disciplined, outside in, text-based, concerned with technique, and more suitable for the stage.

This chapter begins with a question: if those binary differences between acting by American and British actors are true, then how is it that a noticeably large number of British (and Irish) actors have been achieving success in contemporary US film and television? While such transnational creative labor flow is nothing new,[5] recent years have seen an unprecedented number of British and Irish actors secure prominent roles in high-profile US productions. One particularly noteworthy example is HBO drama *Game of Thrones* (2011–present), which hosts a plethora of established and emerging British and Irish actors, whose work has been met with acclaim, including five nominations for the Screen Actors Guild Award for Outstanding Performance by an Ensemble in a Drama Series. The chapter will focus on this telefantasy show, which revolves around the power struggles between different noble families within the fictional world of Westeros. It will specifically examine the work of Northern Irish actor Conleth Hill (who plays Varys, a scheming eunuch concerned with the protection of the realm) and Irish actor Liam Cunningham (who plays Davos Seaworth, loyal right-hand man to Stannis Baratheon), to consider the transatlantic success of British and Irish actors.

There is a nexus of industrial factors informing this transatlantic casting that are worth briefly noting.[6] Many British and Irish actors feel Hollywood's gravitational pull, desiring to be involved in "quality" television drama such as that associated with HBO, whose brand image as a premium cable channel is hinged around notions of distinction and a culture of production emphasizing high production values and creative risk-taking. British and Irish actors, in turn, may offer both high cultural capital and "productive anonymity" to US productions.[7] This means that these actors can endow their productions with the prestige connotations of the British stage and British drama school training, while enhancing verisimilitude and realism. Indeed, through their limited leverage for salary negotiation, their casting can also help to reduce labor costs, so their anonymity is doubly productive. More broadly, the transatlantic casting of such actors is facilitated by a shift in US industry practices following the success of another HBO drama to feature a host of British and Irish actors (including Damian Lewis, Michael Fassbender, Tom Hardy, and James McAvoy), namely *Band of Brothers* (2001). This acclaimed miniseries set a catalyzing precedent that helped shift attitudes and perceptions concerning the suitability of Anglophone actors from east of the Atlantic. In this century, such actors' employment opportunities in the United States have been located within and enabled by a complex transatlantic framework that features both strategic alliances between talent agencies and the use of digital/mobile technology such as Skype to save time, labor, and costs during the casting process.[8]

These industrial factors are significant reasons why so many British and Irish actors have been cast across the Atlantic; however, by themselves, they represent an incomplete picture. What has not yet been considered sufficiently regarding this transatlantic actor flow is how the work produced by the actors in question may inform this. Julian Petley identified a problem of performance for British actors in the 1970s and 1980s, who in his view often exhibited awkward, theatrical acting styles, struggling to work out the widely perceived nature of acting for the camera, namely "how to *look* without appearing to *act*."[9] More recently, Trevor Rawlins, using the transatlantically coproduced miniseries *Burn Up* (BBC2 / Global Television, 2008) as his case study, has noted that "it is the background of American actors and American acting culture that has furnished the American actor with the techniques to explore screen performance in ways that can put them ahead of their British counterparts."[10] However, with US network, cable, and streaming television as well as blockbuster film franchises featuring British and Irish actors in leading parts since the early 2000s, US actors cannot be understood to have been ahead of their counterparts from east of the Atlantic for close to two decades; and the problem of performance cannot apply to British and Irish actors working in contemporary US film and television. Indeed, Christine Becker explores the cultural rhetoric of British superiority that has circulated within press and industry discourses in recent years, which frames British actors as the more suitable for (US) prestige drama, not least because of their approach to acting.[11]

It is therefore timely that this chapter considers in detail how the work of Liam Cunningham and Conleth Hill in *Game of Thrones* both confirms and problematizes some common assumptions about British acting, and thus by extension notions of difference between British and American acting. The chapter will ground its discussion in the close analysis of specific moments from *Game of Thrones* and will pay particular attention to vocal performance. One reason for this is the "relative neglect of the voice" in scholarship noted by Adrian Garvey.[12] Garvey's point refers specifically to cinema, but is even more acute for television. Another reason is that strong vocal technique is what both British and Irish actors have traditionally been acclaimed for and what allows such actors to mask their origins when playing US roles with convincing US accents, which places them within a wider trajectory of "unmarked transnationalism."[13] The chapter's analysis will combine the scholar and practitioner perspectives, which will add a valuable awareness of and emphasis on process and the reality of practice to our analysis.

Game of Thrones and Cunningham and Hill make appropriate case studies for this chapter, as they address issues of national identity, and, as the chapter will show, critical engagement with their work produces insights that aid our understanding of the work of British and Irish actors in US film and television more broadly. *Game of Thrones'* high-profile status as flagship drama offers an opportunity to make a conspicuous inter-vention into ongoing discourses about British acting. It is an HBO production adapting US author George R. R. Martin's source novels (which themselves draw heavy inspira-tion from British history, culture, and geography) and shooting in different locations (including the Titanic Studios in Belfast, and the United Kingdom, the United States, Iceland, and Malta) with an international cast and crew. It has been a global export jug-gernaut, attracting a considerable international fan base (which it has sought to activate and reward via, for example, an interactive touring exhibition). As such, *Game of Thrones* is a transnational program that raises questions concerning the specificity and boundaries of national television culture and notions such as "Britishness" and "Americanness."

So too do the actors employed on the show. In fact, the two actors under scrutiny in this chapter make questions concerning the borders of "British acting" especially acute:[14] because of a distance of roughly 150 miles between their respective places of birth and certain geopolitical historical contingencies, Hill is Northern Irish and thus British, while Cunningham is Irish. However, Cunningham's career is significantly intertwined with British film, television, and theater; to exclude him and fellow Irish actors from discussions of British acting would risk marginalizing their work, depriving discussions of acting in British contexts and misrecognizing the traditions of and approaches to acting east of the Atlantic. So the presence of these actors in *Game of Thrones* reminds us that the term "British acting" is not only highly unstable,[15] but also an umbrella term into which Irish actors are usually, and far from unproblematically, subsumed, an umbrella term that contains (if not obscures) the fluid (if not liminal) identities of a number of actors.

The work of Hill and Cunningham in *Game of Thrones* is also illuminating for the wider presence of British and Irish actors in the United States in ways that link to genre. *Game of Thrones*, as a telefantasy show, could be assumed to privilege a certain kind of heightened performance style, one commonly labeled "theatrical" and with which British and Irish actors have traditionally been associated. Historical fantasy films and programs have often cast British and Irish actors to deliver a performance style deemed suitable for the genre and the epic tone for which so many of its exponents strive. However, *Game of Thrones* is not such a telefantasy text. Anchored within realism, its tone and performance style are more comparable to gritty dramas like its HBO brethren *The Sopranos* (1999–2007) and *The Wire* (2002–2008) than, for example, *The Lord of the Rings: The Fellowship of the Ring* (Peter Jackson, 2001). Thus, critical engagement with the performances within *Game of Thrones* is illuminating for the work of British and Irish actors in other US shows and films, such as, for example, Idris Elba's performance in *The Wire* or Alan Cumming's in *The Good Wife* (CBS, 2009–2016).

As for the specific actors chosen for our analysis, it may be tempting to assume that the acting by Conleth Hill could be understood as the one more representative of the kind of traditional British performance style associated with the telefantasy genre. Likewise, Liam Cunningham could be assumed to be more aligned with American acting (or conventional views thereof). Such assumptions could refer to a number of factors that would help to discursively position Cunningham and Hill at different ends of the US-UK acting binary. When interviewed, Hill has insisted that he is "not a method actor at all" and cited as points of reference for his work British actors who have received particular acclaim for their stage performances, namely Judi Dench, Michael Gambon, and Maggie Smith.[16] Prior to being cast as Varys, Hill had an especially successful stage career, winning the 2001 and 2005 Olivier Awards (for *Stones in His Pockets* and *The Producers*) and 2001 and 2008 nominations for Tony Awards (for *Stones in His Pockets* and *The Seafarer*). Liam Cunningham, on the other hand, has named two US performers as his favorite actors, Ed Harris and Frances McDormand.[17] His curriculum vitae includes significant screen roles, such as in the Stephen Poliakoff drama *Shooting the Past* (BBC2, 1999) and independent films *The Wind That Shakes the Barley* (Ken Loach, 2006) and *Hunger* (Steve McQueen, 2008)—winning Irish Film and Television Awards for the last two—as well as smaller roles in high-budget feature films, such as US blockbuster *The Mummy: Tomb of the Dragon Emperor* (Rob Cohen, 2008). However, such assumptions would be erroneous. As our detailed analysis will demonstrate, something much more complex and nuanced is at stake in Hill's and Cunningham's acting, and their supposedly different performance styles in *Game of Thrones*—respectively, outside in versus inside out, disciplined use of technique versus organic "shooting from the hip"—reveal themselves to share significant commonalities. These reflect both actors' equally nuanced approaches to performance, confounding easy assumptions about their work and challenging binary distinctions in discourses on acting.

Before we begin our close analysis of Hill's and Cunningham's acting in *Game of Thrones*, it is worth reflecting on the fact that the binary view concerning British and American acting has proven so resilient. One reason for this is that it goes to the core of discourses about acting per se, famously captured in Diderot's paradox of acting. To sketch out, nineteenth-century French philosopher Denis Diderot identified the paradox of the actor in the opposition of sensibility and premeditated physical technique. As Robert Gordon sums up:

> Diderot was concerned to discover whether great acting was produced by the exercise of "sensibility," through which the actor feels the emotions of the role he [*sic*] is

playing, or by the mechanical application of an external technique, by means of which the actor's intelligence exercises control over his corporeal instrument.[18]

As Gordon further notes, "Diderot eventually decided that great acting was produced by the exercise of technique alone," referencing acclaimed eighteenth-century British actor David Garrick as the paradigmatic example of an actor using this approach.[19] However, like so many of his professional peers,[20] Garrick proves to be an unstable point of reference, for he thought of acting as a combination of both sensibility and technique. Just as Garrick refused such a distinction, so the actors whose interview testimony has been invoked to articulate the distinction between British and US acting complicate this binary. Lindsay Crouse interjected into her thoughts quoted at the beginning of this chapter that she works closely on the text, "to be able to speak it, to know that my voice has the range to handle it, to know that I have enough breath control for it."[21] Similarly, John Lithgow, who undertook some actor training in Britain, followed his comments about how US actors are considered to be acting "from the guts" with the reflection: "I act from the inside and the outside simultaneously, my own hybrid. Also, every actor has to act according to the project and the material and the director."[22]

The practitioner perspective concerned with the reality of practice problematizes the Cartesian dualist logic that underlies Diderot's seminal writing as well as binary views concerning the difference between British and US acting. Here, our discussion is informed by the fact that one of us is a drama school-trained actor with years of professional experience, and located within a Western, broadly Stanislavskian approach to the analysis of performance. This offers an understanding of acting as a holistic process in which the outside-in approach emphasizing technique and the inside-out approach emphasizing feeling can, and should, complement and support each other. Individually, each one carries risks: the outside-in approach could produce contrived results lacking in "emotional truth." The inside-out approach does not necessarily provide screen actors with the tools they need to contend with on-set challenges (e.g., close proximity of crew and filmic apparatus, prescriptive technical cues, short bursts of activity). When both approaches work together, an actor can reach a certain state of double consciousness, in which organic choices driven by "emotional truth" are supported by a framework of technique and attention to the text.[23] It is this understanding of acting as a holistic process, which runs counter to long-standing binary views concerning British and US acting, that will now drive and, in turn, be articulated via concrete example by our analysis of Hill's and Cunningham's performances in *Game of Thrones*.

For Conleth Hill's performance, we have decided to anchor our analysis in the scene in the episode "And Now His Watch Is Ended" (S3, E4) in which Varys tells Tyrion

Lannister (Peter Dinklage) how he was made a eunuch. To briefly contextualize, Varys is the principal spymaster for the King, who in the cutthroat world of Westeros at this point is Joffrey, the nephew of Tyrion Lannister. Despite having recently saved the capital, King's Landing, from an attack by Stannis Baratheon, Tyrion has been removed from his position as Hand of the King (the second in command). In this scene, Tyrion visits Varys to find out what Joffrey's mother, his sister Cersei, is currently plotting against him. Varys, however, is preoccupied with telling Tyrion how he was, as a boy, castrated by a sorcerer, whom he has tracked down after decades. Varys tells his tale while slowly opening a crate containing the bound and gagged sorcerer.

Hill's performance supports conventional expectations pertaining to British acting. The scene is driven by and exemplifies Hill's use of disciplined technique, especially in terms of his voice. As Varys tells Tyrion the story of his castration, Hill deploys the whole register of his mellifluous voice, modulating within and across individual sentences (e.g., he lowers his pitch during "always in confidence"). He lingers on the sharp, sibilant sounds (e.g., "sliced me," see figure 9.1; "nastiness"), deploys a distinct stress pattern (e.g., "he *burned* my parts," "I *still* dream of that night"), and imposes an unusual syntactical rhythm (e.g., "a-symbolic-revenge," "small-council-chamber"). Pausing at the end of lines to let the meaning of his words set in, Hill also delivers several long sentences with strong breath control, with neither his volume dropping nor his diction losing precision. Through this technical strength, which he gained and honed during the voice training at the Guildhall School of Music and Drama and subsequent professional experience

FIGURE 9.1 Sibilant sounds: Conleth Hill as Varys

(including several years in repertory theater), Hill's acting brings considerable texture to and enlivens his dialogue.

It is important here to be mindful of the existing scholarship on the significance of sound technology for screen acting. Pamela Robertson Wojcik has noted in relation to film performance that "the voice must never be considered as emanating in any simple way from its visual source."[24] As she rightly points out, vocal performance is deeply intertwined with sound technology (in production, postproduction, and exhibition), in such a way that manipulation and design are effaced and disavowed. We are not claiming that Hill necessarily delivered all of his vocal performance in this scene on set or in continuous order, or that the use of the particular microphones deployed or postproduction sound work undertaken (including the possible use of ADR [additional dialogue recording]) does not affect the final product on screen. Of course, Hill's performance needs to be understood as "existing within, for, and through mediation" within the show's sound design.[25] However, just as it is important not to efface the role of technology, so it is crucial to sufficiently recognize the significance of actorly craft, skill, and labor within the nexus of vocal performance and sound design; and our points above about Hill's performance apply regardless, not least because ADR also requires considerable skill on the part of the actor.

With technology intertwined with his acting in complex ways, some of which exceed his creative agency, Hill nevertheless displays a level of technical skill and craft that are commonly associated with British acting. This indubitably involves a level of preparation on his part, which is arguably something not quite captured by Robertson Wojcik's argument that "film acting as such does not exist prior to mediation."[26] Screen acting always necessarily involves an element of preparation and rehearsal. (Even though formal rehearsal time has become scarce, actors commonly rehearse their lines and prepare scenes by themselves—Gary Oldman has called this his "kitchen work".)[27] Such preparation and rehearsal exist prior to mediation and form an intimate relationship with what actors do during production; and from a practitioner's perspective, which is concerned with process, acting cannot be considered separately from preparation and rehearsal. Hill's mediated performance in this scene and across the series is built on his prior work with the text, which likely involved trying out and marking up different variations, in order to work out the texture of the dialogue and "find ways to interpret the character behind the lines."[28]

When doing so, Hill would have especially considered his use of punctuation: faced in this scene with, effectively, one long speech, Hill has to work with several long sentences that are more than one line long. He tackles these by vocally signaling that even though he is reaching the end of a line, the sentence continues, through playing commas well with his breath (e.g., the sentence when he refers to "dream[ing] of the voice from the flames"). This is a technique commonly used by actors to speak (especially Shakespearean) verse, which Hill here employs to make the script his own, but without turning the script into verse. This technique connects Hill's acting to two notions strongly associated with British acting, namely the theater and Shakespeare, and interestingly, the use of mise-en-scène in *Game of Thrones* bears out a sustained intertextual linking of Varys with Shakespeare. At one point during this scene, Varys washes his hands in front of a mirror, looking at his own reflection while speaking in near direct address to the camera within a ghostlike framing (see figure 9.2). The references to *Macbeth* and (with a person hidden in a trunk) *Cymbeline* sit within a trajectory of scenes in several other episodes that present Hill's Varys within a Shakespearean frame of reference. Clearly the production team seeks to place Hill's Varys within a particular paradigm, informed by a general indebtedness to Shakespeare and an awareness of Hill's adeptness for soliloquizing.

However, Hill's adeptness and the deployment of a Shakespearean frame notwithstanding, Hill's performance, although somewhat heightened, does not read as awkward or "theatrical," with no trace of the problem of performance identified by Petley.[29] This is because Hill's acting choices are appropriate within the context of the role, and work toward the characterization of Varys. The role of the scheming eunuch lends itself to a particular acting approach that foregrounds attention to control, precision, and performance. That Hill deploys his voice and body in a carefully controlled way, whereby his vocal precision is coupled with a careful use of his face and body—he hardly blinks within the shots; he uses the crowbar for punctuation and emphasis (see figure 9.3)—reflects

FIGURE 9.2 Shakespearean framing: Varys soliloquizes

FIGURE 9.3 Precision and control: Hill uses a crowbar for punctuation and emphasis

and underscores the need for Varys to remain in control at all times, even when he is about to take revenge on the sorcerer for his castration. A more organic "shoot from the hip" approach to acting would be unlikely to serve a character whose continued survival in the game of thrones depends on his self-control and his successful performance of himself as an omniscient, quietly powerful, and somewhat unfathomable figure.

With the character playing the role of the mysterious schemer, Hill's drawing on a certain degree of performativity reads on the level of characterization and not of acting; and this is supported by Hill's use of technique not drawing attention to itself, becoming noticeable only upon scrutiny. For a role such as this, these would be appropriate acting choices for any actor, whether British, American, or from elsewhere. Hill's work in *Game of Thrones* is in this way not dissimilar to, for example, Alan Cumming's in legal drama *The Good Wife*. For his performance as political consultant Eli Gold, Cumming draws on strong vocal technique, not only in his use of an American accent, but more importantly in the way in which he interjects rhythms into and places emphases within his lines, maintaining crisp diction throughout the soliloquies he delivers on the show. Cumming displays some heightened elements through this controlled use of voice as well as his fluid body movements and facial expressions, but these read as fitting to his character, who is constantly scheming and continually performing. Both Hill and Cumming pitch the level of performativity (which links to theatricality) in their characterization appropriately to their specific roles, without crossing into the realms of "elevated" acting with which British and Irish actors have traditionally been associated. When doing so, their acting choices are informed by their genre contexts (gritty telefantasy and legal drama) but not necessarily "straitjacketed" by them: so, for example, in legal drama *Suits* (USA Network, 2011–present), Hill displays a strong and controlled use of voice, while at the same time exhibiting more of a "shoot from the hip" approach to his performance, which is appropriate to his particular character. This exemplifies and underscores John Lithgow's earlier noted point concerning specificity, namely that "every actor has to act according to the project and the material and the director."[30]

So Conleth Hill as Varys confirms some of the conventional assumptions about British acting by displaying technique, discipline, and close engagement with the text. Simultaneously, however, he problematizes these assumptions by demonstrating that such technical strength does not only work toward acting better suited for the stage, but can be embedded into characterization for screen-based acting. Let us now turn our attention to Liam Cunningham, whose acting also presents an interesting (and differently inflected) challenge to such conventional assumptions. The scene we have chosen takes place in episode "Breaker of Chains" (S4, E3) and concerns a confrontation between Davos and Stannis (Stephen Dillane) upon the news that King Joffrey is dead. Of the noble family Baratheon, Stannis sees himself as the legitimate heir to the throne instead of his incestuously conceived nephew Joffrey. Driven by the pursuit of duty and honor at all costs, Stannis previously both rewarded low-born former smuggler Davos with a knighthood for his loyal service during a siege and punished him for smuggling by shortening the fingers of one of his hands. Recently defeated at King's Landing, Stannis is now trying to rebuild his forces with Davos serving as his Hand of the King. In the scene, Stannis shows Davos a letter with the news of Joffrey's demise and chastises him for having raised insufficient troops thus far, while Davos is against Stannis's leaning toward the use of dark magic.

What is striking in this scene is that, as an Irish actor who needs to be understood as belonging to the paradigm of "British acting," Cunningham's performance noticeably counters traditional assumptions about the lesser spontaneity and aptitude for "acting from the guts" or "shooting from the hip" supposedly found within British acting. Such notions of spontaneity and of being "in the moment" run through Cunningham's acting choices. Reflecting the fact that Davos only recently started learning how to read, Cunningham moves his lips while reading the letter announcing Joffrey's demise (see figure 9.4). While this action might be indicated in the script, the way in which Cunningham executes it avoids making it come across as though it is a preconceived "spiel": he varies the pronouncedness of the lip movement, letting it recede and flare up, thus signaling Davos's moment-to-moment absorption in the contents of the letter.

Cunningham then moves through a series of quick gear changes across the rest of the shots. His face slackens and his eyes look into the middle distance, as his character

FIGURE 9.4 In the moment: Liam Cunningham as Davos

FIGURE 9.5 Wrong-footed by Stannis: Davos rouses

is stunned by the news and needs a moment to process it. Cunningham then shifts side-ways (see figure 9.5) to indicate that his character wakes from this moment as Dillane's Stannis angrily approaches him, literally wrong-footed by Stannis's rebuke. Cunningham continues this physical articulation of Davos's discomfort when his (unimpressive) list of houses that have confirmed support for Stannis's cause is met with dry sarcasm by Stannis. Since sarcasm is not Stannis's modus operandi, Cunningham expresses the unexpectancy of this response, which his character is unsure how to deal with, by not standing with both feet firmly on the ground, literally caught off-balance. By the time Stannis has made the withering joke that there are not enough men "to raid a pantry," Cunningham signals with a rise in his energy and a rallying arm movement that Davos has recovered sufficiently to refocus his attention on discussing ways forward, and spends the rest of the scene urging Stannis to focus on obtaining more soldiers instead of using dark magic.

What Cunningham succeeds at within and across the different shots here is to produce "the illusion of the first time," a significant challenge for screen and stage actors working within realism articulated by William Hooker Gillette in 1915. Gillette wrote:

> Unfortunately for an actor (to save time I mean all known sexes by that), unfortunately for an actor he knows or is supposed to know his part. He is fully aware . . . of what he is going to say. The character he is representing, however, does *not* know what he is going to say, but, if he is a human being, various thoughts occur to him one by one, and he puts such of those thoughts as he decides to, into such speech as he happens to be able to command at the time. Now it is a very difficult thing . . . for an actor who knows exactly what he is going to say to behave exactly as though he didn't; to let his thought (apparently) occur to him as he goes along, even though they are there in his mind already; and (apparently) to search for and find words by which to express those thoughts, even though these words are at his tongue's very end.[31]

Through his gear changes across the scene and his focus upon unanticipatingly reacting (to both the news of Joffrey's death and Stannis's anger), Cunningham certainly makes it seem as though his character is experiencing this moment for the first time. What is particularly noteworthy in this regard is the verbal interplay between Cunningham and Dillane: Dillane clips some of Cunningham's lines, and Cunningham lets two of his lines die out. In this way, they work well together to let their "thoughts apparently occur to them as they go along" and reflect a sense of listening well, making this encounter look unrehearsed (in the positive sense).

Interestingly, Cunningham has stated that the spontaneity of his performance in *Game of Thrones* is enabled by avoiding the George R. R. Martin novels on which the show is based:

> If we were making a movie I would have read it—I think. But I like the rollout of this, the fact that we're shooting season by season, and in a sense, it helps me as an actor to not know what's coming next; I deal with the problems that we have when we're given the scripts. Obviously I know season to season, but I don't really follow that, or want that. It takes the spontaneity out of it, and I don't want to be playing what's two books

ahead. . . . I want things to be surprising to me. Charles Dance and Peter [Dinklage] haven't read them either.[32]

This approach is further shared by Conleth Hill, who has commented:

I can't wait to read them when I'm finished. . . . But the reason I didn't is because I wasn't doing the books. I didn't want to read a brilliant scene in the books that wasn't in the TV series and worry about it. Or vice versa.[33]

As these observations reflect, the challenge of the illusion of the first time for television acting is inflected by television's diachronic potential, especially for shows based on preexisting source material. To help them stay focused on being in the moment and produce the illusion of the first time, actors such as Cunningham and Hill purposefully avoid reading the novels and, as Cunningham indicates, stay focused on the present tense even within the span of a season.[34] Of course, for Hill as Varys, the challenge of the illusion of the first time is very particular, in that—unlike Davos, who as Stannis's right-hand man often *reacts* to events—Hill must indicate that his scheming character frequently *plans* his actions carefully and often carries his words "at his tongue's very end." Crucially, he must do so without the actor making it look like he is mechanically moving through a list of preplanned actions.

Meeting the challenge of the illusion of the first time, Cunningham clearly calls into question conventional assumptions about British acting by producing "shoot from the hip" acting that is generally understood as suitable for screen-based performance and traditionally more associated with US actors. Crucially, however, Cunningham does so in a way that draws on strong technique, which is so frequently associated with acting for the stage and British acting. In the scene with Stannis, Cunningham's acting is in the moment and exudes spontaneity, yet there is still modulation and technique detectible upon scrutiny. Not dissimilar to Hill, Cunningham injects a particular stress pattern into the dialogue, emphasizing certain words on the beat (e.g., "*Soldiers* win wars, *soldiers* on the ground. It's . . . *dirty* on the ground!"). He moves his left hand somewhat like a conductor, underscoring his vocal beat pattern (see figure 9.6), and his head jerks repeatedly to reinforce his urging. Cunningham modulates his sentences well, managing to keep them vocally powerful throughout via strong breath support. Even when in the moment and delivering his lines rapidly, he does not lose the crispness of his diction, but maintains a melodic quality that makes his lines interesting to the ear.[35] This adds a lyricism to the spontaneity—for "shooting from the hip" that lacks variation and nuance is hardly an actor's aim. Trained at the Oscar Theatre School in Dublin, with professional experience on both stage and screen, and often praised by critics for his "invisible" acting style,

FIGURE 9.6 Precision and control: Cunningham visually underscores his vocal beat pattern

Cunningham certainly uses subtly present technique to help him deliver "shoot from the hip" acting.

Cunningham's work in *Game of Thrones* is comparable to that of many British and Irish actors cast in contemporary US film and television. For example, when playing drug kingpin Russell "Stringer" Bell in *The Wire*, Idris Elba displays a strong "shoot from the hip" quality in his performance, which gives a sense of being based on improvisation—his physical mannerisms read as spontaneous, his vocal intonation is both fluid and disjointed—but which, as showrunner David Simon has pointed out, is in fact not.[36] In *The Americans* (FX, 2013–2018), Matthew Rhys's performance as KGB agent Philip Jennings shares this organic quality in, for example, the way in which Rhys sometimes drags parts of his lines. This reads as a naturalistic speech pattern, mirroring how people may slow down parts of their sentences to give themselves time to think while talking, and benefits from Rhys's breath control and precise vocal technique. It also can be read as adding an additional layer of meaning, in that Rhys may be subtly signaling that his character is not a native speaker and might need more time to ensure he expresses himself correctly and idiomatically.[37] So, in the work of Cunningham, Elba, Rhys, and their professional peers, the use of external technique and an inner approach are in a close dialogue in ways that binary views of British and US acting styles do not accommodate.

To move toward a conclusion, we note Robert Gordon's comment from 2006:

Although there are differences between the younger generation of contemporary British actors and their American counterparts, these are not as noticeable as they were in the 1950s. This might be viewed as an effect of the postmodern tendency to efface differences between the local and the global.[38]

We share his view that noticeable differences between the acting by British and by US actors have reduced over time; however, we understand this not via recourse to post-modernism, but instead as part of the continual development of acting and actor training within shifting sociocultural contexts, industrial practices and evaluative discourses. In the United Kingdom, recent approaches to acting have been marked by the rising influence of Stanislavskian principles since the 1960s and, as David Shirley notes, the Meisner tech-nique for the last two decades,[39] as well as increasing provisions for screen-based acting in British drama school environments. Not only have actor-training traditions deriving from Jacques Copeau and Michel Saint-Denis thus been importantly complemented, but, with the decline of British repertory theater, British actors work on stage much less than used to be the case.[40] Thus, they find themselves less in the "default mode" of stage-based acting, which Petley identified as one of the issues behind the problem of performance he discussed.[41] As a consequence of these shifts, it is not surprising that contemporary British and Irish actors "know how to *look* without appearing to *act*."[42]

However, as the broader history of successful nontheatrical performances by British and Irish actors in the United States (and beyond) and our analysis of Conleth Hill's and Liam Cunningham's work in *Game of Thrones* more specifically show, British and Irish actors are and have long been more versatile than discourses and employment opportunities have necessarily acknowledged or accommodated. Certainly, the high cultural capital of British theater and especially Shakespeare has been a persisting influ-ence on actor training in Britain and (self-) perceptions of British acting. The discursive link to the prestige of the British stage has contributed to the resilience of the reductive binary that sees British actors as less accomplished at screen acting, yet it also plays a factor in the current strategic casting of British and Irish actors by US "quality" drama for their usable high cultural capital.[43] As one of us has argued elsewhere, following the shift in mindset by industry personnel in the United States and United Kingdom that, triggered by the success of *Band of Brothers*, led to the development of closer transatlantic working relationships,[44] British and Irish actors have found high-profile employment opportunities that allow them to showcase their abilities on an unprecedented scale.

As two of many acclaimed British and Irish actors who were expressly drawn by "quality" HBO shows such as *The Sopranos*, the work of Hill and Cunningham in *Game of Thrones* to some extent supports conventional expectations pertaining to British acting and at the same time raises important questions concerning such assumptions. Crucially, their acting demonstrates the essentially holistic nature of acting, in which "theatrical" acting choices can be closely embedded into truthful screen-based characterization; and technical strength and "acting from the guts" need not be opposed but actually work to support one another. Tendencies toward binary thinking and generalizing assumptions about national differences in acting have hung over debates on performance for a long time, aided by the instability of much of the critical terminology. We agree with Zucker's view:

> *Through repetition*, this generalized and rather cliched view of British and American performance has taken on the status of truth. Unfortunately, such statements do not begin to account for the vigor, authority, complexity, and emotional depth of performances by British actors.[45]

Future engagement with acting stands to gain much from an increased emphasis on specificity and process, and it is especially significant to recognize actors' processes across preproduction, production, and postproduction. Here, our discussion has found two particularly interesting points that deserve further attention, namely process in terms of the relationship between voice and mediation, and process in terms of the relationship between the illusion of the first time and television seriality. With its emphasis on detailed textual analysis informed by the scholar and practitioner perspective, we hope that our chapter offers a useful intervention into debates about British and American acting that will help to put the binary views of British and US acting that are no longer appropriate into the bins of history. This will benefit scholarship on performance, including the burgeoning field of writing about television, as well as on transatlantic television. The pronounced presence of British and Irish actors in US film and television already adds a significant transatlantic dimension to these productions. With the work produced by these actors a key reason for their transatlantic casting, understanding their acting as complex holistic processes that problematize generalizing assumptions and US-UK binaries makes an illuminating contribution to critical engagement with such transatlantic film and television.

NOTES

1. Virginia Wright Wexman, "Masculinity in Crisis: Method Acting in Hollywood," in *Movie Acting: The Film Reader*, ed. Pamela Robertson Wojcik (New York: Routledge, 2004), 127.
2. Carole Zucker, *Figures of Light: Actors and Directors Illuminate the Art of Film Acting* (New York: Plenum Press, 1995), 17.
3. John Lithgow in Zucker, *Figures of Light*, 87–88.
4. "Emotional truth" is an unstable, slippery term to be found within practitioner discourses on actor training and acting, especially within Stanislavskian-informed contexts. We use it to refer to acting that

imaginatively utilizes an actor's personal experiences to produce a performance that is read as believable by an audience.

5. See, for example, *Journeys of Desire: European Actors in Hollywood—a Critical Companion*, ed. Alastair Phillips and Ginette Vincendeau (London: BFI, 2006).

6. For a comprehensive discussion, see Simone Knox, "Exploring the Casting of British and Irish Actors in Contemporary US Film and Television," in *Exploring Television Acting*, ed. Christopher Hogg and Tom Cantrell (London: Bloomsbury, 2018), 154–170.

7. Elke Weissmann, *Transnational Television Drama: Special Relations and Mutual Influence between the US and UK* (Houndmills: Palgrave, 2012); 171; Christopher Holliday, "The Accented American: The New Voices of British Stardom on US Television," *Journal of British Cinema and Television* 12:1 (2015): 64.

8. Neither Cunningham nor Hill is part of the package deal that must have played a part in a sizable number of actors represented by United Agents getting cast on *Game of Thrones*.

9. Julian Petley, "Reaching for the Stars," in *British Cinema Now*, ed. Martin Auty and Nick Roddick (London: British Film Institute, 1985), 122.

10. Trevor Rawlins, "Screen Acting and Performance Choices," *Networking Knowledge: Journal of the MeCCSA Postgraduate Network* 3:2 (2010): 22.

11. Christine Becker, "Accent on Talent: The Valorization of British Actors on American Quality Television," in Hogg and Cantrell, *Exploring Television Acting*, 140–153.

12. Adrian Garvey, "'Steely Velvet': The Voice of James Mason," *Journal of British Cinema and Television* 12:1 (2015): 84.

13. Michele Hilmes, *Network Nations: A Transnational History of British and American Broadcasting* (New York: Routledge, 2012), 257. While Cunningham and Hill do not play US characters in *Game of Thrones*, they nevertheless use accents that are "foreign" to them: Northern Irish Hill adopts a southern English accent for Varys, and North Dubliner Cunningham has received praise for his northeastern English accent when playing Davos. In this way, their work offers an interesting inflection to debates on unmarked transnationalism.

14. "British acting" is an unstable, fluid term because approaches to acting and actor training in Britain bear out a long history of complex (often transnational) influences, in close dialogue with developments within cultural media, especially theater. British theater has long been associated with an emphasis on the text, technique, and vocal delivery but has also been marked by a myriad of practices that have challenged or diverged from that emphasis, including those influenced by Bertolt Brecht, Jerzy Grotowski, Jacques Lecoq, and the Living Theatre. Moreover, the binary view concerning the differences between British and US acting also does not accommodate the shifting relationships that approaches to acting east (and west) of the Atlantic have had with ideas concerning two notoriously flexible and relative terms: realism and naturalism. For a further discussion, see Robert Gordon, *The Purpose of Playing: Modern Acting Theories in Perspective* (Ann Arbor: University of Michigan Press, 2006).

15. Of course, the same applies to American acting, especially given that "Method" is a term with contested meanings, often used synonymously with American acting, which helps to uphold binary views concerning British and American performance styles.

16. Liz Hoggard, "Hill's Alive with the Sound of Music," *The Observer*, November 14, 2004, 8.

17. Part of a long history of individual actors exerting or absorbing influence across the Atlantic, Cunningham's choices here highlight and reinforce the instability of terms such as British acting and American acting (and the borders between them). This history can be gleaned in *Actors on Acting*, ed. Toby Cole and Helen Krich Chinoy (New York: Crown Publishers, 1974).

18. Gordon, *The Purpose of Playing*, 12.

19. Gordon, *The Purpose of Playing*, 13.

20. As the epigraph to this chapter attests, Olivier has been frequently invoked as a point of reference in discussions concerning the differences between British and US acting. As the founding director of the National Theatre, he readily serves as an embodiment of the link between acting and the theater in Britain, and understood himself as "emphasizing a physical technique of characterization through voice and movement rather than an 'inner' technique of psychological preparation for inhabiting the

role" (Gordon, *The Purpose of Playing*, 373 n. 4). However, Olivier has also been described as a mercurial screen actor, and he and his fellow "theatrical knights" John Gielgud and Michael Redgrave had a more positive relationship with Stanislavsky than is commonly assumed (see Cole and Chinoy, *Actors on Acting*, 403–408). Even deeply ingrained points of reference bear nonfixity, often discursively reduced to one aspect of their work.

21. Zucker, *Figures of Light*, 17.
22. Zucker, *Figures of Light*, 88.
23. This understanding resonates with the work of Konstantin Stanislavsky, which—despite the connotations of scientific precision of the term "system" that is attached to it—constitutes the single most influential and unstable point of reference in contemporary Western discourses on acting. Gaining prominence in the United Kingdom later than in the United States, Stanislavsky's views on acting developed as he "continually tested and revised his ideas ... in a dialectical process" (Gordon, *The Purpose of Playing*, 39). He has been most associated with his earlier ideas, which emphasized "the inner world of the character, what he called the 'logic of emotions'" (Zucker, *Figures of Light*, 2), and which were influential on the Method as taught by Lee Strasberg. However, in the 1930s, Stanislavsky's notion of the method of physical action sought to synthetize "'the actor's inner work on himself' (the psycho-technique) and 'the actor's outer work on his body' (physical technique)" (Gordon, *The Purpose of Playing*, 39). For a discussion of this method, see Sharon Marie Carnicke, "Stanislavsky's System: Pathways for the Actor," in *Actor Training*, 2nd ed., ed. Alison Hodge (New York: Routledge, 2010).
24. Pamela Robertson Wojcik, "The Sound of Film Acting," *Journal of Film and Video* 58:1–2 (2006): 75.
25. Robertson Wojcik, "Sound of Film Acting," 78.
26. Robertson Wojcik, "Sound of Film Acting," 75.
27. See Trevor Rawlins, "Studying Acting: An Investigation into Contemporary Approaches to Professional Actor Training in the UK" (PhD diss., University of Reading, 2012), 147.
28. Gianluca Sergi, "Actors and the Sound Gang," in *Screen Acting*, ed. Alan Lovell and Peter Krämer (New York: Routledge, 1999), 128.
29. Petley, "Reaching for the Stars," 122.
30. Zucker, *Figures of Light*, 88.
31. Cole and Chinoy, *Actors on Acting*, 564–565.
32. Jessica Chandra, "Love Ser Davos on *Game of Thrones*? Read Our Interview with Liam Cunningham," *Popsugar*, June 30, 2014, http://www.popsugar.com.au/celebrity/Liam-Cunningham-Interview-Game-Thrones-Ser-Davos-35098536.
33. Kate Aurthur, "Everything You Need to Know about the Man behind Lord Varys," *BuzzFeed*, September 15, 2015, https://www.buzzfeed.com/kateaurthur/game-of-thrones-conleth-hill-a-patch-of-fog?utm_term=.tg9BgmGgN#.eb4pnDjny.
34. This interestingly intersects with ideas concerning the construction of characters in long-running dramas discussed by Tom Cantrell and Christopher Hogg, "Returning to an Old Question: What Do Television Actors Do When They Act?," *Critical Studies in Television* 11:3 (2016): 283–298.
35. Regardless of the fact that the shots in the scene were not necessarily filmed in a continuous order and that ADR may have been involved, Cunningham manages to deliver a lot of (often rapid) dialogue for each shot. Evidencing strong breath control, he places his breath on the beat and thus has his breath support the melodic quality of his dialogue.
36. See Sara Ramshaw, "'McNulty' on the Small Screen: Improvised Legality and the Irish-American Cop in HBO's *The Wire*," in *Law and Justice on the Small Screen*, ed. Peter Robson and Jessica Silbey (Oxford: Hart Publishing, 2012), 365–366.
37. As an undercover spy, Rhys's character takes on different guises and alter egos, but, unlike Hill's Varys, his continued survival depends on no trace of performativity being evident to the onlooker.
38. Gordon, *The Purpose of Playing*, 359.
39. David Shirley, "'The Reality of Doing': Meisner Technique and British Actor training," *Theatre, Dance and Performance Training* 1:2 (2010): 200.
40. See Rawlins, "Studying Acting."

41. Interestingly, Petley thought that the problem of performance could be resolved through improved support for actors from directors. It is worth noting that both the *Game of Thrones* episodes this chapter has discussed were directed by Alex Graves, an experienced director who had previously worked on *The West Wing* (NBC, 1999-2006), a series showcasing a strong ensemble performance.
42. Petley, "Reaching for the Stars," 122.
43. Weissmann, *Transnational Television Drama*, 171.
44. See Knox, "Exploring the Casting."
45. Carole Zucker, "British Film, Stage, and Television Performance: Training, Praxis, and Culture," *CineAction* 44 (1997): 48, emphasis added.

Transatlantic Fans and Audiences

INTRODUCTION

Audience studies has been interested in the "export" of meaning for decades; the international success of the original US TV series *Dallas* (CBS, 1978– 1991), for example, and debates surrounding American cultural imperialism in the 1980s, sparked empirical audience studies aimed at unpicking *Dallas*'s glocalization by European as well as other international audiences and fans.[1] But the analysis of UK audiences for US TV drama—and vice versa—has sometimes been obscured by a focus on the fandoms surrounding popular transatlantic telefantasy and cult TV, from Henry Jenkins's *Textual Poachers* (1992) onward, which has considered fan-cultural activity without fully addressing American and British cultures of transnational reception.[2] More recently, work on transcultural fandom has explored how national identities might be overwritten (although not entirely) by affiliations with specific media fandoms, while work such as *Crossing Fandoms* has considered how British and American TV dramas can be mashed up via GIF sets and fanfiction—thus treating fandom more explicitly in relation to US and UK TV readings and reputations.[3] And the transnational nature of fandom has become increasingly evident via the normalization of industry promotion at major Comic-Cons such as San Diego. For example, British fans of *Doctor Who* (BBC, 1963–1989, 1996, 2005–) protested vocally online when this US convention was first to show footage from the BBC TV series' fiftieth-anniversary episode in 2013; the issue of BBC America promoting the program on US soil ahead of UK TV license fee payers seeing footage was still being referred to in *Broadcast* magazine months later in Britain.[4]

Contemporary audience studies, unlike the burst of work following *Dallas*'s popularity in the 1980s, has focused less on US cultural imperialism than on the everyday nature of transculturalism that has emerged in the wake of Web 2.0,[5] as well as the issue of audience piracy via downloading or streaming. It could be argued that earlier work on transnational TV and audiences necessarily focused on the formal economy of regulated, official media flows, whereas in the contemporary media context of "user-led transnationalism,"[6] informal economies of audience-generated media flow are just as significant and exist in a dynamic relationship with formal TV circulations such as those via NATPE, MIPCOM, and MIP-TV trade fairs.[7]

Piracy has been one major form of audience-led transnationalism, enabling audiences to view on demand rather than awaiting broadcasters' scheduling decisions, thus "curating" their own television schedules and senses of personalized televisual "flow."[8] As M. J. Robinson has argued, such

> curatorial culture is global but not globalizing. Because it is created by a long tail distribution it does not operate in an environment in which scarce spectrum space is saturated by foreign programming. Online distribution platforms can and do offer programming from all countries' professional and amateur producers in the same long tail and that tail has endless opportunities for expansion.[9]

Simultaneously, audiences and fans are unofficially, informally accessing programming from beyond their national territories, sometimes even with fan-created subtitles, helping to realize a multilayered "transnational cultural economy."[10] Kate MacNeill suggests that unauthorized downloading is "consistent with the behaviour of dedicated fans . . . [who] wish to purchase . . . digitally and pay the creative talent, but if this is not possible within optimal timeframes will download . . . with the intention of making a legitimate purchase at a later stage."[11] It is partly to guarantee these "optimal" time frames for fan access, and so combat piracy, that US and UK broadcasts for TV shows (especially those known to have sizable online fanbases) have become increasingly synchronized across the past few years. And although the media industry has sought to frame and define piracy in terms of its criminality, for many fans and audience members piracy is instead viewed as an "ethical act of rebalancing within an otherwise distorted market."[12] Nor can it be assumed that the transnational pirating of high-profile US or UK TV shows inherently damages the brands concerned:

> Tolerating some level of piracy can make economic sense . . . as a fan base purchases complementary products such as books and other merchandise. . . . HBO officials themselves appear to endorse this view with David Petrarca, the . . . director [of *Game of Thrones*] acknowledging that the piracy created a "buzz" and Jeff Bewkes, CEO of Time Warner (the parent company of HBO), observing that piracy doesn't hurt sales and "is more valuable than an Emmy!"[13]

Here, formal economies of media export, merchandizing, and US-UK flow interact with the informal economy of unauthorized transnational downloading in a way that very much positions these audience practices as brand-reinforcing. And if formal and informal media economies have started to blur together, then so too have fan and audience identities.

When John Fiske introduced and defined fandom in his 1992 chapter of *The Adoring Audience*, he argued that the fan was "an 'excessive reader' who differs from the 'ordinary' one in degree rather than kind."[14] But this relationship of difference from the "more 'normal' audience member"[15] may no longer be so clearly sustainable in an era of streaming and binge watching. Djoymi Baker has discussed these developments:

> In the contemporary era, bingeing in particular need not be characterized as a fandom practice per se any more but simply as a contemporary viewing norm . . . [M]arginal fan activities tend to become mainstream over time, and indeed are increasingly encouraged as a promotional strategy. . . . The ongoing transition towards normalization is important to the way in which we conceptualize binge-viewing—and indeed fandom—because associations with excess become more difficult to sustain.[16]

Indeed, partly by way of contesting the "excessive" ascriptions of binge viewing, both Baker and Lisa Perks rename this mode of (arguably pathologized) viewing via more positive terms: "epic-viewing" and "media marathoning," respectively.[17] This mainstreaming of fandom appears to break down the distinction between "fans" and "audiences," but as an overarching cultural narrative it rather problematically assumes that "the mainstream" operates as a monolithic, singular category, whereas the antimainstream can be subculturally diverse. And yet the "mainstream" itself is something of a shifter, appearing differently in a range of academic arguments. Adrian Athique, writing in *Transnational Audiences*, argues that fan cultures actually moved into the mainstream decades before the advent of streaming and binge watching "and offered substantial commercial opportunities. The vast range of merchandise associated with the popularity of the Beatles is a prime example of this shift. . . . By the 1970s, not only musical acts, but also mainstream . . . television shows would commonly be augmented with a whole range of 'tie-ins.'"[18] And Maria San Filippo notes that Netflix's release strategy of "dropping" entire series runs in one go—in order to incite speedy binge watching—is not simply a co-optation of fannish and detail-oriented modes of viewing, but "takes its cue less from a participatory media model and more from the . . . blockbuster mentality in its reliance on demographic-targeting, saturation-booking, word-of-mouth and sink-or-swim expectations to perform."[19] Any notion of the "mainstream" is thus multiplied here, either temporally (Athique) or intermedially (San Filippo), suggesting that the idea that fans and audiences using streaming have become coterminous can only stand as a somewhat unhelpful simplification. The "mainstream," as "spatial and geographical imagery,"[20] always has a degree of looseness, while at the same time giving rise to "a complex space that encompasses a multitude of practices."[21]

In relation to this multiplicity of the mainstream, while analyzing the formal, global distribution of TV texts via trade fairs, Denise Bielby and C. Lee Harrington observe that in "contrast to the slippery presence of television *viewers* at TV trade fairs, increasingly spotlighted are television *fans*."[22] Unlike generalized viewers, fans are a niche market sought by producers and programmers of "global TV" flowing across national borders: "The question of consumers' imaginative capacity for fanship precontextualises the reception of programming in new cultural markets, and thus the deals that are made at the site of distribution."[23] The fact that "fans are now being actively courted not just at the level of production but again and *differently* at the level of global distribution"[24] suggests one of the complexities behind the "mainstreaming of fandom" argument: namely that fans are a kind of audience seen as specifically desirable in contemporary (social) media contexts, where they can act as both brand champions and repeat consumers, that is, twinned sources of cultural capital ("buzz") and economic capital for producers and distributors. In this instance, fandom's supposed mainstreaming occurs not merely via the normalization of streaming or binge watching in US and UK contexts, or via the fan as consumer, but also via practices of formal distribution and their imagined and projected fandoms.

UK and US fans might be seen as offering a plausible focus for transatlantic "efforts to construct a fan following in new cultural markets,"[25] given a reasonably high degree of "cultural proximity" between the two nations,[26] as well as versions of American TV having been positioned as "quality" media in the United Kingdom, and vice versa.[27] However, Joseph Straubhaar has considered how issues of cultural proximity (and cultural discount) are not objective givens, but can instead vary according to audiences' and fans' levels of Bourdieuian cultural capital.[28] If forms "of cultural capital, in terms of what people know about other countries and cultures, can lead them toward or away from cultural proximity," then it is feasible to suggest that educated and socialized global elites "acquire a more globalized sense of personal identity, and pursue what they see as more cosmopolitan or global media choices."[29] Relatedly, established transatlantic fan cultures, such as those focused on generic or thematic proximities linked to telefantasy or cult TV, might also pursue more "cosmopolitan" TV consumption via unauthorized downloading and streaming, as well as via formal economies of TV distribution, hence reconfiguring their relations of cultural proximity to transatlantically disseminated content. Indeed, a Web 2.0–enabled sense of transnational "mainstream" cult or quality TV may even become sustainable for a range of fan niches. Rather than fandom simply being "mainstreamed," transcultural fandoms can be argued to imagine and project a new sense of mainstream culture via the transnational coalition of audiences gathered around digitally shared and national-boundary-crossing TV content. This neomainstream, comprising different national niche audiences, can also be facilitated by the status of types of US and UK television drama, where an array of "complex" Netflix and broadcast serials have taken on a value as cultural capital in their own right.[30]

This situation calls for television studies to definitively break with "methodological nationalism"[31] at the same time as considering how national meanings of TV drama continue to be powerfully meaningful for fans and audiences in a transnational cultural economy. There have already been some good examples of work addressing audiences in this manner. For instance, Elke Weissmann has explored online audience reviews for a number of different US and UK "crime drama[s] using forensic methodology for investigation purposes," such as *CSI: Crime Scene Investigation* (CBS, 2000–2015), *Silent Witness* (BBC, 1996–), and *Waking the Dead* (BBC, 2000–2011).[32] Weissmann argues that

> despite the fact that most television consumption occurs now in transnational comparisons, supposed national differences are constantly reiterated in discourses about dramas. In other words, even if national differences are eroded as television markets increasingly globalize . . . , the category of national origin offers viewers an experience of variety and thus differentiation.[33]

This is not a scenario of "postnational [TV] flow" for audiences; rather, "physical networks and borders, along with the asymmetries they generate, are recognized to persist in transnational media culture . . . [and the] relations of transcultural . . . fan communities."[34] US and UK TV dramas are presumed to work in certain ways, and they are identified as such by genre audiences in terms of evaluation and contextualization. And though these national flags or markers of TV textuality may be partly imagined (or, indeed, caricatured and stereotyped), they nonetheless point to a hybridization of national and transnational audience receptions.

Faye Woods makes a similar argument not for TV crime drama, but instead for teen TV. Like Weissmann, she observes how "the transatlantic boundaries between [US] teen TV and British youth television are permeable, but at the heart of this relationship are potentially irreconcilable tensions. Whilst British youth drama bears the influence of the US form, it is fundamentally structured in opposition to it."[35] And Woods also focuses on the asymmetries that can persist in the transatlantic disseminations of US and UK TV drama, noting that "British consumers and press are fluent in US culture and thus need no translation [of US teen TV], whereas British culture is conceived of (whether correctly or not) as 'foreign' to a US mainstream population, as suffering a cultural discount."[36] Consequently, Woods suggests that fluency in "British cultural products . . . serves as a form of cultural capital in the US, with British originals [of US adaptations] accessed via cable broadcast and online peer-to-peer flow."[37] In line with Straubhaar's arguments, however, this operation of television drama *as* cultural capital may itself hinge on the deployment of US audiences' and fans' preexistent cultural capital, thereby placing such transatlantic audiencing within circuits of cultural reproduction.

The following chapters engage in a series of ways with transatlantic TV drama's simultaneous permeability and instantiation of "British" versus "American" discourses, exploring how audiences and fans negotiate this transnational cultural economy. In chapter 10, Matt Hills considers Charlie Brooker's *Black Mirror* as a "Netflix Original" which was in fact originally a Channel 4 production in the United Kingdom, analyzing how the show's fans on Reddit engaged with series 3. Explicitly nation-oriented readings seem to be frowned upon here, partly in line with Brooker's mocking dismissal of notions of "Americanization." At the same time, differences between the show's Channel 4 and Netflix incarnations are gestured to by fans in coded ways, while their communal interest in reading the anthology series, via hidden "Easter eggs," as part of an overarching narrative universe works to displace accounts of its "Britishness." Indeed, Brooker seemingly responded to these fan interpretations in series 4, both by incorporating snarky Easter eggs directly targeting fans,[38] and also by creating a story, "Black Museum," that more explicitly tied together different episodes and series. By licensing fan readings that treat the different productions of *Black Mirror* as a diegetic whole, Brooker is able to (relatively) dematerialize real-world issues of (trans)national meaning-making. But as Ramon Lobato has recently argued, in the era of transnational Netflix catalogs and series "drops," it remains important to continue addressing well-established "questions in media and communication studies about the direction and intensity of audiovisual flows,"[39] as well as established questions about transnational audience identities, forms of (televisual) cultural capital, and discourses of national difference.

Chapter 11, from Paul Rixon, puts the issue of cultural capital front and center by focusing on how "quality" American TV drama is positioned for UK viewers and readers via the professional labor of TV critics at *The Guardian*. Here, the category of national origin is discursively constructed and maintained by cultural intermediaries, with specific American TV dramas being positioned as "touchstones of excellence." Although professional TV critics' work takes on the status of "fan-like opinion," these critics still retain a position of symbolic power in relation to members of the public (including fans) who comment on *Guardian* blogs. Rixon discerns a generally celebratory tone to critics' and fans' contributions alike, arguing that *The Guardian*'s TV blogs perform a significant role by transforming niche tastes in American "quality" TV into a legitimated part of dominant British culture. In this sense, US television drama as cultural capital for UK audiences is partly generated by *The Guardian*'s blogging and reviewing as a cultural intermediary, with readers and audiences also sustaining this collective act of legitimation.

Lincoln Geraghty examines very different cultural intermediaries of brand management in chapter 12, as well as reversing the polarity of transatlantic flow to address how British TV brands have been promoted at San Diego Comic-Con. Geraghty explores the contemporary US-UK transnational cultural economy for "blockbuster" TV, with certain UK television dramas taking on a status similar to that of Hollywood franchises by appearing in the famously expansive Hall H at SDCC. National origin is simultaneously drawn on and rendered permeable or even interchangeable here, as British and American TV shows form a shared category of hyped TV that's promoted to, and merchandized for, a transnational fanbase that is also copresent at the con. Geraghty reflects on the value that "being there" at SDCC can have for fans, showing how the physical immediacy of attendance can generate not just symbolic proximity to US and UK TV brands, but also a kind of imagined or projected media "insider" status. Just as trade fairs allow producers to imagine audiences, and especially fans, events like SDCC can enable fans, in turn, to imaginatively "enter" the transcultural worlds of TV production and branding.

The final two chapters focus more centrally on digital fan practices and creativities. In chapter 13, Lori Morimoto, a leading scholar of transcultural fandom, sets out the ways in which fandom's "imagined community" can be called into question when different nationalities of fans encounter one another and critique national discourses (and forms of cultural knowledge) that are in play within "widely accessible" or dominant online fan spaces.[40] Morimoto explores how national differences can become marked in fanfiction through tiny diegetic details, leading to the "nitpicking" of fans' constructions of national (US/UK) settings that they are not wholly familiar with, as well as (re)circulating stereotyped or limited meanings of national identity, such as constructions of "American monoculture," within the online spaces of otherwise transnational/transcultural fandoms. Her chapter then concludes by expanding the meanings of "transatlantic" television drama, specifically addressing the position of *Coronation Street* (Granada/ITV, 1960–) fans in Canada.

Paul Booth builds on his previous study of *Crossing Fandoms* (2016) in chapter 14, considering a fan-created hybridization of US and UK TV drama in the form of *SuperWhoLock*, which mashes up *Supernatural* (WB/CW, 2005–), *Doctor Who*, and *Sherlock* (BBC, 2010–2017) via GIF sets and other fan creations. This is a kind of televisual flow quite unlike the standard model of formal distribution that has been studied in the past, where official TV productions move across national borders. Instead, in this case, fans combine bits of meaning from these UK and US TV shows to create their own counterfactual, liminal "text." *SuperWhoLock* treats presumed national differences between US and UK TV drama as radically permeable, potentially downplaying categories of national (TV) origin in favor of a shared, transcultural fan identity or community. Yet importantly, the transnational cultural economy of US and UK TV drama is actively produced (or perhaps co-created) by fans in this instance, rather than fandom merely acting as a kind of (supposedly mainstreamed) audience that receives and interprets US and UK television. Meaning might be "exported" via *SuperWhoLock*, but so too is the economy of formal distribution imported into fans' informal distribution of alternative textualities. Partly shaped via GIF sets, *SuperWhoLock* also challenges us to ponder exactly where "television" is now circulating digitally, culturally, and creatively.

Taken together, these five chapters make the case for a new wave of audience and fan studies focused more intently on British and American cultures of transnational TV reception, rather than assuming that these audiences can be treated as indistinguishable in the era of globalizing Netflix and "quality" TV, or presumed to be proximate enough to render the analysis of cultural difference(s) insignificant. On the contrary, Hills, Rixon, Geraghty, Morimoto, and Booth all, in their varied ways, demonstrate how transatlantic fans and audiences (with these viewer categories themselves blurring together) can reward detailed theorization as they participate in the permeability and discursive activity of today's "story of transnational cultural economy."[41]

NOTES

1. Ien Ang, *Watching "Dallas": Soap Opera and the Melodramatic Imagination* (London: Methuen, 1985); Tamar Liebes and Elihu Katz, *The Export of Meaning: Cross-Cultural Readings of "Dallas"* (Cambridge: Polity Press, 1993).
2. Henry Jenkins, *Textual Poachers* (New York: Routledge, 1992).
3. Lori Hitchcock Morimoto and Bertha Chin, "Reimagining the Imagined Community: Online Media Fandoms in the Age of Global Convergence," in *Fandom: Identities and Communities in a Mediated World*, 2nd ed., ed. Jonathan Gray, Cornel Sandvoss, and C. Lee Harrington (New York: New York University Press, 2017); Paul Booth, *Crossing Fandoms* (Basingstoke: Palgrave Macmillan, 2016).
4. Matt Hills, *"Doctor Who": The Unfolding Event* (Basingstoke: Palgrave Macmillan, 2015), 30–32.
5. Andreas Hepp, *Transcultural Communication* (Oxford: Wiley Blackwell, 2015), 212.
6. Adrian Athique, *Transnational Audiences* (Cambridge: Polity Press, 2016), 149.
7. Denise D. Bielby and C. Lee Harrington, *Global TV: Exporting Television and Culture in the World Market* (New York: New York University Press, 2008), 157.
8. Ksenia Frolova, "'We Pretty Much Just Watched It All Back to Back!': Parenting, digital Television Viewing Practices and the Experience of Television Flow," *Critical Studies in Televisions* 12:3 (2017): 248.
9. M. J. Robinson, *Television on Demand: Curatorial Culture and the Transformation of TV* (New York: Bloomsbury Academic, 2017), 151–152.
10. Michele Hilmes, *Network Nations: A Transnational History of British and American Broadcasting* (New York: Routledge, 2012), 5.

11. Kate MacNeill, "Torrenting *Game of Thrones*: So Wrong and Yet So Right," *Convergence* 23:5 (2017): 548.

12. MacNeill, "Torrenting *Game of Thrones*," 558.

13. MacNeill, "Torrenting *Game of Thrones*," 557.

14. John Fiske, "The Cultural Economy of Fandom," in *The Adoring Audience*, ed. Lisa A. Lewis (New York: Routledge, 1992), 46.

15. Fiske, "Cultural Economy of Fandom," 46.

16. Djoymi Baker, "Terms of Excess: Binge-Viewing as Epic-Viewing in the Netflix Era," in *The Age of Netflix: Critical Essays on Streaming Media, Digital Delivery and Instant Access*, ed. Cory Barker and Myc Wiatrowski (Jefferson, NC: McFarland, 2017), 36.

17. Baker, "Terms of Excess," 38; Lisa Glebatis Perks, *Media Marathoning: Immersions in Morality* (Lanham, MD: Lexington Books, 2015), ix.

18. Athique, *Transnational Audiences*, 139.

19. Maria San Filippo, "Doing Time: Queer Temporalities and *Orange Is the New Black*," in Barker and Wiatrowski, *The Age of Netflix*, 81.

20. Alison Huber, "Mainstream as Metaphor: Imagining Dominant Culture," in *Redefining Mainstream Popular Music*, ed. Sarah Baker, Andy Bennett, and Jodie Taylor (New York: Routledge, 2013), 9.

21. Sarah Baker, "Teenybop and the Extraordinary Particularities of Mainstream Practice," in Baker, Bennett, and Taylor, *Redefining Mainstream Popular Music*, 23.

22. Bielby and Harrington, *Global TV*, 159.

23. Bielby and Harrington, *Global TV*, 159.

24. Bielby and Harrington, *Global TV*, 160.

25. Bielby and Harrington, *Global TV*, 159.

26. Joseph D. Straubhaar, *World Television: From Global to Local* (London: Sage, 2007), 200.

27. See Trisha Dunleavy, *Complex Serial Drama and Multiplatform Television* (New York: Routledge, 2018); and Elke Weissmann, *Transnational Television Drama: Special Relations and Mutual Influence between the US and UK* (Basingstoke: Palgrave Macmillan, 2012).

28. Straubhaar, *World Television*, 197.

29. Straubhaar, *World Television*, 203.

30. See Michael Z. Newman and Elana Levine, *Legitimating Television* (New York: Routledge, 2012); and Kim Toft Hansen and Anne Marit Waade, *Locating Nordic Noir: From "Beck" to "The Bridge"* (Basingstoke: Palgrave Macmillan, 2017), 117.

31. Kevin Robins and Asu Aksoy, "Whoever Looks Always Finds: Transnational Viewing and Knowledge-Experience," in *Transnational Television Worldwide: Towards a New Media Order*, ed. Jean K. Chalaby (New York: I.B. Tauris, 2005), 19.

32. Weissmann, *Transnational Television Drama*, 117.

33. Weissmann, *Transnational Television Drama*, 139.

34. Sandra Annett, *Anime Fan Communities: Transcultural Flows and Frictions* (Basingstoke: Palgrave Macmillan, 2014), 205.

35. Faye Woods, *British Youth Television: Transnational Teens, Industry, Genre* (Basingstoke: Palgrave Macmillan, 2016), 109.

36. Woods, *British Youth Television*, 108.

37. Woods, *British Youth Television*, 108.

38. Huw Fullerton, "Charlie Brooker Trolls Fans Hunting for *Black Mirror* Easter Eggs," RadioTimes.com, January 3, 2018, http://www.radiotimes.com/news/on-demand/2018-01-03/black-mirror-netflix-easter-eggs-season-4-insults/.

39. Ramon Lobato, "Rethinking International TV Flows Research in the Age of Netflix," *Television and New Media* 19.3 (2018), 249.

40. Lori Hitchcock Morimoto, "Transnational Media Fan Studies," in *The Routledge Companion to Media Fandom*, ed. Melissa A. Click and Suzanne Scott (New York: Routledge, 2018), 286; see also Louisa Ellen Stein, "Tumblr Fan Aesthetics," in Click and Scott, *Routledge Companion to Media Fandom*, 89.

41. Hilmes, *Network Nations*, 5.

10

BLACK MIRROR AS A NETFLIX ORIGINAL

Program Brand "Overflow" and the Multidiscursive Forms of Transatlantic TV Fandom

MATT HILLS

In this chapter I'll argue that thinking about transatlantic TV drama, from a fan/audience studies perspective, needs to be complicated in relation to a whole series of "trans" shifts and developments. Industrially, the rise of streaming services— offering a way to access program brands that circumvents conventional digital and cable TV—means that we need to consider afresh the role that national identities and territories might play. For example, the "ubiquity" of on-demand subscription TV might, in part, have been overly hyped; geoblocking and nation-specific releases still run up against the turn to supposedly "global" simultaneous releases whereby a drama series can "drop" internationally on a set date.[1] Similarly, the nonlinear nature of binge watching on demand, as opposed to following a network/digital TV weekly schedule, might also have been exaggerated. It can be argued that services such as Netflix and Netflix UK continue to enact "TV" scheduling of a sort—albeit relocated in relation to cycles of seasonality or holiday periods, rather than via daily or weekly schedules.

As well as considering this book's focus, the "transatlantic," we therefore also need to address what might be termed the *transtelevisual*, whereby practices linked to linear, broadcast television carry over in modified but recognizable ways into the cultural worlds of "on demand" and streaming.[2] At the same time, the multiplatformed era of on-demand television creates an environment where program brands themselves can take on a newfound significance and mobility, being sold from one broadcaster to another platform, and thus moving from US network TV to Netflix or Showtime (e.g., *Arrested Development, Twin Peaks*), or from a public service broadcaster in the United Kingdom to Netflix, as occurred with the sale of Charlie Brooker's *Black Mirror* and its move from Channel 4. In such a context, we also need to consider the *transtextual*, that is, how program brands are rearticulated in the "interval" of their textual movements between platforms.[3] And we might need to simultaneously consider *transfandom*, as fans display a greater self-reflexive sense of moving between and across versions of their fan objects. At the same time that fans can use social media to articulate and perform how they have followed a fan object across TV networks and streaming services, industry players such as Netflix can use data analytics and algorithms to trace, and exploit, audiences' pathways across their various offerings. The result, as I will go on to argue, is that fandom can act multidiscursively, both as a lived experience *and* as a data-driven phenomenon.

What becomes apparent here is that tracking transatlantic TV drama at such a moment carries a considerable degree of audience and fan complexity: the "transatlantic" is one kind of boundary-crossing among many others. As analysts and scholars, we must address this array of interrelated contexts and discourses, analyzing how transatlantic meanings, practices, and receptions are related to, and inflected by, the transtelevisual and the transtextual, as well as activities of transfandom. In order to do justice to all of this, I will split my chapter into two main sections. First, I want to consider what I'll term a "Netflix discourse" of targeting and identifying multi-niche fandoms. The aim of this opening discussion is to pin down how fandom is potentially being implied, identified, and generalized by the likes of Netflix's algorithmic practices. It is useful to hold on to Adrian Athique's cautionary note that in "the digital aftermath of cultural studies ... audiences are not data."[4] There is a danger of replaying and intensifying the state of affairs set out in Ien Ang's *Desperately Seeking the Audience,*[5] with (fan) audiences being ever more intently and discursively figured in line with forms of industry power and ambition.[6] *Contra* scholarly arguments that have positioned Netflix UK as assimilating into the United Kingdom's TV ecology or argued that Netflix in the United States represents a destabilizing attack on the cultural mainstream of America's national imagined community, I will suggest that the "Netflix discourse" of algorithmically driven audience evaluation seeks to sustain a particular position on Athique's "transnational spectrum" whereby "different scales of transnational orientation are interdependent."[7] Rather than various national "mainstreams" being superseded by transnational—in this case, transatlantic—fandom, or the national TV industry remaining a key context through which Netflix UK should be understood, the national and the transnational instead continually inform one another at a range of levels, operating relationally.

Second, I will then go on to explore the darkly satirical and science-fictional anthology drama *Black Mirror* as a specific case study, analyzing its move from Channel 4 (2011–2014) to Netflix (2016–) after two seasons and a Christmas special, along with fans' reactions on Reddit at https://www.reddit.com/r/blackmirror/. In its emblematically "trans" move from terrestrial TV to streaming, and from being a UK-based show to having a "global" release as a Netflix Original, *Black Mirror* plays out tensions for its fans surrounding Netflix's association with binge watching, as I'll consider, and surrounding the coherence of the program brand when it is rearticulated in a new industry context. Fans often seek to read Netflix's *Black Mirror* as of a piece with the established show they had become affectively invested in, contesting shifts in the program's tone and seeking to install an "extended universe" by placing all of *Black Mirror*'s individual stories within a single storyworld and timeline. As such, I will argue that fans seek to tame, or contain, the "overflow" in *Black Mirror*'s meanings as it moves from Channel 4 to Netflix, and from linear broadcast to nonlinear "on demand" television, thereby displacing US or UK nation-based interpretations even while these are implicitly drawn on.[8] Analyzing the *Black Mirror* subreddit as naturally occurring data means that I am necessarily looking at a range of different fan nationalities, with many posters tending to identify as American or British. Such a transatlantic fandom also contains both US and UK fans who were invested in the C4 version of the show prior to its Netflix production. This incarnation was passed over by US network TV, but was shown on DirecTV in the States from 2013, prior to Netflix picking it up from December 1, 2014. Indeed, the Christmas special episode, "White Christmas," remained a DirecTV exclusive when it was shown on Christmas Day of 2014. Netflix's involvement undoubtedly raised the program's profile and also meant that the company was able to base its decision to enter into a production deal on proprietary audience data. There has thus been a kind of "three-step transatlantic movement" of this TV drama, first to DirecTV's US satellite TV service, then subsequently *onto* Netflix in America, and ultimately *into* a Netflix production.

Before I address the particular case of *Black Mirror*, though, how has Netflix itself sought to reconfigure discourses of fandom? Focusing on this question means not only discussing fan responses to, or engagements with, transatlantic TV drama, but arguing instead that fandom has become distinctively *multidiscursive* within current contexts of transatlantic television flow. As such, bingeing the Netflix-produced *Black Mirror* can certainly allow audiences to position it transtelevisually and transtextually as nonlinear, on-demand, and original drama. But bingeing can also be linked to specific fan readings that simultaneously *dematerialize the program's transatlantic production and reception trajectories* in favor of treating it as a unified diegetic whole, even while national discourses remain in play, albeit in disavowed ways. The multidiscursive operation of fandom will therefore link together my two sections, maintaining a focus on how transatlantic TV drama's meanings are consistently articulated through relational combinations of the transnational and the national.

OVERFLOW (I): NETFLIX AND A "FUTURE BASED FUNDAMENTALLY ON FANDOM"?

Will Brooker introduced the concept of television "overflow," noting in 2001 that scholarship was "at a point where we have to reconsider what it means to engage with a television programme, to 'follow' a specific show."[9] Brooker had in mind a movement toward

> an immersive, participatory engagement with the programme that crosses multiple media platforms and invites active contribution; not only from fans, who after all have been engaged in participatory culture around their favored texts for decades, but also as part of the regular, "mainstream" viewing experience.... [W]e will need new terms to discuss the shifting nature of the television audience. The concept of overflow helps to establish this new vocabulary.[10]

For Brooker, then, "overflow" offered an initial way of thinking about how "the text of the TV show is no longer limited to the television medium,"[11] circulating online and via participatory audience engagements. This was one way into what has since been dubbed transmedia storytelling,[12] but Brooker was also interested in themed merchandising that could be tied into a show, and not only the expansion of a cross-platform narrative universe. Significantly, Brooker's concept of overflow involves a blurring of fan practices with "mainstream" viewing activities. Thus, although it is supposedly the TV text that is overflowing the bounds of its originating medium in Brooker's account, there is arguably a related overflowing of fandom, whose characteristic participatory practices begin to migrate beyond fan discourses and outside of self-described fan identities.

More recent work on binge watching and Netflix has tended to reiterate Brooker's focus on "fan mainstreaming," suggesting that on-demand streaming services might themselves give rise to a kind of *fan overflow*. Writing in the book *Media Marathoning*, Lisa Glebatis Perks rejects the term "binge watching" for its potential pathologization of such audiences, arguing that the "insulated flow" of marathoning, along with its "intensity and immersiveness[,] ... can ... be a gateway to fandom, but marathoning does not predetermine fan identification or behaviors. Marathoners temporarily adopt fan practices."[13] And Mareike Jenner similarly views Netflix as facilitating a situation where

> the lines between fans and non-fans [are] increasingly blurred, [and] the practice of binge-watching, despite its etymological links to unhealthy behaviour, signifies a socially legitimised excess, the luxury of time and "quality" television combined in implicit fan activity. As such, it may imply the agency commonly associated with fans, but conceptualises this as inherent to V[ideo]O[n]D[emand]. . . . [B]inge-watching is . . . a way to describe "watching VOD." . . . If viewed this way, then the line between fans and non-fans lies mostly in . . . self-identification.[14]

Binge watching thus appears as a kind of temporary fandom, or as a set of practices that are effectively coterminous with fandom—"implicit fan activity"—lacking only a framing fan discourse: "the willing adoption of the fan label and participation in a community may be the most significant distinction between fans and non-fans who watch, or binge, VOD."[15]

This temporality-based and practice-based erosion of the division between fandom and nonfandom finds its counterpart in Netflix's official stance on fandom—namely, that it can generate fan audiences, or at least a newfound self-recognition of fandom. Netflix's Chief Content Officer, Ted Sarandos, has discussed the process that led to *House of Cards* being commissioned:

> "We read lots of data to figure out how popular Kevin Spacey was over his entire output of movies. How many people actually highly rate four or five of them?" Then the same thing was done for David Fincher films, where if audiences had highly rated multiple titles then "you're probably a Fincher fan—you probably don't know it, but you are."[16]

Drawing on their proprietary audience data, Netflix could therefore supposedly identify Spacey or Fincher "fans" purely on the basis of their recorded and transtextual viewing practices rather than on any sense of self-described fandom. Resembling Perks's analysis, where bingeing proffers a "gateway" into fandom, Netflix—via Sarandos—was in effect claiming that its data could anticipate fandom (or identify viewing practices and ratings that were basically indistinguishable from fan investment, as in Jenner's scholarly discussion).

Tim Wu has most clearly expressed what I'll term somewhat crudely (yet in line with the brand's typical self-aggrandizement) this *Netflix discourse* of fan "overflow"—that is, the notion that fandom can be predictively identified and innovatively targeted as a result of big data and its associated analytics. Wu argues that Netflix are engaged in nothing less than an act of pop-cultural redefinition: "If modern American popular culture was built on a central pillar of mainstream entertainment flanked by smaller subcultures, what stands to replace it is a very different infrastructure, one comprising islands of fandom."[17] Wu's elaboration on this displacement of a shared "mainstream" via Netflix-configured multiniche fan audiences has been reiterated in more recent academic work; the same quotation from his 2013 article appears in both Casey McCormick's excellent analysis of binge viewing *House of Cards* and Amanda Lotz's key discussion of postnetwork television in the United States.[18] Wu himself conveys a sense of uncertainty, noting that although "smaller communities of fans, forged from shared perspectives, offer a more genuine sense of belonging than a national identity born of geographical happenstance . . . [w]hether a future based fundamentally on fandom is superior in any objective sense is impossible to say."[19] And yet this rhetorical hesitancy belies an argument that the Netflix discourse of predictive and targeted niche fandom will necessarily erode shared national identity: "At a deeper level, a country already polarized by the echo chambers of ideologically driven journalism and social media will find itself with even less to agree on."[20] *Contra* arguments that fandom may itself be transcultural—thus working without reference to lines of national identity/difference[21]—Wu instead positions corporate data-driven fandom as an inevitable attenuation of national "imagined community."[22] In a sense, then, Tim Wu is arguing that the Netflix discourse will both weaken national imaginaries and create transnational (or more significantly transatlantic) imaginaries in their place. An alleged "future based fundamentally on fandom" is simultaneously one in which community based on "geographical happenstance" declines in importance in relation to fannish affinities.

There are, of course, rival ways of positioning Netflix and its algorithmically extended fandoms, where "forms of knowledge can now circulate outside of subcultural groups and . . . find a new audience through algorithmic processes."[23] For example, Sam Ward has analyzed the media-cultural and brand positioning of Netflix UK (launched in January 2012), arguing that far from eroding national identity in favor of transnational or transatlantic imaginaries, it has actively sought "acceptance . . . by the British television establishment."[24] Ward sets out how Netflix UK has positioned itself as an importer of overseas quality programming, akin to Sky Atlantic and "has also sought to integrate its service with the everyday technological objects of British television viewing through its partnerships with Virgin and YouView,"[25] thereby adopting a conventional bridging and mediating role between national and global marketplaces, as well as looking to establish a nonthreatening, "domesticated" British brand. Indeed, one might go further than Ward does with this argument, suggesting that the commissioning of *The Crown*—a dramatization of the reign of the current Queen[26]—was a direct attempt to occupy and challenge the BBC's role as a source of nationally unifying stories and conversations,[27] while Netflix UK's categorization of specific content as "British drama and comedy" also permits "British TV" consumption to be tracked as a microgenre in Netflix's terms.

In the summer of 2017, the BBC actually began a slate of coproductions with Netflix, including a prestige drama serial, *Collateral* (BBC/Forge, 2018), penned by playwright and national institution David Hare,[28] just at the very moment that BBC Drama seemed to feel that it had to discursively differentiate its offerings from those of Netflix UK:

> Controller of [BBC] drama commissioning Piers Wenger . . . told the congregated TV industry guests that he wants the BBC to provide an "antithesis" of "an algorithmic, data-driven approach to commissioning." . . . Said Wenger: "In a world where . . . it can feel like your taste is being curated for you, it's never been more important for BBC Drama to deliver the unexpected and for us to be clear and strong on what sets us apart. . . . We know that the biggest risks deliver the biggest hits."[29]

For the BBC to stridently set out its stall in this way, via an anti-Netflix positioning of expert-created "unexpectedness" versus "data-driven" content,[30] was especially ironic just as the BBC iPlayer was potentially about to be reconfigured via notions of personalization, that is, when the BBC was apparently on the verge of being able to gather data on audiences' online viewing practices that it hoped could be used in ways akin to Netflix's deployment of proprietary big data. While Netflix and the BBC appear to be involved, objectively, in an industrial and transnational dance of mutual appropriation and poaching, each nonetheless needs to assert its brand difference (somewhat artificially or schematically) at the same time.

I would argue that the reality of Netflix's "fandom overflow" most likely falls somewhere between Sam Ward's industry-assimilationist argument and Tim Wu's "national-cultural game-changer" hyperbole. Whereas Wu's argument is definitively transnational and transatlantic in scope, Ward very much returns to national imaginaries and constructions of meaning. By seeking to plot a middle path between these binary options, I am drawing on Adrian Athique's notion of a "transnational spectrum" whereby national and transnational levels of meaning-making continue to remain relationally in play.[31] For, as Ed Finn has argued in *What Algorithms Want: Imagination in the Age of Computing*, Netflix's "process of 'making fans' draws together creative and algorithmic production."[32] Consequently, it is difficult to see Netflix's refinement of "'how fans are made,' as Sarandos puts it,"[33] as simply being of a piece with established UK broadcasters' branding strategies, even while

Wu's grand narrative regarding the collapse of national mainstream cultures sounds suspiciously like an apotheosis of fan- (and brand-) related hype.

Rather than positing particular relationships between national identity and fan culture, and hence positioning Netflix as inherently nation-oriented or as transnationally focused, Finn argues persuasively that reading

> Netflix itself as a series of algorithms, interfaces, and discourses is far more instructive for understanding its role as a culture machine than reading the cultural products produced by the system. . . . [W]hen we consider[, for example] *House of Cards* as a creation that is in part algorithmic, designed for and structured within the broader abstraction aesthetic of Netflix, particular traces of this corporate, computational authorship emerge in the show itself.[34]

And such traces can be symptomatically decoded from Netflix shows even in the absence of official Netflix statements. Uses of data "collection and interpretation permeate many aspects of [the company's] corporate decision making, from the vetting of potential acquisitions to the shaping of the context of acquired properties," and this can include Netflix exerting "a lot of casting influence," in Ted Sarandos's words, over various shows like *Orange Is the New Black*.[35] Although no Netflix statements have framed, say, *Stranger Things* in this way, it seems highly unlikely that Winona Ryder would have been cast without a data-derived sense of how she might bring specific audiences to this 1980s-nostalgia horror series. However, rather than *Stranger Things* being positioned as actively shaped by audience data, unlike *House of Cards*, which very much functioned as a calling card for Netflix's production of brand difference, it has instead been imbued with an auteurist sensibility. The show's creators, the Duffer brothers, paratextually insist, "We're just nerds really, so we love all this stuff," emphasizing their homages to Spielberg, King, and Carpenter *et al.*, as if to authenticate their proximity to fandom and reassure horror fans, rather than the series being called into question as an instrumentally composited creation shaped or supported by Netflix data.[36] (It should be noted that a similar process occurs in relation to Charlie Brooker's authorship of *Black Mirror*, and this is something that I'll consider in the next section.)

And yet, traces of "corporate, computational authorship" persist, being recognized in acafan Dan Hassler-Forest's response to the show:

> Aided and abetted by Netflix's full-drop season mechanism, I spent the day wallowing in this almost-too-perfect collision of nostalgia, geek culture, and "Peak TV." But as much as I did enjoy it, there was also something uncanny about *Stranger Things*

that I found even more unsettling than the "Demogorgon," the faceless monster that terrorizes the precocious pre-teens within the series' story realm. It was the sense that there was something mechanical, something pre-programmed, even something truly inevitable about my first response to the show: almost literally as if it had been tailor-made just for me.[37]

Hassler-Forest's ambivalent reaction recognizes how Netflix, and *Stranger Things* in particular, addresses cult, horror, and SF fans as "identifiable niche groups with particular passions, proclivities, and predilections, and increasingly churns out material that appeals to them with what seems like laser-targeted precision."[38] Rather than a fan "subculture of active resistance and appropriation," fandom instead comes to occupy "a key position within our media landscape" in terms of precisely being targeted and co-opted as a form of "brandom" or brand evangelism.[39] But Hassler-Forest's feeling of uncanniness combines textual appreciation with anxiety about being all-too-accurately anticipated in terms of his fan tastes. Rather than Netflix recognizing or harmoniously predicting fandom here, there is a sense that it is being algorithmically co-opted from the outset. Feelings of "something pre-programmed" work against an organic, authentic sense of finding a new fan object for one's self, or through trusted social contexts, instead too overtly becoming a matter of popular culture "finding-us," as David Beer puts it.[40] But such uneasiness also highlights the "affective measures"[41] that tend to accompany algorithmic cultural targeting—that is, how we feel about our tastes, fandoms, and passions being quantified, coded, and subjected to "new data relations."[42] Rather than fandom folding neatly, without excess, into a Netflix discourse of "how fans are made," there is instead an affective *tension* between the lived experiences of fandom and algorithmic predictions aimed at eliciting fan responses. What uncannily "pre-programmed" shows like *Stranger Things* illuminate is not any uncontested success of the Netflix discourse, but rather that *fandom is highly multidiscursive*, framed both subculturally and industrially at the same time. Arguably, fan studies began in the early 1990s by adopting a monodiscursive view of subcultural fandom, and it is the lingering legacy of this that has been challenged by a counterdiscourse of convergent "fan subcultures and mainstream audiences . . . [where] the contemporary 'mainstream' is . . . actually a vast field of overlapping fan cultures."[43]

But "fan overflow" does not just reposition fandom as outside established fan discourses—for example, being verified by Netflix data ahead of one's self-description. Rather, it renders fandom visibly multidiscursive, subjected to "affective measures" as much as performed through affective investments; and capable of being framed as a corroding challenge to national identity as much as an assimilationist articulation of national "imagined community."[44] That is, the shift to a focus on fans' lived experience versus algorithmic prediction leaves Athique's "transnational spectrum" in play.[45] Netflix is neither rendered as leading to an inevitable erosion of (audiences') national identities, nor as merely replaying established national contexts. Instead, the interplay between fans' identities and Netflix's "affective measures" must necessarily leave space for the interplay of national and transnational meanings at different levels, for example, between fans' preexistent senses of national identity (as well as transatlantic fan affinities via localizing receptions of Hollywood cinema, etc.) and Netflix's canny targeting of fan tastes assumed to be transnational.

In the following section I want to move on to further analyze this multidiscursive quality of contemporary fandom by taking Netflix's *Black Mirror* as a case study. Thanks to its move from terrestrial TV to streaming, and from a UK public service broadcaster (Channel 4) to Netflix, *Black Mirror* can be read as emblematic of current transatlantic industry developments and brand intervals or mobilities. But how do its fans seek to recontain the "overflow" of this program brand as it moves, perhaps jaggedly, across new contexts and production/national cultures?

OVERFLOW (II): *BLACK MIRROR* AND "AN ELABORATE EASTER EGG FOR VIEWERS . . . IN THE FUTURE"?

Black Mirror has not been subjected to extensive academic analysis to date; its anthology structure has mitigated against this, in part, given that each episode necessarily comprises entirely new characters and scenarios. As Alberto N. García has observed:

> Despite such notable precedents such as *The Twilight Zone* (CBS, 1959–64) and *Alfred Hitchcock Presents* (CBS/NBC, 1955–65; NBC/USA Network, 1985–89), the anthology is quite rare in contemporary television, due . . . to the production demands of the format. . . . Still, one of the surprises of recent years on British television—*Black Mirror* . . . , a dystopia imagined by Charlie Brooker—offers a collection of . . . separate stories each season, united only by [a] certain generic theme and feel.[46]

However, specific installments have attracted some scholarly commentary, particularly "The National Anthem" and "White Bear."[47] And Greg Singh has productively explored the show's overarching themes: "Consumer culture and free market logic are repeated targets of Brooker's satire, especially when coupled with the schadenfreude of reality TV . . . , or with data archival and retrieval . . . , or with political apathy and the insidiousness of the public relations industry."[48] Singh argues that the Channel 4 version of *Black Mirror* uses technological dystopia as a (by now) generic way into exploring morality tales that are focused on the human aspect of "what happens to intersubjective recognition and trust when our judgement is mediated through telepresence and data surveillance."[49]

Black Mirror's brand overflow from the United Kingdom's public service broadcaster Channel 4 to Netflix has also attracted commentary. Bryant Sculos argues that the program's presence on this subscription streaming site, along with its anthology format, renders the concept of seasons "largely unnoteworthy," and he consequently places the term "season" consistently "in quotes . . . because that is how the show is organized on Netflix, which now produces and distributes the show."[50] It can certainly be argued that Netflix's "nonlinear affordance" both erodes the concept of seasons and "also enables greater flexibility in program length"[51]—with "Hated in the Nation" being feature-length at ninety-nine minutes, compared to the fifty-seven-minute runtime of, say, "Playtest." And given the typical difference between US and UK season lengths (e.g., twenty or more episodes in a network US TV season versus perhaps six in a UK season, or even half that in the case of *Black Mirror*) it might also be suggested that streaming helps to remove industrial obstacles to transatlantic circulation. However, TV seasons remain more than merely "unnoteworthy," and more than barriers to transatlantic exchange that have now been overcome. For one thing, Netflix often drops programs in season-long blocks, implicitly utilizing the cultural associations of times of year and their broader seasonality. As Derek Johnston has pointed out, "American approaches to seasonal television horror differ from British ones . . . in the season most associated with the supernatural."[52] The US favors Halloween as a time for TV horror specials, whereas the United Kingdom has had a Christmas tradition of ghost stories. It was therefore likely to be no accident that the first season of *Black Mirror* as a Netflix Original dropped on October 21, 2016, a release similar to that of *Stranger Things'* season 2, which was scheduled for October 27, 2017. In such cases, a US-inflected cultural and industrial norm is generalized to transnational (fan) audiences. The expectation is seemingly that dedicated fans will dive straight into each show, but Halloween-themed viewing can also be arranged by delaying briefly, and more general audiences looking for Halloween-oriented genre viewing may pick up on these kinds of releases. The short gap between a season dropping and Halloween arriving also allows for online buzz and "hot takes" to paratextually shepherd All Hallow's Eve audiences to such Netflix offerings as deliberately transnational and "seasonal" horror. And although Derek Johnston's argument, that there has been a US/UK divide between seasonal TV horror, is certainly sound—after all, the final broadcast of *Black Mirror* on Channel 4 was itself a Christmas special, "White Christmas," rather than a Halloween one—such a transatlantic televisual separation has arguably become less marked itself as Halloween has become increasingly commercialized (and celebrated) in the United Kingdom.

Black Mirror also continues to be discussed and recalled in terms of its different seasons by fans, suggesting that the nonlinear availability of episodes (just as they were previously available on DVD) does not significantly alter the dominance of TV "season" discourses. The subreddit focused on *Black Mirror* follows the common cross-fandom convention of identifying episodes by season/series and episode order, for example "S3E4" for the "Episode Discussion" thread on "San Junipero" and so on.

The transatlantic overflow of *Black Mirror* as a program brand also cannot be clearly or reductively read as a switch from "UK" to "US" identity, even if US settings are used for the likes of "Nose Dive" and "San Junipero." Charlie Brooker discussed this decision as a creative one within a Reddit AMA, or "Ask Me Anything" interview: "San Junipero set in the United Kingdom wouldn't have been so evocative of the era. . . . We did actually discuss it—could we set it in Brighton in the 80s we wondered—but a sort of notional California just seemed *right*."[53] But he has also explicitly framed the setting of "San Junipero" as a deliberate challenge to audiences potentially looking to criticize the program's Americanization: "When Netflix picked us up, people were going, 'Oh that means [the show is] going to be Americanised.' I thought it would be a funny to f**k with those people by literally writing an episode set in California."[54] Brooker's reflexively transnational baiting demonstrates how TV drama can be subjected to predictably "nationalizing" containments of meaning. But even prior to the program's shift from Channel 4 to Netflix, it was already playing with notions of US quality television by casting Jon Hamm as a lead in "White Christmas" and hence intertextually referencing *Mad Men* in the process. Part of this special's "special" status was thus its casting of a high-profile US TV star, a fact that was worthy of paratextual publicity:

So how did one of the biggest TV stars on the planet end up in a small-scale British TV show? "I downloaded *The National Anthem* . . . and suffice to say, I'd never seen anything like that in my life," says Hamm. ". . . After that, I watched all the others in order, loved their originality and asked my agent to get in touch with these guys."[55]

Hamm's involvement is therefore authenticated, as it was in Channel 4's press release for "White Christmas," by virtue of his own fandom: "I had been a fan of *Black Mirror*, and Charlie Brooker, because I have a strange predilection for offbeat British things."[56] Hamm's involvement is, in fact, discursively distanced from the TV industry and industrial decision-making: "It came about in this very odd way, with me asking . . . if I could meet Mr Brooker. I didn't know he was even working on . . . a Christmas special or anything, it was simply that I . . . really wanted to meet the guy."[57]

This discourse of fandom (as external to the industry) helps to displace the notion that Channel 4's *Black Mirror* was already repositioning itself at this stage as US-targeted—Hamm approached them rather than the series seeking out an American star intertext—by drawing on a supporting discourse of "offbeat British things" or discerning Anglophilia.[58] (In fact, Hamm already had transatlantic form in this respect, having appeared along with Daniel Radcliffe in Sky Art's 2012–2013 dark comedy *A Young Doctor's Notebook*, which can readily be interpreted as another "offbeat British" production, albeit one based on adapting Russian literary source material.) As Jeffrey Miller has argued with regards to the reception of UK TV drama in America, there can be an Anglophilic "desirability of difference" that demarcates at least some UK (public) broadcasting as having an "elite status"[59] distinguished from US commercial models, even residually in the era of American quality TV and premium cable. A similar concept of cult value, where *Black Mirror* stands in for "British TV" and its "offbeat" attractions, has even been argued to underpin Netflix's take-up of the program:

> At the Sundance film festival in 2015, [Ted] Sarandos was challenged on his data trawling by the American academic Tim Wu, who noted that most of Netflix's biggest-budget, highest-profile shows involved a cult creator—from Fincher's *House of Cards* through to Charlie Brooker's *Black Mirror*. Was Netflix's algorithm actually Ted? "In practice, it's probably a 70/30 mix," Sarandos admitted. "Seventy is the data and 30 is judgment—but the 30 needs to be on top, if that makes sense."[60]

Setting to one side the slightly quirky numeracy involved in claiming that a 30 percent element can be "on top" of a 70 percent data-driven commission, this exchange highlights the extent to which Netflix's business model may be rather less revolutionary than its paratexts and brand mystique would otherwise like to claim. Sarandos's commissioning, as Chief Content Officer, is supposedly "all down to algorithms and data"[61] and the competitive edge granted by secret, proprietary data.[62] But as he discusses here—and like established patterns in media industry decision-making—there is a sense in which "the gut feeling of the expert" remains highly significant,[63] along with judgment calls that are premised on unquantified cultural connotations and taste cultures of "cultish" program brand value.

Thus, Brit TV fandom can seemingly play a role, however exnominated, in Netflix's commissioning machineries rather than merely being attributed to its paying consumers.[64] However, *Black Mirror* had already appeared in the United States, thanks to DirecTV, before Ted Sarandos acquired it for Netflix; hence it possessed a pre-Netflix American fandom, albeit one that was smaller and more cultish, as well as involving audiences' "user-led transnationalism," or illegal downloading. It therefore very much made sense for Tim Wu to position *Black Mirror*'s hyphenate, Charlie Brooker, as a "cult creator" in the US context rather than, say, discussing him as a well-known TV critic and satirist (as a UK-based commentator might have done).

As Elke Weissmann has noted, the "nation as a mark of authentication, then, remains a central construct for marketing, [commissioning,] audiences and critics in order to evaluate and make sense of television in an industrial context which has become distinctly transnational."[65] This can be true even for a program brand that is repositioned transnationally, with *Black Mirror* presumably being valued by Netflix for bringing a distinctively "British" (and "auteurist") sensibility to its lineup via the show's darkly satirical focus.[66] And although the "cultural identity of a work is typically guaranteed by the nationality of its author," this obscures an even more deep-rooted sense of "cultural influence . . . across lines of many different kinds of which the nation is only one,"[67] as *Black Mirror* itself is arguably greatly indebted to US cult telefantasy in the form of *The Twilight Zone*.[68] Indeed, Charlie Brooker has acknowledged and praised Rod Serling's work on this as "uncompromising in its own vision—for want of a less wanky word,"[69] suggesting that cult telefantasy has enduringly offered one important transnational mediation between US and UK television industries and cultures. Hence both Netflix algorithms and *Black Mirror*'s blurring of US and UK contexts work to keep Athique's "transnational spectrum" in play,[70] as levels of national-auteurist and transnational-cultist meaning operate in relation to one another. Fandom similarly mediates between levels of the national and the transnational, readily embracing Brooker's auteur status at the same time as recognizing a transatlantic "canon" of cult quality TV. Rather like the ending of "White Christmas" where (spoiler alert!) the snow globe world is constantly re-embedded within itself in a never-ending ontological loop, we might suggest that despite pervasive national discourses of authentication, *Black Mirror* as a text and a brand is always-already *recursively transatlantic* in advance of its reflexively baited Netflix "Americanization." "White Christmas" already gestures strongly toward an American quality TV lineage, and even if we track right back to *Black Mirror*'s season 1, then Rod Serling's influence can surely be felt. Foreclosing cross-cultural influences via Charlie Brooker's embodied "Britishness" and legitimating authorship means relying on an artificial construct of national identity that (re)contains multiple lines of cult and quality influence in favor of perceiving homogenous blocs of "British" quirkiness versus "American" corporate data.[71] And as Mareike Jenner has pointed out, we should not underestimate "just how much Netflix ties in with an already existing discourse surrounding 'cult' and 'quality' TV."[72]

As well as dismissing objections of Americanization, Charlie Brooker has also focused, perhaps unsurprisingly in terms of television branding, on the "fit" between Netflix and *Black Mirror*. In response to the technology magazine *Wired*'s question as to whether there was "an irony in your signing up with Netflix," Brooker observed that there was "definitely something fitting. . . . Somebody watching an episode of *Black Mirror* who's also watched *House of Cards*, you could show them a different scene."[73] Seeking to blatantly integrate Netflix's audience data into the show's production and textuality, Brooker is evidently fascinated by the possibilities that are opened up. He also paratextually posited the idea of "an elaborate Easter egg for viewers who'd played [the episode "Playtest"] a second time," whereby scenes would be substituted, including the lead character Cooper (Wyatt Russell) "seeing things from other previous episodes and it goes really bizarre and . . . he starts smashing the screen that you're watching him on."[74] A further concept involved asking "Netflix if it was possible to have Cooper's tether to reality, Katie (played by Wunmi Mosaku), address viewers in different cities, to break the [fourth] wall even further."[75] Ultimately, none of these plans for "meta" content were implemented; using audience data on viewing patterns, repeat watching, and geolocation all proved to be "extremely expensive and a logistical nightmare. We had to abandon the idea but that's not to say we wouldn't in the future go forward and do . . . a more vaguely interactive thing."[76] The brand "fit" between *Black Mirror* and Netflix that Brooker recurrently emphasized was hence one based on the innovative, creative exploitation of technology, albeit not in a markedly commercial sense—indeed Brooker has argued that his writing tends to "shy away from that side of things"[77]—and certainly not in a dystopian vein, however present that remained in *Black Mirror*, but rather as a matter of breaking "the fourth wall completely."[78] This also strongly resonates in an auteurist sense with how James Brassett and Alex Sutton have characterized Brooker's political satire as typically "urging viewers to deconstruct . . . [the] illusory division between audience and media."[79]

However, it has been argued by fans and critics alike that a significant part of Netflix's model does not actually fit *Black Mirror* very well at all—namely, dropping a season's worth of episodes at one go and inviting binge watching. Writing in the United Kingdom's *Independent* newspaper after season 3's release, Christopher Hooton set out the position that

> by their very nature, anthology shows aren't about that "ooo I must watch the next episode straight away" vibe, especially one as varied as *Black Mirror*. Each story was completely different in terms of genre, setting (both time and location) and theme, and the world could have comfortably spent a week unpacking the issues each episode hints at. It's a damn shame.[80]

Netflix's stress on binge watching "as a marketing tool, exploiting this form of series reception as a unique selling point," tends instead to relate more comfortably to what Jason

Mittell has termed "complex TV," that is, long-form serial drama where bingeing allows fans to "immerse themselves more deeply in the fictional worlds" concerned.[81] By contrast, on the face of it *Black Mirror* offers no such bingeable world-building or immersive potential given that every episode represents an entirely new narrative. Having said that, I will argue that both binge watching and particular kinds of fan interpretation construct *Black Mirror* as an immersive, coherent text that can exceed and evade national production contexts. As Lisa Glebatis Perks has noted:

> The marathoning practice marks the intersection of lived and fictive space, but the fictive world holds greater power in marathoning than in other media engagement patterns. . . . [M]edia marathoning creates a more stable and solid [fictional] world . . . made of narrative brick and reader mortar to create a stronghold in which readers blissfully play.[82]

When such a storyworld "stronghold" has been created, both fandom and practices of bingeing suspend national(izing) discourses of production in favor of focusing on *Black Mirror* as diegesis. This maneuver maintains the program's position within a "transnational spectrum,"[83] but it does so by temporarily bracketing off "the category of national origin."[84] To be sure, this renders *Black Mirror* as transatlantic TV drama, but it does not do so positively—that is, by arguing for its hybrid or transcultural status—so much as *negatively*, via the absenting of US and UK identifiers.

Bingeing a supposedly less bingeable show also allows *Black Mirror* fans to reinstate a sense of "distinction from mainstream audiences in the consumption of [this] cult . . . series,"[85] especially when bingeing itself has increasingly become normative for fans of texts positioned as "quality" TV. By treating bingeing as a culturally masculinized test, and hence as a way of displaying a high level of toughness and tolerance for some of the series' intensely downbeat and nihilistic material, dedicated *Black Mirror* fans are able to performatively restore a sense of bingeing's fan-cultural difference. Discussions of bingeing recur on the *Black Mirror* subreddit, and it is notable that Reddit's overarching online culture has been discursively dominated by a "geek masculinity"[86] according with cult fandom.[87] For instance, this is apparent in a thread titled "To all my fellow binge watchers, how you guys holding up?" which ponders whether there "are . . . any tough eggs out there who lasted all six episodes [of season 3] already?" (Poster 1).

Given that binge watching had become perceived as a challenge, the subreddit hosted a season 3 survey that asked people not just to rank the episodes but also to detail their viewing patterns. Featuring 1,382 responses, the survey details that 58 percent of respondents had binged the 2016 Netflix Original episodes, while a surprisingly high

19.7 percent had planned to do so but then had to stop after being disturbed by an episode. Such statistics starkly emphasize the emotional difficulty of watching multiple *Black Mirror* stories back to back, with posters commenting outside the survey thread that bingeing "was such a terrible idea. . . . I couldn't sleep at night, it kept fucking with my head" (Poster 2), and "I can't binge *Black Mirror*. I've tried. It's just too depressing" (Poster 3).

The survey question "If you stopped during binge watching, which episode was the cause?" garnered 656 responses. "Shut Up and Dance" (S3, E3) was the leading answer, given by 39.2 percent, and "Playtest" (S3, E2) was second with 24.5 percent. Unusually for the show, "Shut Up and Dance" has no fantastical elements, with one UK newspaper review noting, "I have some bad news about Shut Up and Dance: it's not really science fiction . . . [and] it's not giving much away to say that it's unrelentingly bleak."[88] The lack of a science-fictional modality may have made this "terrifyingly plausible version of what already exists" more disturbing for viewers.[89] Added to this, the episode's bleak reveal is that the young man we've been following, Kenny (Alex Lawther), who has been cyber-blackmailed after webcam footage of him masturbating was recorded and stolen, was in fact viewing child pornography. In response to the observation that "after the first two, I had to take a break. . . . Rest of the series was actually pretty light, but I still feel like I get more enjoyment out of watching two a day max and taking some time in-between to digest" (Poster 4), another subredditor writes, "Just finished ep3. Jesus, if that is your idea of light I'm going to need a puppy and a pint of ice cream to get through this season" (Poster 5). Others similarly chime in, opposing the idea that season three makes for less challenging viewing than the previous Channel 4 incarnation: "I think the third episode was by far the most hard-hitting episode in the season and maybe even the series as a whole" (Poster 6); "I actually had to take a day off after that one . . . episode three fucked me up" (Poster 7).

It should be noted that 22.4 percent of the season 3 survey respondents said that they didn't binge this group of *Black Mirror* episodes; binge viewing is evidently a somewhat divisive issue for these fans (though it remains part of a dominant fan discourse, given that 77.7 percent either binged season 3 or planned to). Some fans reinforce *Black Mirror*'s "quality" and cultural distinction by stressing that it "is a brilliant show but I have to take mental breaks between episodes because it gets 'too real' which is a good thing . . . but definitely not binge material" (Poster 8). And a fellow fan concurs, "Same here, each miniature existential crisis requires a period of reflection for me. Not the most bingeable show but quality like this is what I'm paying my Netflix subscription for" (Poster 9). In this case, rather than binge watching being articulated with "complex" serialized TV drama, *Black Mirror* is positioned as an affectively powerful version of "quality" whose bingeable nature is therefore disputed. At the same time, is it worth recalling that more than three-quarters (77.7 percent) of the survey's respondents either binged season 3 or said that they had initially wanted to do so; the fan-cultural importance of bingeing is seemingly rooted in the fact that it offers one way to render *Black Mirror* as transatlantic TV, suspending debates around national origin in favor of storyworld immersion. The transtelevisual move from broadcast TV to streaming thus supports a productively negative stance for these fans on transatlantic TV drama. That is, transatlanticism is not explicitly argued for or defended, but it remains tacitly valued by fans through their dematerialization of national discourses, running alongside a more direct emphasis on the show's storyworld.

In line with this suspension of national(izing) responses to *Black Mirror*'s brand "overflow," and its move to Netflix, fans often reacted in a way that didn't posit Americanization as an issue, but which nevertheless sought to restore a key element of the program's pre-Netflix format. Charlie Brooker has stated that he

> wanted to reinvent what I thought a *Black Mirror* episode was, because I'd read people grumbling, "Oh the show's going to Netflix. *What if it gets all Americanized!?*" I thought, "Right." Mugging, Brooker gives the double Vs sign. . . . And then I wanted to give . . . ["San Junipero," the first of the Netflix episodes to be written] a very different tone, almost as a sort of clearing of the pipes.[90]

By varying *Black Mirror*'s tone and gifting the two female leads in "San Junipero" "a happy ending,"[91] Brooker was also avoiding the possibility that this initial run of six Netflix episodes would feel repetitive if every installment was radically downbeat. By contrast, shorter three-episode seasons on Channel 4 didn't seem to call for such marked variation in tone.

However, one redditor (Poster 10) argued that "San Junipero" actually had a "secret downer ending," and that rather than the lovers Kelly (Gugu Mbatha-Raw) and Yorkie (Mackenzie Davis) being reunited at the end, this bittersweet conclusion was merely a simulation "meant to keep Yorkie happy." Although Brooker forcefully dismissed the theory, it was rapidly iterated and referenced via a range of online stories, demonstrating that the notion of a hidden and even more subversively dark narrative resonated all too well with the program's established (Channel 4–specific) brand.

On the *Black Mirror* subreddit, this theory—which drew on multiple textual details as well as referencing other episodes such as "Playtest" and "White Christmas"—inspired 182 comments. Some fans agreed, writing, "That's what I thought too: Although this ending seems 'happy,' it is only so for the two virtual clones of the main characters. With further analysis however, I'm not so certain anymore" (Poster 11). Others immediately went looking for auteurist material that could be used to support or discount this "San Junipero" fan theory: "Brooker says that there is a slight variance of tone in the third season as opposed to the first two, so I took the upbeat ending to be intentional" (Poster 12). And still others concluded that the appeal of a subtextually dark ending was that it restored "the habitual expectation of *Black Mirror*," which was "to make you think about the darker edges creeping over [any sunshine]. You find yourself thinking, 'What's the catch?'" (Poster 13).

Contra "variance in tone" in the first run of Netflix-original stories, positing a "secret downer ending" works to resurrect the tonality of Channel 4's *Black Mirror*, hence containing the program's brand overflow by reactivating fans' "habitual expectation." On the whole, this desired fan recontainment was not directly concerned with the show's Americanization, however, although the issue did fleetingly surface in some subreddit comments: "Then again the third season was commissioned by an American production house, which is why one shouldn't generally expect the trademark British dark satire of the first two seasons" (Poster 14). This was rapidly rebuffed via ripostes such as that season 3's "episode 2 disagrees" (Poster 15). Explicitly attacking "Americanization" is seen by fans as lacking in both nuance and fan cultural capital—just as Brooker himself has insistently mocked such a reading—while at the same time seeking to intelligently and subtextually reinstall a resolutely bleak version of the program (through which is *implied* a pre-Netflix version) remains an alluring fan strategy. As a performance of "good" fandom, the "secret downer ending" theory provoked extensive philosophical debate between redditors regarding what the difference might be between a simulated or "real" Kelly, as well as facilitating a detailed discussion of whether textual evidence could be marshaled either way. Although some remained concerned by the fact that "this episode was wholly inconsistent in tone with the rest of the season," let alone preceding seasons (Poster 16), others concluded that there was "not much to definitively rule out a 'secret downer ending' . . . , but on the other hand, nothing is inconsistent with an optimistic ending, either. Perhaps watching *Black Mirror* has made us too cynical!" (Poster 17). Even here, the lingering notion was that fans looking for a darker narrative were doing so because (UK / Channel 4) *Black Mirror* had trained them to do so. National TV distinctions are at play, again operating as a "mark of authentication . . . in an industrial context which has become distinctly transnational,"[92] but they are very much coded within this fan theory and its Reddit discussions. In effect, the "secret downer ending" supports a kind of "secret" UK-versus-US TV binary. Surrounding fan discourse—aligned with Brooker's "mugging . . . V signs"—dictates that this should not be made explicit as an anxiety surrounding "Americanization."

By downplaying or bracketing off this concern, *Black Mirror* fans are able to draw on "supposed national differences . . . constantly reiterated in discourses about dramas,"[93] but without directly or transparently being seen to do so. Such coding perhaps recognizes a progressive value to transatlanticism-as-internationalism, and hence to not being blinkered by nation(alizing) discourses. It is very much of a piece with the way in which bingeing enables a suspension of nation-based evaluations in favor of storyworld immersion, and I want to return to this issue now in greater detail.

Alongside the "secret downer ending" idea, then, another type of fan theory works to displace the program's production context(s) and questions of its tonality. This is the fan-cultural reading of *Black Mirror* not as an anthology show made up of separate stories, but rather as a case of coherent world-building. In these fan theorizations and hypotheses, all *Black Mirror* episodes, whether hailing from Channel 4 or Netflix, form part of the same storyworld. Just as *Star Trek*'s fans read seriality into and from its episodic nature,[94] projecting a consistent, serialized world where this was not always evident from TV material, so too do *Black Mirror* fans discuss, debate, and project a singular world for the program. Such a mode of reading is one that enables dedicated fans to distinguish themselves from other audiences, supporting fan-cultural distinction. This kind of fan theory has again been put to Charlie Brooker, although unlike the Kelly-Yorkie affair, he is more tolerant in this instance: "So is there something of a *Black Mirror* extended universe? Yes, and it's connected with 'string,' jests Brooker. Furthering that idea, he notes the status update from Prime Minister Michael Callow ('National Anthem') on a phone in season 3's 'Nosedive.' "[95] By specifically drawing attention to an "Easter egg," that is, a fleeting reference in the Netflix version of the show that ties back to the very first episode on Channel 4, Brooker emphasizes *Black Mirror*'s ongoing continuity (as well as his own authorial mastery).

The notion that all the program's episodes exist in one "extended universe" can also work to boost the idea that it is independent of production contexts in either the United States or the United Kingdom, symbolically severing a projected, singular diegesis from matters of national origin and trajectory. In this mode of fan interpretation (and auteurist play), regardless of how *Black Mirror* is funded, produced, or symbolically located as transatlantic TV drama, it supposedly retains a hyperdiegetic integrity that remains articulated with Brooker as creator-writer.[96] (And although this could be taken to suggest that the series always remains "British" by virtue of Brooker's embodied nationality, such a style of fan reading is very much implicit rather than being directly stated, akin to the way in which fears surrounding "Americanization" are arguably coded.) Erin Whitney has also picked up on the "theory that all *Black Mirror* episodes take place in the same universe," writing for *Screen Crush*:

Fans . . . may have noticed callbacks between the episodes of the first two seasons. The most obvious is the news network UKN, which appears in *almost* every episode. But in Season 3, Brooker has scattered even more hidden clues. I combed through all 13 episodes to find every Easter egg I could and ended up with . . . 24.[97]

And although Charlie Brooker is said not to subscribe to the theory, telling Thrillist the episodes are "probably all in the same psychological universe' à la *The Twilight Zone*, rather than one connected one," he does not oppose it outright in the way that he pointedly countered supposed misreading of "San Junipero." Instead, this is a "fan theory itch"[98] that Brooker seems happy to encourage, even making more exaggerated use of it in season 3, and again in season 4, perhaps in order to reassure fans that the Netflix commission of *Black Mirror* remains an authentic iteration of the "extended universe" they are fascinated by.

Indeed, when Charlie Brooker and Annabel Jones took part in a Reddit AMA to promote season 3 (an online interview where redditors could pose questions and discuss their answers), Brooker teased fans by asking them, "Which Easter eggs did you notice? There's one (in one former ep) that no-one's ever found."[99] As Inger-Lise Kalviknes Bore has pointed out, "The reddit community platform encourages irreverent and collaborative fan engagement in AMAs,"[100] and this was certainly the case when *Black Mirror* redditors scrambled to respond to Brooker's challenge. One fan's quick-fire response recognized the fannish currency of Easter egg-spotting: "And that's how he got Reddit to shut down the Netflix server in one evening" (Poster 18).

Fans are clearly interested in the program's "national identity" at certain moments, with one AMA question launching straight into the topic: "How is it transferring a show from being a pure British one to an American/British mix? Any noticeable differences?" (Poster 19). But at the same time as pondering this "transfer" and its potential consequences, the subreddit group is simultaneously invested in hunting for references that can be used to support an "extended universe." Such coherent world-projecting coexists with contradictory nation-based authentications and concerns around US-UK hybridity precisely because it sustains fan difference from other kinds of audiences who, however much they may enjoy *Black Mirror*, will tend to read it purely as an anthology show. Coherent world-projecting, as Lisa Glebatis Perks has argued,[101] can at the same time be intensified by bingeing, meaning that although binge watching is contested and complicated by *Black Mirror*'s redditors, attempting a binge of season 3—as so many of the subreddit survey contributors did—can allow fans to *discursively dematerialize national production trajectories* in favor of immersively occupying *Black Mirror*'s storyworld. This means that both fan interpretation and (associated) Netflix bingeing can navigate the "transnational spectrum" posited by Adrian Athique,[102] restoring an *implicit* British national identity to the Netflix-produced series at the level of Charlie Brooker's embodied auteurism *and* the program's "extended universe," as well as tacitly supporting *Black Mirror* as transatlantic TV. Consequently, the "fan theory itch" is itself incoherent, both positing a coherent *Black Mirror* storyworld that exists outside of concerns over nation-based interpretations and yet coding national "authentication" into readings of "San Junipero" as an unusual episode, or via Brooker himself.

In this chapter I've sought to do two main things. First, I've considered how Netflix, in its entry to the United Kingdom, has provoked and participated in a multidiscursive positioning of fandom. Whereas fan studies really began with a monodiscursive approach to subcultural fandom, Netflix's targeting of multi-niche fandoms means that fans' discourses of lived experience now uncannily run up against data-driven discourses that assume the power to "unveil" fan practices, even when audiences do not self-identify as media fans. Likewise, targeted fandoms can find their tastes and cultures mirrored back to them in ways that demonstrate "computational authorship" even in the absence of Netflix paratexts confirming this. The use of auteurist paratexts and legitimations, whether via the Duffer brothers for *Stranger Things* or Charlie Brooker for *Black Mirror*, seeks to reassure fans that Netflix Originals possess an authorial authenticity rather than being wholly data-driven and computationally composited.

Second, I've also taken *Black Mirror* as a case study, given its transtelevisual movement from the United Kingdom's public service broadcaster Channel 4 to newfound status as a Netflix Original in 2016. This symbolic, transatlantic relocation within the TV industry confronted *Black Mirror*'s fans with the possibility that their fandom could become transtextual, moving across different sets of UK and US episodes, and that some version of transfandom may even characterize this experience. I looked at the *Black Mirror* subreddit and Reddit AMA to consider how season 3 was received, given the volume of comments and responses to a naturally occurring season survey (1,382 participants). Partly grounded in the continuity of Charlie Brooker's involvement as an embodied (UK) auteur, as well as in his mockery of audiences decrying potential "Americanization," these fans sought to recontain *Black Mirror*'s brand "overflow." By focusing on the show's "extended universe," they often tuned out national production changes altogether, and by positing a "secret downer ending" to a more bittersweet or upbeat season 3 episode ("San Junipero"), fans could also restore the show's previously unremittingly bleak tone without directly attacking Americanization. Transatlantic TV fandom continues to operate multidiscursively here, implicitly drawing on national markers of authentication while at the same time deprioritizing nation-based responses.

NOTES

1. Mark Stewart, "The Myth of Televisual Ubiquity," *Television & New Media* 17:8 (2016), 691–705.
2. Chuck Tryon, *On-Demand Culture: Digital Delivery and the Future of Movies* (New Brunswick, NJ: Rutgers University Press, 2013); Sam Ward, "Streaming Transatlantic: Importation and Integration in the Promotion of Video on Demand in the UK," in *The Netflix Effect: Technology and Entertainment in the 21st Century*, ed. Kevin McDonald and Daniel Smith-Rowsey (New York: Bloomsbury Academic, 2016).
3. Celia Lury, *Brands: The Logos of the Global Economy* (London: Routledge, 2004), 9.
4. Adrian Athique, *Transnational Audiences: Media Reception on a Global Scale* (Cambridge: Polity Press, 2016), 169.
5. Ien Ang, *Desperately Seeking the Audience* (London: Routledge, 1991).
6. For an excellent analysis of this, see Vilde Schanke Sundet, "Still 'Desperately Seeking the Audience'? Audience Making in the Age of Media Convergence (the *Lilyhammer* Experience)," *Northern Lights* 14 (2016), 11–27.
7. Athique, *Transnational Audiences*, 172 and 186.
8. Will Brooker, "Living on *Dawson's Creek*: Teen Viewers, Cultural Convergence, and Television Overflow," *International Journal of Cultural Studies* 4:4 (2001), 456–472.
9. Brooker, "Living on *Dawson's Creek*," 457.
10. Brooker, "Living on *Dawson's Creek*," 470.
11. Brooker, "Living on *Dawson's Creek*," 457.
12. Henry Jenkins, *Convergence Culture* (New York: New York University Press, 2006).
13. Lisa Glebatis Perks, *Media Marathoning: Immersions in Morality* (Lanham, MD: Lexington Books, 2015), ix, xxii, 8.
14. Mareike Jenner, "Binge-Watching: Video-on-Demand, Quality TV and Mainstreaming Fandom," *International Journal of Cultural Studies*, online first, September 18, 2015, 14.
15. Jenner, "Binge-Watching," 14.
16. Ted Sarandos quoted in Tim Wu, "Netflix's War on Mass Culture," *New Republic*, December 5, 2013, https://newrepublic.com/article/115687/netflixs-war-mass-culture.
17. Wu, "Netflix's War."
18. Casey J. McCormick, "'Forward Is the Battle Cry': Binge-Viewing Netflix's *House of Cards*," in McDonald and Smith-Rowsey, *The Netflix Effect*, 113; Amanda D. Lotz, *The Television Will Be Revolutionized*, 2nd ed. (New York: New York University Press, 2014), 271.
19. Wu, "Netflix's War."
20. Wu, "Netflix's War."
21. Bertha Chin and Lori Hitchcock Morimoto, "Towards a Theory of Transcultural Fandom," *Participations* 10:1 (2013), 92–108.
22. Benedict Anderson, *Imagined Communities* (London: Verso, 1991).
23. David Beer, *Popular Culture and New Media: The Politics of Circulation* (Basingstoke: Palgrave Macmillan, 2013), 96.
24. Ward, "Streaming Transatlantic," 219.
25. Ward, "Streaming Transatlantic," 231.
26. Chris Hallam, "*The Crown*: Big Feature," in *TV Bingebox* 2 (2016): 13.
27. Trevor Johnston, "Drama Queen," *Sight and Sound* 26:12 (2016): 47; Benji Wilson, "How Netflix Changed the Way We Watch," *Daily Telegraph*, November 21, 2016, 26.
28. Nancy Tartaglione, "Netflix Boards BBC Two's 'Collateral'; Billie Piper & More Join David Hare Thriller," *Deadline Hollywood*, April 6, 2017, http://deadline.com/2017/04/netflix-collateral-bbc-two-david-hare-billie-piper-john-simm-nicola-walker-carey-mulligan-1202063340/.
29. Georg Szalai, "BBC Drama Chief Vows to Back Britishness and the "Unexpected" over Algorithms," *Hollywood Reporter*, May 5, 2017, http://www.hollywoodreporter.com/news/bbc-drama-chief-vows-back-britishness-unexpected-algorithms-1000476.

30. Neta Alexander, "Catered to Your Future Self: Netflix's 'Predictive Personalization' and the Mathematization of Taste," in McDonald and Smith-Rowsey, *The Netflix Effect*, 92.

31. Athique, *Transnational Audiences*, 172.

32. Ed Finn, *What Algorithms Want: Imagination in the Age of Computing* (Cambridge, MA: MIT Press, 2017), 103.

33. Finn, *What Algorithms Want*, 103.

34. Finn, *What Algorithms Want*, 103.

35. Blake Hallinan and Ted Striphas, "Recommended for You: The Netflix Prize and the Production of Algorithmic Culture," *New Media & Society* 18:1 (2016): 128.

36. Daniel Fienberg, "The Duffer Brothers Talk 'Stranger Things' Influences, 'It' Dreams and Netflix Phase 2," *Hollywood Reporter*, August 1, 2016, http://www.hollywoodreporter.com/fien-print/duffer-brothers-talk-stranger-things-916180.

37. Dan Hassler-Forest, "Global Capitalism, Fan Culture, and (Even) Stranger Things," rowmaninternational.com, August 30, 2016, https://www.rowmaninternational.com/blog/global-capitalism-fan-culture-and-even-stranger-things/.

38. Hassler-Forest, "Global Capitalism, Fan Culture."

39. Matthew Guschwan, "Fandom, Brandom and the Limits of Participatory Culture," *Journal of Consumer Culture* 12:1 (2012), 19–40.

40. Beer, *Popular Culture*, 95; see also Finn, *What Algorithms Want*, 107; John Cheney-Lippold, *We Are Data: Algorithms and the Making of Our Digital Selves* (New York: New York University Press, 2017), 7–8.

41. David Beer, *Metric Power* (Basingstoke: Palgrave Macmillan, 2016), 189.

42. Helen Kennedy, *Post, Mine, Repeat: Social Media Data Mining Becomes Ordinary* (Basingstoke: Palgrave Macmillan, 2016), 11.

43. Athique, *Transnational Audiences*, 153.

44. Wu, "Netflix's War"; Ward, "Streaming Transatlantic."

45. Athique, *Transnational Audiences*, 172.

46. Alberto N. García, "A Storytelling Machine: The Complexity and Revolution of Narrative Television," *Between* 6:11 (2016): 7.

47. Camil Ungureanu, "Aestheticization of Politics and Ambivalence of Self-Sacrifice in Charlie Brooker's *The National Anthem*," *Journal of European Studies* 45:1 (2015), 21–30; Pierluigi Musarò, "Reality Show and Pop Politics: Who Holds Power in the Network Society?," *Mediascapes Journal* 6 (2016), 115–127; Javier Cigüela Sola and Jorge Martínez-Lucena, "Screen Technologies and the Imaginary of Punishment: A Reading of *Black Mirror*'s 'White Bear,'" *Empedocles: European Journal for the Philosophy of Communication* 7:1 (2016), 3–22.

48. Greg Singh, "Recognition and the Image of Mastery as Themes in *Black Mirror* (Channel 4, 2011–Present): An Eco-Jungian Approach to 'Always-On' Culture," *International Journal of Jungian Studies* 6:2 (2014): 121.

49. Singh, "Recognition," 121.

50. Bryant W. Sculos, "Screen Savior: How *Black Mirror* Reflects the Present More Than the Future," *Class, Race and Corporate Power* 5:1 (2017), http://digitalcommons.fiu.edu/classracecorporatepower/vol5/iss1/4.

51. Amanda Lotz, *Portals: A Treatise on Internet-Distributed Television* (Ann Arbor: Michigan Publishing, 2017), 57.

52. Derek Johnston, *Haunted Seasons: Television Ghost Stories for Christmas and Horror for Halloween* (Basingstoke: Palgrave Macmillan, 2015), 11.

53. In Charlie Brooker and Annabel Jones, "We're Charlie Brooker and Annabel Jones, the showrunners of Black Mirror. Ask us anything. As long as it's not too difficult or sports related," October 25, 2016, https://www.reddit.com/r/IAmA/comments/59cppq/were_charlie_brooker_and_annabel_jones_the/.

54. Thomas Ling, "*Black Mirror* Season 3 on Netflix: Full Episode Guide," radiotimes.com, October 21, 2016, http://www.radiotimes.com/news/2016-10-21/black-mirror-season-3-on-netflix-full-episode-guide.

55. Simon Lewis, "On the Set Of *Black Mirror* with Jon Hamm," *ShortList* (2014), http://www.shortlist.com/entertainment/tv/on-the-set-of-black-mirror-with-jon-hamm#art.

56. Alex Fletcher, "When Is Jon Hamm's Christmas *Black Mirror* Airing?," *Digital Spy*, November 25, 2014, http://www.digitalspy.com/tv/black-mirror/news/a612386/when-is-jon-hamms-christmas-black-mirror-airing/#~oWJHZOnNPVnz7d.

57. Fletcher, "Jon Hamm's Christmas."

58. Barbara Selznick, *Global Television: Co-producing Culture* (Philadelphia: Temple University Press, 2008), 84.

59. Jeffrey S. Miller, *Something Completely Different: British Television and American Culture* (Minneapolis: University of Minnesota Press, 2000), 182.

60. Stephen Armstrong, "Has TV Gone Too Far?," *Sunday Times—Culture*, January 15, 2017, 17.

61. Armstrong, "Has TV Gone Too Far," 17.

62. Jonathan Gray, "Reviving Audience Studies," *Critical Studies in Media Communication* 34:1 (2017), 79–83.

63. Contra Alexander, "Catered," 92; and Michael D. Smith and Rahul Telang, *Streaming, Sharing, Stealing: Big Data and the Future of Entertainment* (Cambridge, MA: MIT Press, 2016), 140.

64. Jenner, "Binge-Watching," 10.

65. Elke Weissmann, *Transnational Television Drama: Special Relations and Mutual Influence between the US and UK* (Basingstoke: Palgrave Macmillan, 2012), 185.

66. James Brassett and Alex Sutton, "British Satire, Everyday Politics: Chris Morris, Armando Iannucci and Charlie Brooker," *British Journal of Politics and International Relations* 19:2 (2017): 257.

67. Michele Hilmes, *Network Nations: A Transnational History of British and American Broadcasting* (New York: Routledge, 2012), 310.

68. Roberta Pearson, "Cult Television as Digital Television's Cutting Edge," in *Television as Digital Media*, ed. James Bennett and Niki Strange (Durham, NC: Duke University Press, 2011), 119.

69. Ian Berriman, "Charlie Brooker Talks *The Twilight Zone* and Technology," *GamesRadar*, February 1, 2013, http://www.gamesradar.com/charlie-brooker-talks-the-twilight-zone-and-technology/.

70. Athique, *Transnational Audiences*, 172.

71. Michael Z. Newman and Elana Levine, *Legitimating Television: Media Convergence and Cultural Status* (New York: Routledge, 2012).

72. Mareike Jenner, "Is This TVIV? On Netflix, TVIII and Binge-Watching," *New Media & Society* 18:2 (2016): 270.

73. James Temperton, "Through a Glass, Darkly," *Wired: UK Edition*, November 2016, 80.

74. Audra Schroeder, "'Black Mirror' Creator on Easter Eggs and the Show's Connected Universe," *Daily Dot*, October 28, 2016, https://www.dailydot.com/upstream/black-mirror-charlie-brooker-annabel-jones/.

75. Schroeder, "'Black Mirror' Creator."

76. Schroeder, "'Black Mirror' Creator."

77. Temperton, "Through a Glass, Darkly," 83.

78. Schroeder, "'Black Mirror' Creator."

79. Brassett and Sutton, "British Satire, Everyday Politics," 257.

80. Christopher Hooton, "*Black Mirror* Season 3's Netflix Release and Why Dropping Every Episode at Once Isn't Always Best," *The Independent*, November 3, 2016, http://www.independent.co.uk/arts-entertainment/tv/features/black-mirror-season-3s-netflix-release-and-why-dropping-every-episode-at-once-isnt-always-best-a7395926.html.

81. Lothar Mikos, "Digital Media Platforms and the Use of TV Content: Binge Watching and Video-on-Demand in Germany," *Media and Communication* 4:3 (2016): 157; Perks, *Media Marathoning*, 8; Jenner, "Binge-Watching," 9.

82. Perks, *Media Marathoning*, 8.

83. Athique, *Transnational Audiences*, 172.

84. Weissmann, *Transnational Television Drama*, 139.

85. Mikos, "Digital Media Platforms," 157.

86. Adrienne L. Massanari, *Participatory Culture, Community and Play: Learning from Reddit* (New York: Peter Lang, 2015), 16.
87. Inger-Lise Kalviknes Bore, *Screen Comedy and Online Audiences* (London: Routledge, 2017), 142.
88. Alex Hern, "Shut Up and Dance," *The Guardian*, October 25, 2016, https://www.theguardian.com/tv-and-radio/2016/oct/25/reflections-on-black-mirror-by-those-for-whom-science-fiction-became-reality.
89. Hern, "Shut Up and Dance."
90. Kristy Puchko, "*Black Mirror* Creator Responds to San Junipero Fan Theory," *Nerdist*, November 4, 2016, http://nerdist.com/black-mirror-creator-responds-to-san-junipero-fan-theory/.
91. Puchko, "*Black Mirror* Creator Responds."
92. Weissmann, *Transnational Television Drama*, 185.
93. Weissmann, *Transnational Television Drama*, 139.
94. Henry Jenkins, *Textual Poachers* (New York: Routledge, 1992), 98–99.
95. Schroeder, "'Black Mirror' Creator."
96. This makes it unsurprising that Brooker would have picked up on the "Mirrorverse" fan theory and reinforced it via season 4's "Black Museum."
97. Erin Whitney, "24 Easter Eggs from All Three Seasons of 'Black Mirror,' Plus a Timeline Connecting Every Episode," *Screen Crush*, October 26, 2016, http://screencrush.com/black-mirror-easter-eggs-theory/.
98. Whitney, "24 Easter Eggs."
99. In Brooker and Jones, "We're Brooker and Jones."
100. Bore, *Screen Comedy*, 145.
101. Perks, *Media Marathoning*, 8.
102. Athique, *Transnational Audiences*, 172.

11

CONTEXTUALIZING "QUALITY" US TELEVISION PROGRAMS FOR THE UNITED KINGDOM

The Guardian's Media Blog and the Role of Critics

PAUL RIXON

In this chapter I explore the way British newspapers' digital strategies are affecting the popular and critical discourse they produce around "quality" American television programs, a discourse that plays an important role in contextualizing American programs for the British viewer. To provide a focus for this work, I will be concentrating on the role of newspaper-based blogs. As I do this I will explore three main questions: First, what form of critical and popular coverage is appearing with these new means of writing about television? Second, what is the resulting discourse on American quality television programs? And last, what role is there for the television critic in this new phase of newspaper television coverage? To undertake this analysis I will look at one of the most influential and trusted newspaper websites in the United Kingdom, www. guardian.com, which belongs to the *Guardian*.[1] This is not to suggest that the *Guardian*'s coverage dominates and shapes the discourse around television in Britain, but that the nature of its digital strategy is indicative of changes happening in the media and the changing nature of television coverage provided by the United Kingdom's main national newspapers. As part of the theoretical framework for this work, I will utilize some of the concepts of Pierre Bourdieu, especially those closely related to the issues I am exploring here, such as taste groups, cultural dispositions, cultural intermediaries (critics), and cultural distinction.[2] Indeed, as Bourdieu argues in *Distinction* (1984), tastes, values, and forms of cultural distinction are not static; there is a continual process of struggle occurring over these,[3] something we need to understand in relation to television at this moment of digital and cultural change. Accordingly, shifts in the *Guardian*'s coverage of US TV, especially as it has become increasingly fan-like, may be readable as part of the cultural intermediation of forms of "emerging cultural capital" that treat specific strands of American television drama as being among "the 'very best' of popular culture."[4]

THE *GUARDIAN*'S DIGITAL STRATEGY

The *Guardian* was one of the first UK newspapers to develop a digital strategy, soon followed by other British newspapers.[5] One of its main objectives was to view its digital web-based activities as an integral part of how the *Guardian* would operate in the future, and not as some add-on to the normal production of the newspaper.[6] Indeed, it was the first paper to announce, in June 2006, that it "would publish stories first to the web . . . indicating a new phase in UK Journalism."[7] For some, these developments are leading to a fundamental shift in journalism, from writing and delivering news to providing more opinion and comment.[8] As part of this strategy, the *Guardian* began to experiment with and develop new forms of coverage and interaction, such as using embedded videos and audio in its web pages as well as allowing the public the ability to comment on almost all of its output.[9] The aim has been to create a form of coverage more conducive to what it thinks its readers and users, who are often well educated, young, and technologically savvy, might want from an online newspaper site.[10] And as Mike Savage has argued, in *Social Class in the 21st Century*, "Younger people have their own kind of distinctive cultural capital which jostles with that of their elders,"[11] with these (twenty- and thirty-something) British TV audiences being more likely to valorize a range of "quality" popular cultural texts. Similarly, Tony Bennett *et al.*, in a Bourdieuian analysis of contemporary cultural distinctions in Britain, found that well-educated, younger, and middle-class TV viewers tended to favor the kind of television described as "quality" American TV drama.[12] Shifts in the *Guardian*'s television coverage can thus be argued to mirror—and perhaps even to reinforce or professionally and culturally consecrate—generational struggles over forms of (TV-oriented) cultural capital.

As part of these developments, the *Guardian* started to experiment with blogs, which have now become an important part of its provision.[13] These divide into two main types, live blogs focusing on ongoing events, usually with a temporary life span, such as covering the November 2015 shootings in Paris,[14] and others of a more permanent and ongoing nature, focusing on such areas as education, politics, arts, and culture.[15] The blogs are made up of regular posts, many of which are quite short and are usually more informal than traditional forms of journalism. Within these blog posts hyperlinks are provided, connecting the post to news sources and stories either on the *Guardian* site or elsewhere on the Web. This helps to deliver a more innovative news experience, and one that moves from just presenting "knowledge about events"[16] to one where readers are guided "along paths of exploration"[17] to engage with the actual information sources. The majority of the permanent *Guardian* blogs are either linked to a particular journalist, such as George Monbiot and his blog on environmental issues,[18] or is the output of various contributors. Both forms allow the public to share blog posts on social media sites and to leave comments. A number of these permanent blogs focus on television and other media industries, such as the *Guardian*'s media blog, which encompasses a large range of different areas, for example, radio, television, PR, film, and the like.[19] The *Guardian* also has a further blog that focuses purely on television and radio,[20] whose coverage of American television I will now explore in more detail.

THE *GUARDIAN*'S TELEVISION AND RADIO BLOG

The *Guardian*'s television and radio blog has been going since 2006 and had, according to the search function on its website, over 7,240 posts by September 2, 2016. This would be an average of around 700 per year, or around 2 a day. As the blog cannot be searched separately from the rest of the *Guardian*'s coverage, for this analysis I have had to use a different approach for finding relevant posts. To do this I looked at all the headings of the 7,000-plus posts appearing on the blog and have read all those relating to American TV programs or American television. For the public interactions I have looked at one month's worth per year for the last ten years, focusing on the number of times posts have been shared and the comments appearing on a selection of these posts.

I have divided up the following analysis of the blog's coverage of quality American programs into two parts, with the first focusing on the actual blog posts by contributors relating to American programs and then the second part exploring the public engagement with posts. For the analysis of the contributors' blog posts, I initially looked at the meta level, at titles and content of the posts, and used this information to identify three main tensions or issues, which I consider below: first, the nature and form of the posts, whether they are short or long, celebratory or critical; second, the discourse appearing around the quality American drama programs concerned; and, last, the different touchstones of excellence that are drawn on to position specific texts as "quality" US TV. After exploring these posts, I then move on to look at the public's interaction with the television and radio blog, considering which posts they shared, how many times, whether readers made comments, and the resulting discussions that occurred.

BLOG POSTS AND AMERICAN TELEVISION PROGRAMS

While this blog might be viewed, as other blogs, as part of the democratization of the media and mediated debates, it also works to shape and limit access and the resulting discussion. For example, for the TV and radio blog only *Guardian* contributors can publish posts, including the *Guardian*'s TV critics, reviewers, or previewers, though occasionally an outsider will also be allowed to contribute, such as the author Jane Bussmann.[21] Therefore, it is their professional, taste-making views that will tend to shape the issues being raised on the blog, along with any subsequent reader debates. Such critics thus act, as Pierre Bourdieu and others argue, as cultural intermediaries, selecting, filtering, and positioning cultural artifacts for the reader.[22] The blog has also been structured and designed to work for the strategic needs of the *Guardian*.[23] For example, while many of the posts have embedded hyperlinks, many aim at other parts of the *Guardian* and thus help to keep the reader on the website. The blog, therefore, is designed to work for the *Guardian* while offering an innovative and interactive experience for the types of readers who make up much of its particular readership demographic, which is younger and more educated than that of most other British newspapers.[24] Indeed, the blog form, with its ability to offer in-depth coverage of a specific topic or issue, presented in an interactive form, is able to offer a novel form of journalism, comment, and discussion—what might in fact be thought of as a form of *broadsheet newspaper narrowcasting*. Therefore, the blog is able to present coverage of relatively specialized topics like American television dramas, and serve, refract, reinforce, and potentially consecrate these emergent British taste cultures on a scale, and with a scope, that traditional UK broadsheet newspapers have not been able to offer in the past.

From News to Fan-Like Opinion: The Form and Nature of Blog Posts

From an initial look at the posts it is obvious that many of them have a fan-like feel to them, perhaps reflecting the more informal nature of blogs. Looking at those focusing on American television, one sees that many of the blog writers concentrate on American programs that mean something to them, rather than, as a traditional critic might do, critiquing a program that has been broadcast and around which there is public debate or interest, and which they thus feel a necessity or an obligation to write about.[25] For example, Vicky Frost writes about being obsessed with *CSI* (2000–2015), noting that "FiveUS has become a default setting on my telly (and yes, I am probably the only person who has ever uttered those words), and I am some kind of crime-drama zombie with eyes only for Gil Grissom."[26] There is often little attempt to present a critical argument about the program or to approach it in some neutral or objective way; instead the *Guardian's* TV bloggers write subjectively about why they like or "love" the program. One point emerging in many of these posts relates to how protective bloggers are of "their" US program, discussing how badly treated it has been by its UK broadcaster, for instance, perhaps being moved around the schedule or being shown in an unpopular slot or on a little-watched channel, thus stopping the program concerned from building the substantial audience and recognition they think it deserves. Blog writers seem to feel they have a right to criticize the United Kingdom's broadcasters and distributors for this, in a practice that is very similar to how Henry Jenkins views fans as acting to protect their "common cultural property."[27] For example, Owen Van Spall complains that a series he likes, *Breaking Bad* (2008–2013), compared to series like *Mad Men* (2007–2015), "has been unfairly denied the limelight. It has been aired in the United Kingdom only on FX so far, and a region two box-set of the first season isn't due until December."[28] Given the number of *Guardian* posts on this issue relating to American programs, it would seem that US TV dramas are, perhaps, more prone to this problem of inaccessibility than broadly comparable British ones, which are usually commissioned by and broadcast on the main UK channels.

However, while many of these blog posts are informal, some take a more serious approach and are penned from within an established critical tradition, often critiquing a particular American program or related topic. For example, Mark Lawson's pieces about the problem of British television in the face of the American industry's success stories work in this vein.[29] These more serious or critical posts are, in some ways, like traditional pieces about television written by a TV critic rather than by a fan or advocate. They explore a particular issue, often in some depth, supported by evidence and reasoned argument framed by dominant cultural values; it would seem that such writers, utilizing their very much established rather than "emerging" cultural capital,[30] are writing in such a way that their commentary will be positioned within the accepted cultural hierarchy as a piece of serious criticism.[31] Two main reasons might explain the appearance of these critical forms on the blog: one, that the pieces were originally written as articles or reviews that have then been posted onto the blog or, two, that the writers wished to convince the reader of their views using an accepted, persuasive way of writing about television. As Bourdieu points out, newspapers have tended to employ critics who share values and outlooks with the main readership, [32] and who are not there solely to serve a niche audience. However, as this chapter explores, this situation is changing as newspapers gain traction in new virtual spaces that can instead service niche readerships and their associated, emerging tastes. In such a transitional moment, professional TV critics such as Mark Lawson might find themselves representing a form of older, "highbrow" cultural capital, somewhat at odds with generational, social-media-savvy expressions of new televisual and pop-cultural taste cultures, as Bennett *et al.* have begun to demonstrate via their updating of Bourdieu's work.[33]

One of the dominant forms of posting on the *Guardian* blog, especially in recent years, has been the episodic guide. These blog posts provide weekly updates on a particular series, helping viewers to keep up to date with what is happening, something that is especially useful for long, complex series, with many story arcs, as well as allowing room for discussion between fans and viewers. Many programs, both on radio and TV, now have these episodic guides, but American TV dramas, because of their number of episodes, which are normally far greater than in British series—and also perhaps because many attract glowing plaudits—have tended to be dominant, for example, *The Wire* (2002–2008), *Battlestar Galactica* (2004–2009), and *Game of Thrones* (2011–). One of the first episodic guides for an American series on the blog was written by Steve Busfield about *The Wire*, which he started in 2008 when season 5 was being broadcast on FX.[34] Busfield begins his initial post by discussing why he is starting an episodic guide, noting that because access to *The Wire* in Britain has been through so many different means—DVDs, downloads, and now FX—rather than through regular scheduled broadcasts, it has been hard to share watercooler moments when UK viewers can discuss the show together. He goes on, "I'd like to make this a forum for those who are watching it at the same time: during its British TV premiere on FX on Monday nights. If you are one of those people, please read on and share the debate."[35] Such guides provide an important and regular presence for American television on the blog. In many ways, they help in the creation of a feeling of community around such programs, generating a *Guardian*-oriented and yet US quality TV fan base of sorts.[36] It is here that you can go to discuss or read about "your" American show as a British fan; it is as if an American program that attracts a niche UK audience can now also sustain a related "niche" area of criticism and discussion on the *Guardian* blog, a space tailored just for it, though one still connected to television's wider transatlantic discursive spaces. Arguably, the result is not merely a mirroring of emerging cultural capital by the *Guardian*'s cultural intermediaries, but also a consecration of these televisual tastes as part of the "very best" of popular culture,[37] implicitly endorsed by professional journalists even as they write in more personalized, fan-like, or fan-friendly ways.

US Quality TV? An Uncontested Discourse on "the Greatest TV Shows"

From my analysis of the blog posts it would seem that where American programs constitute the main part of a post, they are covered almost invariably in a favorable way. However, it is interesting to note that when discussing the standing of these programs, most of the posts rarely use the formal-sounding and much-debated term "quality,"[38] tending instead to use more informal and reader-friendly ways of writing about the selected US TV shows. For example, Sarah Hughes refers to *Lost* as "groundbreaking television,"[39] and Ben Marshall on January 17, 2007, calls *24* "bloody good television,"[40] whereas Jon Wilde writes of *The Wire*, *The Shield* (2002–2008), and *Deadwood* (2004–2006) that they represent "some of today's greatest TV shows," though he wonders why three of the greatest-ever TV series are virtually unheard of among British viewers.[41] Such discussions are framed much more in the language of a fan or advocate than that of traditional critics, who would usually attempt to appear more balanced in their critique, perhaps utilizing the term "quality" as a measured reference to the critical standing of a program rather than deploying informal phrases such as "great" or "fantastic."

Yet there are some posts that take issue with these sentiments. For example, Steven Wells criticizes the American remake of *The Office* (2005–2013), seeing it as a "shadow of the original,"[42] and Stuart Heritage in 2010 writes about his disappointment with the series *FlashForward* (2009–2010): "The whole thing's a knotted mess of unresolved strands and irrational new strands, performed by a set of characters who are impossible to root for, in a format that's been stripped of all dramatic tension."[43] However, looking through all the posts on this blog that relate to American programs, only a few, in their entirety, are overtly critical. The overwhelming number of posts on the blog either ignore American programs, focusing on British and, increasingly, European shows, or express positive views about the US TV dramas that are focused upon. Perhaps the dominance of supportive posts among those on American television can be put down to writers tending to write about what they like, about programs that fit their tastes, and programs they are prepared to track down in a multichannel UK environment.[44] Where posts are more critical of American television and its impact on British culture, they tend to focus less on individual programs, instead taking issue with the general discourse of excellence that surrounds American television and the view that it produces programs that are much better than their British counterparts. For example, Ben Myers laments the alleged demise of British television drama and its replacement with fashionable, lauded American TV drama, a form that he argues can in reality only tell us about "life in America. [O]nly the British can truly comment on Britain."[45] In some ways, these two opposing views— being supportive of American "quality" programs, or being critical of their newfound influence over the British industry—have come to dominate much of the UK debate and discussion around American television dramas over the last decade or so, at least on the *Guardian*'s TV and radio blog, although views in favor of US TV have predominated. Such discursive interactions signal what Bourdieu would call a symbolic struggle as different groups try to (re)position American and British television programs within shifting or possibly even fragmenting cultural hierarchies.[46] This scenario has been further complicated by the arrival of lauded European programs, led by those from Scandinavia, which, for some, have offered another new, rival form of "quality" television drama.[47]

Touchstones of Excellence (and Mediocrity)

Within the "quality US TV drama" discourse found on the blog, comparisons are regularly made between new American programs and other more established programs that I will call "touchstones of excellence." Interestingly, the neocanonical touchstones invariably used, for American programs, are other American series rather than British shows. One argument why this happens is that the two television industries and systems remain sufficiently different, with the result that it is easier to use programs that have the same characteristics to make comparisons. For example, a blog post by Jim Shelley explores the standing of *The Wire* by using two other American programs as reference points: "The Wire, The Sopranos' HBO stable-mate, which finished its fourth series on FX last night, has for nearly four years been so dark, complex and involving, it's made David Chase's mob family look as simplistic and all-American as a modern-day Waltons."[48] In turn, British programs are mostly compared to other British TV dramas, partly as they share similar histories and have common characteristics that are likely to be known to most British viewers, and also perhaps because American "quality" TV programs often remain less watched or known by the majority of British viewers.[49]

However, some posts do attempt to compare better-known American programs with British examples, often within a wider discussion comparing the state of the two national systems. An example of this can be seen where Tim Lusher raises the question of why the American system produces *The Wire*, whereas the British system generates and sustains TV dramas like *Casualty* (1986–).[50] As he argues, "The only way to produce sophisticated, rich, long-running drama like The Wire or even ER is to use a team of writers who collaborate under a showrunner, a system the US studios has cracked."[51] There seems to be a division in how American and British television and their respective programs are written about, reflecting, in some ways, the different television tastes and cultural dispositions of the contributors and, perhaps, readers.[52] Certain versions of "mainstream" or popular British TV drama, such as BBC1's long-running Saturday night medical drama

Casualty, are devalued and othered in relation to celebrated US "quality" TV, working as touchstones of mediocrity rather than televisual excellence. As noted earlier, blogs are able to create discursive spaces for specific readers to discuss and valorize the cultural forms they enjoy, such as particular American TV dramas.

INTERACTING WITH THE *GUARDIAN'S* TV AND RADIO BLOG

Given the relative ease with which anyone can create a blog or contribute to a social media site, these communication forms have been seen as a sign of a newfound equality between media producers and consumers.[53] As Bar-Ilan argues, "In most blogs readers can comment on the postings, thus engage in active discussion and become part of the blogspace."[54] No longer do users just consume what they are presented with. Now, if they want, they can create their own blog content; they can act as prosumers.[55] Therefore, in relation to television, the public no longer has to quietly accept a mediated public debate shaped and dominated by professional television critics. They now have the ability to create content, to write their own reviews, stories and ideas, and to publish these in places where other members of the public can read and engage with them.[56] For blogs, this function tends to operate in three main ways: the public can post on their own blogs or on those where they are allowed to do so; they can share a post if they want; and if the comments function is enabled, they can write comments on a blog, engaging in discussion with the writer and other contributors. However, on the *Guardian* TV and radio blog the public's interaction is limited to sharing and commenting on the posts, as only *Guardian*-endorsed contributors can post. I now want to explore how such interactions on the blog act as part of a UK-oriented discourse around quality American TV dramas. First, I will look at the way the *Guardian* blogs are shared and then, second, I'll analyze the comments and discussions of blog readers.

Sharing: Creating Information Clusters or a Brand-Specific Niche

The *Guardian*'s TV and radio blog posts can be easily shared on social media and through email via buttons provided on the top left-hand side of the page for Facebook, Twitter, email, LinkedIn, and Google+. By clicking these links, the user is taken to the corresponding site where additional information can be added before blog posts are shared on that platform. The restricted number of platform links included on the *Guardian* page does not limit users, who can copy the piece and post it where they want to, but it does signify the social media that the *Guardian* currently views as being of importance. By sharing the piece, the user helps link the *Guardian* site to a wider cluster of information, news, and television websites, helping to promote the *Guardian*, raising its profile, and perhaps attracting more web users to its site, while also helping to circulate the television discourse found on its blog.

A sample of posts, a month's worth of around thirty posts each year since 2006, makes it evident that most posts had been shared infrequently, if at all. The reasons for this in the first couple of years, 2006 through to 2008, could very likely be because the *Guardian* site was still relatively new at the time, and user numbers were still growing. This is supported by the fact that many posts also had few comments across this period.[57] For example, Jenny Colgan's post on *24* (2001–2010) has only three comments and no shares.[58] However, in relation to American programs, the limited number of shares in this period could also be linked to a less visible debate about American shows on the blog at this point in time, along with the limited ability of people, including contributors, to gain access to the TV programs that were mentioned, some of which were often only available through DVDs, subscription channels, or downloads.[59] As more posts on American programs start to appear after 2009, helping the discourse around American series to become more visible, so the number of shares increases slightly. For example, a post by Sarah Hughes on *Masters of Sex* (2013–) was shared twenty-four times in 2013.[60] Overall, the number of shares for posts about American programs on the whole of the blog is small in number per blog post. This compares unfavorably to British drama programs that, overall, have far more shares, including one of the highest number, which was for a post in 2013 on David Suchet's final *Poirot* (1989–2013) episode, shared 1,944 times.[61] However, many current posts, whether about British or American programs, still receive 10 shares or less. Perhaps, for American programs, this might be linked to the still relatively small and niche-like audience they attract in Britain, and the continual problem of gaining access to them.[62] This has meant that the blog, through its limited number of shares, is not strongly linked to a wider cluster of social media sites on the Web, and therefore it acts more as a single information node, a one-stop branded space where a reader can discuss particular niche areas like American "quality" programming.

Engaging the Public: Celebratory and Comparative Comments

Looking over the seven thousand or so posts on this *Guardian* blog reveals a notable divergence between the large number that have received ten comments or under and the relative few that have gained hundreds of comments. On the first main page of the blog's history, covering the period October 24 to November 7, 2006, there are thirty posts, of which nineteen received comments, with the highest number of comments being ten, while the lowest was zero.[63] It would seem that this early in the life of the blog few readers wanted to engage with posts, though this might have been linked to the limited number of early adopters attracted online to the *Guardian's* website.[64] However, of the thirty posts appearing in April 2011, all received between 10 and 183 comments.[65] For the period July to September 2016, by contrast, all of the thirty-five posts had comments, ranging between 1 and 1,012.[66] While many of those with comments were on posts about British programs, such as *Top Gear* (1977–) with 1,012,[67] American programs, such as *Preacher* (749 responses), also received a considerable number of comment.[68] Over time, it would seem that readers have started to engage with the blog in far greater numbers, though the number of comments, even with more popular posts, is still relatively small compared to the *Guardian's* official number of unique online users: this had hit twenty-six million by 2016.[69] Also, there is a question of how many readers will lurk on such pages reading the posts and comments but not engaging.[70]

While the comments on a diverse series of posts about American programs range widely, a few observations can be made. Most of the comments about American shows are positive, with much of the debate being about the comparative standing of the programs being discussed. For example, engaging in a debate about *The Shield*, one reader commented that "this season of The Shield has been riveting, intense, exciting and powerful,"[71] while another wrote, "I have no doubt that the final episode of this fantastic show is going to be one of the best pieces of television ever."[72] Many of the comments are very short—supporting or, in a few cases, opposing the view of the original post—or they further explore the ideas raised by the initial post, such as the comments from pandemoniana,[73] who, in some depth, argued that *The Wire* was a better program than *The Shield*. These views were, however, opposed by those supporting the *Guardian* journalist's position, who suggested that such comparisons with *The Wire* should stop.[74] Interestingly though, as noted earlier, there was no attempt to compare *The Shield* with British programs; American programs remain the "quality" touchstone that all the contributors seem to understand and share. Some of the comments appear as a dialogue between members of the public, rather than as a critical engagement with debates or with *Guardian* contributors, giving the impression that this interaction is between members of a community of sorts, one defined by their interest in "the best . . . ever" American programs. And while there is some overlap and commonality across the public comments on the blog, no one clear view or public opinion emerges. This might relate to the lack of any key mediator being in place to engage with the comments and to bring out any shared points or elements in order to create a consensus that could then be brought back into wider public discussion. Instead, readers of these somewhat fragmentary comments are left, in many ways, to decide for themselves the significance of the "US quality TV drama in Britain" debates.

The blog is structured in such a way that the original posters—usually a professional journalist—are placed in a position of power. They are able to present their views, in some depth if they wish, and it is their topic that sets the focus for any ensuing readership debate. Acting as cultural intermediaries, they help to "construct value, by framing how others . . . engage with goods, affecting and effecting others' orientation towards those goods as legitimate."[75] The public is left to react to such postings, and their comments, often short in length, are hidden at the bottom of the page, even requiring the click of a link to bring them up. Therefore, such blogs do not somehow democratically allow the voices of the public to replace those of professional critics, but instead allow established TV journalists and neocritics, those who now write regularly (in fan-like ways) about television for online media, to play an important role in continuing to shape the public US-UK TV debate emanating from the *Guardian* newspaper through its online presence. At the same time, such fan-friendly TV journalism in the UK national press (or its online extensions) has typically worked to legitimate the emerging cultural capital of "quality" American TV for younger, well-educated, middle-class, and social-media-savvy audiences.

CONCLUSION: A DIVIDED NATIONAL TELEVISION DISCOURSE?

I have analyzed the *Guardian*'s TV and radio blog, delineating and exploring its discourses surrounding "quality" American TV dramas. Through this examination I have shown that the *Guardian*'s blog posts, and their related discourses, have been dominated by an informal approach, indeed one that is almost fan-like in places. Posts on American programs tend to be written by contributors who passionately advocate for them and who often write subjectively while trying to persuade readers to watch these shows or engaging with those that are already doing so. The dominant discourse is typically framed in terms of these programs' undisputed excellence, of their success and their quality, backed up by illustrations and examples of the complexity of storyline arcs, the quality of scripts, the high production values, and the realistic characters. In supporting such views, many of the posts use other American TV programs as examples, drawing on them as uncontested touchstones of excellence. For many of those posting on the blog about American programs, these are quite simply the best things on British television, even if (and sometimes especially because) they have attracted very small niche audiences in the UK context, audiences who are thus able to perform their cultural distinction and discerning taste.[76] There are few dissenting views that engage critically with these assessments, though many posts ignore American programs altogether and focus purely on British and other European programs. It is as if there is a taste-cultural divide in this national television discourse between those who are positively and selectively in-terested in the "greatest" American programs and those who are more interested solely in domestic British TV output, although some *Guardian* contributors and readers move be-tween these two interpretive positions. The blog offers a place where readers who enjoy US programs, and often watch them in different ways at different times, can come to-gether as a community to gain regular information, share views, and join discussions with like-minded people, helped by the regular posts of episodic guides. Such online spaces provide a place where similar views and values can be exchanged, where existing cultural dispositions can be refined, where new taste groups can emerge or become self-knowing, and where existing, albeit emergent, taste cultures can seek a new position and legitimacy in the cultural hierarchy.[77]

Overall, the presence of posts about American programs and television on the blog remains relatively high, at around 30 percent of all posts,[78] with most being supportive in tone. Public interactions with posts are more limited in character; the number of shares to other social sites is still fairly low, though the number of comments has increased over the years, and contemporary posts regarding flagship British shows, for example *Top Gear*, *Poirot*, or *Sherlock*, can typically receive more than a thousand comments. Most of the comments on posts relating to American programs occur between readers who like the specific program or American TV drama in general. The debate is less about whether American programs are excellent—this seems often to be unquestionably accepted—than about whether a specific program under discussion is up to the same level of quality as other canonized US TV programs. The discourse around American programs, at least on the relevant posts on this blog, is still dominated by professional critics and writers, who are the only ones able to post. It would seem that, unlike their forebears writing be-tween the 1950s and 1980s,[79] TV critics find American programs far more suited to their tastes, perhaps more so than would be the case for the majority of the British public, who still mostly watch domestic programs, as seen by their domination of top-thirty viewing charts.[80]

In some ways, *Guardian* contributors are, on the one hand, writing for a taste culture of younger, well-educated, social-media-savvy readers who enjoy and watch "quality" American programs: an audience niche in the United Kingdom who have needed a place to gather. Thus, *Guardian* writers, and the discourse they help to shape, contextualize such programs for this group, reinforcing it as a discerning and knowledgeable cadre of educated British viewers. On the other hand, the *Guardian*'s TV and radio bloggers also present a view of US TV programs to readers and members of the public who do not watch these shows, or are less obsessed by them, yet who are still interested in their pres-ence on British screens and in British culture. Increasingly, critics and neocritics, as the newspaper's online television coverage increases in scale and scope, can focus on niche programs, that is, programs they value, rather than ones the mainstream viewing public is watching. Accordingly, these critics have played—and continue to play—a role in the symbolic struggle around types of US television drama in the United Kingdom, seeking to elevate "quality" American television so that it becomes part of the dominant culture, or at least so that it can act as a marker of its fan audiences' generational and cultural distinction when set against other social and cultural groups and the wider population.[81] The legitimation of showrunner-led or supposedly complex TV occurs here not merely due to textual attributes or industrial promotion, but rather through the situated actions of specific, consecrating cultural intermediaries and associated community formations.[82] This knowing, self-reflexive act of distinction fits very well with the strategy of British national newspapers like the *Guardian*, keen to attract specific audience demographics to its website while also generating and sustaining a brand-specific blog community.

APPENDIX: TELEVISION PROGRAMS CITED

Battlestar Galactica. Sci-Fi Channel. 2004–2009.

Breaking Bad. AMC. 2008–2013.

Casualty. BBC. 1986–.

CSI. CBS. 2000–2015.

Deadwood. HBO. 2004–2006

ER. NBC. 1994–2009.

FlashForward. ABC. 2009–2010.

Game of Thrones. HBO. 2011–.

Lost. ABC. 2004–2010.

Mad Men. AMC. 2007–2015.

Masters of Sex. Showtime Networks. 2013–.

Office. NBC. 2005–2013.

Poirot. ITV. 1989–2013.

Preacher. AMC. 2016–..

The Shield. FX. 2002–2008.

The Sopranos. HBO. 1999–2007.

Top Gear. BBC. 1977–.

24. Fox. 2001–2010.

The Waltons. CBS. 1971–1981.

The Wire. HBO. 2002–2008.

NOTES

1. Jim Hall, "Online Editions: Newspapers and the 'New' News," in *Pulling Newspapers Apart: Analysing Print Journalism*, ed. Bob Franklin (London: Routledge, 2008), 23; *Guardian*, "CheatSheet," August 2016, http://advertising.theguardian.com/assets/img/audience/Cheatsheet-August-2016-pdf.pdf.

2. Pierre Bourdieu, *Distinction: A Social Critique of the Judgement of Taste*, trans. Richard Nice (Cambridge, MA: Harvard University Press, 1984).

3. Bourdieu, *Distinction*, 244–256.

4. Mike Savage, *Social Class in the 21st Century* (London: Pelican, 2015), 115.

5. Kevin Williams, *Read All about It! A History of the British Newspaper* (London: Routledge, 2010), 239–241; Hall, "Online Editions," 216.

6. Williams, *Read All about It*, 239–241.

7. Kim Fletcher, "The Web Trail," *Media Guardian*, June 12, 2006, https://www.theguardian.com/technology/2006/jun/12/news.mondaymediasection.

8. Williams, *Read All about It*, 240–241.

9. Hall, "Online Editions," 219–222.

10. Bob Franklin, "Introduction: Trends and Developments," in Franklin, *Pulling Newspapers Apart*, 3–5; *Guardian*, "CheatSheet."

11. Savage, *Social Class*, 126.

12. Tony Bennett, Mike Savage, Elizabeth Silva, Alan Warde, Modesto Gayo-Cal, and David Wright, *Culture, Class, Distinction* (New York: Routledge, 2010), 145.

13. Richard Van der Wurff, "The Impact of the Internet on Media Content," in *The Internet and the Mass Media*, ed. Lucy Kung, Robert G. Picard, and Ruth Towse (London: Sage, 2008), 81.

14. Claire Phipps and Kevin Rawlinson, "Paris Attacks," *Guardian*, November 14, 2015https://www.theguardian.com/world/live/2015/nov/13/shootings-reported-in-eastern-paris-live.

15. Meg Pickard, "Announcing Some Exciting Changes to Blogs and Commenting," *Guardian*, August 19, 2008, https://www.theguardian.com/help/insideguardian/2008/aug/19/blogsandcommenting; Neil Thurman and Anna Walters, "Live Blogging—Digital Journalism's Pivotal Platform?," *Digital Journalism* 1:1 (2013): 82–101.

16. Van der Wurff, "Impact of the Internet," 81.

17. Matheson cited in Van der Wurff, "Impact of the Internet," 81.

18. George Monbiot, "Environmental Blog," *Guardian*, https://www.theguardian.com/environment/georgemonbiot.

19. https://www.theguardian.com/media/media-blog.

20. https://www.theguardian.com/culture/tvandradioblog.

21. Jane Bussmann, "Top 10 Reasons to Love Californication and David Duchovny," *Guardian*, July 29, 2010, https://www.theguardian.com/tv-and-radio/tvandradioblog/2010/jul/29/californication-david-duchovny-10-reasons.

22. Bourdieu, *Distinction*, 325.

23. Hall, "Online Editions," 221; Pickard, "Announcing Some Exciting Changes."

24. *Guardian*, "CheatSheet."

25. Amanda Lotz, "On 'Television Criticism': The Pursuit of the Critical Examination of a Popular Art," *Popular Communication* 6:1 (2008): 30.

26. Vicky Frost, "My CSI obsession," *Guardian*, August 31, 2007, https://www.theguardian.com/culture/tvandradioblog/2007/aug/31/mycsiobsession.

27. Henry Jenkins, *Textual Poachers: Television Fans & Participatory Culture* (London: Routledge, 1992), 88.

28. Owen Van Spall, "Breaking Bad: The Finest Thing You Haven't Seen," *Guardian*, August 21, 2009, https://www.theguardian.com/culture/tvandradioblog/2009/aug/21/breaking-bad.

29. Mark Lawson, "TV Matters: Britain and America's Special Relationship," *Guardian*, November 22, 2007, https://www.theguardian.com/culture/tvandradioblog/2007/nov/22/tvmattersbritainandamerica;

Mark Lawson, "The State of British TV: Drama," *Guardian*, March 22, 2011, https://www.theguardian.com/tv-and-radio/tvandradioblog/2011/mar/29/state-british-tv-drama.

30. Savage, *Social Class*, 113.

31. Paul Rixon, *TV Critics and Popular Culture* (London: I.B. Tauris, 2011), 67–100; as Bourdieu argues, newspapers tend to employ critics that reflect their readers' values: *Distinction*, 240–241.

32. Bourdieu, *Distinction*, 240–241.

33. Bennett et al., *Culture, Class, Distinction*, 145–146; see also Savage, *Social Class*, 113.

34. Steve Busfield, "*The Wire*: Season Five: Episode One," *Guardian*, July 22, 2008, https://www.theguardian.com/media/organgrinder/2008/jul/22/thewireseasonfiveepisodeo.

35. Busfield, "*The Wire*."

36. Nancy K. Baym, "Interpreting Soap Operas and Creating Community: Inside an Electronic Fan Culture," in *Culture of the Internet*, ed. Sara Keisler (Mahwah, NJ: Lawrence Erlbaum Associates, 1997), 103–120.

37. Savage, *Social Class*, 115.

38. Janet McCabe and Kim Akass, eds., *Quality: Contemporary American Television and Beyond* (London: I.B. Tauris, 2007).

39. Sarah Hughes, "Has *Lost* Lost It?," *Guardian*, November 17, 2006, https://www.theguardian.com/culture/tvandradioblog/2006/nov/17/haslostlostit.

40. Ben Marshall, "*24*'s Means Don't Justify Its End," *Guardian*, January 17, 2007, https://www.theguardian.com/culture/tvandradioblog/2007/jan/17/24smeansdontjustifyitsend.

41. Jon Wilde, "From *Deadwood* to *The Wire*," *Guardian*, February 8, 2007, https://www.theguardian.com/culture/tvandradioblog/2007/feb/08/fromdeadwoodtothewire.

42. Steven Wells, "Why the Original *Office* Is a Shadow of the Original," *Guardian*, May 10, 2010, https://www.theguardian.com/culture/tvandradioblog/2008/sep/23/television.ustelevision.

43. Stuart Heritage, "*Flashforward* Television Series Loyalty," *Guardian*, May 10, 2010, https://www.theguardian.com/tv-and-radio/tvandradioblog/2010/may/10/flashforward-television-series-loyalty.

44. Lotz, "On Television Criticism," 32.

45. Ben Myers, "Realism to 'Reality': TV Drama's Sad Demise," *Guardian*, June 10, 2008, https://www.theguardian.com/culture/tvandradioblog/2008/jun/10/keepingitrealwhatsbecomeo.

46. Bourdieu, *Distinction*, 244–256, 309–310.

47. Paul Rixon, "The Interaction of Broadcasters, Critics and Audiences in Shaping the Cultural Meaning and Status of Television Programmes: The Public Discourse around the Second Series of *Broadchurch*," *Journal of Popular Television* 5:2 (2017): 225–243.

48. Jim Shelley, "*The Wire* Makes *The Sopranos* Look Like *The Waltons*," *Guardian*, May 9, 2007, https://www.theguardian.com/culture/tvandradioblog/2007/may/09/thewiremakesthesopranoslo.

49. See the Broadcasters Audience Research Board for recent viewing figures: www.barb.co.uk.

50. Tim Lusher, "They Get *The Wire*, We Get *Casualty*," *Guardian*, October 29, 2009, https://www.theguardian.com/media/organgrinder/2009/oct/29/the-wire-us-television.

51. Lusher, "They Get *The Wire*."

52. Bourdieu, *Distinction*, 1984.

53. Judit Bar-Ilan, "Information Hub Blogs," *Journal of Information Science* 31:4 (2005): 299.

54. Bar-Ilan, "Information Hub Blogs," 299.

55. Martin Lister, Jon Dovey, Seth Giddings, Iain Grant, and Kieran Kelly, *New Media: A Critical Introduction* (London: Routledge, 2003), 33.

56. John Corner, "'Criticism': Notes on the Circulation of Cultural Judgement," *Journal of Journalism, Media and Cultural Studies*, November 4, 2013, 7–8, https://publications.cardiffuniversitypress.org/index.php/JOMEC/article/view/342/348.

57. *Guardian* unique users were 3.6 million in 2008 (Comscore, http://www.comscore.com/Insights/Press-Releases/2009/5/U.K.-Newspaper-Sites-Aattract-Visitors-from-Around-the-World) compared to over 24 million by 2016 (*Guardian*, "CheatSheet").

58. Jenny Colgan, "Open Late, *24* Heaven," *Guardian*, November 28, 2006, https://www.theguardian.com/culture/tvandradioblog/2006/nov/28/24.

59. Will Dean, "FX Is the Best Import Channel on TV. But Is Anyone Watching It?" *Guardian*, October 7, 2009, https://www.theguardian.com/tv-and-radio/tvandradioblog/2009/oct/07/television-wire.

60. Sarah Hughes, "*Masters of Sex* Recap: Season One, Episode Four—Catherine," *Guardian*, November 5, 2013, https://www.theguardian.com/tv-and-radio/2013/nov/05/masters-of-sex-episode-five-catherine.

61. Mark Lawson, "David Suchet's Final *Poirot* Episodes: The End of One of TV's Great Castings," *Guardian*, October 23, 2013, https://www.theguardian.com/tv-and-radio/tvandradioblog/2013/oct/23/david-suchet-poirot-tv-great-casting.

62. Dean, "FX Is the Best"; Paul Rixon, *American Television on British Screens: A Story of Cultural Interaction* (Houndmills, Basingstoke: Palgrave Macmillan, 2006), 51–57.

63. TV and Radio Blog, "Page 207," *Guardian*, June 8, 2010, https://www.theguardian.com/culture/tvandradioblog?page=207.

64. ComScore 2009; *Guardian*, "CheatSheet."

65. TV and Radio Blog, "Page 100," *Guardian*, August 20, 2013, https://www.theguardian.com/culture/tvandradioblog?page=100.

66. TV and Radio Blog, "Page 1," *Guardian*, https://www.theguardian.com/culture/tvandradioblog.

67. Stuart Heritage, "*Top Gear*: The Verdict on the First Post-Clarkson Season," *Guardian*, July 4, 2016, https://www.theguardian.com/tv-and-radio/tvandradioblog/2016/jul/04/top-gear-verdict-first-season.

68. Luke Holland, "The Problem with *Preacher*: Why No One's Talking about the Best Show of the Year," *Guardian*, July 18, 2016, https://www.theguardian.com/tv-and-radio/tvandradioblog/2016/jul/18/the-problem-with-preacher-why-no-ones-talking-about-the-best-show-of-the-year.

69. *Guardian*, "CheatSheet."

70. Sonja Utz, "Social Identification with Virtual Communities," in *Mediated Interpersonal Communication*, ed. Elly Konijn, Sonja Utz, Martin Tanis, and Susan Barnes (London: Routledge, 2008), 264.

71. Comments by darren73 on Ben Sillis, "*The Shield*: A Quality TV Cop Show without the Hype," *Guardian*, November 19, 2008, https://www.theguardian.com/culture/tvandradioblog/2008/nov/19/television-theserial-thewire-cop-shows.

72. Comments by Ichit on Sillis's 2008 post.

73. Comments by pandemoniana on Sillis's 2008 post.

74. Comments by bazmc86 on Sillis's 2008 post.

75. Jennifer Smith Maguire and Julian Matthews, "Are We All Cultural Intermediaries Now? An Introduction to Cultural Intermediaries in Context," *European Journal of Cultural Studies* 15:5: (2012): 551.

76. Dean, "FX Is the Best"; Rixon, *American Television*, 51–57.

77. Bourdieu, *Distinction*, 246–256, 309–310.

78. This is based on an analysis of titles of the seven thousand posts and whether they refer to American television in some way.

79. Rixon, *TV Critics*, 135–161.

80. See www.Barb.co.uk.

81. Bourdieu, *Distinction*, 309–310; Bennett et al., *Culture, Class, Distinction*, 145–146; Savage, *Social Class*, 112–118.

82. Michael Z. Newman and Elana Levine, *Legitimating Television: Media Convergence and Cultural Status* (New York: Routledge, 2012).

/// 12 /// FANS, FEZZES, AND FREEBIES

Branding British Television Series at the San Diego Comic-Con

LINCOLN GERAGHTY

Following Russell T. Davies's successful 2005 reboot of *Doctor Who* and the popularity of Mark Gatiss and Steven Moffat's *Sherlock* in 2010, the BBC has become a major exporter of quality television to the world. Both series are global brands, and their titular central protagonists are now akin to global television superheroes— iconic, clever, and ever resourceful. With that said, it is no surprise that *Doctor Who* and *Sherlock* form the bedrock to BBC America's successful TV schedule—the cable network was launched in 1998 and restructured in 2007. Alongside *Doctor Who*, it screens multiple popular UK series, not just from the BBC but also from Sky, ITV, and Channel 4, ensuring a continued British alternative to the dominance of US series and US channels in an increasingly global television market. One sign of the recent success of UK television in the United States has come at the annual San Diego Comic-Con, where for the last eight years BBC America has made a concerted effort to attract and build a loyal American audience. *Doctor Who, Sherlock, Torchwood, Being Human, Bedlam,* and *Orphan Black* (among others) have all had popular previews, panels, and merchandise launches in San Diego—with the Eleventh Doctor achieving a Comic-Con first for the BBC in 2011 by having its *Doctor Who* panel held in the famous Hall H (a seven-thousand-seat auditorium usually reserved for big Hollywood premieres, attracting star names and very long queues).

This chapter seeks to analyze the importance of San Diego Comic-Con in the transatlantic circulation of popular British television texts within the American media industry. Where once Comic-Con was entirely American in its focus (dominated by DC and Marvel, US comic book artists and film and TV series) the organization has become a global nexus for all types of popular media and international texts: British science fiction, Japanese anime and computer games, Spanish and Mexican horror, Canadian superheroes, Belgian adventurers, and Danish toy companies stand side-by-side with established American comics icons such as Superman and major Hollywood studios such as Warner Brothers. Comic-Con International (to give it its proper title) provides a space for the promotion of UK television brands, where American and British fans can meet, and international media companies can compete with US conglomerates. There is clearly a transatlantic trade relationship between the US and UK TV industries, and it is at Comic-Con where the BBC and television series such as *Doctor Who* compete with content from networks such as CBS and HBO through the targeted promotion of British brands.

For Celia Lury, brands are important communicators of meaning—promoting products as well as introducing qualities that are meant to be experienced by the target audience. She argues that the brand is an object of new media, drawing attention to modes of production as well as communication: the brand is "a site . . . of interactivity . . . promoting and inhibiting 'exchange' between producers and consumers."[1] In calling attention to this "exchange," the physical location of BBC America at Comic-Con allows producers and consumers to interact. On the one hand, BBC America is clearly presented as a producer of *Doctor Who*, the media text enjoyed by fans for over five decades. However, on the other hand, BBC America is also a brand in itself, marketed to convention attendees as offering unique content compared to other media producers in the exhibition hall. Thus *Doctor Who*, as a long-running science fiction series, plays an important role in communicating BBC America's distinctive type of programming, as well as conveying more traditional qualities associated with British television. For Barbara Selznick, *Doctor Who* "can be viewed as a superbrand that, if put together properly, could generate international sales of the program as well as ancillary media and merchandise."[2] Its presence at Comic-Con allows it to do both of these things. Furthermore, as Christine Becker argues, "BBC America has tried to portray itself as a hybrid of the best of British and American television, and has marketed its superiority on that basis."[3] At Comic-Con, both BBC America and *Doctor Who* are media brands; relying on physical and online marketing, they promote quality of content, genre, and, most importantly, the notion of Britishness. The convention offers a popular and well-established platform from which both producer and text can communicate with fans while at the same time continuing to promote their brands in an international market.

COMIC-CON AS A SPACE FOR THE GLOBAL ENTERTAINMENT INDUSTRIES

Founded as the "Golden State Comic Book Convention" in 1970 at the Grant Hotel in downtown San Diego, San Diego Comic-Con has become the premier site for fans and global companies to meet and share in all manner of popular media (including comics, film, television, and computer games). Moving to the convention center in 1991, Comic-Con now attracts more than 130,000 people a year. So, from a hotel lobby hosting comic book dealers attracting roughly three hundred die-hard collectors, the site for comics and the superhero stories contained within has changed dramatically to incorporate industry, artists, producers, directors, celebrities, journalists, and fans. Booths that sell rare comic books or reissued toys from Mattel or Hasbro, autograph tables that offer fans the chance to meet their favorite actors, and giant rooms used by Hollywood executives to publicize the latest blockbuster to thousands of attendees—all represent locations where fans, collectors, dealers, and the industry can interact. While, inside, the convention center space offers opportunities for the reconfiguration or intensification of fan hierarchies, the city space outside also becomes part of the Comic-Con experience. The streets are postered with adverts for new series, costumed volunteers hand out freebies on street corners, and local businesses welcome attendees by decking out their shops with cult merchandise. As a result, the San Diego Convention Center, the hotels and the city itself become familiar places returned to every year, where fans can get spoilers, see special screenings, buy new collectibles, and meet their favorite stars for the duration of the event.

What this means for the actual products being launched in San Diego is that they are no longer aimed at a niche audience—they are mass-market commodities, with enduring comic book superheroes from DC and Marvel competing with new characters from the worlds of television, film, and anime. Generations of fans collide at Comic-Con, offering producers, directors, artists, and industry tycoons ample opportunity to market their brands and continue the shelf life of their comic book, film franchise, or television series—whether in paper, electronic, or computer game forms. An exhibition space, as described by Umberto Eco in *Faith in Fakes*, "assumes the form of an inventory," and thus Comic-Con can be a seen as an inventory of the popular.[4] Stan Lee, renowned comic book writer and legendary creator of Marvel Comics' most iconic characters, says of San Diego Comic-Con: "The thousands of convention-goers are grown-ups, adults who are interested in movies, television, DVDs, and, of course, comic books. . . . These fans are tremendously important to the comic book business, just as they are to any creative endeavour."[5] These comments mirror Henry Jenkins's opinion of the convention, in that "fans have become the leading edge of the studio's promotional campaigns" and that trying to win over crowds in San Diego may lead to greater success for new television series set to launch that autumn or blockbusters gearing up for battle the next summer.[6] For Rebecca Keegan, "Comic-Con remains a force" in terms of making hits out of smaller features and turning fans into powerful promoters of brands and franchises. Her article in *Time* about fan bloggers who report on what's new, and which blockbuster to look out for, highlights how in 2006 only a few minutes of advance footage from *300* (2006) shown to a largely unfamiliar audience could go viral and create a buzz ultimately resulting in box office receipts of $450 million worldwide.[7]

Seeking higher esteem within the Comic-Con pecking order, Hollywood studios compete to get their new film or television show into Hall H. Running from dawn to dusk, with queues often forming days in advance to get into the most popular panels, the mixed program of film launches and television series' plot-reveals attracts not only thousands of fans during Comic-Con but also the world's press, who flock to interview stars and get an angle on what new content will be released the following year. The big superhero franchises, like *Avengers* and *Spider-Man*, start off in Hollywood but make their way through San Diego to gather momentum and hopefully set up a lucrative box-office return. In 2010 Hall H hosted panels to launch Disney's *Tron: Legacy* and Marvel's *Captain America*; in 2011 *The Twilight Saga: Breaking Dawn Part 1* and *The Adventures of Tintin*, with a rare appearance by Steven Spielberg, were joined by television luminaries such as those from *Glee* and *Doctor Who*; and in 2012 television seemingly took over, with panels for *The Big Bang Theory* and *The Walking Dead* proving very popular in addition to another appearance by *Doctor Who*. The expansion of Hall H's program to include science fiction television as well as the usual superhero and blockbuster films further signals Comic-Con's shift to promote global popular arts beyond the comic book. Indeed, in his analysis of Comic-Con and the future of popular culture, Rob Salkowitz argues that the forces responsible for the popularization of comics in the twenty-first century are on full display at the San Diego Comic-Con every summer, among them

> the lure of digital technology, dragging publishers into an uncertain marketplace; the centrifugal force of consolidation, as corporate pop culture conglomerates attempt to wave their diverse holdings into a coherent portfolio across all media; the amplification of individual creative voices connecting directly with their audience; and the aspirations of fans who want to participate in a culture that is rich, spectacular, exciting, familiar, and uniquely theirs.[8]

John Fiske described the traditional fan convention, most famously illustrated by big franchises like *Star Trek* and *Star Wars*, as a space where "cultural and economic capital come together."[9] Fans' love for, and valuing of, the text is expressed alongside their financial investment in it, represented by their spending money on expensive tickets, souvenirs, and memorabilia. The BBC's *Doctor Who* attracts thousands of fans dressed as Daleks and Doctors to Comic-Con, illustrating the global audience for this traditionally British science fiction television franchise.[10] The fact that *Doctor Who* and its fans can fill Hall H means its cult reputation has reached America. And, as I have argued elsewhere, this helps to transform its central character (the Doctor) into an international superhero icon who sits side by side with his American cousins, such as Superman and Captain America.[11] BBC America, as the network that carries and markets series like *Doctor Who* in the United States, plays an important role in the transatlantic trade of British television at Comic-Con.

BBC AMERICA AT COMIC-CON

Given its cultural centrality for fandom, it is no surprise that BBC America now uses Comic-Con to build an audience for UK programs in a crowded international television market. The network was launched on March 29, 1998, and rebranded in 2007 as part of the BBC Worldwide brand. Distributed in association with the Discovery Network, it is available on both satellite and cable through subscription. With a New York HQ, BBC America has had a number of American executive officers with experience working on US niche cable networks, including MTV and Comedy Central. Deriving most of its content from the BBC and other UK broadcasters means that BBC America offers an interesting mix of drama, genre programming, and documentaries, but it has also aired classic American series such as *Battlestar Galactica* (2003–2009) and *Star Trek: The Next Generation* (1987–1994). As a result, BBC America is an inherently transatlantic company, and thus its presence at the San Diego Comic-Con again suggests that it is becoming a key site for global media interaction and particularly US-UK international promotion.

While BBC America has attempted to provide distinctive programming in a highly competitive US market, it has also relied on more traditional modes of advertising to attract new audiences. Gareth James argues that from the outset BBC America has been marketed to an Anglophile audience, promoting British culture by using traditionally popular British television genres such as the sitcom, lifestyle, and the news in order to provide a solid schedule through which it could then launch more primetime series.[12] Cult television came later to the network, with *Doctor Who* and *Torchwood* providing subsequent cornerstones to its programming. Having been sold to America's Sci-Fi Channel at first, *Doctor Who* didn't come to BBC America until 2007 and was quickly followed by the more adult-themed *Torchwood* series. The latter, according to James, was a perfect fit for BBC America in terms of building a brand in the United States because it emphasized a "cool but high quality" identity.[13] Similarly, Catherine Johnson outlines how the BBC's partnership with Red Bee Media to produce a new logo and credits for Matt Smith's first series as the Doctor reflected the corporation's search for a brand image "that could function both as a central aspect of the title sequence and as a trade-marked sign that could be utilised across a wide range of *Doctor Who* products."[14] This new logo, the letters DW forming the body of the TARDIS, could also be recycled in transatlantic spaces, providing a familiar design that worked to promote BBC America as the home for "cool", quality UK TV programming.

BBC America has publicized *Doctor Who* heavily on the air. In 2010 the Christmas special was broadcast on the channel on Christmas Day for the first time.[15] In 2011, to create a sense of anticipation among the American audience for the series, the network aired new episodes at the same time as the BBC in the United Kingdom. *Doctor Who's* simultaneous broadcast followed an experiment by the BBC a year earlier to transmit episodes of the ten-part *Torchwood: Miracle Day* series in the United States before UK audiences could see them. This was, in part, due to the fact that *Miracle Day* was a coproduction between the BBC and Starz (a US-based subscription channel that has produced series such as *Spartacus* and *Camelot*).

Doctor Who's marketing has been specifically targeted at American audiences too. Matt Hills argues that BBC America adapted trailers and promos for series 5 and 6, promoting and branding the show as American through noirish imagery and a focus on the Doctor as a cool action hero.[16] However, such a focus on the US market, and on attracting new audiences through a presence at Comic-Con, indicates that *Doctor Who* and its spin-offs are core to the BBC's international brand, targeting multiple markets and multiple audiences.[17] Of course, *Doctor Who* has had a longer history of traveling across the Atlantic. The original series first aired in 1977 on US television and by 1984 was being shown on 112 American PBS stations.[18] Following declining ratings on both sides of the Atlantic and cancellation in 1989, the franchise was reborn in the form of a 1996 television movie, again a coproduction (between the BBC, Universal Studios, and Fox Television) that was broadcast in America a week before UK audiences could watch it, and which was intended as a test to "gain sufficiently high North American ratings to make a future series viable."[19]

BBC America's presence at Comic-Con includes panel events with the cast and creators of *Doctor Who*, BBC America's top-rated series, supported by a centrally located booth in the main exhibit hall that attracts hordes of fans and passers-by eager to purchase the latest *Doctor Who* merchandise and grab exclusive Comic-Con freebies. For example, in 2015 toy company Titan released a special vinyl figure of the Tenth Doctor complete with the fez he wore in *The Day of the Doctor*, and in 2012 fans could get a free foam Dalek hat to wear around San Diego, displaying their fandom with pride. Such blatant commodification of the series chimes with how the BBC has changed its institutional focus over the past two decades. Catherine Johnson argues that through the original run of *Doctor Who* (1963–1989) the BBC was not interested in coordinating its merchandising efforts. Seen as more peripheral to the broadcaster's activities, merchandising at this time was typically limited to books, audio, and video (later followed by DVD). However, by "the 2000s the extension of television programmes onto other media [. . . had] become a central strategy for the BBC . . . leading to greater emphasis on the need to manage and coordinate activities."[20] As well as representing the BBC's shift from national broadcaster to international content provider, BBC America's physical presence at Comic-Con is also significant because it represents the changing nature of the event as it has moved away from solely being a celebration of American popular culture toward the promotion of transatlantic media.

While American-produced television, film, and comic book franchises battle for space in the panel rooms, exhibit hall, and event program, smaller transatlantic companies like BBC America act as alternative brands within the main convention space; here fans can seek out new texts and more exclusive items, attaining a higher position within the hierarchies of fandom. Following Lury's definition of a brand, BBC America uses its physical location at the heart of the exhibition hall to literally reach out to *Doctor Who* fans and other attendees: "This prevents the product simply becoming a commodity that is bought (and sold on) by an intermediary."[21] Moreover, the production and distribution of freebies such as the Dalek foam hat or the exclusive vinyl figure fits with how the series has been marketed on BBC America since its reboot, tying into the youthful exuberance and quirkiness personified by the Matt Smith's Eleventh Doctor, who was very keen on wearing a silly hat himself. Becker argues that "BBC America explicitly separated itself from traditional network television, as well as from the traditional BBC image, and aligned with those cable channels identified with hip, quality programming, such as HBO."[22] In this way, we can see the BBC America booth, situated next to other booths sponsored by Starz (promoting its series *Spartacus* and *Black Sails*) and AMC (promoting *The Walking Dead*), as the physical embodiment of the network's attempts at standing out, being innovative, and taking risks. It also fits with how Selznick has viewed the changing characterization and rebranding of the series post-reboot, allowing the show to work in a US context: "By fitting into the cool brand of Britishness, the program offers a fresh image of *Doctor Who* for the fragmented U.S. audience in the midst of the niche-focused environment of the contemporary U.S. television industry."[23]

DOCTOR WHO AS TRANSATLANTIC CONVENTION EVENT

In this age of online branding and transmedia storytelling, the presence of BBC America at Comic-Con, with *Doctor Who* as its tent-pole series, proves the importance of "event" status to the continued popularity of genre programming within the popular media arts.[24] Fans gathering together en masse in San Diego to attend the panel in Hall H and see the likes of Matt Smith, Peter Capaldi, and Steven Moffat create a buzz of media hype that helps promote the series to an international audience, and offers a promotional spring-board for the latest episodes soon to air on television. It is a viral event where attendees can tell their friends through social media and word of mouth about spoilers, previews, and what is yet to come for the Doctor. The convention experience, and "insider infor-mation" gleaned, places fan-attendees at the center of production activity, albeit for a brief moment. During that moment they can share their enthusiasm for the series be-yond Comic-Con and via social media—thus making their Comic-Con experience valu-able within today's mediatized fan culture. Comic-Con is an economically viable way of generating buzz, and accordingly, fans are active participants in the making and remaking of *Doctor Who* as a transatlantic television brand for international audience consump-tion.[25] However, some would disagree with this position. Henry Jenkins contends:

> Today, one of my big ambivalences about Comic-Con is how much it now emphasizes fans as consumers rather than fans as cultural producers . . . [It] puts the professionals in the center and [leaves] the subcultural activities the [. . . convention] was based on at the fringes.[26]

In spite of this, when creating buzz for an industry determined to market products, fans are not just pawns in the greater pursuit of promotion and profit, as Jenkins might argue. These fans are creative in the ways that they engage with the industrial discourses of Comic-Con: they are subcultural producers who transform the *Doctor Who* text, much like the poachers described by Jenkins in his seminal work.[27] Fans dressed in original cosplay outfits display their subcultural creativity: there are "Southern Belles" with dresses made from cut-up TARDIS costumes; female Doctors (well in advance of Jodie Whittaker's casting) with their own sonic screwdrivers; undead zombie Doctors that take part in a Zombie Walk through the city. Fans are also rewarded for making the effort to be there. To honor lead actor Peter Capaldi's first appearance at Comic-Con in 2015, Titan published a special issue of the *Doctor Who* comic that featured original artwork of the Twelfth Doctor (played by Capaldi) and Clara Oswald (Jenna Coleman) on alter-nate front covers. Inside, an exclusive story focused on the Doctor and Clara themselves traveling to Comic-Con for a break, only to get embroiled in a plot concocted by the evil Lady Neverness, who wanted to destroy all life on earth. Diegetic and extradiegetic realities are playfully blurred together here: fans can read about the Doctor encountering fictional fans at the fictionalized yet recognizable convention, while at the same time witnessing Capaldi's first visit to San Diego. In an interview for BBC America's website in the build-up to the event, Capaldi clearly recognized the cultural significance and industrial importance of Comic-Con:

> Tales of San Diego Comic-Con are told in awe on every set around the known fantasy/sci-fi production world. It's become a fabled kingdom. One I am thrilled to find myself heading for. And to appear in the legendary Hall H is a further twist to the cosplay and comic madness I may never recover from.[28]

The transatlantic flavor of the Doctor is also emphasized by the diversity of attendees in Hall H. They come from all four corners of the globe, enabling American fans to claim moral ownership of "their" show just as much as UK audiences. Hall H is hence a boon to convention organizers as well as to BBC America. *Doctor Who* gains status through its presence in the hall, being supported by and billed alongside colossal Hollywood franchises that use Comic-Con to premiere blockbuster releases. Yet, as Comic-Con diversifies its market and cult audience to include *Doctor Who* fans prepared to travel thousands of miles to get the unique convention experience, the appeal of the convention experience grows, resulting in more people wanting to attend. Therefore, *Doctor Who*'s "mainstream" presence is the product of multiple transatlantic television trends, cultural exchanges, and fan interactions.

In 2013, the year in which the BBC celebrated the fiftieth anniversary of the series, Comic-Con also commemorated this event. Given all the popular media franchises that congregate in San Diego, the fact that *Doctor Who* got such special attention is indicative of its cultural standing as well as, perhaps, the transatlantic "special relationship" between the United Kingdom and America. Starting with these celebrations, *Doctor Who*'s presence at Comic-Con also expanded beyond the confines of Hall H, with BBC America hiring space in a nearby bar to hold an official "Fan Meetup." This is now an annual event that attracts hundreds of fans to line up hours before opening in order to get the best vantage point inside. The location affords fans an opportunity to get closer to the actors: Jenna Coleman and Matt Smith were there in 2013 to answer questions about the then-upcoming special, and fans could also win merchandise, donated by local businesses, for the best cosplay and scene re-enactment.[29] It has been well documented by Matt Hills that the BBC used the anniversary as a strategic event both to fulfill its public service remit, celebrating quality, and to capitalize on the series in creating a multimedia brand and transmedia story. The show's public value was reasserted, positioning the anniversary "as a moment of collective memory" while at the same time promoting the "BBC's distinctiveness" through the mobilization of high-profile BBC personalities, docudrama in the guise of *An Adventure in Space and Time* (2013), and other transmedia paratexts that paved the way for the movie-length anniversary episode simulcast in cinemas around the country and at London's ExCeL.[30] The 2013 event was part of the BBC's long-established history of commemorating its flagship series. From celebrations that lacked a specific targeting of fan audiences through to campaigns that served as extended branding and marketing opportunities for the BBC, Hills argues that *Doctor Who* anniversary celebrations "can be variously categorised as naive, hybrid, niche and hyped TV events, intersecting with television's ages of scarcity, availability and plenty, as well as being inflected by shifting fan discourses."[31] This being said, the importance of Comic-Con's transatlantic tribute should not be overlooked. Recognition of the series' cultural impact and televisual longevity highlights the changing role that Comic-Con has taken on in terms of celebrating popular media franchises from film, television, video games, as well as comics, that originate from outside the United States.[32]

However, the most striking evidence of *Doctor Who*'s transatlantic status is provided by the souvenir book and event guide given out to all attendees at Comic-Con. Every year these paper publications are handed out to fans as they register and pick up their tickets. Both of the front covers offer the chance for budding comic book artists and well-established comic book companies to display their art and publicize their brands. Articles in the souvenir book focus on famous artists, characters, and developments in the comic book industry; each is introduced by the organizers of Comic-Con, and original artwork inspired by a range of popular media texts fills the pages. The cover art is almost always American in both origin and inspiration. In 2010, the book featured DC's big three superheroes (Superman, Batman, and Wonder Woman) to celebrate seventy-five years of the company, while the event guide had an indie twist on iconic characters from *Peanuts*, Charlie Brown and Snoopy. The 2011 book featured specially commissioned cover artwork from DC, representing the new Justice League, and the guide had artwork celebrating the twentieth anniversary of independent comic book character Bone, created by the American artist Jeff Smith. Marvel received recognition in 2012, as the cover of the book celebrated fifty years of some of its most iconic characters, including Spider-Man, Hulk, and Iron Man. The corresponding event guide celebrated one hundred years of Edgar Rice Burroughs's *Tarzan*. In 2013 Comic-Con finally turned its attention to more international texts: the book featured DC's *Sandman*, created by the United Kingdom's Neil Gaiman, celebrating twenty-five years of the character, and the event guide had artwork celebrating the fiftieth anniversary of *Doctor Who* (reinforcing the importance of anniversary discourses within this major component of Comic-Con publicity).

Perhaps unsurprisingly, the image used on the front cover of the guide was the TARDIS, depicted in front of Gallifreyan writing and an emblem by artist Brian Miller. The familiar Converse shoes worn by David Tennant's Tenth Doctor can just be seen entering through the open police box door. Largely devoid of detail, and choosing not to display all incarnations, or even the most recent incarnation, of the Doctor, this cover art follows the BBC's use of the TARDIS to stand in for the entirety of the series in its marketing—a point made by Catherine Johnson in her discussion of the change in the actor playing the Doctor in 2009.[33] It is also a pop-cultural icon, a visual symbol of the show's cultural resonance and longevity. Feature articles in the souvenir book follow the celebration of *Doctor Who*'s fiftieth anniversary on the front of the guide, including a history of the Doctor's regenerations, an autobiography of a fan growing up watching the show and passing on his fandom to his son, and an analysis of the Doctor as Byronic hero. Interspersed between these pieces are various comic book artists' own visual tributes to the series. One might have been forgiven for thinking that only the Doctor and Sandman were celebrating significant birthdays in 2013, but further examination of the souvenir book reveals that more homegrown popular culture icons were also being recognized, for example, seventy-five years of DC's Superman, fifty years of Marvel's Avengers, X-Men, and Doctor Strange comics, and twenty years of Bongo Comics (publisher of *The Simpsons*).

The surprising absence of Superman, a transatlantic symbol of American popular culture, or the Avengers and X-Men, now major film franchises, on either cover is interesting considering the original purpose of Comic-Con—to promote comic book culture in the United States. It is perhaps a sign of the international shift that has been made by Comic-Con's organizing body to support the popular arts beyond comics and beyond national boundaries. In terms of the BBC's strategy to market *Doctor Who* across the Atlantic, a presence at Comic-Con—endorsed at the level of the event's souvenir book and guide—serves as a sign of US brand awareness and success. As Simone Knox claims, increasing DVD sales and iTunes downloads in America showed that there was a growing audience for the series, at least partly attributable to its representations of Britishness and "heritage as cool" through the quirky fashion style of the Eleventh Doctor, played by Matt Smith.[34] This point is further illustrated by Smith's warm reception from predominantly US fans in Hall H in 2011. Selznick makes a similar argument in relation to how the new series was promoted on BBC America, via promos that emphasized the youthfulness of Rose as the first new companion and the show's London-bound locations: "The result of the shift to the cool brand is to create a *Doctor Who* that is decidedly British and still appealing to younger U.S. and international television viewers."[35] However, I would argue that precursors for a "*Doctor Who* at 50" themed Comic-Con event guide and souvenir book in 2013 can be seen in the planned and promoted presence of the series several years earlier: for example, personal appearances were made by the stars (Smith along with Karen Gillan, and then Capaldi with Jenna Coleman), and the series' showrunner (Moffat), while the BBC America booth began selling official merchandise. *Doctor Who* had already become a Comic-Con mainstay before the anniversary, but its celebration was evidence of its transatlantic success on the popular culture world stage.

CONCLUSION

As a cable network, BBC America is clearly keen to build on *Doctor Who*'s cult television status, marketing merchandise as "exclusive" to fans who attend the convention and organizing events both within and outside the convention center. BBC America extends the *Doctor Who* brand across Comic-Con much in the way Celia Lury describes the brand as a "new media object": "[It is] performative, open-ended, distributed in time and space. It is a *dynamic platform or support for a variety of practices*."[36] For example, the static booth, the well-attended and heavily hyped panel in Hall H, freebies circulated around the convention center, fans dressed up and posing for pictures, personal appearances from the cast and crew, and the printed promotional material given out to attendees all represent this brand performativity—promoting *Doctor Who* as quality British television and BBC America as a distinctive content provider. It is clear that the San Diego Comic-Con acts as a "dynamic platform" and a "support for a variety of practices" involving both fans and producers.

However, much is done to promote the channel and its content before BBC America even arrives in San Diego. Indeed, *Doctor Who* is part of a wider and more complex trend in transatlantic cultural exchange that BBC America has been displaying and following in recent years. In the same year that *Who*'s fiftieth anniversary was being celebrated at Comic-Con, BBC America was busy launching a new section on its website called "Anglophenia," designed to promote British content to an American audience. Anglophenia, a term coined by YouTube presenters Siobhan Thompson and Kate Arnell for their channel of the same name, describes the love of British culture with an American emphasis. The YouTube channel attracts almost nine million viewers, including videos produced by BBC America such as "One Woman, 17 British Accents" and "If Shakespearean Insults Were Used today."[37] As a space on BBC America's site, Anglophenia promotes British shows and actors, as well as US films and television starring British talent, using interviews and videos to situate the content as quirky, exclusive, and unique. *Doctor Who* takes the top spot in newsfeed and stories, routinely trending within the top five searched-for items on the site. Where Knox talks about BBC America's strategy to attract younger audiences with British content and a brand based on "cool," Anglophenia specifically uses *Doctor Who*, its cast, and online exclusives to distinguish the channel in a highly competitive (and here, anglophile) global television landscape.[38] Transatlantic cultural exchange therefore happens in the *run-up* to Comic-Con, with reports on who will be there, *during* Comic-Con through appearances in Hall H and local venues, and *following* Comic-Con through exclusive photos, interviews, and videos of what fans may have missed.

Doctor Who's presence at Comic-Con and how BBC America has used the event to brand its British content for a transatlantic market offer us insights into how contemporary television channels and genre texts disperse across international platforms and media networks. That BBC America works hard to tie fans into the physical experiences offered at the booth and utilizes the show's personalities through panel appearances and online promotions suggests that the text, its marketing, and the channel are interconnected; there are visual and thematic links between all components that make up the whole *Doctor Who* brand. In this sense, Comic-Con is the physical manifestation of what Jennifer Gillan terms "television brandcasting," which describes American television as a medium for branded storytelling. Throughout history, television has had to adapt to changing viewing technologies and competition from other entertainment forms; in response, content providers developed ways in which they could offer audiences new content while promoting and extending their brand through advertising, visual experimentation, and merchandising. Gillan describes this as a "content-promotion hybrid." She argues that "television programs are not simply entertainment products in their own right because they always also function as platforms for promoting other entertainment content, consumer products, and brands, whether those of stars, sponsors, advertisers, networks, studios, or media conglomerates."[39] In this way, Comic-Con offers a physical space for "content-promotion hybrids," which in turn help to "construct and maintain a network or studio brand and encourage viewers to identify with its output and recommend it to others."[40]

As I have argued throughout this chapter, Comic-Con provides a space for the promotion of UK television, where American and British fans can meet and international media companies can compete on an equal footing with larger US conglomerates. The transatlantic television and media trade relationship between the United States and United Kingdom not only extends to promoting series like *Doctor Who* as BBC America's flagship show, but is also about the celebration of this national institution on an international stage. Physically being there at Comic-Con is important to fans and network executives alike, providing an exclusive experience, but also one they can share through social media. Yet the channel itself and online spaces such as "Anglophenia" also promote UK television as exclusive and distinctive. BBC America is the provider of that exclusive content, and its brand is all about promoting Britishness as epitomized by a series like *Doctor Who*.

NOTES

1. Celia Lury, *Brands: The Logos of the Global Economy* (London: Routledge, 2004), 6.
2. Barbara Selznick, "Rebooting and Re-branding: The Changing Brands of *Doctor Who*'s Britishness," in *Ruminations, Peregrinations, and Regenerations: A Critical Approach to "Doctor Who"*, ed. Chris Hansen (Newcastle: Cambridge Scholars Publishing, 2010), 79.
3. Christine Becker, "From High Culture to Hip Culture: Transforming the BBC into BBC America," in *Anglo-American Media Interactions, 1850–2000*, ed. Joel H. Wiener and Mark Hampton (Basingstoke: Palgrave Macmillan, 2007), 289.
4. Umberto Eco, *Faith in Fakes: Travels in Hyperreality*, trans. William Weaver (London: Vintage, 1998), 292.
5. Stan Lee quoted in Morgan Spurlock, *Comic-Con: Episode IV—A Fan's Hope* (New York: Dorling Kindersley, 2011), 5.
6. Henry Jenkins, "Superpowered Fans: The Many Worlds of San Diego's Comic-Con," *Boom: A Journal of California* 2:2 (2012): 25.
7. Rebecca Keegan, "Boys Who Like Toys," *Time* 169:18 (2007): 67.
8. Rob Salkowitz, *Comic-Con and the Business of Pop Culture: What the World's Wildest Trade Show Can Tell Us about the Future of Entertainment* (New York: McGraw-Hill, 2012), 235.
9. John Fiske, "The Cultural Economy of Fandom," in *The Adoring Audience: Fan Culture and Popular Media*, ed. Lisa A. Lewis (London: Routledge, 1992), 43.
10. See also Selznick, "Rebooting and Re-branding."
11. For an analysis of the Doctor as a British superhero among other national superheroes see Lincoln Geraghty, "Heroes of Hall H: Global Media Franchises and the San Diego Comic-Con as Space for the Transnational Superhero," in *Superheroes on World Screens: Global Exchanges in Superhero Texts*, ed. Rayna Denison and Rachel Mizsei Ward (Jackson: University Press of Mississippi, 2015), 75–93.
12. Gareth James, "'Cool but High Quality': *Torchwood*, BBC America and Transatlantic Branding, 1998–2011," in *"Torchwood" Declassified: Investigating Mainstream Cult Television*, ed. Rebecca Williams (London: I.B. Tauris, 2013), 38–39.
13. James, "Cool but High Quality," 48.
14. Catherine Johnson, "*Doctor Who* as Programme Brand," in *New Dimensions of "Doctor Who": Adventures in Space, Time and Television*, ed. Matt Hills (London: I.B. Tauris, 2013), 102.
15. David Budgen, "'Halfway out of the Dark': Steven Moffat's *Doctor Who* Christmas Specials," in *Doctor Who: The Eleventh Hour. A Critical Celebration of the Matt Smith and Steven Moffat Era*, ed. Andrew O'Day (London: I.B. Tauris, 2014), 98.
16. Matt Hills, "Hyping *Who* and Marketing the Steven Moffat Era: The Role of 'Prior Paratexts,'" in O'Day, *Doctor Who*, 190.
17. Matt Hills, *Triumph of a Time Lord: Regenerating "Doctor Who" in the Twenty-First Century* (London: I.B. Tauris, 2010), 67–69.
18. Nicholas J. Cull, "Tardis at the OK Corral: *Doctor Who* and the USA," in *British Science Fiction Television: A Hitchhiker's Guide*, ed. John R. Cook and Peter Wright (London: I.B. Tauris, 2006), 61–62.
19. Peter Wright, "Expatriate! Expatriate! *Doctor Who: The Movie* and Commercial Negotiation of a Multiple Text," in *British Science Fiction Film and Television: Critical Essays*, ed. Tobias Hochscherf and James Leggott (Jefferson, NC: McFarland, 2011), 128.
20. Johnson, "Programme Brand," 107.

21. Lury, *Brands*, 46.
22. Becker, "From High Culture," 280.
23. Selznick, "Rebooting and Re-branding," 84.
24. See also Matt Hills's *Doctor Who: The Unfolding Event* (Basingstoke: Palgrave, 2015), which analyzes the program's official fiftieth anniversary convention at the ExCeL London in these terms.
25. Peter Coogan, *Superhero: The Secret Origin of a Genre* (Austin, TX: MonkeyBrain Books, 2006), 6.
26. Jenkins, "Superpowered Fans," 25. See also Anne Gilbert, "Live from Hall H: Fan/Producer Symbiosis at San Diego Comic-Con," in *Fandom*, 2nd ed., ed. Jonathan Gray, Cornel Sandvoss, and C. Lee Harrington (New York: New York University Press, 2017); and Anne Gilbert, "Conspicuous Convention: Industry Interpellation and Fan Consumption at San Diego Comic-Con," in *The Routledge Companion to Media Fandom*, ed. Melissa A. Click and Suzanne Scott (New York: Routledge, 2018).
27. Henry Jenkins, *Textual Poachers* (New York: Routledge, 1992).
28. Peter Capaldi quoted in Kevin Wicks, "'Doctor Who': Peter Capaldi to Make San Diego Comic-Con Debut," BBC America, http://www.bbcamerica.com/anglophenia/2015/05/doctor-who-peter-capaldi-to-make-san-diego-comic-con-debut, paragraph 2.
29. Kevin Wicks, "San Diego Comic-Con 2013: Day Three Gallery, 'Doctor Who' Fan Meetup Recap," BBC America, http://www.bbcamerica.com/anglophenia/2013/07/san-diego-comic-con-2013-day-three-gallery-doctor-who-fan-meetup-recap, paragraph 1.
30. Matt Hills, "The Year of the Doctor: Celebrating the 50th, Regenerating Public Value?," *Science Fiction Film and Television* 7:2 (2014): 174.
31. Matt Hills, "Anniversary Adventures in Space and Time: The Changing Faces of *Doctor Who*'s Commemoration," in Hills, *New Dimensions*, 231.
32. Highlighting both the importance of Comic-Con for promoting the *Doctor Who* brand and the significance of Jodie Whittaker's first panel in Hall H, in 2018 BBC America screened a special "Cardiff to Comic-Con" video on its website that traced the journey of Whittaker from Wales to San Diego, seguing into her actual appearance live on stage in front of thousands of fans.
33. Johnson, "Programme Brand," 102.
34. Simone Knox, "The Transatlantic Dimensions of the Time Lord: Doctor Who and the Relationships between British and North American Television," in O'Day, *Doctor Who*, 115.
35. Selznick, "Rebooting and Re-branding," 83.
36. Celia Lury, *Consumer Culture*, 2nd ed. (Cambridge: Polity Press, 2011), 151.
37. Carly Lanning, "#WCW Anglophenia: British Culture with an American Accent," *Daily Dot*, July 8, 2015, http://www.dailydot.com/upstream/bbc-anglophenia-british-wcw/, paragraph 2.
38. Knox, "Transatlantic Dimensions," 116.
39. Jennifer Gillan, *Television Brandcasting: The Return of the Content-Promotion Hybrid* (New York: Routledge, 2015), 11.
40. Gillan, *Television Brandcasting*, 10.

FROM IMAGINED COMMUNITIES TO CONTACT ZONES

American Monoculture in Transatlantic Fandoms

LORI MORIMOTO

In English-language scholarship on media fandoms, lacking any indicators to the contrary, we tend to assume a default Anglo-American orientation. Defined less by geography or culture than by a common language, such an orientation can flatten differences within both fandoms and fan studies itself. This, in turn, lends itself to a broad conceptualization of fandom as not simply comprising, but being defined by, a community-based framework. There is, of course, no question that fandoms may be understood as communities of affect. Particularly as experienced online, they map neatly onto what Benedict Anderson has termed "imagined communities," defined by certain commonalities—of language, culture, religion, race, and, in the case of fandom, fan object—held by geographically dispersed people and enabled through globalized mass media.[1] Indeed, the correspondence of Anderson's imagined communities to online fandoms is such that it has been a seminal framework in media fan studies as a whole for conceptualizing how fans congregate and communicate.

At the same time, this emphasis in fan studies on imagined communities as intensified spatiotemporal convergence obscures its politics, namely the theorization and analysis of how such communities lend themselves to nationalist ideologies. As theorized by Anderson, imagined communities are "distinguished, not by their falsity/

genuineness, but by the style in which they are imagined,"[2] a style that is necessarily constrained by the borders that surround and define a given community. Thus, while a framework of imagined community enables us to understand online fandoms as determined largely, if not solely, by shared interest in a given fan object between geographically dispersed people, it might equally foreground *how* such communities are formed: who does and does not qualify for membership and why; how common rules of engagement are determined and the centripetal assumptions they overlay. That is to say, while the first, spatiotemporally convergent understanding of imagined communities supports and reinforces a paradigm of generally cohesive "community," the second, more political approach does the opposite, drawing attention to the possibility of friction and fissure within fandoms.

In the context of "normative" Anglo-American fandoms, broadly defined by English language and cultural commonalities, such fissures become visible when we take into account their transatlantic locus, comprising not only the United States and the United Kingdom, but also such places—media markets and industries—as Canada, Scandinavia,[3] and Mexico, each with its own idiosyncratic relationship to the others.[4] An imagined community framework can help us see these differences, even if it remains inadequate to the task of understanding the lines of tension and axes of difference that can nonetheless occupy ostensibly coherent fan communities.[5] It is here that a turn to Mary Louise Pratt's theory of "contact zones" is salient: Pratt argues that Anderson's imagined communities are "strongly utopian, embodying values like equality, fraternity, liberty, which the societies often profess but systematically fail to realize."[6] She might just as easily be speaking of fan communities that, like the nation-states of Anderson's work, similarly privilege "principles of cooperation and shared understanding" that assume "all participants are engaged in the same game and that the game is for all players."[7] A contact zones perspective enables us to push the political critique of Anderson's imagined communities further along, understanding them as "social spaces where cultures meet, clash and grapple with each other, often in contexts of highly asymmetrical relations of power."[8] In a fan studies' context, thinking of fan communities through a contact zones model thus facilitates "attention to what divides fans from one another, [rather than celebrating or assuming] fans' identical interests and similar interpretations of popular cultural products."[9] Indeed, how these cultures are understood in the context of a given fandom depends largely on the perspective adopted by scholars: cultures of nation, race, ethnicity, gender, class, and so on are all potential sites of difference and disjuncture even where normative fan practices and assumptions predominate (interfandom points of affinity notwithstanding).

With this in mind, how might we alter our understanding of seemingly normative, monolithic Anglo-American fandom through a contact zones approach to transatlantic television fandoms? What insights does it afford us? In what follows, I will explore how a contact zones framework foregrounds the cultural diversity inherent in transatlantic fandoms. I am particularly concerned with how perceptions of what one fan productively terms "American monoculture" inform both conflict and cultural capital within these fandoms.[10] Less invasive cultural imperialism than a totalizing and pervasive popular cultural backdrop, American monoculture is that de facto mass or "mainstream" popular culture against which fans of all nationalities define both themselves and the media they consume. As I discuss below, fan resistance to any association with American monoculture is enacted sparticularly through assertions of local specificity, and it is in this way that even American fans may differentiate their consumption of American media from mainstream monoculture. If anything, American fans' attempts to distance themselves from American monoculture suggest that online transatlantic fan engagement, as much as any other kind of fan interaction, is informed by those same hierarchies of authenticity and taste that comprise subcultural self-identity. In this sense, we might understand fans' attempts to distance themselves from American monoculture less as a uniquely transcultural phenomenon than as symptomatic of the ways fans assert identity *through* local specificity and against the consumption of seemingly undifferentiated "mainstream" popular culture.

This essay thus explores both how and to what ends transatlantic television fans perceive and distance themselves from American monoculture, first by considering transculturally articulated fan frictions that emerge within the contact zones of online transatlantic television fandom, followed by an examination of how fans' eagerness to distance themselves from American monoculture informs and drives transatlantic fan fiction community practices of "Britpicking" and its ancillary "American-picking, Ameri-picking, and Yank-wanking" offshoots.[11] Finally, I will look at the Canadian popularity of Granada Television's long-running UK soap opera, *Coronation Street*, particularly as it encompasses a liminal axis of transatlantic television fandom not commonly considered in scholarship. At once neighboring the United States and part of the British Commonwealth, Canada occupies a unique position in relation to both the United States and the United Kingdom—one that plays out through *Coronation Street* fandom as it, too, is inflected by a backdrop of American monoculture. In approaching these varied phenomena through a contact zones lens that foregrounds the potential for transcultural conflict within the spaces of fandoms, this chapter demonstrates both the constancy of transatlantic fan resistance to American monoculture as overlaying broader concerns with subcultural identity, and the culturally specific ways in which this resistance is performed.

MONOCULTURE, AUTHENTICITY, AND SUBCULTURAL
CAPITAL IN TRANSATLANTIC TV FANDOMS

In June 2015, I solicited a small sampling of Tumblr-based fans' experiences of transatlantic television fandom. Self-selected primarily from my own Tumblr "followers," these
fans were invited to describe instances of transcultural friction, accommodation, and so
forth, as examples of fan interactions that exceeded a "community" orientation. Ultimately,
three Americans, three British fans, and one Canadian responded with detailed accounts
of their experiences, enabling me to identify at the anecdotal level two generalizable points
of felt transcultural friction: fandom Americanization as experienced by non-U.S. fans, and
British cultural gatekeeping as experienced primarily by American fans. Americanization,
or American cultural imperialism, perceived by non-American television viewers is certainly not a new phenomenon. Ien Ang's seminal study of Dutch viewers of the American
television show *Dallas* described how the specter of the show's Americanness loomed
large over viewers' perceptions of it. In particular, among those who disliked or even hated
the show, she discerned a strongly anti-American discourse that understood American television shows "as a threat to one's own national culture and as an undermining of high-
principled cultural values in general."[12] As one dissenter commented, "I find it a typical
American programme, simple and commercial, role-affirming, deceitful."[13]

What distinguishes contemporary non-American fans' sense of the intrinsic
Americanness of both American television and, in particular, fans, from such overtly ideological criticism is its firmly affective nature; as one of my survey respondents observed,
"Perceived American monoculture is probably something that annoys almost all fans from
outside it to some degree."[14] Indeed, many of the responses from British fans of UK television shows emphasized how it *feels* when Americans fail to comprehend or acknowledge
cultural differences, ranging from a simple "It does jar a bit when . . ."[15] to exclamations of
"It just bloody well irks me!"[16] and "What is up with some of them? The sheer intoxicated
self-righteousness of it."[17] For these fans, it is the Americanization of fandom through
American fans' assumptions of a hegemonic, US-centric fandom value system (already
embodied in US media exports) that underlies transatlantic fan frictions, frictions that
are exacerbated within fandom contact zones "by the fact that we are similar enough to
be able to argue about our differences in the first place, and to assume that each should
know what the other means when actually they don't."[18] That is, in the absence of overt
markers of difference, online fans tend to assume congruence between fan and language
communities, often where little exists. To be sure, as with Ang's anti-fan respondents *avant
la lettre*, there is an ideological side to these frustrations with perceived American monoculture, despite the colorations and attachments of fan affect. Yet where Ang's respondents

actually employ ideological explanations to obscure and distance themselves from visceral reactions to *Dallas*,[19] these fans begin from a place of affect, which in turn may lead to recognition of the ideological work that their responses perform.

American fans' monocultural assumptions and concomitant ignorance of British cultural specificity are also a flashpoint in transatlantic television fandoms. As one Welsh fan points out,

> Our TV is very regional, originally broadly divided into "Granada land" (the North) and "BBC land" (the South) and the TV company that makes a show impacts its perception (in the same way that ITV = slightly "lesser" than BBC traditionally) it [*sic*] irks me that I'm supposed to "know" what it "means" when Americans say a "CW Show" but American fans lump all "British TV" as equal.[20]

At the same time, such distinctions, and non-American (primarily British) fans' insistence on registering them, provoke in some non-British (primarily American) fans the perception of "a cultural power imbalance between [the United States and Great Britain] that persists even in the face of American-led globalization."[21] Sarah Thornton has argued that what she terms "subcultural capital is embodied in the form of being 'in the know,' "[22] much of which is demonstrated through displays of cultural authenticity that, "in its full-blown romantic form . . . suggests that grassroots cultures resist and struggle with a colonizing mass-mediated corporate world."[23] Within Thornton's subcultures and transatlantic fandoms alike, such authenticity is grounded in an oppositional relationship to what is posited as "American monoculture," with subcultural or fan-cultural value determined by its distance from "mainstream" US culture. When British fans complain about the frustrations of "trying to have discussions about 'British shows' with American fans who don't try and understand [us]," American fans may perceive this as a spurious British assumption of American cultural homogeneity in the face of their own cultural specificity. In turn, this can provoke counterassertions of American cultural diversity from US fans, a discursive strategy that enables American fans to distance themselves from perceived American monoculture.[24] In such fan exchanges and discussions, both UK *and* US fans therefore construct a (globalized, culturally imperialist) US "mainstream" as other to their own fan-cultural identities.

Transformative fandom's already presumed oppositional and nonhegemonic self-identities further complicate this calculus. As one American fan of *Doctor Who* writes:

> The first conflict I ran across . . . was the divide between Old and New Who fans, or rather between those who knew both canons and those who didn't. (Authentic vs.

fake geek discourse, anyone? Less obviously gendered, but still gatekeeping.) Early on, in particular, this seemed more prevalent among those who identified Who (Old or New) as Their Culture, as something especially Brit [*sic*] that Americans could not possibly understand.[25]

There are at least two oppositional axes of authenticity at work here. First, from a trans-atlantic perspective, the British-American axis privileges Britishness as more authentic. Second, from a gendered perspective concerning online *Doctor Who* fandom, an axis of distinction runs between "real" long-established male fans and "fake" squeeing fangirls new to the show—a spurious distinction already challenged within fan studies. Given the hurdles of fan-cultural authenticity that fans must negotiate in order to be deemed "real" or "true" fans—in both a transatlantic and gendered sense—my respondent identifies these frictions as kinds of fan "gatekeeping." Even so, the specificity of the transatlantic conflict does not disappear altogether, as this respondent goes on to note:

> Exclusionary politics aside, they did have a point. I hadn't watched much UK TV, or any TV, for years; a lot of RTD's [Russell T. Davies's] cultural coding (especially on Who) did go right over my head on first viewing—just following the accents and dia-logue was challenging enough without parsing the cultural politics. It took a while to realize that RTD was taking something like a beloved sacred cow and reinventing it; he was doing it with a Doctor with a Northern working-class accent and a Companion who came from a council estate, had a black boyfriend and a "chav" accent, and was not incidentally played by the UK equivalent of Britney Spears.[26]

Understood in this way, American monoculture within transatlantic fandoms is not necessarily synonymous with a monolithic, outward-directed American imperialism. While for non-American fans it appears implicated in ideologies of American cultural he-gemony, it equally might be understood, particularly in a fan context, as signifying a more generalizable American-dominated cultural mainstream against which even American fans define themselves—just as my respondent notes that fandom gatekeepers, despite their problematic exclusionary cultural politics, actually had "a point," and that it required some time to learn the "cultural coding" of (i.e., accumulate the "authentic" subcultural capital called up by) showrunner Russell T. Davies's reinvention of *Doctor Who* in 2005.

If such staples of fan activity as textual interpretation might thus be under-stood as equally likely to divide as unite fans within a transatlantic television context, foregrounding the kinds of intercultural clash intrinsic to contact zones, how do such differences play out within the (arguably) oppositional spaces of fan fiction reading and writing? As transformative work, fan fiction (re)creates its diegetic milieu, but what happens when such spaces are foreign to the writer creating them? In what follows, I will explore how British and American fans alike mobilize local specificity in fan fiction, both as a distancing tactic from perceived American monoculture and as a means of fixing the non-American authenticity of fan objects often created or revised according to the imperatives of transnational media industries.

SUBCULTURAL AUTHENTICITY AND TRANSATLANTIC FAN FICTION: BRITPICKING AND BRIT-FIXING

The practice of "Britpicking" is thought to have begun circa 2003 with the online prolif-eration of *Harry Potter* fan fiction.[27] A play on the word "nitpick," it typically involves non-British fan fiction writers consulting with British fans to ensure their work corresponds culturally and linguistically to the British locus of UK television shows, books, and films. Although there may be multiple factors underpinning the emergence of Britpicking practices, it seems safe to say that one significant reason has been British fans' vocal indig-nation and irritation with erroneous cultural and linguistic details in UK-set fan fiction created by non-British writers. As "Alison," a contributor to the *Fanfic Symposium* website, wrote in 2004:

> I've been reading in The Professionals fandom for a number of years and, on the whole, I'm impressed by the effort made to get Bodie and Doyle and their environ-ment as authentic as possible. The trouble is I've just started reading Harry Potter fan fiction and, apart from being astounded at the vast amount of stories out there, I'm becoming more and more irked by the fact that there are far too many writers who are not bothering to learn about the culture that Harry and his friends and foes live in, despite having the books as reference material.[28]

The Professionals aired in the early 1980s; in the early 2000s its fans were likely to have been adults. In contrast, by 2004 *Harry Potter* had effectively introduced a new genera-tion of younger fans to the pleasures of fan fiction. Thus, an expectation that *Harry Potter* fandom would or should reflect the same attention to authenticity demonstrated by fans of *The Professionals* may well have been optimistic (as well as implicitly challenging the fandom bona fides of young fan fiction writers). As one American respondent observes:

> I strongly suspect that H[arry] P[otter] was the gateway UK fandom for a lot of US Who/TW [Torchwood] fans—certain [*sic*] in my circles, it was. There may have

been a generational effect in play; one asks more sophisticated questions later in one's life as a fan and with more adult content in the canon.[29]

"Alison" asserts above that "there are far too many writers who are not bothering to learn about the culture that Harry and his friends and foes live in, despite having the books as reference material." Yet the books sold by Scholastic, a publisher specializing in children's and young adult markets, were localized for the American market with "the spellings, terms, and idioms used by British speakers [translated] into their American equivalents so the audience was not put off or confused."[30] Thus, American fan fiction writers *were* using the books available to them in the US marketplace as reference material, given a context-dependent understanding of "the books." Nonetheless, Scholastic's American localization or "domestication" of the *Harry Potter* books lends itself to an implicit fan critique of American monoculture based on the British-American axis of authenticity within which transatlantic fan fiction writing (concerning UK-centered media texts) often occurs.

Other British fans' nods to cultural common sense seem equally divorced from the material conditions of transnational production and distribution. In a 2013 post by British LiveJournal user wellingtongoose, entitled "More Tea Please, We're Sherlocked," purporting to teach fans "how to write a good Sherlock fan fiction featuring this glorious brew," she asserts unequivocally that "BBC Sherlock was made very much for British audiences."[31] Yet, as a coproduction between BBC Wales, Hartswood, and WGBH, the Boston member station of American public broadcaster PBS, *Sherlock* is at least materially transnational. Indeed, as Michele Hilmes argues, we might also understand it as a transcultural text, insofar as such television coproductions involve providing capital for program production "in exchange for distribution rights *as well as for some degree of creative input into the production*."[32] In the case of *Sherlock*, Hilmes notes that

> properties (like *Sherlock*) that already have transnational recognition and can work . . . imaginary identification into their narrative focus . . . [carry] qualities that mark the most successful co-productions, and . . . draw together transnational publics.[33]

Within Britain, reactions to such practices might be considered analogous to those that gave rise to Britpicking practices:

> On the British side, this has involved accusations of cultural dilution, of using the television license fee paid by all British TV viewers on programs made for Americans.

Implied here is that making programs that appeal to Americans somehow weakens their essential Britishness.[34]

Alternatively, as in the case of wellingtongoose's LiveJournal post that substitutes "Sherlocked" for "British," transnationally conceived, marketed, and consumed programs may also be *re*contextualized by fans as fundamentally British. Such discourse amounts to what might be termed *Brit-fixing*, where Britishness is fixed by fans as a marker of textual authenticity. That said, what underpins many British fans' reactions to British-American television coproductions and transatlantic fan fiction writing communities is an implicit perception of American monoculture as the Great Homogenizer—an approach grounded in historical perceptions (in the United Kingdom and Europe) of American popular culture as intrinsically immature, generic, and hypercommercial. Even here, however, the material conditions of *Sherlock*'s transnational production are displaced, implying that related transformative works should conform to a British cultural sensibility.

We might assume from this that the British relationship to American monoculture— played out in practices of Britpicking and Brit-fixing within transatlantic fandoms—is defined by the threat of American cultural hegemony and a resulting "dilution" of British cultural distinction. As noted above, the similarities between such a discourse and that employed by Dutch viewers who disliked *Dallas* in the 1980s are clear, both reflecting familiar concerns over American cultural imperialism. But it is not only non-Americans whose online transatlantic fan activities are affected by perceptions of American monoculture. Whereas Britpicking is now a recognized aspect of English language fan fiction, the opposite—proofreading for cultural accuracy in fan fiction set in an American milieu—remains far rarer, despite errors by non-US writers provoking similar irritations in some American fans to those expressed by the British fans above. As one American fan of the CW show *Supernatural* ("SPN") observes:

> It grates on me when British fic authors of Supernatural fic make no attempt to get the British-isms out of their writing. They're writing characters who are, like, THE epitome of Americana, and then they have Dean say something like "thanks ever so" and it's very jarring. I'm sure British fic authors get just as annoyed at Americans writing Sherlock, but I feel like at least we mostly try? I'm not sure British SPN authors even try.[35]

Indeed, *Supernatural*, one of the biggest Anglo-American online media fandoms, is something of a lightning rod for cultural clashes in the context of transatlantic television. As noted on the (predominantly Anglo-American-centered) fandom wiki Fanlore, responses to a LiveJournal-based workshop on Americanisms and *Supernatural* fan fiction were decidedly mixed and contentious. The workshop itself, hosted by two non-Anglophone European fans,[36] began from the perspective that

> Supernatural deals not only with two brothers fighting heaven and hell, it also deals with a country and its culture. In some ways, Supernatural is one of the most "American" shows out there, because unlike the majority of other shows, it is not restricted to a specific town, or city building, or even room. . . . In traveling through the Midwest and the small towns, and via literally [*sic*] using the backroads of the US, Supernatural is as American as it gets.[37]

Notably, responses to this statement, as well as the content of the workshop post itself, closely reflect those of the fans discussed above. While many non-American fans thanked the posters for putting together such a resource, others were critical of the posters' flattening of "American" culture and resulting failure to address local and regional differences. This reflected the same concerns with local specificity often voiced by British fans: "In reading over the comments, I have to say I agree with what I've read— the US is a place of contradictions and complexities that aren't easy to understand— even for those of us who live here!"[38] In this way, then, the drive to distinguish oneself from American monoculture is repeated by Americans in transatlantic *Supernatural* fandom, underscoring the extent to which American monoculture might just as easily be considered through a lens of mainstreamed commercial homogeneity as nationality. The suggestion that non-American writers conform to an "American" style of writing and, in particular, characterization is seen by one fan as a "bafflingly exclusionary vision of Americanness," particularly in the context of *Supernatural*'s own problems with multicultural representation ("for a start . . . [what about] Black, Hispanic, and Asian American people").[39] Taken as a whole, however, the similarities in fan conversations concerning Britpicking and "American-picking" suggest that they both play out along two different axes: one of cultural verisimilitude and one of fandom in/authenticity. Considered against the latter, exhortations to demonstrate adequate knowledge of other cultures in fan fiction echo subcultural identity claims that are centered on fan authenticity. As the commenter in the previous section observed, criticism of "American" writing based around UK-based storyworlds seems analogous to "fake geek" discourses in fandom more generally.[40]

Reinforcing this is a tendency in fan fiction, whether it has been US or UK culturally nitpicked or not, to index insider knowledge through certain (show-specific or national) cultural markers. In *Sherlock*, for example, John Watson mentions milk exactly once, in a scene towards the end of "The Great Game" when he tells Sherlock in frustration, "Uh, milk. We need milk," in hopes that Sherlock will buy it instead of him. In *Sherlock* fan fiction, however, it's become something of a recognized trope to have John Watson somehow involved in the purchasing of milk from Tesco, often against his will: "John trudged up the steps to their flat the [*sic*] Tesco bag with milk and honey in one hand."[41] When John demands that Sherlock get the milk, he often fares differently in the unfamiliar wilderness of the shop:

> Entering the sliding doors of Tesco, Sherlock grabbed a carrier basket and strode back to the dairy section. There, he was confronted with a dizzying array of possible choices: whole, semi-skimmed, skimmed, non-homogenized, organic, soymilk, goat's milk. How did anyone ever choose when all they needed was just "milk?"[42]

Broadly speaking, milk here serves a generic purpose; appended to "Tesco" it becomes a marker of some baseline level of cultural and fandom authenticity. Whether fully Britpicked or not, its inclusion in a story signals, however marginally, the author's awareness of the show's British setting. This tendency seems equally reflected in non-American fan fiction of shows such as *Supernatural* as well; as one fan comments, "I know I've read some DeanCas fics where people who are unfamiliar with the US [nevertheless] write about the landmarks—like the Great Ball of Twine, etc."[43]

Further, the more specialized the landmark, the greater the degree of performed cultural familiarity and authenticity, as seen in the opening of a *Harry Potter* story by American fan asecretchord:

> Harry Potter made his way to the narrow alley where the rubbish bins were stored. The theatres at the National would be emptying soon, disgorging their audiences in a flood that would sweep along the South Bank before spilling into the Underground. If he could just find something to eat—a half-eaten sandwich from Eats or a forgotten takeaway box from Wagamama—he'd be set for the night and could head for home.[44]

Similarly, in her discussion of Britpicking in Anglo-American fandoms, Erin Horáková observes of one British *Sherlock* fan fiction:

> Unfortunately no preparation, no community, however helpful can match the effortless, brief description of breakfast at a café in Hounslow after a rough flight. . . . There is, perhaps, also something inimitable about the local specificity the Lancastrian Hall shows in the ensuing clipped discussion of "a Yorkshireman's refusal to admit to

excellence in anything originating from the other side of the Pennines," even in [the author's] choice to stage a scene in this shoddy, little-known corner of London.[45]

Here, then, we have three kinds of fan fiction localization: (1) baseline use of British culture or brands; (2) specialized non-British use of specific British landmarks; and (3) British inhabitation of cultural experience. Yet all three perform fan authenticity in ways that highlight the specific role played by American monoculture in transatlantic television fandoms. "Britishness" is figured here as oppositional to transatlantic cultural homogeneity, and as marginalized by US-centric transnational popular culture—something we often are inclined to view through a lens of American cultural imperialism. At the same time, Britishness also sits at the top of fan hierarchies of authenticity within fandoms of British television shows. Exhortations to "Ameri-pick" non-American fan fiction of US television shows similarly position Americans at the apex of this fandom hierarchy, but only when American national or local specificity is foregrounded. Regarding her feelings of irritation with the kinds of American monoculturalism she sees in transatlantic fandoms generally, one British respondent notes:

> This undeniably gives me the pleasure of perceiving myself as a sensible British person who has a sense of proportion which the American doesn't. . . . Making that kind of judgment no doubt plays to my stake in the British idea of Americans as spoilt children.[46]

In this way, and analogous to American fans' attempts to distance themselves from a hegemonic American monocultural center by way of local specificity, in which they—like this fan—are better than or different to the undifferentiated American mainstream, the two axes of opposition to American monoculture and support for fan authenticity become one and the same. In each, authentic fandom has to struggle against a threat of inauthenticity, whether marked out by unknowing fans lacking US or UK cultural awareness, or homogenized American monoculture. In doing so, these authenticity claims collapse together to demarcate and fix "real" fan identity. Indeed, I would argue that attempts to fix "true" fandom (often based around US and UK cultural authenticities, where paradoxically both construct and other American monoculture) are a defining aspect of transatlantic television fandom.

My focus up to this point on British-American fan intersections and clashes within the contact zones of *Doctor Who, Sherlock,* and *Supernatural* online fandoms might imply that they are synonymous with transatlantic television fandoms. Certainly, the strength of American and British TV shows overseas in these two markets reinforces such an understanding. Yet, as noted in the introduction, it is important to explore transatlantic television fandoms outside a strict Anglo-American framework. Given the great popularity of the British soap opera *Coronation Street* in Canada, as well as the utter lack of such fandom in the United States, what follows is an exploration of its specific contours as an example of transatlantic television fandom.

TRIPARTITE TRANSATLANTIC FANDOM: CANADIAN FANS OF ITV'S *CORONATION STREET*

In Canada, the popularity of the long-running British soap *Coronation Street* is such that it was the topic of a 2010 documentary aired on the Canadian Broadcasting Corporation (CBC) entitled *Corrie Crazy: Canada Loves Coronation Street*.[47] A subsequent newspaper article about the return of *Coronation Street* to nightly broadcasts on the CBC observed that, in the end, "there was no plausible explanation" given by the documentary for the show's Canadian reception.[48] The article specifically dismisses fans' claims that "believable characters" and "real people in real situations" were the reason they loved the show, arguing, "With respect, this is nonsense. Coronation Street is not realistic. . . it is tin-pot television, ludicrously melodramatic, mannered and corny."[49]

This writer does identify at least one impetus for such fandom, however: "It's true that many of the actors look like regular British people and bear little resemblance to the cookie-cutter handsomeness one sees in U.S. network TV." He continues:

> Part of its appeal in Canada is rooted in the peculiar mix of the familiar and the exotic that it offers. We are colonially familiar with much of Brutish [*sic*] culture and, simultaneously, the texture of that culture is not ours.[50]

Writing in *Shakespeare in Quebec: Nation, Gender, and Adaptation*, Jennifer Drouin is more specific:

> English Canada's Anglophilia, which distinguishes Canada culturally from the United States, manifests itself not only in notions of "the classics" and "refinement" but also in popular culture. Colonial longing for the mother country must provide at least a partial explanation why 775,000 viewers tune in nightly to CBC Television to watch *Coronation Street*.[51]

As with the specter of American monoculture in US-British transatlantic television fandoms, here Canadian-British cultural affinity, on the one hand, and shared oppositionality to American monoculture, on the other, are credited both for *Coronation Street*'s extraordinary showing on Canadian television, and its expression of English-speaking Canadian national identity. As one male Tumblr user and Canadian *Coronation Street* fan explained in more affective detail, the show's Canadian popularity

> definitely comes from the "not-American" sense of it. . . . [T]o be an English-speaking Canadian is to be a foreigner in your own country at times. The cinemas are all American movies, our highest rated TV shows are American, the pop music is generally American. This is largely due to popular tastes and largely because Canada doesn't produce enough TV and movies to dominate the airwaves. . . . There's also a bit of an inferiority thing going on. Canada could produce a fine police procedural which does ok but viewers also have the choice of, like, five US based police procedurals, all with bigger budgets and stars. So Corrie comes into that in as much as culturally, *some* Canadians feel a stronger connection to that than they do to US stuff. And it's a well-produced show.[52]

There is no one axis of Canadian interest in *Coronation Street*—no one reason why Canadians seem to like it so much. Neither is there a singular binary or relation underpinning the show's popularity (unlike "UK versus US" fan authenticity claims). Rather, *Corrie*'s fandom has multiple points of semiotic entry that are at least tripartite: British affinity, the felt weight of American monoculture, and English-speaking Canada's liminal position between UK and US cultures.

The "inferiority thing" described by this respondent demonstrates the differences in transatlantic relationships mentioned at the beginning of this chapter. If both Canada and the US share a colonial relationship to the United Kingdom, their paths nonetheless diverged when the US declared independence. Thus Canadian money is imprinted with the image of Queen Elizabeth II, and English word spellings overwhelmingly conform to British standards. At the same time, Americans and Canadians share not only a land border, but driving norms, popular culture, and a myriad other minutiae of cultural identity. They speak similarly accented English, such that Americans sometimes adopt an informal guideline of claiming to be Canadian when traveling overseas in order to avoid the negative associations of Americanness abroad. In this sense, English-speaking Canada is not simply culturally "Canadian," but also not/British and not/American: a liminal and hybrid subjectivity that lends itself to a differently positioned oppositionality to American monoculture. Reflecting this, Canadian fans of *Coronation Street* do not claim "Britishness" *per se*, but instead occupy a unique position in relation to the show. As the above respondent writes:

> The fandom in Canada is so different because it exists outside the celebrity [world of] . . . the UK. We don't see the stars of the show on chat shows or supermarket magazines or Strictly Come Dancing. We just have the show, aired every weeknight, on the CBC. . . . I think the difference between Canadian and UK fans is that Corrie is more like a club you belong to in Canada whereas in the UK, it's just a big show that's been on the air for more than 50 years.[53]

Indeed, given the ubiquity of the show in the United Kingdom and its absence from transatlantic markets outside Canada, he observes:

> It's funny: I never thought of Corrie as being part of a fandom because it's not a "genre" thing. . . . It's not Sherlock or Star Trek or Buffy. But when I realize I run a Corrie based Twitter and used to contribute to a Corrie based blog, then I see that it's totally a fandom.[54]

Existing outside both the British-American axis and the aegis of what normative cult or genre TV fandom typically understands *as* fandom, the Canadian fandom of *Coronation Street* gives the lie to definitions of transatlantic media fandom as necessarily bidirectional between the United States and the United Kingdom. Further, it complicates an understanding of American monoculture within transatlantic fandom as being somehow synonymous with American cultural imperialism. While it is absolutely the case that American media continue to dominate global markets and, therefore, American mainstream pop culture remains a key node within the contact zones of transatlantic fandom, multiple other subjectivities—in particular, transcultural fan identities—also inflect who we are as fans and how we position ourselves relative to border-crossing media that we embrace and love.

CONCLUSION: FROM BRITPICKING TO US UNIVERSALISM

To this point, the perception of, and distancing from, American monoculture in transatlantic television fandoms has been confined primarily to issues of media interpretation, the production of fan fiction, and "authentic" fan identity. Yet it's worth noting that other survey respondents voiced different ways of understanding how American monoculture asserts itself in transatlantic fandoms. Particularly in the case of racial representation, a topic that is heavily debated in Tumblr and Twitter-centered online fandoms, American monoculture may be understood as American fans' insistence on understanding social relations solely through a US sociohistorical lens. As the Welsh respondent quoted above writes, one characteristic of US-centric fan culture concerns "Race/Ethnicity/what is or isn't offensive issues. These abound in watching American drama and having fan discussions about them. See also: we are not all English over here and it's really important."[55] Another British respondent notes:

> The transformation of fanspace into a kind of social justice ragespace feels like a specifically American development, and an Americanising of the space, because the obsession with cultural privilege is in itself an American leftist one. . . . "Blatant intra-American racism = I'm not surprised black American fans are angry but I'm not quite sure why white fans think this plays identically to the whole world."[56]

Here, rather than fan/cultural authenticity, what characterizes these interactions is a kind of presumed American universalism—or the critical recognition of it by non-US fans—that is at least perceived to play a determining role in the formation of, and participation in, online transcultural fandoms writ large.

It is these kinds of culturally complex intersections that are ineffectively served by fan studies' continued reliance on cohesive, or even simply imagined, "community" frameworks. As noted in the introduction to this chapter, this is not to say that fans cannot feel a sense of community in inherently transcultural fandoms: the common refrain among online fans that "fandom" is where they found like-minded friends and a sense of social belonging is common because it's a legitimate fannish experience. But as with all (sometimes seemingly universal) experiences, felt community is subjective and uneven, particularly as it plays out in those "contexts of highly asymmetrical relations of power"[57] that characterize contact zones. Fandom may be "beautiful,"[58] but the singular "fandom" common to much fan studies' work hints at the problems inherent in assuming that all experiences of it are alike and generalizable. Particularly where differences hide in plain sight, as in the case of Anglophone transatlantic fandoms, beginning from the assumption of fandoms not as cohesive communities, but as always-already transcultural, and as therefore vulnerable to the kinds of frictions presumed in a contact zones model, would enable fan studies to more adequately highlight and interrogate the very real conflicts and struggles that punctuate transatlantic media fandoms.

NOTES

1. Benedict Anderson, *Imagined Communities: Reflections on the Origins and Spread of Nationalism* (London: Verso, 1991), 6.
2. Anderson, *Imagined Communities*, 6.

3. Strictly speaking, "Nordic noir" does not neatly map onto a transatlantic framework. Nonetheless, given the literally overseas orientation of its transborder popularity (particularly in the United Kingdom), it seems suited to interrogation as a transatlantic phenomenon.

4. Rebecca Wanzo, "African-American Acafandom and Other Strangers: New Genealogies of Fan Studies," *Transformative Works and Cultures* 20 (2015): 2.1.

5. Piotr Siuda, "Fan Cultures: On the Impossible Formation of Global and Transnational Fandoms," in *Is It 'Cause It's Cool? Affective Encounters with American Culture*, ed. Astrid M. Fellner, Susanne Hamscha, Klaus Heissenberger, and Jennifer J. Moos (Münster: LIT Verlag, 2014), 296.

6. Mary Louise Pratt, "Arts of the Contact Zone," *Profession* (1991): 38.

7. Pratt, "Arts," 38.

8. Pratt, "Arts," 34.

9. Siuda, "Fan Cultures," 297.

10. Tumblr User P, solicited response by author, June 2015.

11. Erin Horáková, "Britpicking as Cultural Policing in Fanfiction," in *Play, Performance, and Identity: How Institutions Structure Ludic Spaces*, ed. Matt Omasta and Drew Chappell (New York: Routledge, 2015), 135.

12. Ien Ang, *Watching "Dallas": Soap Opera and Melodramatic Imagination* (London: Methuen, 1985), 93.

13. Ang, *Watching Dallas*, 91.

14. Tumblr User P.

15. Tumblr User W, solicited response by author, June 2015.

16. Tumblr User M, solicited response by author, June 2015.

17. Tumblr User P.

18. Tumblr User P.

19. Ang, *Watching Dallas*, 92–93.

20. Tumblr User M.

21. Horáková, "Britpicking as Cultural Policing," 135.

22. Sarah Thornton, *Club Cultures: Music, Media, and Subcultural Identity* (London: Polity Press, 1995), 11.

23. Thornton, *Club Cultures*, 116.

24. Tumblr User M.

25. Tumblr User G, solicited response by author, June 2015.

26. Tumblr User G.

27. "Brit-pick," Fanlore, July 9, 2014, https://fanlore.org/wiki/Brit-pick.

28. "The Americanisation of British Fandoms," Alison, June 29, 2004, http://www.trickster.org/symposium/symp157.html.

29. Tumblr User G.

30. Horáková, "Britpicking as Cultural Policing," 136.

31. "More Tea Please, We're Sherlocked," wellingtongoose, April 3, 2013, http://wellingtongoose.livejournal.com/21577.html.

32. Michele Hilmes, "Why Co-produce? Elementary, Holmes," *Antenna: Responses to Media and Culture*, March 11, 2014, http://blog.commarts.wisc.edu/2014/03/11/why-co-produce-elementary-holmes/.

33. Hilmes, "Why Co-produce."

34. Hilmes, "Why Co-produce."

35. Tumblr User GP, solicited response by author, June 2015.

36. "Cultural Imperialism in Fandom," Fanlore, December 7, 2011, https://fanlore.org/wiki/Cultural_Imperialism_in_Fandom.

37. "Workshop: Faking It Pretending You're a US Citizen When You're an Ocean Away," Legoline and benitle, November 28, 2009, http://spnroundtable.livejournal.com/187754.html.

38. nighean_isis, comment, November 29, 2009, http://spnroundtable.livejournal.com/187754.html.

39. 22by7, comment, November 29, 2009, http://spnroundtable.livejournal.com/187754.html.

40. Tumblr User GP.

41. "Married Ones," tealeavesandmoonlight, April 9, 2016, http://archiveofourown.org/works/379683.

42. "Milk and Beans," Botan, May 25, 2016, http://archiveofourown.org/works/6966382.

43. Anonymous, personal correspondence.

44. "No Sign of Love," asecretchord, June 22, 2012, http://archiveofourown.org/works/441213.

45. Horáková, "Britpicking as Cultural Policing," 139.

46. Tumblr User P.

47. Jennifer Drouin, *Shakespeare in Quebec: Nation, Gender, and Adaptation* (Toronto: University of Toronto Press, 2014), 204.

48. John Doyle, "What's up with Canada's *Coronation Street* Obsession?," August 31, 2012, *Globe and Mail*, http://www.theglobeandmail.com/arts/television/whats-up-with-canadas-coronation-street-obsession/article4513162/.

49. Doyle, "Canada's *Coronation Street* Obsession."

50. Doyle, "Canada's *Coronation Street* Obsession."

51. Drouin, *Shakespeare in Quebec*, 204.

52. Tumblr User S, solicited response by author, June 2015.

53. Tumblr User S.

54. Tumblr User S.

55. Tumblr User M.

56. Tumblr User P.

57. Pratt, "Arts," 34.

58. Francesca Coppa, "Fuck Yeah, Fandom Is Beautiful," *Journal of Fandom Studies* 2:1 (2014): 73.

/// 14 /// CROSSING OVER THE ATLANTIC

SuperWhoLock as Transnational/Transcultural Fan Text

PAUL BOOTH

In one image, a man texts, "Dean, Samuel, The Doctor has asked me to relay this message to you. The angels are coming, and you must not blink. Take from it what you will, I suppose. SH." In art posted on DeviantArt, a blue police box and a black Chevrolet Impala are parked outside of 221B Baker Street. In a more blatant GIF, three figures embrace, two with their back to the camera; superimposed on each of their heads are the titles *Doctor Who, Sherlock,* and *Supernatural*.

For the uninitiated, these pieces of fan art are just small contributions within a vast, intertextual, and subcultural fan crossover universe called *SuperWhoLock*.[1] *SuperWhoLock*, as the name suggests, is a combination of the canon within (and the fandom surrounding) the television shows *Supernatural* (2005–, United States, CW), *Doctor Who* (1963–1989, 1996, 2005–, United Kingdom, BBC), and *Sherlock* (2010–, United Kingdom, BBC). Constructed from characters, images, symbols, situations, and subtexts from these three shows, *SuperWhoLock* both reveals transatlantic connections between the three and demonstrates "transfannish" commonalities between their fan audiences.[2] In this chapter, I want to explore the connective tissues at the heart of *SuperWhoLock* to examine the way that multiple fan audiences both cohere and differ in an era of global entertainment and transcultural fandom.[3] Examining fandom through a transcultural lens allows researchers to analyze transatlantic *texts*, but fan sentiment reveals transatlantic *fandoms* as well.

In this update to my book *Crossing Fandoms*,[4] I want to expand upon my examination of *SuperWhoLock* fan audiences in order to investigate the ebb and flow of fan sentiment and to reveal specific textual and transatlantic connections between the three original texts via fan activity. The following chapter therefore uses two different methodologies to investigate fan activity, sentiment, and connectivity surrounding *SuperWhoLock*. After discussing the history and impact of *SuperWhoLock*, I analyze the transatlantic dimensions of the fandom through a series of interviews with fans collected at three different fan conventions—two in the United States (for *Doctor Who* and for *Supernatural*) and one in the United Kingdom (for *Sherlock*). This section will argue that, more than any of the official media texts can by themselves, *SuperWhoLock* reveals the transatlantic connections undergirding many of today's major cult media products in what Hills has called a "transfandom" experience.[5] Contemporary fandom itself becomes a vehicle for making these specific transatlantic exchanges.

Following on from this initial argument, I then use Crimson Hexagon, a social media analytics engine, to analyze sentiment regarding *SuperWhoLock*. Crimson Hexagon deploys a social media data library of over 500 billion posts, and includes searches of posts from social networks such as Twitter, Tumblr, and Facebook as well as blogs, forums, and news sites.

My aim in this chapter is to reveal transatlantic connections within, and to evidence site-specific differences between, US and UK popular cultural fandoms. While specifically focused on the *fandom* of the crossover between these texts, it also reveals the fandom's dependence *on* these texts. Sentiment changes for *SuperWhoLock* over time also reveal a deepening resentment across multiple fandoms for *SuperWhoLock* and its specific fandom, which may only partly be mitigated by the appearance of the shows themselves. Through an investigation and analysis of *SuperWhoLock* as a transatlantic fandom, I elucidate changing patterns of fan affect and explore how transfandom develops in the digital age.

SUPERWHOLOCK AS TRANSFAN INTERTEXT

The preponderance of fan-created mashup and remix texts—Questarian fandom,[6] *Inspector Spacetime* fandom,[7] *SuperWhoLock* fandom[8], among others—portends a shift in the character of fandom and fannishness in the transmedia era. In traditional fan studies' literature like Jenkins's *Textual Poachers*, fans serve as "poachers" who "operate from a position of cultural marginality and social weakness"—they are powerless in the eyes of media corporations, as they lack "direct access" to the means of production, but at the same time reflect an impassioned and engaged audience of creators who produce their own work.[9] Fans' creative work often challenges mainstream media representations, offering new versions of texts that expand character sexuality or narrative timeline. In a transnational context, fans can be faced with additional challenges—or opportunities—of critique: Iain Robert Smith notes that because of the preponderance of American and Eurocentric texts across the world, fans from one culture can present a "tension between oppositional critique and mimetic reverence" of another—and they can "illustrate . . . one of the many layers of ambivalence that lie at the heart of transnational processes of cultural exchange."[10] Both critiquing the original but also presenting an homage to it, the *Star Trek* fan films Smith describes highlight the instability in fannish critique that transnational fandom can present. *SuperWhoLock* may not be a commercially available media text, but for followers of this crossover the connections between the three requisite texts are highlighted by fans on social media. Unlike a television show that may have a premiere date, multiple start dates for *SuperWhoLock* can be found. Google indicates that "the first inklings of *SuperWhoLock* appeared in January 2012."[11] In an email interview with me, *SuperWhoLock* fan Martina Dvorakova said that she created *SuperWhoLock* art even earlier, in December 2011. And Crimson Hexagon first notes the term "*SuperWhoLock*" from May 2011, in a single tweet talking about "epic [fan] crossovers."

All of these various "start dates" fall within about a ten-month period, though, and this highlights an important connection between the three shows: *SuperWhoLock* emerges first when the three shows have recently been on the air. In May 2011, BBC Wales's *Doctor Who* was in the middle of its sixth series. By January 1, 2012, *Sherlock* had premiered its second series, and *Supernatural* was in the middle of its seventh season. By October 2012, *SuperWhoLock* had become well known enough for Aja Romano, a popular culture critic, to publish a piece called "WTF Is SuperWhoLock?," a short article that detailed the origins and discussion of the fan-created text.[12] However, according to Crimson Hexagon's social media monitoring, *SuperWhoLock* exploded in popularity in December 2014—it jumped from about 140 mentions a day to 10,000 mentions a day during the latter half of 2014 and early 2015, hitting a peak of 51,000 mentions on April 5, 2015, and garnering 423,000 over a one-week period.

Why this sudden jump in numbers of mentions?

Ironically, it appears as though the number is because of *other* content not *SuperWhoLock* related. Posts during that time talk about a *That's So Raven / Suite Life of Cody and Zach/Hannah Montana* crossover (a Disney Channel triumvirate of the early 2000s) and a *Gravity Falls / Steven Universe / Over the Garden Wall* crossover (a Cartoon Network connection), using *SuperWhoLock* as an example of a *previous* fan-generated crossover. *SuperWhoLock* during this time became a reference point, a comparison or touchstone fan crossover, meaning that it had already become so well known that it could be used as a contrast. The high number of mentions could also be attributed to a post by a Tumblr user with "superwholock" in her name about pop star Taylor Swift that had been reblogged multiple times. Interestingly, then, by the time of its highest number of mentions, *SuperWhoLock* was already a part of popular conversation.

SuperWhoLock is not the first crossover text, a "fictional creation that imagines those stories all reside in the same universe, where the characters can interact with each other and go on adventures"[13]—think of Spock being transported aboard the TARDIS or Edward Cullen going to school at Sunnydale. If crossover fic is a type of fan fiction genre,[14] then *SuperWhoLock* is a representation of that crossover within fan audiences. Matt Hills describes this movement as a kind of "transfandom": "people who are moving across different fandoms . . . most likely you'd be combining, moving across these different forms of fan knowledge."[15] In other words, transfandom refers to crossover *fans* (as opposed to crossover *fiction*). *SuperWhoLock* is both a type of fiction and a type of fandom, however, and as such it manifests these crossover dimensions in both textual and fannish spheres.

Also relevant to *SuperWhoLock* is Bertha Chin and Lori Morimoto's concept of "transcultural" fandom, given the transatlantic nature of the text. Tellingly, both of the British shows that are part of *SuperWhoLock* could be considered *heritage* television,[16] and both bring with them connections to historical fan cultures. *Supernatural*, on the other hand, is relatively new (Eric Kripke created it in 2005) but has cultivated a vast and vocal fan audience through social media (especially Twitter and Tumblr). For Chin and Morimoto, a transcultural fandom moves beyond notions of nation; they examine "border-crossing fandoms . . . and with them the unique insights they offer about the ways that fans interpret and interact with both media and one another in an ever-intensifying global media marketplace."[17] Moving not just between national borders, but also digital ones, *SuperWhoLock* fandom is thoroughly transcultural: despite the nationalistic impetus of the original UK and US texts, the fan audience itself is global and dispersed. Fan identities in the digital age are always "'in progress,' and constantly shifting within and outside the (artificial) boundaries placed on fan context."[18] Using social media and online tools, the fan audience for *SuperWhoLock* emerges not necessarily from the intersection of national contexts, but instead from the fannishness that develops out of the texts themselves.

TRANSATLANTIC DIMENSIONS OF THE FANDOM: FANTASTICAL ANGLOPHILIA FOR TRANSCULTURAL AUDIENCES

For many of the fans I spoke with at conventions on both sides of the Atlantic, *Doctor Who*, *Sherlock*, and *Supernatural* were both similar in many ways and yet vastly different from each other. The similarities can be superficial—all three feature good-looking men, all three deal with supernatural (or superhuman) elements, and all three shows share a relation to what Louisa Stein refers to as "feels culture," an aspect of millennial fan culture that "combines an aesthetics of intimate emotion . . . with an aesthetics of high performativity."[19] There is a heightened emotional component to each of the shows, as each focuses on family and friendship amidst the turmoil of genre-induced monstrosities. Emily, one of the people I interviewed, noted this aspect of feels culture: *SuperWhoLock* "makes you think in terms of . . . relationships." Some *SuperWhoLock* fan texts make these connections explicit: for example, in the online video "*SuperWhoLock* trailer," which I describe in *Playing Fans*,[20] repeated allusions from all three shows emphasize their common elements—repetition of the names Amy Pond (a character in both *Doctor Who* and *Supernatural*) and Sherlock Holmes (referenced in all three shows), for instance—but also focus on the emotional impact of each drama.

Both *Doctor Who* and *Sherlock* are produced by the BBC and—at least for series 6 to 10 of *Who* (2010–2017)—feature the same showrunner, Steven Moffat. Moffat, in fact, is one of the key elements that tied *SuperWhoLock* together for many fans. Ashley noted, "*Sherlock* and *Doctor Who* have the added benefit of the same person heading things," highlighting that as a fan of one of the showrunner's programs, you might also be a fan of the other. Pat, a Sherlock Holmes fan for decades, also uses Moffat to link the shows: "I watch *Doctor Who* as I see the crossover. I watch it because I think Moffat gives me clues about what's going on in *Sherlock* in *Doctor Who*."

But for many fans, textual *differences* actually make *SuperWhoLock* viable. Key to understanding *SuperWhoLock* lies in the way that assorted fans construct varying textual differences between the three texts. Each group I spoke to noted variant differences between the three shows, and for the "fans of *SuperWhoLock*, joining together the three texts becomes a sort of identifier; the characters and situations utilized in each *SuperWhoLock* story or image come from a corpus of elements and are reconstructed in new patterns that deliberately reflect the fans' preferences."[21] For instance, many fans tended to see *Sherlock* as the "odd text out," arguing that it didn't fit into the science fiction or supernatural genre—Colleen noted, "*Sherlock* I guess is weird, because it has nothing to do with sci-fi." Other fans saw *Supernatural* as the most different, noting that of the three, *Supernatural* was the only US TV show. For example, one of my interview subjects, Sarah, noted that "*Supernatural* is America to me. . . . For some reasons that doesn't match the English for *Sherlock*, and for *Doctor Who*." And while other fans also tended to see *Supernatural* as the outlier, this wasn't just because it was American. Some certainly saw that as a major difference, but others perceived the difference as one of heritage—as Ben put it, "Certainly over here [in the United Kingdom], *Doctor Who* and *Sherlock* are institutions, which *Supernatural* isn't." *Supernatural* has "only" been on the air for fourteen years, whereas

Doctor Who has been around for more than half a century, and the Sherlock Holmes canon for over a century. Others saw the differences as being constructed through fan audiences—*Supernatural* was seen as having an older audience (Diana notes that "it's more mature . . . and I think that most of the people that like SPN [*Supernatural*] have matured along with the show").

SuperWhoLock fans thus cross the Atlantic with their fandom, despite the obvious differences between the three texts. For many of the American fans I interviewed, part of the love of *Sherlock* and *Doctor Who* was precisely that Britishness which Dylan Morris hails as "Young American nerds appropriat[ing] Britain as a second heritage."[22] This form of Anglophilia is different from, but plays on, the tropes of "British heritage" discussed by Claire Monk.[23] The heritage tropes of British period films emphasize an English, pastoral, upper-class and bourgeois-type of "quality" filmmaking;[24] such films developed a political rewriting of British history that highlighted a Thatcherite view of the past.[25]

In contrast, the Anglophilia of Morris posits a more institutionalized magical realism that is threaded through British cultural history, filtered through the lens of Carroll, Tolkien, Lewis, and Rowling: "Every American young nerd I surveyed grew up reading the classics of British children's fantasy. . . . A vision of the British Isles as a land of whimsy and fantasy shapes their passion."[26] The pastoral imaginings of British history are superseded by fantastical imaginings of a literary past: because "America is a country without a (fantastical) medieval European past. There are no castles, no stories of American knights, kings and queens," and literature from the United Kingdom takes the place of this mythology for Anglophile readers.[27] For his project, Morris interviewed a number of self-professed "Anglophile nerds" about their love of British literature, and for some it relied more on imagined connections than on real ones.

SuperWhoLock plays on its Anglophilic nature to its American audience. For instance, Fatenah notes, "I do consider myself a fan of more British shows than . . . American shows. And I think for me it's because the British just plays with my mind and intelligence a lot more, and makes me think." And for Reannon, "Half of [why I watch] is [that the shows are] British." At the same time, other fans are put off by the "Britishness" of the two BBC shows—Jennifer, a fan at the *Supernatural* convention, said, "I'm not a . . . fan, and I tried it, as much as I loved sci-fi, it's the British sci-fi [I don't like], I guess..."

Importantly, just as much as the "Anglo" nature of *Doctor Who* and *Sherlock* attracted some American audiences, the US-centric nature of *Supernatural* both attracted and alienated British fans. Most of the British fans I interviewed were attending "Sherlocked," the first *Sherlock* convention, held in London in April 2015. Thom argues that "there's quite a big following of people for *Supernatural* in the UK." Certainly, *Supernatural* has fans in the United Kingdom, and UK fan conventions like Asylum 16, 17, and 18 have featured many *Supernatural* stars. Ben, alternately, had never thought of *Supernatural* in the same genre as the other two shows, arguing, "I don't think *Supernatural* has as big a presence over here in the UK as it does in the US." Indeed, it has had trouble finding a TV home, having been broadcast on ITV2, Living TV, Sky Living, and Channel 4.

The Anglophilia that accompanies *Sherlock* and *Doctor Who* in the United States can be attributed to fans' general feeling that British television has greater "quality" than the equivalent US variety. This is not just a US-centric sentiment, as some of the Brits I interviewed also noted that *Supernatural* wasn't quite in the same league as the other two texts. But of course, as Elisa Tamarkin notes, Anglophilia is both "a fetish and nostalgia that is just as much [about] politics and aspiration" and "tells a story of English culture and society that is . . . an expression of the anxieties and wishes of someplace else."[28] Although Tamarkin doesn't mention television, the larger context here is relevant to *SuperWhoLock*—the quality of British media products can be linked to general dissatisfaction with American network and genre television rather than any inherent quality therein. *Doctor Who* and *Sherlock* give the appearance of "quality" to viewers seemingly used to more pedestrian American fare.

SuperWhoLock, with its transatlantic character, takes on these Anglophilic characteristics of *Sherlock* and *Doctor Who* and translates them via *Supernatural* to a transcultural audience. The fandom of one text is hailed by particular qualities and characteristics of the other texts to form a transatlantic fan culture. As a fan-created text, *SuperWhoLock* exists at the periphery of each of the three original and "official" texts. Boundaries between texts become blurred, as fans place different signifiers within different contexts. Some icons are more embedded in one text rather than others; it is hard to see a blue police box without thinking of *Doctor Who* (and of the United Kingdom). Others are more mutable—does a man in a trench coat symbolize *Supernatural*'s Castiel or Holmes? Does a deerstalker hat reference Holmes or the Doctor in "The Snowmen"? By deliberately mixing and matching referents within the fan-created text, *SuperWhoLock* makes the whole larger than the sum of its parts. At the same time, conceptualizing *SuperWhoLock* as "more than the sum of its parts" comes with inherent complications, and in the following section I want to examine in more detail how *SuperWhoLock* manifests characteristics of remix, as well as situating fan sentiment about *SuperWhoLock* within the spectrum of reactions to the remix genre. Along with the excitement that the crossover creates, many fans also feel anger and resentment that "their" favored text is being "used" by other fans as a part of *SuperWhoLock*. In addition, because of antagonistic fan behaviors, *SuperWhoLock* fandom cannot be conceptualized solely as a positive contribution to the fan landscape; it has been divisive as well, and brings with it a type of fan anger about perceptions of fandom.[29]

FANDOM AS REMIX CULTURE

As a fan-created "mashup" of three different texts, *SuperWhoLock* in many ways brings together characteristics of digital media studies, or "media studies 2.0," as key traits of contemporary fandom. For William Merrin, media studies 2.0 is a way of studying contemporary digital media as a complete paradigm shift, the "digital experience [being] fragmented and proliferated" across multiple screens, technologies, and audiences.[30] Media studies 2.0 is an "open-source media studies" that "invites students in" to the academic world.[31] Similarly, *SuperWhoLock* and the fandom that created it are helping to change the fan landscape as well. To understand *SuperWhoLock* as an emblem of the digital (fan) media environment means noting the saliency of fan work (and fanworks) in a media studies 2.0 format—that is, that fans are formative and generative.

One cultural concept that has been usefully proffered to understand fandom in the digital age is remix culture.[32] Remix has been defined in multiple ways and in multiple contexts; there is not space here to fully unpack the term. However, the gist of remix culture is the relationship between texts and the people that consume and use them. Remix is the act of combining multiple textual sources into one complete whole. The term has been used in relation to fandom to describe the "practice of taking cultural artifacts and combining them in new and creative ways."[33] Media scholars like Lev Manovich and David Gunkel have focused on remix in order to understand larger shifts in the culture and audiences for digital media.[34] When remix is involved, participation increases and the fan of multiple texts becomes a producer of one.

As Kristina Busse and Alexis Lothian point out, remix is not just about audiences and reception; it can also be about practice.[35] They look at vidding as a remix practice that involves multiple skills across a range of abilities. For Virginia Kuhn, remix is also a rhetorical strategy, a "digital argument that is crucial to the functioning of a vital public sphere."[36] In these senses, remix does more than just bring together multiple texts; it acts as a digital speech act, a critical intervention into understanding "resistant practices that question the grand narratives of our time."[37] Kuhn goes on to acknowledge that

> at a basic level, viewing remix as a digital speech act would rid us of terms like appropriation and recycling, which suggest the primacy of an original author or text. This view resists the hierarchies that champion big media and make fannish efforts a secondclass mode of discourse, the realm of the amateurish and the trivial.[38]

This is important for fan studies in general, and *SuperWhoLock* more specifically, as it focuses on the fan at the heart of digital production. *SuperWhoLock* is this rhetorical methodology made manifest; literally neither the work of a single creative auteur (e.g., Kripke or Moffat), nor the work of a single fan, *SuperWhoLock* remixes fandom and fan cultures. To better understand the remix fandom attributes of *SuperWhoLock*, I have used the social media analytics engine Crimson Hexagon to develop a profile of the types of fan interest in this crossover text. The reason analyzing social media content can reveal aspects of remix here is due to the way that individual fan voices construct the text. *SuperWhoLock* doesn't exist except in the minds and practices of the fans. The textual examples we have are therefore concrete manifestations of ideas; there is no "canon" of *SuperWhoLock* except what individual fans create for themselves. Analyzing the social media surrounding *SuperWhoLock* reveals the remixing of fannish multivocality that surrounds this unusual textual experience.

Crimson Hexagon, I should note, is one of many social media analytic tools, and as such it can be used to analyze aspects of any topic online. It analyzes social media posts for demographic information, sentiment about a topic, and related topics, among other elements. It is also, however, notably imperfect, and so I offer the following analysis with caveats: analyzing social media posts is only as useful as the information provided on social media, and despite the best efforts of programmers, demographics and sentiment can be difficult to discern through the type of quantitative analysis that Crimson Hexagon thrives on. It is hard, for example, to take into account changing slang terms. Furthermore, Crimson Hexagon uses related terms to discern demographics, but not only do these connections depend on statistical generalizations that might not be applicable in any specific case, they are also culturally constructed terms that, in practice, may not necessarily mean what they are assumed to.

That being said, Crimson Hexagon reveals important data about *SuperWhoLock* and ties it into remix culture, illuminating the voices of fans bringing *SuperWhoLock* to life. From its first mention in May 2011 to the end of August 2016, Crimson Hexagon found over three million total relevant *SuperWhoLock* posts (this counts reblogs on Tumblr and retweets on Twitter). Of these posts, 94 percent came from Tumblr, and of this subset, 8 percent were marked "basic positive" (meaning the sentiment associated with the post was a positive one), and 27 percent were labeled "basic negative." Although this appears to indicate that more posts about *SuperWhoLock* were negative than positive, as I discuss below, that would constitute a rather misleading finding. Fifty-seven percent of the posts were considered to do with "emotion." Of the emotions associated with *SuperWhoLock*, joy is by far the number one, with 57 percent of posts expressing it; this is followed by no emotion expressed (43 percent), sadness (21 percent), anger (10 percent), disgust (9 percent), and fear (3 percent), with surprise coming in last at 0 percent—evidently no one was surprised at *SuperWhoLock*.

Posts that express joy tend to affirm not just *SuperWhoLock* but also fandom itself as a meaningful part of one's life. For instance, one post on Tumblr is of a photograph of a sign that reads, "If you're going to be weird, be confident about it." The poster has written underneath, "I love and live by this" and has then hashtagged a number of fannish things like #doctorwho and #superwholock, among others. In contrast, negative posts expressing fear tended to use fear to talk at least somewhat playfully about the experience of becoming part of fandom. For example, one post exclaimed, "Now that my bf dragged me into watching supernatural i am very scared of becoming a superwholock." The fear here isn't associated with *SuperWhoLock* in particular, but is (potentially humorously) linked to perhaps establishing oneself as part of this fandom. Similarly, another post reads, "Im already in the [*Supernatural* fandom], but I'm gonna start watching the sister shows & join superwholock. Im scared for my sanity (what's left of it)." Again, the fear isn't about *SuperWhoLock* but is instead about being part of a fandom. In both these cases—and in many more in the social media stream—the sentiment expressed (fear) seems to be far more tongue-in-cheek rather than an appeal to any actual fear, marking the limits of such sentiment analysis.

Certainly, however, some posts did express a negative reaction to *SuperWhoLock*. For instance, one post on Tumblr reads:

> Whenever i come across a superwholock blog that's still active it's a bit like when you have what you think is a really weird/bad dream but then find out later that it was real. it happened. it was not a dream.

Here the poster seems to regret *SuperWhoLock*, echoing the "fandom is childish" discourse apparent throughout representations of fans in the popular press.[39] This sort of negativity was also described by some of the fans I spoke with. For instance, Nicole noted that she was into *SuperWhoLock* at first, but then lost interest:

> You just start separating. At the very beginning I was like, "Yeah, this mashed my three favorite shows together." And then it just gets to the point where it's like, "Well, I don't want to put them together any more."

Colleen described *SuperWhoLock* as "the silliest thing ever. There's no way that anyone would ever agree to do that." However, she later argued that "it would be fun. I do really like all the fanwork that people create with that, especially the mashups. Those are some of my favorite things that people make." And Tanya said, "I only have a certain amount of time, and I decide to channel my fan energy into one thing. . . . There's not enough space in my life for three fandoms." At the same time, the cosplayer Johnslynn (her cosplay name) noted that "people will like only one or two of the shows and not like one of the other shows, and just, like, hate [*SuperWhoLock*] and not want it to happen. . . . I've seen a lot of people who just hate the idea of crossovers because they like the idea of the shows separately and they don't want to see them together."

Perhaps this, then, is the most relevant way of looking at *SuperWhoLock* as a transnational fan-text that in turn has become transcultural as it conveys fantastical Anglophilia across fandoms. It has become so widely known that it's no longer seen by many fans as a simple play on the three shows and has developed its own fan animosity.

CONCLUSION

Crimson Hexagon also uses a "word cluster" that can show what other topics are being discussed in relation to *SuperWhoLock* and how popular they are. The most popular connecting word associated with *SuperWhoLock* is "Tumblr," although that may be because many of the posts are on Tumblr, and it is seen as a Tumblr-centered fan practice. Other connecting terms include "fandom," "people," and "vanished." It is easy to see how some of these terms are connected to *SuperWhoLock*, but I want to end this chapter by discussing the last one: "vanished."

By any stretch of the imagination, *SuperWhoLock* has not entirely vanished. Although not as often talked about as it was in 2012 and 2014, the term still has hundreds of mentions a week. New *SuperWhoLock* art is produced each day. But many fans from both inside and outside the fandom feel as though *SuperWhoLock*'s time has passed. On Tumblr, one post seems to sum this up by connecting the "disappearance" of *SuperWhoLock* to the passing of multiple fandoms at once, and it is from this source post that the term "vanished" seems to have taken root, given that it has been shared and reblogged hundreds of times. The post starts, "I would pay top dollar for a comprehensive, source-supported explanation of how Superwholock *vanished*. . . . [It] was the core of tumblr in 2013."

Replies tie into contemporary fan antagonisms and flashpoints of fan cultural memory. One reply notes, "I think you can pinpoint the disappearance to the month following Dashcon"—a Tumblr fan convention that, rather infamously, was incredibly hyped but seemed to fail miserably. Another reply ties in the vanishing to "hiatuses and competition," as all three shows went on hiatus and then "fans became more critical." Here, the author notes that *SuperWhoLock* disappeared because the *SuperWhoLock* fans were becoming annoying on Tumblr and at the same time the fandom criticized all three shows for their treatment of women. A third rationale argues that "the users on this site [Tumblr] have matured some, pushing the average age older," linking *SuperWhoLock* again to a discourse of childishness.

Perhaps like *Sherlock* itself, a series that now seems likely to be on a permanent hiatus, the time for *SuperWhoLock* may have passed—but it's precisely because of the type of transfandom that it represents that this fan-engineered "show" has been eclipsed by newer fan creations. The aforementioned *Gravity Falls / Steven Universe / Over the Garden Wall* crossover might be the next big thing, or something else that hasn't even appeared yet. *SuperWhoLock* is a truly transatlantic text that spans three shows, two nations, and a huge swath of fandom. It reveals the way that fan audiences can come together in a remix culture to create something new from something old. Fandom enables these pop-cultural mutations and exchanges. But *SuperWhoLock* also doesn't represent any kind of endpoint for fan creativity in the digital age. If anything, it helped bring Tumblr into the limelight as a fan-centric social media site. The popularity of *SuperWhoLock*, at least for a brief moment in time, heralded a view of fan creativity not just as "poaching" the leftovers from mainstream media, but as developing original texts through fannish means. Or, as my interview subject Reannon noted, *SuperWhoLock* is really just "a bunch of people getting together, commenting on something on Tumblr . . . [w]ho decided . . . to smoosh the words together, and it worked and we were like OK! We're just going to go with it! Because that's what fans do."

NOTES

1. Paul Booth, *Crossing Fandoms: SuperWhoLock and the Contemporary Fan Audience* (London: Palgrave, 2016); Nistasha Perez, "GIF Fics and the Rebloggable Canon of *SuperWhoLock*," in *Fan Phenomena: "Doctor Who,"* ed. Paul Booth (Bristol: Intellect, 2013), 148–157; Dean Howard Short, "*SuperWhoLock*: An Analysis of Subculture in a Microblogging Setting" (MA thesis, University of Central Florida, 2014).

2. Matt Hills, "Fandom as an Object and the Objects of Fandom," interview with Clarice Greco, *MATRIZes* 9:1 (2015): 147–163.

3. Bertha Chin and Lori Hitchcock Morimoto, "Towards a Theory of Transcultural Fandom," *Participations* 10:1 (2013): 92–108.

4. Readers interested in more in-depth discussion of my ethics and methodology, in terms of interviewing fans at US and UK conventions, should consult Booth, *Crossing Fandoms*.

5. Hills, "Fandom as an Object."

6. Matt Hills, "Recognition in the Eyes of the Relevant Beholder: Representing 'Subcultural Celebrity' and Cult TV Fan Cultures," *Mediactive* 2:2 (2003): 59–73; Lincoln Geraghty, *Living with "Star Trek": American Culture and the "Star Trek" Universe* (London: I.B. Tauris, 2007).

7. Paul Booth, "Reifying the Fan: Inspector Spacetime as Fan Practice," *Popular Communication* 11:2 (2013): 146–159; Paul Booth, *Playing Fans: Negotiating Fandom and Media in the Digital Age* (Iowa City: University of Iowa Press, 2015).

8. Perez, "GIF Fics"; Booth, *Playing Fans.*

9. Henry Jenkins, *Textual Poachers: Television Fans and Participatory Culture* (New York: Routledge, 1992), 27.

10. Iain Robert Smith, "'Beam Me up, Ömer': Transnational Media Flow and the Cultural Politics of the Turkish *Star Trek* Remake," *Velvet Light Trap* 61 (2008): 3.

11. Booth, *Crossing Fandoms*, 9.

12. Aja Romano, "WTF Is SuperWhoLock?," *Daily Dot*, October 5, 2012, http://www.dailydot.com/up-stream/superwholock-fandom-supernatural-sherlock/.
13. Romano, "WTF Is SuperWhoLock?"
14. Natalia Samutina, "Fan Fiction as World-Building: Transformative Reception in Crossover Writing," *Continuum*, 30:4 (2016): 433–450.
15. Hills, "Fandom as an Object," 160–161.
16. Claire Monk, "From 'English' Heritage to Transnational Audiences: Fan Perspectives and Practices and Why They Matter," in *Screening European Heritage*, ed. Paul Cooke and Rob Stone (London: Palgrave, 2016), 209–234.
17. Chin and Morimoto, "Towards a Theory," 93.
18. Booth, *Crossing Fandoms*, 5.
19. Louisa Stein, *Millennial Fandom* (Iowa City: University of Iowa Press, 2015), 158.
20. Booth, *Playing Fans*, 28.
21. Booth, *Crossing Fandoms*, 19.
22. Dylan Morris, "Britain as Fantasy: New Series *Doctor Who* in Young American Nerd Culture," in Booth, *Fan Phenomena: Doctor Who*, 51.
23. Monk, "English Heritage."
24. Monk, "English Heritage."
25. Christina Goulding, "The Commodification of the Past, Postmodern Pastiche, and the Search for Authentic Experiences at Contemporary Heritage Attractions," *European Journal of Marketing* 34:7 (1998): 835–853.
26. Morris, "Britain as Fantasy," 51.
27. Morris, "Britain as Fantasy," 51.
28. Elisa Tamarkin, *Anglophilia: Deference, Devotion, and Antebellum America* (Chicago: University of Chicago Press, 2007), xxiv.
29. Derek Johnson, "Fan-tagonism: Factions, Institutions, and Constitutive Hegemonies of Fandom," in *Fandom: Identities and Communities in a Mediated World*, ed. Jonathan Gray, Cornel Sandvoss, and C. Lee Harrington (New York: New York University Press, 2007), 285–300; Matt Hills, "'Twilight' Fans Represented in Commercial Paratexts and Inter-fandoms: Resisting and Repurposing Negative Fan Stereotypes," in *Genre, Reception, and Adaptation in the "Twilight" Series*, ed. Anne More (Farnham: Ashgate, 2012), 113–130; Booth, *Crossing Fandoms*.
30. William Merrin, *Media Studies 2.0* (London: Routledge, 2014), 4.
31. Merrin, *Media Studies 2.0*, 5–6.
32. Kristina Busse and Alexis Lothian, "Scholarly Critiques and Critiques of Scholarship: The Uses of Remix Video," *Camera Obscura* 26:2 (2011): 139–146; Zephra C. Doerr, "Abridged Series and Fandom Remix Culture," in "Fan/Remix Video," ed. Francesca Coppa and Julie Levin Russo, special issue, *Transformative Works and Cultures* 9 (2012), doi:10.3983/twc.2012.0396; Virginia Kuhn, "The Rhetoric of Remix," in "Fan/Remix Video," ed. Francesca Coppa and Julie Levin Russo, special issue, *Transformative Works and Cultures* 9 (2012), doi:10.3983/twc.2012.0358; Andrew M. Whelan and Katharina Freund, "Remix: Practice, Context, Culture (editorial)," *M/C Journal* 16:4 (2012), http://journal.media-culture.org.au/index.php/mcjournal/article/view/694.
33. Jen Scott Curwood, "Fan Fiction, Remix Culture, and the Potter Games," in *Teaching with "Harry Potter": Essays on the Classroom Wizardry from Elementary School to College*, ed. Valerie Estelle Frankel (Jefferson, NC: McFarland, 2013), 84, here talking about crossover fic.
34. Lev Manovich, "What Comes after Remix?" (2007), http://remixtheory.net/?p=169; David Gunkel, *Of Remixology* (Cambridge, MA: MIT Press, 2016).
35. Busse and Lothian, "Scholarly Critiques."
36. Kuhn, "The Rhetoric of Remix," 1.5.
37. Kuhn, "The Rhetoric of Remix," 5.1.
38. Kuhn, "The Rhetoric of Remix," 2.1.
39. Jenkins, *Textual Poachers*.

GLOSSARY

BBC. British Broadcasting Corporation, the United Kingdom's public service broadcaster since 1922. Non-commercial, supported by universal license fee.

BBC America. A cable television and satellite television channel available in the United States and co-owned by BBC Worldwide and AMC (with a 49.9 percent share). It is not funded by the BBC universal license fee (which only operates in the UK) and focuses on British programming, including UK programs and coproductions from broadcasters other than the BBC.

BBC Worldwide. The for-profit arm of the BBC, used to sell British programs outside of the United Kingdom. Profits go back into the BBC.

broadcast television. US term; sometimes also over-the-air (OTA), television delivered in the traditional way, using licensed spectrum space to transmit signals from land-based stations, whether public or commercial. In Britain, the term is terrestrial or free-to-air, though this latter term can describe non-OTA services as well.

cable television. Primarily a US term; subscription television service delivered to homes by wire, rather than over-the-air, via special receivers. It offers a mixed service of OTA stations, advertising-based channels, and premium channels. Generally there is only one cable TV provider in any given location: a local monopoly.

carriage negotiation. A negotiation between a cable television company and a content provider over rates for carrying channels or channel bundles on the cable TV company's service.

channel. Historically used to refer to a central source of over-the-air/terrestrial broadcast programming, for example, BBC 1, ITV, NBC, PBS. Currently the term can also refer to cable, satellite, or digital streaming services, for example, AMC, HBO, Sky Atlantic, Netflix.

channel bundle. Groups of related cable or satellite channels owned by a single company.

Channel 4. The UK's publicly-owned commercial public service broadcaster, supported by advertising income, with a remit of catering to diversity and minority tastes..

corporate underwriting. Term used by public broadcasters in the United States to denote income from corporate sponsors in exchange for on-air promotion. It is very similar to advertising on commercial channels except less frequent, less numerous, and softer-sell.

digital streaming service. A program service that is delivered digitally to audiences, via cable TV, satellite, or the internet. It is usually paid for by subscription, as with Netflix, Amazon, and Hulu, but can also include the digital delivery arms of OTA/terrestrial broadcasters.

free-to-air. UK term for over-the-air broadcast television that can be received without paying subscription. fees.

Freeview. The UK's digital terrestrial television platform, providing free-to-air channels.

heritage drama. A term used particularly in the UK to denote high-production-value dramatic television series about Britain's historical heritage, often based on literary properties, and often criticized for glossing over the less comfortable aspects of history.

idents. UK term for sequences between programs displaying the channel logo and allowing for continuity announcements; known as "station identification announcements" or "promos" in the United States.

ITV. The United Kingdom's primary commercial public television service, composed of several different regional entities. It is supported entirely by advertising but operates under the public service mandate.

linear television. A term sometimes used to indicate television delivered on a fixed schedule, usually by broadcasters or cable and satellite channels, as opposed to nonlinear or on-demand programming.

Netflix. A leading SVOD or digital streaming service that has established a significant international presence, becoming known for its promotion of "binge watching" and its practice of series/season "drops," when an entire run of new episodes are made available at one time.

network. Mostly used in US: national TV service providers such as NBC, CBS, and PBS that distribute programs to TV stations linked together by wire or satellite, either owned by or affiliated with a network. Today the term is often used synonymously with channel.

on-demand. Digital streaming services that provide a library of programming that can be accessed at any time, unlike linear television.

over-the-air (OTA). US term for traditional broadcast services; free-to-air or terrestrial in UK.

outsourcing. A term associated with the BBC's efforts to contract with independent producers and creators to make programs, as opposed to producing them in-house.

premium cable channel (also "pay TV"). A primarily US term indicating subscription cable television channels, like HBO and Showtime, with no commercial advertising.

public broadcasting. In the United States, private, nonprofit television and radio funded by government grants, private donations, and corporate underwriting—like PBS.

public service broadcasting (PSB). May be advertising-supported (Channel 4) or noncommercial and funded via the universal license fee (BBC) with a government operating charter and extensive requirements for programming that serves the public interest, including domestic programming quotas.

quality television. A contested term most often applied to shows produced by US premium cable channels, as a result of the fact that they are not subject to the same broadcast regulations as network television. Consequently, premium cable TV shows have established a reputation for being edgier and more risk-taking in terms of content.

satellite television. Subscription television channels delivered via satellite transponder orbiting the earth and received via satellite dishes and special receivers.

series/season. Terms that have historically had a variant usage in the United States and United Kingdom. In America, "seasons" have referred to batches or runs of episodes, while "series" meant the overall TV program. In the UK, "series" has been used to also refer to distinct runs of episodes.

Sky Television. Formerly BSkyB, the UK's largest digital satellite-delivered subscription TV service, with multiple specialized channels and a reach that extends around the world.

station. In the United States, a licensed local transmitter of television signals to local viewers; can be affiliated with a network or be independent. Stations originate local programming and broadcast some syndicated programs.

subscription television. TV service paid for directly by the user, rather than via license fees or advertising.

SVOD. Short for "streaming video on demand" and used to refer to subscription services like Netflix or Amazon video that are delivered on demand, via digital cable, satellite, or internet.

syndicated program. A program sold to individual stations either after its network run or independently.

terrestrial. British term for over-the-air broadcast television.

universal license fee. The annual tax British viewers pay to watch broadcast television, which goes to fund the BBC.

INDEX